FOUNDATIONS OF EDUCATION IN AMERICA

FOUNDATIONS OF EDUCATION IN AMERICA

An Anthology of Major Thoughts and Significant Actions

JAMES WM. NOLL
UNIVERSITY OF MARYLAND

SAM P. KELLY
WESTERN WASHINGTON STATE COLLEGE

HARPER & ROW, PUBLISHERS
NEW YORK, EVANSTON, AND LONDON

FOUNDATIONS OF EDUCATION IN AMERICA:
An Anthology of Major Thoughts and Significant Actions
Copyright © 1970 by James Wm. Noll and Sam P. Kelly

LIBRARY OF CONGRESS CATALOG CARD NUMBER: 76-95838

CONTENTS

PART 3   THE MODERN PERIOD (1800–1900)

THE MODERN PERIOD · MAJOR THOUGHTS

THE MODERN PERIOD · SIGNIFICANT ACTIONS

PART 4   THE CONTEMPORARY PERIOD   (*20th Century*)

THE CONTEMPORARY PERIOD · MAJOR THOUGHTS

THE CONTEMPORARY PERIOD · SIGNIFICANT ACTIONS

PREFACE

This anthology contains nearly a hundred primary documents that have been influential in shaping one or another aspect of American education. The earliest selection is from Plato and the latest from a 1968 state supreme court decision; however, well over half date from the nineteenth and twentieth centuries. Included are major philosophical propositions, educational ideas and proposals, social and psychological propositions, committee presentations, legislative acts, and court decisions. For the most part, the editors have abridged these documents in order to present the essential aspects of each document without requiring the reader to examine it in its entirety. This collection brings together materials often unavailable in restricted or growing libraries and offers the student of education a convenient single source of materials for initial examination.

Primarily, this anthology is intended for undergraduate and graduate courses in the foundations of education, or as a supplement for such courses as the history of education and the philosophy of education. In our time, though, when education as a field of study and concern is demanding the attention of scholars in many disciplines, the contents of this volume will also be relevant to students of sociology, anthropology, and political science. Instructors who use this anthology will no doubt choose among its contents and further support their choices with a text on foundations, or a history of education, or books on particular educational issues or problems. (See the bibliography for suggestions.) No matter what tone or emphasis the instructor may give his course, much of this anthology's contents will be directly useful to him and his students.

Students these days demand issues and ideas as the focus of their study; where can they better start than with the sources of significant ideas and issues —the words of the authors? The editors believe that students can best approach an understanding of the dimensions and significance of important issues confronting American education through an examination of these sources that have exerted major formative influence on our educational system and its practices. Of the dozens of other contemporary texts and works on education, most are derivative, not primary, and most are thematic, not developmental. Such books are typical of the common current approach to the study of social institutions; they also demonstrate the urgent need to come directly to grips with the problems which beset contemporary education. However, students must also understand the *roots* of issues and positions, and these are most clearly seen through examination of original and fundamental statements and of their explicit and implicit meanings.

In arranging the contents of this anthology, the editors followed chronology as the primary organizational scheme; the contents progress in time from early Greece to the present. Yet, so that a thematic approach to selections can be followed if the instructor wishes, the editors have also provided an index of issues so that a reader may concentrate his attention on particular themes and problems. Whichever approach is used, the selections are most valuable for their provocativeness and their relevance to the contemporary scene in education.

Of course, no anthology goes totally unchallenged. The editors have included selections that in their judgment have been of major importance. They have not merely attempted to sample here and there, to provide just a flavor of this issue or that topic. Instead, the editors assumed that each selection warranted a place in this anthology according to the criterion of influence it seemingly has exerted. Understandably, it was easier to make such an assessment of Plato or Rousseau, or of certain legislation or court decisions, than of contemporary writers, since current public attention and lasting historical influence are not necessarily won by the same works.

Two other points: (1) Conspicuously absent are such names as Darwin, Marx, and Freud. The crucial question is: "Were these enormously influential men directly concerned with education and did they write pointedly to education, or were their ideas and positions adapted to education by a second generation?" An argument could perhaps be made for each proposal, but the absence of such men in this anthology indicates the editors' viewpoint. (2) No one-to-one correspondence between a single inclusion and an immediate educational consequence is claimed or offered, as even legislation and court decisions take some time to become implemented. The too-easy generalization that "this caused that" has been avoided. On the other hand, had none of these selections ever been produced, contemporary American education would not show either its present structure or all of its present promises and problems. Direct and causal relationships are for the user of this anthology to determine, for the instructor to demonstrate, and for the student to discover through his study of these and other sources.

Selections are arranged by historical periods. The first part contains thoughts which precede the beginnings of education in America; the second encompasses the period 1600–1800; the third contains educational ideas and significant actions of the nineteenth century; and the fourth, by far the most extensive section, covers this present century. The contents in each section are arranged chronologically, except in a few instances where other principles of organization made points more clearly—for example, in showing the close relationship of certain legislation.

Each section begins with three portions of background and organizational materials prepared by the editors: (1) a commentary on "The Social Context" within which the selected ideas and actions occurred, (2) a discussion of "The Educational Issues" which emerged and were debated during the period covered and thereafter, and (3) an "Index of Basic Issues," which provides thematic, nonchronological ways to approach the selections.

The passages on "The Social Context" are meant to provide only a limited general background. Certainly they do not attempt to outline the entire social and cultural context of the four different historical periods into which the selections are grouped. At best, these sections identify some of the major events and issues of the periods concerned, so that the student may place the documents, mentally, into an accurate background of place and events. Readers are urged to turn to a competent history of Western civilization or to a text that discusses educational development against an historical backdrop, in order to provide themselves with more than the basic memory aids offered in the "Social Context" portions.

The "Educational Issues" sections offer a more direct commentary on the selections and upon the interplay among ideas expressed in the selections—but not to the extent of transferring the task of interpretation and understanding from reader to editor. The raising of detailed questions, the presentation and comparison of positions and actions, the sharpening of issues and development—these remain the responsibility of the instructor and the reader.

A "Cumulative Index of Basic Issues" and a categorical bibliography based on that index are included at the end of the anthology.

The editors wish to thank the individuals and publishers who gave permission to use the selections contained in this book, their colleagues at the University of Maryland and Western Washington State College for help in selecting materials, and the editorial staff of Harper & Row for encouragement and constructive criticism.

JAMES WM. NOLL
SAM P. KELLY

PART I

EARLY WRITINGS
(*to 1600*)

THE SOCIAL
CONTEXT

FOR the Greeks the fundamental purpose of education was to produce good citizens; other goals were less important. Since Greek city-states differed in their concepts of what constituted a good citizen, the methods and aims of education varied also and were shaped by the ethos and values of the populations concerned.

Athenian society esteemed freedom and personal development for its citizens. Theirs was a relatively open society—though hardly democratic in our modern sense of the term—which assumed that the state would prosper if its citizens could move freely in thought and action. A reflective creative leadership would strengthen the state. Athenians demonstrated such views by encouraging both open discussion and the individual development of the psychological, physical and artistic nature of individuals. Since the citizen was expected to make wise use of his leisure time (a primary goal of self-development), education aimed at making the individual self-reliant.[1]

Spartan society, on the other hand, placed the state in supremacy over the individual. Prime Spartan values, to be developed through education and training, included subservience to the state, regulation of one's actions and views in accordance with social values and aims, and loyalty to the body politic. Individual development constituted a relatively minor order of interest.

The basis for the curriculum in the early city-states was the national literature of Greece, which was quite religious in nature. Thus, through examination of the ancient epics and the artistic legacy from former times, the curriculum emphasized veneration of the gods. This content was supplemented by such subjects as music, mathematics, and rhetoric, and by strong attention to gymnastics and artistic training.

Nowhere in early Greece was education provided for all youth. Only a minority of young persons attended school for any prolonged period, and most of these were the sons of the wealthy or the well-placed. For girls, a

---

[1] Our word "school" derives from the Greek word for leisure.

3

program of domestic training sufficed. In his writings Plato called for the education of talent whether male or female, though this principle was not followed in the Athens of his day. It is to Athens, not Sparta, and primarily to Plato and Aristotle, that we turn today for relevant statements on the basis for learning and curriculum and for discussion of the relation of education to society.

In his curriculum proposals, Plato called for all children to acquire a measure of schooling and to receive proper social indoctrination. His emphasis on the cognitive aspects of education for the intellectually elite casts a long shadow over similar positions that have been advanced from his time to the present. He also believed the Athens of his time was insensible to enduring values and proper aspirations. To insure an appropriate curriculum in arts and literature, he called for censorship of those materials used by the young, an issue that still recurs today.

Earlier, the state had required that all children of free citizens attend school and obtain at least the rudiments of education and a basis for personal and civic morality. But by Plato's time, these laws were not commonly honored, and the state involved itself mainly with the training of selected older youth. Mistrustful of the influence of the typical home, Plato would nullify its baneful influence by having children raised and educated by the state in approved curricula and according to the individual's potential and society's needs.

In contradistinction to many of Plato's aims were positions taken by certain professional teachers, the Sophists. These teachers offered instruction in such skills as rhetoric and logic, claiming that these would assist young men to success in Athenian society. In Plato's view, the Sophists only weakened the curriculum and the aims of education by providing training that aimed merely at temporal efficiency or pragmatic attainment.

In many respects Aristotle agreed with his mentor, Plato; but he departed from him in some views—those concerning the proper role of education in society and the appropriate methods for learning and teaching. He also differed in certain philosophic positions about the nature of reality and knowledge, and about the ethical premises on which conduct should be based. Though for centuries Plato was the more influential educational spokesman, the ideas of Aristotle were to gain eventual ascendancy.

Plato and Aristotle came to grips with basic issues of education that today still demand attention—for these problems are not yet fully resolved. Both writers based their proposals on their contemporary societies, and attempted to formulate educational approaches to the proper development of society and the individual. Underlying their proposals were positions concerning fundamental questions as to the nature of knowledge and reality, the duties and privileges of the individual and the society, the proper structure of the curriculum, the control of the content of education, the ways of overcoming man's natural tendencies or of capitalizing on these tendencies for man's betterment, the variable treatment of persons with varying capacities and aptitudes, the interplay of social class and opportunity, and the use of education as a safeguard against societal and personal license.

Their writings were prompted by contemporary needs—as they saw these needs. Their societies had problems which had to be attacked. To Plato and Aristotle, education was no abstract entity entirely detached from the daily problems of existence. Instead, it was held to be a primary and most practical approach toward remedying injustices, social excesses, and ignorance or superstition. Education not only developed the individual; it also preserved the state and advanced the state to its optimum condition and structure.

One turns to such writings today simply for their continuing relevance, and for the clarity of the positions enunciated. The influence of such writings continues, because their authors based their representations on theory, logic and observation; and because, though their exact dimensions may differ today, the basic social and individual issues still are relevant.

In early Rome, education was the responsibility of the home. The *pater familias* was charged with instructing his children, particularly his sons. The aim of this education was in harmony with a central social ethic of the Romans: obedience and service to the fatherland. The Roman youth was expected to turn to his father for an exemplar to follow in shaping his conduct and in formulating his values. If the father failed to provide this example or to arrange a proper schedule of instruction and activity, he was liable to public censure. Additional education for a Roman youth came from public life and from experience provided by service to his country.

Few schools existed in early Rome, but toward the second century B.C., and due partly to the influence of Greek models, schools sprang up in several parts of the empire, particularly in Italy. Most of these were private institutions attended by sons of the wealthy, with curricula emphasizing rhetoric and philosophy. Noble youth received advanced education at such famous centers of learning as Athens and Alexandria. With the flowering of Latin literature and thought, the curriculum became more nativistic. A strong moral emphasis was placed on education; this is seen in the prescriptions of Quintilian who describes the aims and means for becoming a model citizen. Toward the end of the Empire, the government closely controlled the schools, and the curriculum was highly centralized. Professions such as engineering, law, and medicine were supported through special institutes.

Roman civilization laid emphasis on practical training, functional arrangements in government, and other aspects of social life. The spread of Roman conquests carried a concomitant spread of Roman institutions and organizations. Rome was the great transmitter of culture of the ancient world, and many of the primary social institutions of today—e.g., law, education, and government—trace much of their present structure from the centuries of Roman cultural and political domination.

To use an oversimplification, one may say that the contrast between Greek and Roman was the contrast between originator and implementer. The Romans built, expanded, and developed systems of government, law, education, public works, commerce, military and civil service. Accompanying this development was a corresponding hierarchical social system, which did, however, permit some entry and upward mobility to those of other than noble birth. Attainment of social grace and of knowledge and skill in the arts marked a well-educated Roman of upper social status. Rhetoric, as in Greece and later in other societies, was the hallmark of the complete education. An ethical character and a sense of devotion to the state were acknowledged goals of education—goals necessary to a society that depended for its vigor and expansion on loyalty to the state, honesty in civil dealings and government service, and coordination of a vast and remote empire.

Though decadence and self-gratification are associated with the late days of Rome, the early centuries of Roman dominance and expansion were possible only through commitment to the fatherland and through the organization, planning, and engineering that allowed Rome to expand and to build but at the same time to control its conquests and absorb a plurality of groups and social inventions. The ethical and political system that permitted this demanded of education that education gear itself to the production of leaders and upholders of the social and cultural aims and of the heritage of Rome. Education thus was more than ornamental; it was socially responsive to the milieu within which it operated.

Into disintegrating Roman civilization came a new moral, philosophical, and theological force: Christianity. To the disciples of this new belief, love and good works provided the ethical basis, and philosophy provided the prop on which Christian doctrines must rest. (It was not until the time of Aquinas, in the late Middle Ages, that a systematic theology was developed.) The early Church fathers turned to previous philosophers, especially to Plato, for a base on which to develop Christian thought. The great influence Christianity exerted in changing both personal values and the design of society can be traced in part to Greek social thinkers and philosophers from whom stemmed much of Christianity's doctrinal foundation and formal theology. Also, however, the early Church drew upon Roman models of organization and administration; it has retained much of this structure even to the present day.

Lacking a literature and a social history of its own, Christianity looked to the heritage of Greek and Roman writings for part of its educational curriculum. Early Church fathers believed that the way to a Christian life on earth was through liberal culture and education, and that this was not incompatible with the primary social aim of a good Christian family as the basic social unit, or with a dominant educational aim of training for the ministry. Both intellect and faith served man and God. Again, as in Greece and Rome, education helped prepare leaders—in this case an educated ministry.

For some time, harmony existed between advancing Christian culture and the pagan literary and rhetorical heritage of the older culture. As well, certain former social and educational emphases were retained; Augustine, for example, held that an emphasis on rhetorical training was acceptable so long as it was kept in its proper relative position, subordinate in aim to the Christian ethical way of life. But by the seventh century, classical study had passed into near oblivion; its traditional goals of self-reliance and individual attainment hardly squared with the primary Christian priorities of humility and forbearance or with the changing concept of the best possible earthly life: absorption in intuitive, personal contemplation of God. During the centuries marked by the barbarian invasion of much of Europe, classical study nearly disappeared except for isolated spots, mainly monasteries, where the Greco-Roman heritage was preserved. Deterioration of language and literary forms and contents occurred rapidly, and soon classical Latin was comprehensible to only a small minority of the population. The number of literate persons kept diminishing and even in the Church it was the exceptional priest or monk who was schooled beyond a rudimentary level. Cultural and social isolation, accompanied by a decentralization of such education as had existed, produced a near oblivion of formal education and the attainment of excellence.

Accompanying the disintegration of classical culture was the diminution of Roman political and administrative influence. Where once Rome had provided near-universal political and social control of the Western world, now a number of semi-autonomous, feudal states appeared, each with its characteristic vernacular tongue, its customs and its regulations. The superstructure that crossed borders and political and social entities now was the Catholic Church, which had its own law (canon law), its own administrative lines of authority, and its own lands and possessions. Looking toward the recreation of a Roman empire, but one based on the Christian ethic and doctrine, the Church for centuries held the balance of power in Europe and provided what over-all stability existed outside the control of local states and agencies.

Following what probably was the lowest ebb of culture and of education the Western world has seen, the crowning of Charlemagne as Holy Roman Emperor was succeeded by a partial revival of learning. An attempt was made to purify Latin and to refine the forms and conventions in current usage. Charlemagne instituted a palace school, bishops' schools and monastery schools. Not only the clergy but also a portion of the upper-class laity became literate, even educated in a restricted sense of the word.

This education consisted for the most part of the liberal arts and some philosophy, prescriptive teachings and rules of the Church, and study of the Scriptures and the writings of early Church fathers. The format included the famous trivium and quadrivium, which had seen their beginnings in former centuries. The trivium included grammar, dialectic, and rhetoric; the quadrivium consisted of geometry, arithmetic, music, and astronomy—more advanced, more specialized subjects. Grammar contained the content and form of literature and demanded of the student some facility in Latin. Dialectic was largely formal logic. Rhetoric was the study of the composition of prose and verse and, as well, the study of law. Geometry also contained what today is considered geography and natural science (such as was then known and acceptable to Church dogma). Arithmetic was quite rudimentary due to the rigidity of the Roman numbering system. Music dealt with sound, harmony, and liturgical music. Astronomy was concerned with the movement of planets and stars—astrology would be a more appropriate term.

Despite the compartmentalization of subject matters, medieval man was not an educational specialist. He saw the whole field of knowledge as unified and approachable through the use of logic, the key to understanding that which was not to be taken on faith alone. This view was in consonance with his vision of the universe: single and purposeful for the over-all benefit of man, having been so created by God. This unified approach was expected of all areas of activity—in government, in religion, in philosophy, in art, in education. All was to be organized to the greater glory of God and to man's fruitful existence on earth. The rules for such organization and for appropriate earthly activity were handed down by the Church. The break with this tradition was a hallmark of the Renaissance.

By the eleventh century, a degree of stability had returned to much of Europe. The invaders had been converted to Christianity. Cities were developing into economic and cultural centers, and trade with the East was increasing. This was a time of relative political and social rest and was marked by Church discipline and control in the areas of belief and behavior. During this period there was a flowering of art and architecture. Great cathedrals were raised to the glory of God; and art, especially that with a religious motif, flourished. The use of vernacular language increased, especially in commercial transactions and ordinary discussion.

Schools, though not uncommon, were available only to the minority. Monastery schools were giving way in importance to cathedral schools because of the former's tendency to concentrate on religious ritual and the latter's dual advantage in offering certain other studies and in being located most often in population and trade centers. Arabic translations of the early Greek writers, especially of Aristotle, were now available for retranslation into Latin. The time was ready for a new educational emphasis: Scholasticism.

Reaching its height in the thirteenth century, Scholasticism was largely an educational and theological revival, though some heightened interest in classical literature was shown. During this movement, the interest of scholars was directed toward examination of the pressing metaphysical questions of Christianity: for example, questions dealing with origins, existence, and the nature of God. Different positions were held and debated vigorously. Formal logic, especially syllogistic reasoning, was the applied method of examination. Disputation proceeded through the dialectic, the statement and analysis of position and counterposition through which resolution of the question was sought.

Against this background, Aquinas performed his synthesis of theology and philosophy. His basis was the systems and structures of Aristotle, which now were available in translation. The field of proper knowledge came to be almost divided between the supreme authorities—Aristotle and the Church. The Church governed belief and conduct; Aristotle was acclaimed the authority on worldly and physical matters.

A great advance in education in the late Middle Ages was the founding of universities. Though some cathedral schools had progressed to the point of becoming what now we would call colleges, it was the universities that were the primary advanced centers of learning and the organizations that prepared and licensed teachers. Many of the early medieval universities were organized much like craft guilds, and for a special purpose: the preparation of teachers of advanced subjects. Gradually, these institutions shaped into a school of liberal arts and one or more advanced schools—law, medicine, theology. Two organizational arrangements were prevalent. In one, the students constituted a guild and hired the faculty, paid their salaries, and retained faculty members or dismissed them according to performance. In the other, teachers constituted the guild.

As many as fourteen years could be spent obtaining a complete education. The first several years were devoted to the study of the trivium. Upon successfully completing examinations, the student received a basic degree: bachelor of arts (*baccalaureus*). The master of arts degree (*magister*) required further study of three or four years in the subjects of the quadrivium. Then, advanced study in one or more of the professional schools led to the doctor's degree, for example in theology. Emphasis was on order and on accepted knowledge, not on investigation and independent inquiry. Instructors read, spoke, or lectured to the students, who listened, took notes, or copied from approved texts. Discussion, though often vigorous, stayed within acceptable bounds.

Schools below university level increased in number. Cathedral and guild schools were becoming relatively common and their curriculum more difficult and demanding. This period also saw the beginnings of municipal schools. Feudal training, in a sense social apprenticeship, formed yet another approach to education, predominantly for elite youth.

By about 1300 A.D., or near the beginning of the Renaissance, established patterns of medieval life were undergoing transformation. Chivalry, feudalism, the guild system, papal authority, the Holy Roman Empire—all these were weakening in authority. Scholastic philosophy was being questioned and in some quarters ridiculed. Throughout much of Europe, Roman law was substituted for various local codes and systems, and canon law declined in importance. Increasingly, criticism was voiced of Church practice and precept.

The causes of these changes were many. The influence of eastern civilizations was felt in Europe as a result of the Crusades and later because of trade with the East. Commerce opened new vistas, and cultural exchange followed hard upon mercantile ventures. The concentration of wealth accruing from trade accelerated the development of cities and towns. The collectivism of the Middle Ages was turning, at least in some quarters, to individualism and to economic independence. There was a surge of interest in the ancient writings and culture. Tied to ancient Rome by geography and an extensive heritage, Italy also possessed the monied leisure class that served as a vanguard to cultural advance and modification.

No abrupt change occurred, for actually much of the interest in classical culture can be traced back to the ninth century or earlier; well before the fourteenth century, Dante, in the *Divine Comedy,* had provided dramatic evidence of classical interests and capabilities, though he served intentionally as an apologist for the Scholastic system of theology and philosophy. In the fourteenth century, Boccaccio and Petrarch gave more impetus to the study of classical forms and contents through their writings and through their translation and collection of ancient works. Toward the end of the century, a foreign scholar was invited to teach Greek at the University of Florence, an event marking formal academic recognition of the value of this ancient language and its literature. Enthusiasm for such study spread throughout southern European centers of learning and eventually northward across the Alps.

The Renaissance hallmark was an integration of man's abilities and interests with a freedom of inquiry and a departure from following the strict injunctions of the Church regarding temporal practices and activities. There was a widespread interest in early Christian writings and sources, in Latin literature and, later, in Greek culture. A consequent humanistic, not spiritual, emphasis followed and individual development of tastes, aptitudes and value positions resulted.

Many schools incorporated into their curricula the writings of ancient authors. Efforts were made to obtain more accurate renditions of classical works and clearer understanding of their contents. The hereafter now shared attention with the present and with man, who increasingly was viewed as perfectible in this world. Hardly all schools and universities were affected, but even cathedral and monastic schools paid considerable homage to such writers as Virgil and Aristotle, according them both affection and esteem. Scholasticism did not disappear; it continued athwart the changing times though not, as before, in a singularly dominant position.

Many humanists saw the older culture and writings as compatible with Christianity (as had early fathers of the Church) and with loyalty to the Church and adherence to the proper temporal life. To such persons the opening up of horizons seemed good; it helped man fulfill both his immediate and eternal destiny. But critics were quick to point out the dangers of a man-centered value system and they argued against the secular content and emphases of the ancient writings. As the Renaissance spread, different positions were espoused by various productive and influential spokesmen. Some, like Erasmus, believed that within a Christian framework the humanism of the early writings could serve to liberate and exalt man and prepare him both for the good life and for eternity. Though critical of much that he saw in Church practice and precept, Erasmus remained within the Church. In France, Montaigne, a skeptic, despaired of attaining final answers from any source. To him, religion and worship were retarding customs. In England, Francis Bacon proposed a different method for examining truth and discovering new knowledge, a method previously outlined by Aristotle but since then given scant attention. This was induction, the development of principles from particulars—the scientific method.

While the Middle Ages had offered a centrality of practice, authority, and doctrine, many leading Renaissance figures now shared the attitude of questioning, of openness to more than a single doctrine or mode of inquiry, and of near veneration of much pre-Christian writing and speculation. New views toward literature, art, politics, philosophy, religion, natural science, and education followed. The increasing tendency to inquire and to experiment produced significant scientific discoveries in the fifteenth and sixteenth centuries.

While the Renaissance promoted an expanded concern with man and his temporal life and individual development, the Reformation produced a spiritual and social reemphasis and called for reform and purification of the Church. The Reformation can be said to be a second stage of the Renaissance, a stage in which peoples mainly north of the Alps played a major role in which the focus was on doctrinal and social freedom from Rome. As well, the Reformation can be labeled a political movement: it was a protest against the policies and rule of the Church and against the contemporary ecclesiastical hierarchy. A return to the earlier, more simplistic ritual and administration of Christianity was of prime importance to such reformers as Luther and Calvin.

Providing background for the Reformation was the decline of the feudal system and the development of early national forms of government. A simultaneous increase in trade and industry was occurring, and the wealth this engendered made certain regions north of the Alps (e.g. the Low Countries) both more self-dependent and more productive with their wealth. There was a concomitant growth of towns and semi-independent political units each desiring more local control of its institutions and social arrangements.

The early Reformation did not encourage learning. Intellectual activity was suspect, even discouraged; Luther called learning the devil's harlot. Fundamentalist Protestantism worked against the increase of either worldly or scientific knowledge. Faith was enough, purified faith based on man's interpretation of God's word as revealed in the Scriptures. Such a posture hardly stimulated higher learning; beyond reading and writing, little more was seen as needed. Scripture, assuming one could read, sufficed. Vocational training was more acceptable; it offered a worthy way to avoid idle hands. But the necessity to read the Bible laid the basis for later elementary education supported by the state, and the subsequent cooperation of church and state strengthened national governments in Protestant lands.

A basic difference between the views of Protestant educators and Catholic educators involved the control of education. Luther was convinced that the state should reign supreme over the temporal affairs of man, education included. He saw the king or prince, through God-given right, as the protector and defender of man as a social being. The school, therefore, should come under civil authority and be supported by the state. Calvin called for a separation of church and state (as did Madison some centuries later) with each functioning differently but with similar ends in view. To Calvin, the church interpreted God's will and the state enforced it. The Catholic position was that the Church was responsible for the education of the people and supreme over the civil government in this regard. Education was the right of the Church, which derived its franchise from God. This fundamental difference provided an issue that still is not totally resolved today.

Gradually some restoration of higher education took place in Protestant lands. Universities were founded or reopened, and schools confiscated from Papal ownership or control were reestablished, often under local authority. For the educated, rhetoric once again became the primary academic subject and Latin the tool. Cicero was considered the model for emulation, the supreme spokesman and exemplar on style and form. In time, "Ciceronianism" became a corrupted version of the earlier humanism which had held as its base a wide-ranging selection of Greek and Roman authors. Programs of education often were formed on a corruption of such views as those of Erasmus, who had called not only for an accenting of classical literature but also for an inquiring and provocative study of its contents. A model for Protestant lands was the Academy at Strasbourg, run by John Sturm. This school, one of the best of its day, was for boys only and was directed primarily to the development of competence in Latin, especially Ciceronian Latin.

In non-Protestant lands, the Catholic Church retained control of education, while at the same time within the Church a counter-reformation took place. The order of the Society of Jesus, the Jesuits, was formed in 1534 and became a force in founding schools, in promoting learning, and in establishing teaching methods and curricula. Into their curriculum, the Jesuits incorporated many elements of the classical heritage of Greece and Rome. The system of Jesuit education was one of divisions and hierarchies, each with a function to perform and a designed area of responsibility. It was a highly centralized system and well coordinated. The quality of education was such that many Protestant students were attracted to the order's colleges and higher schools. The influence of the Jesuit system of education helped shape the educational practices, organization and curriculum of several European countries—e.g., France and Spain—especially at the college and higher secondary levels. The over-all aim of the Jesuit system was to promote the greater glory of God through the propagation of the faith. Probably no other single influence has so shaped the structure and content of Catholic higher education to this day.

The period from the fourteenth to the seventeenth centuries witnessed no universal education. The humble rarely rose through education, or by any other means, to elevated positions in society, commerce or Church. The early influence of the Renaissance deteriorated as the years passed. Yet it must be recalled that this period produced such men as Shakespeare, Luther, Galileo, da Vinci, More, Bacon, Machiavelli, Loyola, Cervantes, Borgia, Rabelais, Copernicus, Columbus, Erasmus, Colet, Henry IV, Richard II, Ferdinand I, Gregory XIII, Boccaccio, and a host of others—men whose individual genius outstripped the social and institutional accomplishments of their times. These were centuries that witnessed significant change: nationalistic beginnings, splintering of religious belief and practice, urbanization to a degree formerly unknown in most of Europe, increased commerce, and much more.

From these centuries dates the still persistent emphasis on classical, humanistic education; the recognition that reading is vital to all, not just the few; the beginnings of schools such as the gymnasium and the English public schools; and other educational institutions, issues and practices of which we are today the inheritors. From this time dates the prelude to modern education and such contemporary questions as the content and arrangement of the various parts of the curriculum; the relationship of Church, state, and education; the support of education; and the secular purposes of education. New times called for new approaches to education and for modifications of existing patterns. While the period just considered hardly could be signaled as a time of great educational advance on all sides, it was a time of educational revision, of educational ferment, and of postulation and argument. The prelude to much of modern education is evident.

THE
EDUCATIONAL
ISSUES

Western educational theory began with the Greek philosophers, particularly Plato and Aristotle. Their conceptions of man, nature, and knowledge, and the suggested relationships between organized education and the state provided basic starting points for the development of education in the occidental civilizations to follow. Many of the educational issues argued in modern America can be traced back to the basic theories and speculations of early Greek philosophers through the refiners and reformers of these early thoughts.

The most encompassing and fundamental issue affecting the shape and texture of contemporary American education is the continuing argument between advocates of the essentialist-basic education position and promoters of the experimentalist-progressive education viewpoint. The former are inclined to believe the best education is that basically intellectual education which uniformly holds to high standards and which concentrates on identifiable blocks of subject matter. The latter are inclined to believe that the best education is that education which is attentive to social and personal-emotional bases of development, which establishes standards more relative to the individual learner, and which focuses on the methodological processes involved in education. The roots of this divided argument extend from Plato and Aristotle, respectively.

Plato depicted a dualistic world of appearance and reality, a world composed of a realm of imperfect material things and a realm of perfect nonmaterial forms or ideas. How this conception of the world determines and relates to the nature of man and knowledge and to the process of education is made clear in his major work, *The Republic*, particularly in the portions represented in this anthology: "The Allegory of the Cave" (p. 22) and "The Stages of Cognition" (p. 19).

The "Allegory" is a graphic presentation of the centrality of education to

14

the development of man and civilization. Plato sees man as a dweller in a cave of delusion, chained down by his ignorance, his unreliable senses, his emotions, his habits, and his unquestioning complacency. He is kept enchained and deluded by society's purveyors of "images"—the teachers, the preachers, the politicians—who shape the thought of their constituents and, knowingly or unknowingly, keep man from attaining a closer approximation of the Truth which resides "outside the cave."

In order for man to develop properly and for society to achieve harmony and purposefulness, at least those men with intellectual ability must be led out of the cave, away from the realm of imperfect illusions and toward the sun, the light of pure reason, . . . toward the contemplation of the abstract forms and ideas which undergird and give meaning and value to the objects of material existence. It is a difficult path to tread, one involving a good deal of external motivation in its initial steps and a high level of mental discipline for its completion. When the journey is done, society is in possession of a "new breed" of leaders and teachers who know the real standards of truth, beauty, and goodness, and who, by then serving society, lend a needed unity and balance to the entire enterprise. The hallmark of this new civilization is reason.

In Plato's presentation of the stages of knowing, the curricular implications of his world view are made more explicit. On his "divided line," the lower two sections deal with beliefs and conjectures about the material world, the world of appearance and change. The lower of these two embraces images, reflections, and representations found in the material world and often presented through media such as art and literature. Such media are highly subjective and tainted by emotion and are, therefore, involved with the lowest type of "knowledge." The higher of these two lower sections includes all natural, physical objects, knowledge of which is dependent upon sensory perception and which, consequently, is still on quite a low level in Plato's taxonomy.

The upper half of the divided line encompasses intellectual understanding and is also subdivided into two sections. The lower of these represents hypothetical knowledge, the generalizations about the natural world which are produced by the sciences. Because of the connection with the changing material world which is necessary on this level, the knowledge obtained here is not "pure." Pure knowledge is obtainable only through pure reason, such as that employed in dialectic thinking, logic, and mathematics; and it occupies the highest level of the line, the level of abstract concepts, first principles, pure ideas. This, then, is the realm of certainty and permanence, the understanding and appreciating of which is the aim of all intellectual education. This is the realm of wisdom.

The controls demanded by this system become more obvious in Plato's discussion of education and the state (p. 29). In his utopian society, under the rule of a wisdom geared to eternal truths and certain knowledge, subjectivity and innovation suffer under a censorship imposed in the name of stability and proper harmony. The individual man, intellectually glorified as he may be, is in a subordinate position to the state.

Aristotle also gives highest priority to the development of reason in his analysis of the nature of man and knowledge, but he sees man as existing in a unified natural world in which man's rationality is a developing, natural endowment that can be nurtured by education. A more down-to-earth, scientific attitude pervades Aristotle's thinking as he describes the interaction of man's reason and man's senses as the basis for the discernment, analysis, ordering, experimentation, and generalization which bring man to an understanding of his world. This natural, experiential basis for knowledge and education is explained by Aristotle in his *Metaphysics* (p. 32). Aristotle insists that education should be directed toward the development of all of the individual's potential "virtues"—the purely intellectual, the practical, the artistic, the moral.

Education, for Aristotle, is an internal process, aided by external agents, in which, primarily through individual activity and effort, potentialities are actualized and happiness is gained. Man is an animal with sensory-emotional needs, but he is, by nature, a rational animal with intellectual needs and, furthermore, a political animal with social needs. Thus we have, in Aristotle's *Politics* (p. 35), an over-all justification for education couched in terms of human needs and judged by the criterion of usefulness or social practicality.

Practicality, especially in the sense of the public results obtained, becomes a hallmark of Roman education. No grand theories were produced by Roman educators, yet many workable suggestions were recorded for posterity, a number of which remain vital even in the modern educational context. Cicero, in his treatise *On the Character of the Orator* (p. 38), presents a lucid justification for a liberal arts education as the most important element in the training of young orators. Quintilian's *Institutio Oratoria* (p. 41) offers a multitude of practical suggestions for teachers and parents and displays an amazing degree of insight into the psychology of the teaching-learning process. A portion of Plutarch's *Moralia* (p. 46) deals with the qualities of a good father and a proper tutor, with deftness and wit. The emphasis in Roman education is training, intellectual training and moral training. The three selections included reveal the thoroughness with which such education was prescribed for the upper strata of Roman youth.

With St. Augustine (p. 52), there is a return to plumbing the depths of human nature and knowledge. He depicts true knowledge in a manner reminiscent of Plato—that is, true knowledge resides within the soul, having been implanted there through spiritual means, and is "brought to the surface"

in water and in solid, smooth and polished bodies and the
...erstand?
...rstand.

...ow, the other section, of which this is only the resemblance, to
...als which we see, and everything that grows or is made.

...u not admit that both the sections of this division have differ-
... truth, and that the copy is to the original as the sphere of
...e sphere of knowledge?
...doubtedly.

...oceed to consider the manner in which the sphere of the intellec-
...ivided.

...manner?

...There are two subdivisions, in the lower of which the soul uses the
...en by the former division as images: the inquiry can only be
...l, and instead of going upward to a principle descends to the other
...e higher of the two, the soul passes out of hypotheses, making no
...ges as in the former case, but proceeding only in and through the
...selves.

...not quite understand your meaning, he said.

...n I will try again; you will understand me better when I have made
...liminary remarks. You are aware that students of geometry, arith-
...d the kindred sciences assume the odd, and the even, and the figures,
...e kinds of angles, and the like, in their several branches of science;
...e their hypotheses, which they and everybody are supposed to know,
...refore they do not deign to give an account of them either to them-
...r others; but they begin with them, and go on until they arrive at last,
...a consistent manner, at their conclusion?

...es, he said, I know.

...And do you know also that although they make use of the visible forms
...eason about them, they are thinking not of these, but of the ideals which
...resemble; not of the figures which they draw, but of the absolute square
...the absolute diameter, and so on—the forms which they draw or make,
...which have shadows and reflections in water of their own, are converted
...hem into images, but they are really seeking to behold the things them-
...es, which can only be seen with the eye of the mind?

...That is true.

...And of this kind I spoke as the intelligible, although in the search after it
...e soul is compelled to use hypotheses; not ascending to a first principle,
...cause she is unable to rise above the region of hypothesis, but employing the
...jects of which the shadows below are resemblances in their turn as images,
...ney having in relation to the shadows and reflections of them a greater
...istinctness, and therefore a higher value.

and made operational through the use of reason, logic, and symbols such as words.

An examination of the Renaissance-Reformation period reveals a Roman-like concern with character development, social duties and graces, practical results (certainly salvation is practical in Luther's terms), and pedagogical method. A composite picture of the education of the well-born is provided by the two works of Erasmus (p. 58) and (p. 61) and by the essays of Montaigne (p. 71) and Bacon (p. 77). The latter two, especially, give hints of the growing importance of individual thinking and inquiry as necessities for the dawning age of science. Martin Luther's letter (p. 66) signals a monumental development in education, the movement toward governmental provision of rudimentary education for all, the details of which are fully enunciated by writers like Comenius (see Part II) and the promise of which was given life in colonial New England—each over a century after Luther's proposals.

St. Thomas Aquinas provided the philosophical and theological positions and constructions upon which the *Ratio Studiorum* (p. 79) of the Jesuits was based. Aquinas seized upon Aristotle's principles of potentiality and actuality for his educational model for man, a viewpoint that welds together sensory and mental knowledge and envisions the learner as a striver toward the actualization of his rational potentiality and, ultimately, his spiritual potentiality. To Greek educational thought he added a spiritual dimension and an ecclesiastical interpretation. The *Ratio* was published after several decades of discussion, revision, and experimentation in colleges and in higher schools maintained by the Society of Jesus. It developed directly from statements of philosophy and positions contained in the "Constitutions" of the Jesuit order, and the "Constitutions" themselves base much of their content on the writings of Aquinas.

The *Ratio* is not so much a statement of educational philosophy as it is a pedagogical document, one dealing minutely with teaching, organization, and the curriculum. It set forth the procedures and curricula followed in the Jesuit schools until the order was disbanded in 1773 A.D., and with later modifications it continued in effect after the restoration of the order in 1814.

INDEX OF
BASIC ISSUES

THE S
OF COG

AUTHOR:

Plato (c. 427–c.

WORK:

THE REPUB

You have to imagine, then, that there are two ru
them is set over the intellectual world, the other
heaven, lest you should fancy that I am playin
suppose that you have this distinction of the visib
your mind?

I have.

Now take a line which has been cut into two u
each of them again in the same proportion, and supp
sions to answer, one to the visible and the other to the
compare the subdivisions in respect of their clearness a
and you will find that the first section in the sphere of t
images. And by images I mean, in the first place, shadow

I understand, he said, that you are speaking of the province of geometry and the sister arts.

And when I speak of the other division of the intelligible, you will understand me to speak of that other sort of knowledge which reason herself attains by the power of dialectic, using the hypotheses not as first principles, but only as hypotheses—that is to say, as steps and points of departure into a world which is above hypotheses, in order that she may soar beyond them to the first principle of the whole; and clinging to this and then to that which depends on this, by successive steps she descends again without the aid of any sensible object, from ideas, through ideas, and in ideas she ends.

I understand you, he replied; not perfectly, for you seem to me to be describing a task which is really tremendous; but at any rate, I understand you to say that knowledge and being, which the science of dialectic contemplates, are clearer than the notions of the arts, as they are termed, which proceed from hypotheses only; these are also contemplated by the understanding, and not by the senses; yet, because they start from hypotheses and do not ascend to a principle, those who contemplate them appear to you not to exercise the higher reason upon them, although when a first principle is added to them they are cognizable by the higher reason. And the habit which is concerned with geometry and the cognate sciences I suppose that you would term understanding, and not reason, as being intermediate between opinion and reason.

You have quite conceived my meaning, I said; and now, corresponding to these four divisions, let there be four faculties in the soul—reason answering to the highest, understanding to the second, faith (or conviction) to the third, and perception of shadows to the last—and let there be a scale of them, and let us suppose that the several faculties have clearness in the same degree that their objects have truth.

I understand, he replied, and give my assent, and accept your arrangement.

THE ALLEGORY OF THE CAVE

AUTHOR:

Plato (*c. 427–c. 347* B.C.)

WORK:

THE REPUBLIC (c. 366 B.C.)

And now, I said, let me show in a figure how far our nature is enlightened or unenlightened: Behold! human beings living in an underground den, which has a mouth open toward the light and reaching all along the den; here they have been from their childhood, and have their legs and necks chained so that they cannot move, and can only see before them, being prevented by the chains from turning round their heads. Above and behind them a fire is blazing at a distance, and between the fire and the prisoners there is a raised way; and you will see, if you look, a low wall built along the way, like the screen which marionette-players have in front of them, over which they show the puppets.

I see.

And do you see, I said, men passing along the wall carrying all sorts of

From *The Republic of Plato,* Book VII, rev. ed., translated by Benjamin Jowett (New York: Willey Book Co., 1901), pp. 209–216. Copyright 1901 by the Colonial Press. Footnotes omitted.

vessels, and statues, and figures of animals made of wood and stone and various materials, which appear over the wall? Some of them are talking, others silent.

You have shown me a strange image, and they are strange prisoners.

Like ourselves, I replied; and they see only their own shadows, or the shadows of one another, which the fire throws on the opposite wall of the cave?

True, he said; how could they see anything but the shadows if they were never allowed to move their heads?

And of the objects which are being carried in like manner they would only see the shadows?

Yes, he said.

And if they were able to converse with one another, would they not suppose that they were naming what was actually before them?

Very true.

And suppose further that the prison had an echo which came from the other side, would they not be sure to fancy when one of the passers-by spoke that the voice which they heard came from the passing shadow?

No question, he replied.

To them, I said, the truth would be literally nothing but the shadows of the images.

That is certain.

And now look again, and see what will naturally follow if the prisoners are released and disabused of their error. At first, when any of them is liberated and compelled suddenly to stand up and turn his neck round and walk and look toward the light, he will suffer sharp pains; the glare will distress him, and he will be unable to see the realities of which in his former state he had seen the shadows; and then conceive someone saying to him, that what he saw before was an illusion, but that now, when he is approaching nearer to being and his eye is turned toward more real existence, he has a clearer vision—what will be his reply? And you may further imagine that his instructor is pointing to the objects as they pass and requiring him to name them—will he not be perplexed? Will he not fancy that the shadows which he formerly saw are truer than the objects which are now shown to him?

Far truer.

And if he is compelled to look straight at the light, will he not have a pain in his eyes which will make him turn away to take refuge in the objects of vision which he can see, and which he will conceive to be in reality clearer than the things which are now being shown to him?

True, he said.

And suppose once more, that he is reluctantly dragged up a steep and rugged ascent, and held fast until he is forced into the presence of the sun himself, is he not likely to be pained and irritated? When he approaches the light his eyes will be dazzled, and he will not be able to see anything at all of what are now called realities.

Not all in a moment, he said.

He will require to grow accustomed to the sight of the upper world. And first he will see the shadows best, next the reflections of men and other objects in the water, and then the objects themselves; then he will gaze upon the light of the moon and the stars and the spangled heaven; and he will see the sky and the stars by night better than the sun or the light of the sun by day?

Certainly.

Last of all he will be able to see the sun, and not mere reflections of him in the water, but he will see him in his own proper place, and not in another; and he will contemplate him as he is.

Certainly.

He will then proceed to argue that this is he who give the season and the years, and is the guardian of all that is in the visible world, and in a certain way the cause of all things which he and his fellow have been accustomed to behold?

Clearly, he said, he would first see the sun and then reason about him.

And when he remembered his old habitation, and the wisdom of the den and his fellow-prisoners, do you not suppose that he would felicitate himself on the change, and pity him?

Certainly, he would.

And if they were in the habit of conferring honors among themselves on those who were quickest to observe the passing shadows and to remark which of them went before, and which followed after, and which were together; and who were therefore best able to draw conclusions as to the future, do you think that he would care for such honors and glories, or envy the possessors of them? Would he not say with Homer,

Better to be the poor servant of a poor master,

and to endure anything, rather than think as they do and live after their manner?

Yes, he said, I think that he would rather suffer anything than entertain these false notions and live in this miserable manner.

Imagine once more, I said, such a one coming suddenly out of the sun to be replaced in his old situation; would he not be certain to have his eyes full of darkness?

To be sure, he said.

And if there were a contest, and he had to compete in measuring the shadows with the prisoners who had never moved out of the den, while his sight was still weak, and before his eyes had become steady (and the time which would be needed to acquire this new habit of sight might be very considerable), would he not be ridiculous? Men would say of him that up he went and down he came without his eyes; and that it was better not even to think of ascending; and if anyone tried to loose another and lead him up to the light, let them catch the offender, and they would put him to death.

No question, he said.

This entire allegory, I said, you may now append, dear Glaucon, to the previous argument; the prison-house is the world of sight, the light of the fire is the sun, and you will not misapprehend me if you interpret the journey upward to be the ascent of the soul into the intellectual world according to my poor belief, which, at your desire, I have expressed—whether rightly or wrongly, God knows. But, whether true or false, my opinion is that in the world of knowledge the idea of good appears last of all, and is seen only with an effort; and, when seen, is also inferred to be the universal author of all things beautiful and right, parent of light and of the lord of light in this visible world, and the immediate source of reason and truth in the intellectual; and that this is the power upon which he who would act rationally either in public or private life must have his eye fixed.

I agree, he said, as far as I am able to understand you.

Moreover, I said, you must not wonder that those who attain to this beatific vision are unwilling to descend to human affairs; for their souls are ever hastening into the upper world where they desire to dwell; which desire of theirs is very natural, if our allegory may be trusted.

Yes, very natural.

And is there anything surprising in one who passes from divine contemplations to the evil state of man, misbehaving himself in a ridiculous manner; if, while his eyes are blinking and before he has become accustomed to the surrounding darkness, he is compelled to fight in courts of law, or in other places, about the images or the shadows of images of justice, and is endeavoring to meet the conceptions of those who have never yet seen absolute justice?

Anything but surprising, he replied.

Anyone who has common-sense will remember that the bewilderments of the eyes are of two kinds, and arise from two causes, either from coming out of the light or from going into the light, which is true of the mind's eye, quite as much as of the bodily eye; and he who remembers this when he sees anyone whose vision is perplexed and weak, will not be too ready to laugh; he will first ask whether that soul of man has come out of the brighter life, and is unable to see because unaccustomed to the dark, or having turned from darkness to the day is dazzled by excess of light. And he will count the one happy in his condition and state of being, and he will pity the other; or, if he have a mind to laugh at the soul which comes from below into the light, there will be more reason in this than in the laugh which greets him who returns from above out of the light into the den.

That, he said, is a very just distinction.

But then, if I am right, certain professors of education must be wrong when they say that they can put a knowledge into the soul which was not there before, like sight into blind eyes.

They undoubtedly say this, he replied.

Whereas, our argument shows that the power and capacity of learning exists in the soul already; and that just as the eye was unable to turn from darkness to light without the whole body, so too the instrument of knowledge can only by the movement of the whole soul be turned from the world of becoming into that of being, and learn by degrees to endure the sight of being, and the brightest and best of being, or, in other words, of the good.

Very true.

And must there not be some art which will effect conversion in the easiest and quickest manner; not implanting the faculty of sight, for that exists already, but has been turned in the wrong direction, and is looking away from the truth?

Yes, he said, such an art may be presumed.

And whereas the other so-called virtues of the soul seem to be akin to bodily qualities, for even when they are not originally innate they can be implanted later by habit and exercise, the virtue of wisdom more than anything else contains a divine element which always remains, and by this conversion is rendered useful and profitable; or, on the other hand, hurtful and useless. Did you never observe the narrow intelligence flashing from the keen eye of a clever rogue—how eager he is, how clearly his paltry soul sees the way to his end; he is the reverse of blind, but his keen eyesight is forced into the service of evil, and he is mischievous in proportion to his cleverness?

Very true, he said.

But what if there had been a circumcision of such natures in the days of their youth; and they had been severed from those sensual pleasures, such as eating and drinking, which, like leaden weights, were attached to them at their birth, and which drag them down and turn the vision of their souls upon the things that are below—if, I say, they had been released from these impediments and turned in the opposite direction, the very same faculty in them would have seen the truth as keenly as they see what their eyes are turned to now.

Very likely.

Yes, I said; and there is another thing which is likely, or rather a necessary inference from what has preceded, that neither the uneducated and uninformed of the truth, nor yet those who never make an end of their education, will be able ministers of the State; not the former, because they have no single aim of duty which is the rule of all their actions, private as well as public; nor the latter, because they will not act at all except upon compulsion, fancying that they are already dwelling apart in the islands of the blessed.

Very true, he replied.

Then, I said, the business of us who are the founders of the State will be to compel the best minds to attain that knowledge which we have already shown to be the greatest of all—they must continue to ascend until they arrive at the good; but when they have ascended and seen enough we must not allow them to do as they do now.

What do you mean?

I mean that they remain in the upper world; but this must not be allowed; they must be made to descend again among the prisoners in the den, and partake of their labors and honors, whether they are worth having or not.

But is not this unjust? he said; ought we to give them a worse life, when they might have a better?

You have again forgotten, my friend, I said, the intention of the legislator, who did not aim at making any one class in the State happy above the rest; the happiness was to be in the whole State, and he held the citizens together by persuasion and necessity, making them benefactors of the State, and therefore benefactors of one another; to this end he created them, not to please themselves, but to be his instruments in binding up the State.

True, he said, I had forgotten.

Observe, Glaucon, that there will be no injustice in compelling our philosophers to have a care and providence of others; we shall explain to them that in other States, men of their class are not obliged to share in the toils of politics: and this is reasonable, for they grow up at their own sweet will, and the government would rather not have them. Being self-taught, they cannot be expected to show any gratitude for a culture which they have never received. But we have brought you into the world to be rulers of the hive, kings of yourselves and of the other citizens, and have educated you far better and more perfectly than they have been educated, and you are better able to share in the double duty. Wherefore each of you, when his turn comes, must go down to the general underground abode, and get the habit of seeing in the dark. When you have acquired the habit, you will see ten thousand times better than the inhabitants of the den, and you will know what the several images are, and what they represent, because you have seen the beautiful and just and good in their truth. And thus our State, which is also yours, will be a reality, and not a dream only, and will be administered in a spirit unlike that of other States, in which men fight with one another about shadows only and are distracted in the struggle for power, which in their eyes is a great good.

Whereas the truth is that the State in which the rulers are most reluctant to govern is always the best and most quietly governed, and the State in which they are most eager, the worst.

Quite true, he replied.

And will our pupils, when they hear this, refuse to take their turn at the toils of State, when they are allowed to spend the greater part of their time with one another in the heavenly light?

Impossible, he answered; for they are just men, and the commands which we impose upon them are just; there can be no doubt that every one of them will take office as a stern necessity, and not after the fashion of our present rulers of State.

Yes, my friend, I said; and there lies the point. You must contrive for your future rulers another and a better life than that of a ruler, and then you may have a well-ordered State; for only in the State which offers this, will they rule who are truly rich, not in silver and gold, but in virtue and wisdom, which are the true blessings of life. Whereas, if they go to the administration of public affairs, poor and hungering after their own private advantage, thinking that hence they are to snatch the chief good, order there can never be; for they will be fighting about office, and the civil and domestic broils which thus arise will be the ruin of the rulers themselves and of the whole State.

Most true, he replied.

And the only life which looks down upon the life of political ambition is that of true philosophy. Do you know of any other?

Indeed, I do not, he said.

And those who govern ought not to be lovers of the task? For, if they are, there will be rival lovers, and they will fight.

No question.

Who, then, are those whom we shall compel to be guardians? Surely they will be the men who are wisest about affairs of State, and by whom the State is best administered, and who at the same time have other honors and another and a better life than that of politics?

They are the men, and I will choose them, he replied.

EDUCATION AND THE STATE

AUTHOR:

Plato (*c. 427–c. 347* B.C.)

WORK:

THE REPUBLIC (c. 366 B.C.)

Here then, I said, is another order which will have to be conveyed to our guardians: Let our city be accounted neither large nor small, but one and self-sufficing.

And surely, said he, this is not a very severe order which we impose upon them.

And the other, said I, of which we were speaking before is lighter still— I mean the duty of degrading the offspring of the guardians when inferior, and elevating into the rank of guardians the offspring of the lower classes, when naturally superior. The intention was, that, in the case of the citizens generally, each individual should be put to the use for which nature intended him, one to one work, and then every man would do his own business, and be one and not many; and so the whole city would be one and not many.

From *The Republic of Plato,* Book IV, rev. ed., translated by Benjamin Jowett (New York: Willey Book Co., 1901), pp. 109–112. Copyright 1901 by the Colonial Press. Footnotes omitted.

Yes, he said; that is not so difficult.

The regulations which we are prescribing, my good Adeimantus, are not, as might be supposed, a number of great principles, but trifles all, if care be taken, as the saying is, of the one great thing—a thing, however, which I would rather call, not great, but sufficient for our purpose.

What may that be? he asked.

Education, I said, and nurture: If our citizens are well educated, and grow into sensible men, they will easily see their way through all these, as well as other matters which I omit; such, for example, as marriage, the possession of women and the procreation of children, which will all follow the general principle that friends have all things in common, as the proverb says.

That will be the best way of settling them.

Also, I said, the State, if once started well, moves with accumulating force like a wheel. For good nurture and education implant good constitutions, and these good constitutions taking root in a good education improve more and more, and this improvement affects the breed in man as in other animals.

Very possibly, he said.

Then to sum up. This is the point to which, above all, the attention of our rulers should be directed—that music and gymnastics be preserved in their original form and no innovation made. They must do their utmost to maintain them intact. And when anyone says that mankind most regard

> The newest song which the singers have,

they will be afraid that he may be praising, not new songs, but a new kind of song; and this ought not be praised, or conceived to be the meaning of the poet; for any musical innovation is full of danger to the whole State, and ought to be prohibited. So Damon tells me, and I can quite believe him; he says that when modes of music change, the fundamental laws of the State always change with them.

Yes, said Adeimantus; and you may add my suffrage to Damon's and your own.

Then, I said, our guardians must lay the foundations of their fortress in music?

Yes, he said; the lawlessness of which you speak too easily steals in.

Yes, I replied, in the form of amusement; and at first sight it appears harmless.

Why, yes, he said, and there is no harm; were it not that little by little this spirit of license, finding a home, imperceptibly penetrates into manners and customs; whence, issuing with greater force, it invades contracts between man and man, and from contracts goes on to laws and constitutions, in utter recklessness, ending at last, Socrates, by an overthrow of all rights, private as well as public.

Is that true? I said.

That is my belief, he replied.

Then, as I was saying, our youth should be trained from the first in a stricter system, for if amusements become lawless, and the youths themselves become lawless, they can never grow up into well-conducted and virtuous citizens.

Very true, he said.

And when they have made a good beginning in play, and by the help of music have gained the habit of good order, then this habit or order, in a manner how unlike the lawless play of the others! will accompany them in all their actions and be a principle of growth to them, and if there be any fallen places in the State will raise them up again.

Very true, he said.

Thus educated, they will invent for themselves any lesser rules which their predecessors have altogether neglected.

What do you mean?

I mean such things as these: —when the young are to be silent before their elders; how they are to show respect to them by standing and making them sit; what honor is due to parents; what garments or shoes are to be worn; the mode of dressing the hair; deportment and manners in general. You would agree with me?

Yes.

But there is, I think, small wisdom in legislating about such matters—I doubt if it is ever done; nor are any precise written enactments about them likely to be lasting.

Impossible.

It would seem, Adeimantus, that the direction in which education starts a man, will determine his future life. Does not like always attract like?

To be sure.

Until some one rare and grand result is reached which may be good, and may be the reverse of good?

That is not to be denied.

And for this reason, I said, I shall not attempt to legislate further about them.

THE EXPERIENTIAL BASIS

AUTHOR:

Aristotle (384–322 B.C.)

WORK:

METAPHYSICS

All men naturally desire knowledge. An indication of this is our esteem for the senses; for apart from their use we esteem them for their own sake, and most of all the sense of sight. Not only with a view to action, but even when no action is contemplated, we prefer sight, generally speaking, to all the other senses. The reason of this is that of all the senses sight best helps us to know things, and reveals many distinctions.

Now animals are by nature born with the power of sensation, and from this some acquire the faculty of memory, whereas others do not. Accordingly the former are more intelligent and capable of learning than those which cannot remember. Such as cannot hear sounds (as the bee, and any other similar type of creature) are intelligent, but cannot learn; those only are capable of learning which possess this sense in addition to the faculty of memory.

Reprinted by permission of the publishers and The Loeb Classical Library from Aristotle, *Metaphysics,* Book I, translated by H. Tredennick (Cambridge, Mass.: Harvard University Press).

Thus the other animals live by impressions and memories, and have but a small share of experience; but the human race lives also by art and reasoning. It is from memory that men acquire experience, because the numerous memories of the same thing eventually produce the effect of a single experience. Experience seems very similar to science and art, but actually it is through experience that men acquire science and art; for as Polus rightly says, "experience produces art, but inexperience chance." Art is produced when from many notions of experience a single universal judgment is formed with regard to like objects. To have a judgment that when Callias was suffering from this or that disease this or that benefited him, and similarly with Socrates and various other individuals, is a matter of experience; but to judge that it benefits all persons of a certain type, considered as a class, who suffer from this or that disease (e.g. the phlegmatic or bilious when suffering from burning fever) is a matter of art.

It would seem that for practical purposes experience is in no way inferior to art; indeed we see men of experience succeeding more than those who have theory without experience. The reason of this is that experience is knowledge of particulars, but art of universals; and actions and the effects produced are all concerned with the particular. For it is not man that the physician cures, except incidentally, but Callias or Socrates or some other person similarly named, who is incidentally a man as well. So if a man has theory without experience, and knows the universal, but does not know the particular contained in it, he will often fail in his treatment; for it is the particular that must be treated. Nevertheless we consider that knowledge and proficiency belong to art rather than to experience, and we assume that artists are wiser than men of mere experience (which implies that in all cases wisdom depends rather upon knowledge); and this is because the former know the cause, whereas the latter do not. For the experienced know the fact, but not the wherefore; but the artists know the wherefore and the cause. For the same reason we consider that the master craftsmen in every profession are more estimable and know more and are wiser than the artisans, because they know the reasons of the things which are done; but we do think that the artisans, like certain inanimate objects, do things, but without knowing what they are doing (as, for instance, fire burns); only whereas inanimate objects perform all their actions in virtue of a certain natural quality, artisans perform theirs through habit. Thus the master craftsmen are superior in wisdom, not because they can do things, but because they possess a theory and know the causes.

In general the sign of knowledge or ignorance is the ability to teach, and for this reason we hold that art rather than experience is scientific knowledge; for the artists can teach, but the others cannot. Further, we do not consider any of the senses to be Wisdom. They are indeed our chief sources of knowledge about particulars, but they do not tell us the reason for anything, as for example why fire is hot, but only that it *is* hot.

It is therefore probable that at first the inventor of any art which went further than the ordinary sensations was admired by his fellow-men, not merely because some of his inventions were useful, but as being a wise and superior person. And as more and more arts were discovered, some relating to the necessities and some to the pastimes of life, the inventors of the latter were always considered wiser than those of the former, because their branches of knowledge did not aim at utility. Hence when all the discoveries of this kind were fully developed, the sciences which relate neither to pleasure nor yet to the necessities of life were invented, and first in those places where men had leisure. Thus the mathematical sciences originated in the neighbourhood of Egypt, because there the priestly class was allowed leisure.

The difference between art and science and the other kindred mental activities has been stated in the *Ethics*; the reason for our present discussion is that it is generally assumed that what is called Wisdom is concerned with the primary causes and principles, so that, as has been already stated, the man of experience is held to be wiser than the mere possessors of any power of sensation, the artist than the man of experience, the master craftsman than the artisan; and the speculative sciences to be more learned than the productive. Thus it is clear that Wisdom is knowledge of certain principles and causes.

THE CRITERION
OF USEFULNESS

AUTHOR:

Aristotle (384–322 B.C.)

WORK:

POLITICS

Now nobody would dispute that the education of the young requires the special attention of the lawgiver. Indeed the neglect of this in states is injurious to their constitutions; for education ought to be adapted to the particular form of constitution, since the particular character belonging to each constitution both guards the constitution generally and originally establishes it—for instance the democratic spirit promotes democracy and the oligarchic spirit oligarchy; and a better spirit always produces a better constitution. Moreover in regard to all the faculties and crafts certain forms of preliminary education and training in their various operations are necessary, so that manifestly this is also requisite in regard to the actions of virtue. And inasmuch as the end for the whole state is one, it is manifest that education also must necessarily be one and the same for all and that the superintendence of this must be public,

Reprinted by permission of the publishers and The Loeb Classical Library from Aristotle, *Politics,* Book VIII, translated by H. Rackham (Cambridge, Mass.: Harvard University Press).

and not on private lines, in the way in which at present each man superintends the education of his own children, teaching them privately, and whatever special branch of knowledge he thinks fit. But matters of public interest ought to be under public supervision; at the same time also we ought not to think that any of the citizens belongs to himself, but that all belong to the state, for each is a part of the state, and it is natural for the superintendence of the several parts to have regard to the superintendence of the whole. And one might praise the Spartans in respect of this, for they pay the greatest attention to the training of their children, and conduct it on a public system.

It is clear then that there should be legislation about education and that it should be conducted on a public system. But consideration must be given to the question, what constitutes education and what is the proper way to be educated. At present there are differences of opinion as to the proper tasks to be set; for all peoples do not agree as to the things that the young ought to learn, either with a view to virtue or with a view to the best life, nor is it clear whether their studies should be regulated more with regard to intellect or with regard to character. And confusing questions arise out of the education that actually prevails, and it is not at all clear whether the pupils should practice pursuits that are practically useful, or morally edifying, or higher accomplishments—for all these views have won the support of some judges; and nothing is agreed as regards the exercise conducive to virtue, for, to start with, all men do not honor the same virtue, so that they naturally hold different opinions in regard to training in virtue.

It is therefore not difficult to see that the young must be taught those useful arts that are indispensably necessary; but it is clear that they should not be taught all the useful arts, those pursuits that are liberal being kept distinct from those that are illiberal, and that they must participate in such among the useful arts as will not render the person who participates in them vulgar. A task and also an art or a science must be deemed vulgar if it renders the body or soul or mind of free men useless for the employments and actions of virtue. Hence we entitle vulgar all such arts as deteriorate the condition of the body, and also the industries that earn wages; for they make the mind preoccupied and degraded. And even with the liberal sciences, although it is not illiberal to take part in some of them up to a point, to devote oneself to them too assiduously and carefully is liable to have the injurious results specified. Also it makes much difference what object one has in view in a pursuit or study; if one follows it for the sake of oneself or one's friends, or on moral grounds, it is not illiberal, but the man who follows the same pursuit because of other people would often appear to be acting in a menial and servile manner.

The branches of study at present established fall into both classes, as was said before. There are perhaps four customary subjects of education, reading and writing, gymnastics, music, and fourth, with some people, drawing; reading and writing and drawing being taught as being useful for the purposes of life and very serviceable, and gymnastics as contributing to manly courage; but as to music, here one might raise a question. For at present most people take part in it for the sake of pleasure; but those who originally included it in education did so because, as has often been said, nature itself seeks to be able not only to engage rightly in business but also to occupy leisure nobly; for—to speak about it yet again—this is the first principle of all things. For if although both business and leisure are necessary, yet leisure is more desirable and more fully an end than business, we must inquire what is the proper occupation of leisure. For assuredly it should not be employed in play, since it would follow that play is our end in life. But if this is impossible, and sports should rather be employed in our times of business (for a man who is at work needs rest, and rest is the object of play, while business is accompanied by toil and exertion), it follows that in introducing sports we must watch the right opportunity for their employment, since we are applying them to serve as medicine; for the activity of play is a relaxation of the soul, and serves as recreation because of its pleasantness. But leisure seems itself to contain pleasure and happiness and felicity of life. And this is not possessed by the busy but by the leisured; for the busy man busies himself for the sake of some end as not being in his possession, but happiness is an end achieved, which all men think is accompanied by pleasure and not by pain. But all men do not go on to define this pleasure in the same way, but according to their various natures and to their own characters, and the pleasure with which the best man thinks that happiness is conjoined is the best pleasure and the one arising from the noblest sources. So that it is clear that some subjects must be learnt and acquired merely with a view to the pleasure in their pursuit, and that these studies and these branches of learning are ends in themselves, while the forms of learning related to business are studied as necessary and as means to other things. Hence our predecessors included music in education not as a necessity (for there is nothing necessary about it), nor as useful (in the way in which reading and writing are useful for business and for household management and for acquiring learning and for many pursuits of civil life, while drawing also seems to be useful in making us better judges of the works of artists), nor yet again as we pursue gymnastics, for the sake of health and strength (for we do not see either of these things produced as a result of music); it remains therefore that it is useful as a pastime in leisure, which is evidently the purpose for which people actually introduce it, for they rank it as a form of pastime that they think proper for free men.

QUALIFICATIONS OF THE ORATOR

AUTHOR:

Cicero (*106–43* B.C.)

WORK:

ON THE CHARACTER OF THE ORATOR (55 B.C.)

It does not escape your observation that what the Greeks call Philosophy is esteemed by the most learned men, the originator, as it were, and parent of all the arts which merit praise; philosophy, I say, in which it is difficult to enumerate how many distinguished men there have been, and of how great knowledge, variety, and comprehensiveness in their studies, men who have not confined their labors to one province separately, but have embraced whatever they could master either by scientific investigations, or by processes of reasoning. Who is ignorant in how great obscurity of matter, in how abstruse, manifold, and subtle an art they who are called mathematicians are engaged? Yet in that pursuit so many men have arrived at excellence, that not one seems to have applied himself to the science in earnest without attaining

From *Cicero on Oratory and Orators,* edited and translated by J. S. Watson (London: Henry G. Bohn, York Street, Covent Garden, 1855), pp. 145–148.

in it whatever he desired. Who has ever devoted himself wholly to music; who has ever given himself up to the learning which they profess who are called grammarians without compassing, in knowledge and understanding, the whole substance and matter of those sciences, though almost boundless? Of all those who have engaged in the most liberal pursuits and departments of such sciences, I think I may truly say that a smaller number of eminent poets have arisen than of men distinguished in any other branch of literature; and in the whole multitude of the learned, among whom there rarely appears one of the highest excellence, there will be found, if you will but make a careful review of our own list and that of the Greeks, far fewer good orators than good poets. This ought to seem the more wonderful, as attainments in other sciences are drawn from recluse and hidden springs; but the whole art of speaking lies before us, and is concerned with common usage and the custom and language of all men; so that while in other things that is most excellent which is most remote from the knowledge and understanding of the illiterate, it is in speaking even the greatest of faults to vary from the ordinary kind of language, and the practice sanctioned by universal reason.

Yet it cannot be said with truth, either that more are devoted to the other arts, or that they are excited by greater pleasure, more abundant hope, or more ample rewards; for to say nothing of Greece, which was always desirous to hold first place in eloquence, and Athens, that inventress of all literature, in which the utmost power of oratory was both discovered and brought to perfection, in this very city of ours, assuredly, no studies were ever pursued with more earnestness than those tending to the acquisition of eloquence. For when our empire over all nations was established, and after a period of peace had secured tranquillity, there was scarcely a youth ambitious of praise who did not think that he must strive, with all his endeavors, to attain the art of speaking. For a time, indeed, as being ignorant of all method, and as thinking there was no course of exercise for them, or any precepts of art, they attained what they could be the single force of genius and thought. But afterward, having heard the Greek orators, and gained an acquaintance with Greek literature, and procured instructors, our countrymen were inflamed with an incredible passion for eloquence. The magnitude, the variety, the multitude of all kinds of causes, excited them to such a degree, that to that learning which each had acquired by his individual study, frequent practice, which was superior to the precepts of all masters, was at once added. There were then, as there are also now, the highest inducements offered for the cultivation of this study, in regard to public favor, wealth, and dignity. The abilities of our countrymen (as we may judge from many particulars) far excelled those of the men of every other nation. For which reason, who would not justly wonder that in the records of all ages, times, and states, so small a number of orators should be found?

But the art of eloquence is something greater, and collected from more sciences and studies than people imagine. For who can suppose that, amid the greatest multitude of students, the utmost abundance of masters, the most eminent geniuses among men, the infinite variety of causes, the most ample rewards offered to eloquence, there is any other reason to be found for the small number of orators than the incredible magnitude and difficulty of the art? A knowledge of a vast number of things is necessary, without which volubility of words is empty and ridiculous; speech itself is to be formed, not merely by choice, but by careful construction of words; and all the emotions of the mind, which Nature has given to man, must be intimately known; for all the force and art of speaking must be employed in allaying or exciting the feelings of those who listen. To this must be added a certain portion of grace and wit, learning worthy of a well-bred man, and quickness and brevity in replying as well as attacking, accompanied with a refined decorum and urbanity. Besides, the whole of antiquity and a multitude of examples is to be kept in the memory; nor is the knowledge of laws in general, or of the civil law in particular, to be neglected. And why need I add any remarks on delivery itself, which is to be ordered by action of body, by gesture, by look, and by modulation and variation of the voice, the great power of which, alone and in itself, the comparatively trivial art of actors and the stage proves, on which though all bestow their utmost labor to form their look, voice, and gesture, who knows not how few there are, and have ever been, to whom we can attend with patience? What can I say of that repository for all things, the memory, which, unless it be made the keeper of the matter and words that are the fruits of thought and invention, all the talents of the orator, we see, though they be of the highest degree of excellence, will be of no avail? Let us, then, cease to wonder what is the cause of the scarcity of good speakers, since eloquence results from all those qualifications, in each of which singly it is a great merit to labor successfully; and let us rather exhort our children, and others whose glory and honor is dear to us, to contemplate in their minds the full magnitude of the object, and not to trust that they can reach the height at which they aim, by the aid of the precepts, masters, and exercises, that they are all now following, but to understand that they must adopt others of a different character.

In my opinion, indeed, no man can be an orator possessed of every praiseworthy accomplishment, unless he has attained the knowledge of everything important, and of all liberal arts, for his language must be ornate and copious from knowledge, since, unless there be beneath the surface matter understood and felt by the speaker, oratory becomes an empty and puerile flow of words.

EDUCATION
OF THE IDEAL ORATOR

AUTHOR:

Quintilian (c. 35–95)

WORK:

INSTITUTIO ORATORIA

. . . It is above all things necessary that our future orator, who will have to live in the utmost publicity and in the broad daylight of public life, should become accustomed from his childhood to move in society without fear and habituated to a life far removed from that of the pale student, the solitary and recluse. His mind requires constant stimulus and excitement, whereas retirement such as has just been mentioned induces languor and the mind becomes mildewed like things that are left in the dark, or else flies to the opposite extreme and becomes puffed up with empty conceit; for he who has no standard of comparison by which to judge his own powers will necessarily rate them too high. Again when the fruits of his study have to be displayed to the public gaze, our recluse is blinded by the sun's glare, and finds everything

Reprinted by permission of the publishers and The Loeb Classical Library from Quintilian, *Institutio Oratoria,* Vol. I, translated by H. E. Butler (Cambridge, Mass.: Harvard University Press).

new and unfamiliar, for though he has learnt what is required to be done in public, his learning is but the theory of a hermit. I say nothing of friendships which endure unbroken to old age having acquired the binding force of a sacred duty: for initiation in the same studies has all the sanctity of initiation in the same mysteries of religion. And where shall he acquire that instinct which we call common feeling, if he secludes himself from that intercourse which is natural not merely to mankind but even to dumb animals? Further, at home he can only learn what is taught to himself, while at school he will learn what is taught others as well. He will hear many merits praised and many faults corrected every day: he will derive equal profit from hearing the indolence of a comrade rebuked or his industry commended. Such praise will incite him to emulation, he will think it a disgrace to be outdone by his contemporaries and a distinction to surpass his seniors. All such incentives provide a valuable stimulus, and though ambition may be a fault in itself, it is often the mother of virtues. I remember that my own masters had a practice which was not without advantages. Having distributed the boys in classes, they made the order in which they were to speak depend on their ability, so that the boy who had made most progress in his studies had the privilege of declaiming first. The performances on these occasions were criticized. To win commendation was a tremendous honor, but the prize most eagerly coveted was to be the leader of the class. Such a position was not permanent. Once a month the defeated competitors were given a fresh opportunity of competing for the prize. Consequently success did not lead the victor to relax his efforts, while the vexation caused by defeat served as an incentive to wipe out the disgrace. I will venture to assert that to the best of my memory this practice did more to kindle our oratorical ambitions than all the exhortations of our instructors, the watchfulness of our *paedagogi* and the prayers of our parents. Further while emulation promotes progress in the more advanced pupils, beginners who are still of tender years derive greater pleasure from imitating their comrades than their masters, just because it is easier. For children still in the elementary stages of education can scarce dare hope to reach that complete eloquence which they understand to be their goal: their ambition will not soar so high, but they will imitate the vine which has to grasp the lower branches of the tree on which it is trained before it can reach the topmost boughs. So true is this that it is the master's duty as well, if he is engaged on the task of training unformed minds and prefers practical utility to a more ambitious program, not to burden his pupils at once with tasks to which their strength is unequal, but to curb his energies and refrain from talking over the heads of his audience. Vessels with narrow mouths will not receive liquids if too much be poured into them at a time, but are easily filled if the liquid is admitted in a gentle stream or, it may be, drop by drop; similarly you must consider how much a child's mind is capable of receiving: the things which are beyond their grasp will not enter their minds, which have not opened out sufficiently to take them in. It is a good thing therefore that a boy should have companions whom he will desire first to imitate and then to surpass: thus he will be led to aspire to higher achievement. I would add that the instructors themselves cannot develop the same intelligence and energy before a single listener as they can when inspired by the presence of a numerous audience.

For eloquence depends in the main on the state of the mind, which must be moved, conceive images and adapt itself to suit the nature of the subject which is the theme of speech. Further the loftier and the more elevated the mind, the more powerful will be the forces which move it: consequently praise gives it growth and effort increase, and the thought that it is doing something great fills it with joy. The duty of stooping to expend that power of speaking which has been acquired at the cost of such effort upon an audience of one gives rise to a silent feeling of disdain, and the teacher is ashamed to raise his voice above the ordinary conversational level. Imagine the air of a declaimer, or the voice of an orator, his gait, his delivery, the movements of his body, the emotions of his mind, and, to go no further, the fatigue of his exertions, all for the sake of one listener! Would he not seem little less than a lunatic? No, there would be no such thing as eloquence, if we spoke only with one person at a time.

The skillful teacher will make it his first care, as soon as a boy is entrusted to him, to ascertain his ability and character. The surest indication in a child is his power of memory. The characteristics of a good memory are twofold: it must be quick to take in and faithful to retain impressions of what it receives. The indication of next importance is the power of imitation: for this is a sign that the child is teachable: but he must imitate merely what he is taught, and must not, for example, mimic someone's gait or bearing or defects. For I have no hope that a child will turn out well who loves imitation merely for the purpose of raising a laugh. He who is really gifted will also above all else be good. For the rest, I regard slowness of intellect as preferable to actual badness. But a good boy will be quite unlike the dullard and the sloth. My ideal pupil will absorb instruction with ease and will even ask some questions; but he will follow rather than anticipate his teacher. Precocious intellects rarely produce sound fruit. By the precocious I mean those who perform small tasks with ease and, thus emboldened, proceed to display all their little accomplishments without being asked: but their accomplishments are only of the most obvious kind: they string words together and trot them out boldly and undeterred by the slightest sense of modesty. Their actual achievement is small, but what they can do they perform with ease. They have no real power and what they have is but of shallow growth: it is as when we cast seed on the surface of the soil: it springs up too rapidly, the blade apes the loaded ear, and yellows ere harvest time, but bears no grain. Such tricks please us when we contrast them with the performer's age, but progress soon stops and our admiration withers away.

Such indications once noted, the teacher must next consider what treatment is to be applied to the mind of his pupil. There are some boys who are slack, unless pressed on; others again are impatient of control: some are amenable to fear, while others are paralyzed by it: in some cases the mind requires continued application to form it, in others this result is best obtained by rapid concentration. Give me the boy who is spurred on by praise, delighted by success and ready to weep over failure. Such an one must be encouraged by appeals to his ambition; rebuke will bite him to the quick; honor will be a spur, and there is no fear of his proving indolent.

Still, all our pupils will require some relaxation, not merely because there is nothing in this world that can stand continued strain and even unthinking and inanimate objects are unable to maintain their strength, unless given intervals of rest, but because study depends on the good will of the student, a quality that cannot be secured by compulsion. Consequently if restored and refreshed by a holiday they will bring greater energy to their learning and approach their work with greater spirit of a kind that will not submit to be driven. I approve of play in the young; it is a sign of a lively disposition; nor will you ever lead me to believe that a boy who is gloomy and in a continual state of depression is ever likely to show alertness of mind in his work, lacking as he does the impulse most natural to boys of his age. Such relaxation must not however be unlimited: otherwise the refusal to give a holiday will make boys hate their work, while excessive indulgence will accustom them to idleness. There are moreover certain games which have an educational value for boys, as for instance when they compete in posing each other with all kinds of questions which they ask turn and turn about. Games too reveal character in the most natural way, at least that is so if the teacher will bear in mind that there is no child so young as to be unable to learn to distinguish between right and wrong, and that the character is best moulded, when it is still guiltless of deceit and most susceptible to instruction: for once a bad habit has become ingrained, it is easier to break than bend. There must be no delay, then, in warning a boy that his actions must be unselfish, honest, self-controlled, and we must never forget the words of Virgil,

So strong is custom formed in early years.

I disapprove of flogging, although it is the regular custom and meets with the acquiescence of Chrysippus, because in the first place it is a disgraceful form of punishment and fit only for slaves, and is in any case an insult, as you will realize if you imagine its infliction at a later age. Secondly if a boy is so insensible to instruction that reproof is useless, he will, like the worst type of slave, merely become hardened to blows. Finally there will be absolutely no need of such punishment if the master is a thorough disciplinarian. As it is, we try to make amends for the negligence of the boy's *paedagogus*, not by forcing him to do what is right, but by punishing him for not doing what is right. And though you may compel a child with blows, what are you to do with him when he is a young man no longer amenable to such threats and confronted with tasks of far greater difficulty? Moreover when children are beaten, pain or fear frequently have results of which it is not pleasant to speak and which are likely subsequently to be a source of shame, a shame which unnerves and depresses the mind and leads the child to shun and loathe the light. Further if inadequate care is taken in the choices of respectable governors and instructors, I blush to mention the shameful abuse which scoundrels sometimes make of their right to administer corporal punishment or the opportunity not infrequently offered to others by the fear thus caused in the victims. I will not linger on this subject; it is more than enough if I have made my meaning clear. I will content myself with saying that children are helpless and easily victimized, and that therefore no one should be given unlimited power over them. . . .

THE EDUCATION OF FREE-BORN CHILDREN

AUTHOR:

Plutarch (*c. 46–120*)

WORK:

MORALIA

Let us consider what may be said of the education of free-born children, and what advantages they should enjoy to give them a sound character when they grow up.

It is perhaps better to begin with their parentage first; and I should advise those desirous of becoming fathers of notable offspring to abstain from random cohabitation with women; I mean with such women as courtesans and concubines. For those who are not well-born, whether on the father's or the mother's side, have an indelible disgrace in their low birth, which accompanies them throughout their lives, and offers to anyone desiring to use it a ready subject of reproach and insult. Wise was the poet who declares:

Reprinted by permission of the publishers and The Loeb Classical Library from Plutarch, *Moralia,* Vol. I, translated by Frank C. Babbitt (Cambridge, Mass.: Harvard University Press).

The home's foundation being wrongly laid,
The offspring needs must be unfortunate.

A goodly treasure, then, is honorable birth, and such a man may speak his mind freely, a thing which should be held of the highest account by those who wish to have issue lawfully begotten. In the nature of things, the spirits of those whose blood is base or counterfeit are constantly being brought down and humbled, and quite rightly does the poet declare:

A man, though bold, is made a slave whene'er
He learns his mother's or his sire's disgrace.

Children of distinguished parents are, of course, correspondingly full of exultation and pride. At all events, they say that Cleophantus, the son of Themistocles, often declared to many persons, that whatever he desired was always agreed to by the Athenian people; for whatever he wished his mother also wished; whatever his mother wished Themistocles also wished; and whatever Themistocles wished all the Athenians wished. It is very proper also to bestow a word of praise on the Spartans for the noble spirit they showed in fining their king, Archidamus, because he had permitted himself to take to wife a woman short of stature, the reason they gave being that he proposed to supply them not with kings but with kinglets.

In this connection we should speak of a matter which has not been overlooked by our predecessors. What is this? It is that husbands who approach their wives for the sake of issue should do so only when they have either not taken any wine at all, or at any rate, a very moderate portion. For children whose fathers have chanced to beget them in drunkenness are wont to be fond of wine, and to be given to excessive drinking. Wherefore Diogenes, observing an emotional and crack-brained youth, said, "Young man, your father must have been drunk when he begot you!" So much for my views on the subject of birth. We must now speak of education.

As a general statement, the same assertion may be made in regard to moral excellence that we are in the habit of making in regard to the arts and sciences, namely, that there must be a concurrence of three things in order to produce perfectly right action, and these are: nature, reason, and habit. By reason I mean the act of learning, and by habit constant practice. The first beginnings come from nature, advancement from learning, the practical use from continued repetition, and the culmination from all combined; but so far as any one of these is wanting, the moral excellence must, to this extent, be crippled. For nature without learning is a blind thing, and learning without nature is an imperfect thing, and practice without both is an ineffective thing. Just as in farming, first of all the soil must be good, secondly, the husbandman skillful, and thirdly, the seed sound, so, after the same manner, nature is like to the soil, the teacher to the farmer, and the verbal counsels and precepts like to the seed. I should strenuously insist that all three qualities met together and formed a perfect union in the souls of those men who are celebrated among all mankind,—Pythagoras, Socrates, Plato, and all who have attained an ever-living fame.

Now it is a fortunate thing and a token of divine love if ever a heavenly power has bestowed all these qualities on any one man; but if anybody imagines that those not endowed with natural gifts, who yet have the chance to learn and to apply themselves in the right way to the attaining of virtue, cannot repair the want of their nature and advance so far as in them lies, let him know that he is in great, or rather total error. For indifference ruins a good natural endowment, but instruction amends a poor one; easy things escape the careless, but difficult things are conquered by careful application. One may understand how effective and how productive a thing is application and hard work, if he only direct his attention to many effects that are daily observed. For drops of water make hollows in rocks, steel and bronze are worn away by the touch of hands, and rims of chariot-wheels once bent by dint of labor, cannot, no matter what be done, recover their original lines. The bent staves which actors use it is impossible to straighten; indeed the unnatural shape has, through labor, come to predominate over the natural. And are these the only things which clearly show the potency of diligence? No, but myriads upon myriads. A piece of land is good by nature, but without care it grows waste, and the better it is by nature, so much the more is it spoiled by neglect if it be not worked. Another piece is forbidding and rougher than land should be, but, if it be tilled, straightway it produces noble crops. What trees if they are neglected do not grow crooked and prove unfruitful? Yet if they receive right culture, they become fruitful, and bring their fruit to maturity. What bodily strength is not impaired and finally ruined by neglect and luxury and ill condition? On the other hand, what weak physique does not show a very great improvement in strength if men exercise and train themselves? What horses if they are well broken when young do not become obedient to their riders, whereas if they are left unbroken they turn out stubborn and restive? Why wonder at other instances, seeing as we do that many of the wildest animals are made tame and used to their labors? Well did the Thessalian say, when asked who were the most pacific of the Thessalians, "Those who are just returning from war." But why discuss the matter at length? For character is habit long continued, and if one were to call the virtues of character the virtues of habit, he would not seem to go far astray. I will cite but one more example on this point and then I shall desist from discussing it further. Lycurgus, the lawgiver of the Spartans, took two puppies of the same litter, and reared them in quite different ways, so that from the one he produced a mischievous and greedy cur, and from the other a dog able to follow a scent and to hunt. And then at a time when the Spartans were gathered together, he said, "Men of Sparta, of a truth habit and training and teaching and guidance in living are a great influence toward engendering excellence, and I will make this evident to you at once." Thereupon producing the two dogs, he let them loose, putting down directly in front of them a dish of food and a hare. The one dog rushed after the hare, and the other made for the dish. While the Spartans were as yet unable to make out what import he gave to this, and with what intent he was exhibiting the dogs, he said, "These dogs are both of the same litter, but they have received a different bringing-up, with the result that the one has turned out a glutton and the other a hunter." In regard to habits and manner of life let this suffice.

. . .

When now they attain to an age to be put under the charge of attendants, then especially great care must be taken in the appointment of these, so as not to entrust one's children inadvertently to slaves taken in war or to barbarians or to those who are unstable. Nowadays, the common practice of many persons is more than ridiculous; for some of their trustworthy slaves they appoint to manage their farms, others they make masters of their ships, others their factors, others they make house-stewards, and some even money-lenders; but any slave whom they find to be a wine-bibber and a glutton, and useless for any kind of business, to him they bring their sons and put them in his charge. But the good attendant ought to be a man of such nature as was Phoenix, the attendant of Achilles.

I come now to a point which is more important and weighty than anything I have said so far. Teachers must be sought for the children who are free from scandal in their lives, who are unimpeachable in their manners, and in experience the very best that may be found. For to receive a proper education is the source and root of all goodness. As husbandmen place stakes beside the young plants, so do competent teachers with all care set their precepts and exhortations beside the young, in order that their characters may grow to be upright. Nowadays there are some fathers who deserve utter contempt, who, before examining those who are going to teach, either because of ignorance, or sometimes because of inexperience, hand over their children to untried and untrustworthy men. And this is not so ridiculous if their action is due to inexperience, but there is another case which is absurd to the last degree. What is this? Why, sometimes even with knowledge and with information from others, who tell them of the inexperience and even of the depravity of certain teachers, they nevertheless entrust their children to them; some yield to the flatteries of those who would please them, and there are those who do it as a favor to insistent friends. Their action resembles that of a person, who, if he were afflicted with bodily disease, should reject that man who by his knowledge might be able to save his life, and, as a favor to a friend, should prefer one who by his inexperience might cause his death; or again that of a person who should dismiss a most excellent shipmaster, and accept the very worst because of a friend's insistence. Heaven help us! Does a man who bears the name of father think more of gratifying those who ask favors than he thinks of the education of his children? And did not Socrates of old often say very fittingly, that if it were in any way possible one should go up to the loftiest part of the city and cry aloud, "Men, whither is your course taking you, who give all possible attention to the acquiring of money but give small thought to your sons to whom ye are to leave it?" To this I should like to add that such fathers act nearly as one would act who should give thought to his shoe but pay no regard to his foot. Many fathers, however, go so far in their devotion to money as well as in animosity toward their children, that in order to avoid paying a larger fee, they select as teachers for their children men who are not worth any wage at all—looking for ignorance, which is cheap enough. Wherefore Aristippus not inelegantly, in fact very cleverly, rebuked a father who was devoid both of mind and sense. For when a man asked him what fee he should require for teaching his child, Aristippus replied, "A thousand drachmas"; but when the other exclaimed, "Great Heavens! what an excessive demand! I can buy a slave for a thousand," Aristippus retorted, "Then you will have two slaves, your son and the one you buy." And, in general, is it not absurd for people to accustom children to take their food with their right hand, and, if one puts out his left, to rebuke him, and yet to take no fore-thought that they shall hear right and proper words of instruction?

Now I will tell what happens to these admirable fathers when they have badly brought up and badly educated their sons. When their sons are enrolled in the ranks of men, and disdain the sane and orderly life, and throw them-selves headlong into disorderly and slavish pleasures, then, when it is of no use, the fathers regret that they have been false to their duty in the education of their sons, being now distressed at their wrongdoing. For some of them take up with flatterers and parasites, abominable men of obscure origin, corrupters and spoilers of youth, and others buy the freedom of courtesans and prostitutes, proud and sumptuous in expense; still others give themselves up to the pleasures of the table, while others come to wreck in dice and revels, and some finally take to the wilder forms of evil-doing, such as adultery and bacchanalian routs, ready to pay with life itself for a single pleasure. But if these men had become conversant with the higher education, they perhaps would not have allowed themselves to be dominated by such practices, and they would at least have become acquainted with the precept of Diogenes, who with coarseness of speech, but with substantial truth, advises and says, "Go into any brothel to learn that there is no difference between what costs money and what costs nothing."

Briefly, then, I say (an oracle one might properly call it, rather than advice) that, to sum up, the beginning, the middle, and end in all these matters is good education and proper training; and it is this, I say, which leads on and helps towards moral excellence and towards happiness. And, in comparison with this, all other advantages are human, and trivial, and not worth our serious concern. Good birth is a fine thing, but it is an advantage which must be credited to one's ancestors. Wealth is held in esteem, but it is a chattel of fortune, since oftentime she takes it away from those who possess it, and brings and presents it to those who do not expect it. Besides, great wealth is the very mark for those who aim their shafts at the purse—rascally slaves and blackmailers; and above all, even the vilest may possess it. Repute, moreover, is imposing, but unstable. Beauty is highly prized, but short-lived. Health is a valued possession, but inconstant. Strength is much admired, but it falls an easy prey to disease and old age. And, in general, if anybody prides himself wholly upon the strength of his body, let him know that he is sadly mistaken in judgment. For how small is man's strength compared with the power of other living creatures! I mean, for instance, elephants and bulls and lions. But learning, of all things in this world, is alone immortal and divine. Two elements in man's nature are supreme over all—mind and reason. The mind exercises control over reason, and reason is the servant of the mind, unassailable by fortune, impregnable to calumny, uncorrupted by disease, unimpaired by old age. For the mind alone grows young with increase of years, and time, which takes away all things else, but adds wisdom to old age. . . .

SENSORY AND MENTAL KNOWLEDGE

AUTHOR:

St. Augustine (354-430)

WORK:

CONCERNING THE TEACHER (c. 389)

INTERNAL LIGHT, INTERNAL TRUTH

Now, if regarding colors we consult light; and regarding the other sensible objects we consult the elements of this world constituting the bodies of which we have sense experience, and the senses themselves which the mind uses as interpreters to know such things; and if, moreover, regarding those things which are objects of intelligence we consult the truth within us through reasoning—then what can be advanced as proof that words teach us anything

From *The Greatness Of The Soul, The Teacher* by St. Augustine, translated by Joseph M. Colleran, in The Ancient Christian Writers Series, Volume 9, edited by Johannes Quasten and Joseph C. Plumpe (Westminster, Md.: The Newman Press, 1950), pp. 178–186, footnotes omitted. Reprinted by permission.

beyond the mere sound which strikes the ears? For everything we perceive, we perceive either through a sense of the body or by the mind. The former we call sensible, the latter, intelligible; or, to speak in the manner of our own authors, we call the former carnal, and the latter spiritual. When we are asked concerning the former, we answer, if the things of which we have sense knowledge are present; as when we are looking at a new moon we are asked what sort of a thing it is or where it is. In this case if the one who puts the question does not see the object, he believes words; and often he does not believe them. But learn he does not at all, unless he himself sees what is spoken about; and in that case he learns not by means of spoken words, but by means of the realities themselves and his senses. For the words have the same sound for the one who sees the object as for the one who does not see it. But when a question is asked not regarding things which we perceive while they are present, but regarding things of which we had sense knowledge in the past, then we express in speech, not the realities themselves, but the images impressed by them on the mind and committed to memory. How we can speak at all of these as true when we see they are false, I do not know—unless it be because we report on them not as things we actually see and perceive, but as things we have seen and perceived. Thus we bear these images in the depths of memory as so many attestations, so to say, of things previously perceived by the senses. Contemplating these in the mind, we have the good conscience that we are not lying when we speak. But even so, these attestations are such for us only. If one who hears me has personally perceived these things and become aware of them, he does not learn them from my words, but recognizes them from the images that are stored away within himself. If, however, he has had no sense knowledge of them, he clearly believes rather than learns by means of the words.

Now, when there is question of those things which we perceive by the mind—that is, by means of the intellect and by reason—we obviously express in speech the things which we behold immediately in that interior light of truth which effects enlightenment and happiness in the so-called inner man. And at the same time if the one who hears me likewise sees those things with an inner and undivided eye, he knows the matter of which I speak by his own contemplation, not by means of my words. Hence, I do not teach even such a one, although I speak what is true and he sees what is true. For he is taught not by my words, but by the realities themselves made manifest to him by God revealing them to his inner self. Thus, if he were asked, he could also give answers regarding these things. What could be more absurd than to think that he is taught by my speech, when even before I spoke he could explain those same things, if he were asked about them?

As for the fact that, as often happens, one denies something when he is asked about it, but is brought around by further questions to affirm it, this happens by reason of the weakness of his vision, not permitting him to consult that light regarding the matter as a whole. He is prompted to consider the problem part by part as questions are put regarding those same parts that constitute the whole, which originally he was not able to see in its entirety. If in this case he is led on by the words of the questioner, still it is not that the words teach him, but they represent questions put to him in such a way as to correspond to his capacity for learning from his own inner self.

To illustrate: if I were to ask you whether it is true that nothing can be taught by means of words—the very topic we are discussing now—you would at first think the question absurd, because you could not see the problem in its entirety. Then I should have to question you in a way adapted to your capacity for hearing that Teacher within you. So I should say: "Those things which I stated and you granted as true, and of which you are certain and which you are sure you know—where did you learn them?" You would perhaps answer that I had taught them to you. Then I would rejoin: "Let us suppose I told you that I saw a man flying. Would my words give you the same certitude as if you heard that wise men are superior to fools?" You would, of course, answer in the negative and would tell me that you do not believe the former statement, or even if you did believe it, that you did not know it; whereas you knew the other statement to be absolutely certain. Certainly, the upshot of this would be that you would then realize that you had not learned anything from my words; neither in the case where you were not aware of the thing that I affirmed, nor in the case of that which you knew very well. For if you were asked about each case, you would even swear that you were unaware of the former and that you did know the latter. But then you would actually be admitting the entire proposition which you had denied, since you would now know clearly and certainly what it implies: namely, that whatever we say, the hearer either does not know whether it is true, or knows it is false, or knows that it is true. In the first of these three cases he either believes, or has an opinion, or is in doubt; in the second, he opposes and rejects the statement; in the third, he bears witness to the truth. In none of the cases, therefore, does he learn. The obvious reason is that the one who on hearing my words does not know the reality, and the one who knows that what he has heard is false, and the one who, if he were asked, could have answered precisely what was said, demonstrate that they have learned nothing from my words.

WORDS DO NOT ALWAYS HAVE THE POWER
EVEN TO REVEAL THE MIND
OF THE SPEAKER

Therefore, also in regard to the things which are seen by the mind, it is of no avail for anyone who cannot perceive them to hear the words of another who does perceive them, except in so far as it is useful to believe them, so long as one is not acquainted with them. But anyone who is able to perceive them is in his innermost a pupil of truth and outside himself a judge of the speaker or, rather, of what he says. For often enough he has knowledge of what is said even when the speaker lacks such knowledge. For example, someone who is a follower of the Epicureans and thinks the soul is mortal, sets forth the arguments for its immortality as expounded by wiser men. If one who is able to contemplate spiritual things hears him, he judges that the other is expressing the truth, while the speaker does not know whether the arguments are true; indeed he even thinks them utterly false. Is he, then, to be considered as teaching what he does not know? Yet he is using the very same words which one who does have the knowledge could also use.

Hence, not even this function is left to words, that they at least manifest the mind of the one who speaks them, since it is even uncertain whether he knows as true what he expresses. Take also the liars and deceivers: you can readily see that they employ words not only not to reveal their minds, but even to conceal them. I do not at all doubt, of course, that the words of those who tell the truth represent efforts and, in a way, promises, to manifest the mind of the speaker; and they would be sustained in this and find acceptance by all, if liars were not allowed to speak.

Of course, we have often experienced both in ourselves and in others, that words are uttered which do not correspond to the things thought about. This, I see, can happen in two ways: either a piece of diction that has been committed to memory and frequently repeated passes the mouth of one actually thinking of other things—as often happens to us when we are singing a hymn; or, contrary to our intention and by a slip of the tongue, some words will rush out in the place of others; obviously, in this case, too, what is heard does not represent the things that are in the mind. In fact, those who tell lies also think of what they express, so that even though we do not know whether they are expressing the truth, we nevertheless know that they have in mind what they are saying, if neither of the two things I spoke of applies to them. If anyone contends that these latter things occur only occasionally and that it is apparent when they occur, I make no objection; though they frequently do escape notice and they have often deceived me when I heard them.

But in addition to these there is another class, certainly very extensive, and the source of countless disagreements and disputes: when the one who speaks signifies exactly what he is thinking, but generally only to himself and certain others, while he does not signify the same thing to the one to whom he speaks and to a number of other persons. For example, let someone say in our hearing that man is surpassed in virtue by certain brute animals. We resent that at once, and with great insistence we refute that statement as utterly false and harmful. Yet he may be using the term "virtue" to designate physical strength, and expressing by it what he has in mind; and he would not be lying, nor is he in error regarding the realities, nor is he reeling off words he has memorized, while he ponders something else in his mind; nor does he express by a slip of the tongue something he did not intend to say. But he merely calls the reality of which he is thinking, by another name than we do; and we should at once agree with him regarding that reality, if we could see his thought, which he was not able to manifest to us by the words he had already spoken in proposing his opinion.

They say that a definition can correct this type of error; so that, if in the present case the speaker should define what "virtue" means, it would be made clear, they say, that the dispute concerns not the reality, but the term used. Even granting that this is so, how many are there who can give good definitions? Even with regard to the method of defining, there has been much discussion; but it is not opportune to treat of that here, nor am I entirely satisfied with it.

. . .

But listen to this—I now yield and concede that when words have been heard by one to whom they are familiar, he can know that the speaker has been thinking about the realities which they signify. But does he for that reason also learn whether what is said is true, which is the present point of inquiry?

CHRIST TEACHES WITHIN THE MIND. MAN'S WORDS ARE EXTERNAL, AND SERVE ONLY TO GIVE REMINDERS

Teachers do not claim, do they, that their own thoughts are perceived and grasped by the pupils, but rather the branches of learning that they think they transmit by speaking? For who would be so absurdly curious as to send his child to school to learn what the teacher thinks? But when they have explained, by means of words, all those subjects which they profess to teach, and even the science of virtue and of wisdom, then those who are called pupils consider within themselves whether what has been said is true. This they do by gazing attentively at that interior truth, so far as they are able. Then it is that they learn; and when within themselves they find that what has been said is true, they give praise, not realizing that they are praising not so much teachers as persons taught—provided that the teachers also know what they are saying. But people deceive themselves in calling persons "teachers" who are not such at all, merely because generally there is no interval between the time of speaking and the time of knowing. And because they are quick to learn internally following the prompting of the one who speaks, they think they have learned externally from the one who was only a prompter.

But at some other time, God willing, we shall investigate the entire problem of the utility of words, which, if considered properly, is not negligible. For the present, I have reminded you that we must not attribute to words more than is proper. Thus we should no longer merely believe, but also begin to understand how truly it has been written on divine authority that we should not call anyone on earth a teacher, since *there is One in heaven who is the teacher of all.* What "in heaven" means He Himself will teach us, who has also counselled us through the instrumentality of human beings—by means of signs, and externally—to turn to Him internally and be instructed. He will teach us, to know and love whom is happiness of life, and this is what all proclaim they are seeking, though there are but few who may rejoice in having really found it.

THE CHRISTIAN
EXEMPLAR

AUTHOR:

Erasmus (*1466–1536*)

WORK:

THE EDUCATION
OF A CHRISTIAN PRINCE (1503)

Some princes exercise themselves greatly over the proper care of a beautiful horse, or a bird, or a dog, yet consider it a matter of no importance to whom they entrust the training of their son. Him they often put in the hands of such teachers as no common citizen with any sense at all would want in charge of his sons. Of what consequence is it to have begot a son for the throne, unless you educate him for his rule? Neither is the young prince to be given to any sort of nurse, but only to those of stainless character, who have been previously instructed in their duties and are well trained. He should not be allowed to associate with whatever playmates appear, but only with those boys of good and modest character; he should be reared and trained most carefully and as becomes a gentleman. That whole crowd of wantons, hard drinkers, filthy-

From *The Education of a Christian Prince* by Desiderius Erasmus, translated by Lester K. Born (New York: Columbia University Press, 1936), pp. 142–144, 148–149, 162–163. Footnotes and reference notes omitted. Reprinted by permission.

tongued fellows, especially flatterers, must be kept far from his sight and hearing while his mind is not yet fortified with precepts to the contrary. Since the natures of so many men are inclined towards the ways of evil, there is no nature so happily born that it cannot be corrupted by wrong training. What do you expect except a great fund of evil in a prince, who, regardless of his native character (and a long line of ancestors does not necessarily furnish a mind, as it does a kingdom), is beset from his very cradle by the most inane opinions; is raised in the circle of senseless women; grows to boyhood among naughty girls, abandoned playfellows, and the most abject flatterers, among buffoons and mimes, drinkers and gamesters, and worse than stupid and worthless creators of wanton pleasures. In the company of all of these he hears nothing, learns nothing, absorbs nothing except pleasures, amusements, arrogance, haughtiness, greed, petulance, and tyranny—and from this school he will soon progress to the government of his kingdom! Although each one of all the great arts is very difficult, there is none finer nor more difficult than that of ruling well. Why in the case of this one thing alone do we feel the need of no training, but deem it sufficient to have been born for it? To what end except tyranny do they devote themselves as men, who as boys played at nothing except as tyrants?

It is too much even to hope that all men will be good, yet it is not difficult to select from so many thousands one or two, who are conspicuous for their honesty and wisdom, through whom many good men may be gained in simple fashion. The real young prince should hold his youth in distrust for a long time, partly because of his inexperience and partly because of his unrestrained impulsiveness. He should avoid attempting any considerable enterprise without the advice of tried men, preferably old men, in whose company he should steadily be, so that the rashness of youth may be tempered by deference to his elders.

Whoever will undertake the task of educating the prince, let him ponder again and again the fact that he is undertaking a duty by no means slight. Just as it is the greatest of all [duties], so is it beset with the most trials. In the first place, he should have an attitude of mind befitting his undertaking; he should not contemplate the number of priestly benefices he can gain as a result, but rather in what way he can repay the hopes of his country entrusted to him by giving it a prince heedful of his country's needs. Think, you who would teach, how much you owe your country, which has entrusted the source of its fortunes to you! It rests with you whether you are going to turn out a power for good in your country or visit it with a scourge and plague.

.   .   .

Before all else the story of Christ must be firmly rooted in the mind of the prince. He should drink deeply of His teachings, gathered in handy texts, and then later from those very fountains themselves, whence he may drink more purely and more effectively. He should be taught that the teachings of Christ apply to no one more than to the prince.

The great mass of people are swayed by false opinions and are no different from those in Plato's cave, who took the empty shadows as the real things. It is the part of a good prince to admire none of the things that the common people consider of great consequence, but to judge all things on their own merits as "good" or "bad." But nothing is truly "bad" unless joined with base infamy. Nothing is really "good" unless associated with moral integrity.

Therefore, the tutor should first see that his pupil loves and honors virtue as the finest quality of all, the most felicitous, the most fitting a prince; and that he loathes and shuns moral turpitude as the foulest and most terrible of things. Lest the young prince be accustomed to regard riches as an indispensable necessity, to be gained by right or wrong, he should learn that those are not true honors which are commonly acclaimed as such. True honor is that which follows on virtue and right action of its own will. The less affected it is, the more it redounds to fame. The low pleasures of the people are so far beneath a prince, especially a Christian prince, that they hardly become any man. There is another kind of pleasure which will endure, genuine and true, all through life. Teach the young prince that nobility, statues, wax masks, family-trees, all the pomp of heralds, over which the great mass of people stupidly swell with pride, are only empty terms unless supported by deeds worth while. The prestige of a prince, his greatness, his majesty, must not be developed and preserved by fortune's wild display, but by wisdom, solidarity, and good deeds.

. . .

Let the teacher paint a sort of celestial creature, more like to a divine being than a mortal: complete in all the virtues; born for the common good; yea, sent by the God above to help the affairs of mortals by looking out and caring for everyone and everything; to whom no concern is of longer standing or more dear than the state; who has more than a paternal spirit toward everyone; who holds the life of each individual dearer than his own; who works and strives night and day for just one end—to be the best he can for everyone; with whom rewards are ready for all good men and pardon for the wicked, if only they will reform—for so much does he want to be of real help to his people, without thought of recompense, that if necessary he would not hesitate to look out for their welfare at great risk to himself; who considers his wealth to lie in the advantages of his country; who is ever on the watch so that everyone else may sleep deeply; who grants no leisure to himself so that he may spend his life in the peace of his country; who worries himself with continual cares so that his subjects may have peace and quiet. Upon the moral qualities of this one man alone depends the felicity of the state. Let the tutor point this out as the picture of a true prince!

THE RENAISSANCE MOOD

AUTHOR:

Erasmus (*1466–1536*)

WORK:

COLLOQUIES (1522–1533)

"A LESSON IN MANNERS" (1522)
MASTER, BOY

MASTER. You seem to me to have been born not in a hall but a stall, so crude are your manners. A respectable boy ought to have decent manners. Whenever one of your betters addresses you, stand up straight and uncover your head. Your face should be neither sad nor gloomy nor saucy nor insolent nor changeable but controlled by a pleasant modesty; your gaze respectable, always looking at the person you're speaking to; your feet together; hands still. Don't shift from one foot to the other or gesticulate with your hands or bite your lip or scratch your head or dig out your ears. Also your clothes should be neat, so that the whole dress, expression, posture, and bearing of the body may indicate a sincere modesty and respectful nature.

Reprinted from *The Colloquies of Erasmus,* translated by Craig R. Thompson by permission of The University of Chicago Press. Copyright © 1965 by the University of Chicago.

BOY.   Suppose I practice?

MASTER.   Do.

BOY.   Is this good enough?

MASTER.   Not yet.

BOY.   What if I do it thus?

MASTER.   Almost.

BOY.   How's this?

MASTER.   Yes, that's good. Keep that posture. Don't chatter foolishly or impetuously. Don't let your mind wander but pay attention to what is said. If an answer is required, give it briefly and carefully, addressing the person from time to time by his proper title. Sometimes add his name as a mark of respect, bowing slightly now and then, especially when you make your response. Don't leave without excusing yourself or unless you're dismissed. Come now, give me a demonstration of this kind of thing. How long have you been away from home?

BOY.   Nearly six months.

MASTER.   You should have added "sir."

BOY.   Nearly six months, sir.

MASTER.   Don't you miss your mother?

BOY.   Sometimes, yes.

MASTER.   Would you like to go and see her?

BOY.   I would, sir, with your kind permission.

MASTER.   Now you should have bowed. Good; continue in that fashion. When you speak, take care not to spill the words out too fast or to stammer or to mutter in your throat, but form the habit of uttering words distinctly, clearly, articulately. If you pass an elderly person, magistrate, priest, doctor, or any other man of dignity, remember to uncover your head and don't hesitate to bow. Do the same when you pass a church or crucifix. At a dinner party be gay, but in such a fashion that you remember always what is appropriate to your age. Be the last of all to reach for the dish. If a special dainty is offered, decline modestly; if it is urged upon you, accept and say "Thank you"; after taking a small serving, give the rest back to the one who offered it to you or to the person seated next to you. If anyone drinks, give him a health gaily but drink moderately yourself. If you're not thirsty, raise the cup to your lips anyway. Look pleasantly at those who are speaking; say nothing yourself unless asked. If anything risqué is said, don't laugh but keep a straight face, as though you don't understand. Don't disparage anybody, or put on airs, or boast about your things, or belittle another's. Be cordial even toward companions who are poorly off. Don't accuse anyone. Don't let your tongue run away with you. Thus you will find sincere approval and make friends. If you notice that the dinner's dragged out, excuse yourself, say goodby to the company, and leave the table. See that you bear these things in mind.

BOY.   I'll try, master. Anything else?

MASTER.   Go to your books now.

BOY.   Yes, sir.

"THE ART OF LEARNING" (1529)
DESIDERIUS, ERASMIUS

DESIDERIUS.   How do your studies progress, Erasmius?

ERASMIUS.   I'm not the Muses' darling, apparently. But studies would go better if I could get something from you.

DESID.   Anything you ask, provided it be to your advantage. Just tell me what's the matter.

ERAS.   I'm sure none of the abstruse arts has escaped you.

DESID.   I wish you were right!

ERAS.   I hear there's a certain method that enables a fellow to learn all the liberal arts thoroughly with a minimum of trouble.

DESID.   How's that? Have you seen the book?

ERAS.   I've seen it, but only seen it, because I didn't have the resources of a teacher.

DESID.   What was in the book?

ERAS.   Various figures of animals—dragons, lions, leopards—and various circles with words written in them, partly Greek, partly Latin, partly Hebrew, and others in barbarous tongues.

DESID.   The title promised a knowledge of the arts within how many days?

ERAS.   Fourteen.

DESID.   A splendid promise, surely, but do you know anybody who emerged a learned man through this method of instruction?

ERAS.   No indeed.

DESID.   Neither has anyone else ever seen one, or ever will, unless we first see someone made rich through alchemy.

ERAS.   Well, I wish there *were* a true method!

DESID.   Perhaps because you're reluctant to buy learning at the cost of so much labor.

ERAS.   Of course.

DESID.   But heaven has so decreed. Riches in the ordinary sense—gold, jewels, silver, palaces, a kingdom—it sometimes grants to the slothful and worthless; but it has ordained that what are true riches, and peculiarly our own, must be won by toil. The labor by which wealth so great is achieved should not seem grievous to us when we see many men struggle, through terrible dangers, through countless labors, for wealth that is both temporary and quite ignoble if compared with learning; they don't always get what they seek, either. And the drudgery of studies has a generous mixture of sweetness, too, if you advance a little in them. Now getting rid of a large part of the irksomeness depends on you.

ERAS.   How do I do it?

DESID.   First, by persuading yourself to love studies. Secondly, by admiring them.

ERAS.   How shall this be done?

DESID.   Observe how many men learning has enriched, how many it has brought to the highest honor and power. Reflect at the same time how much difference there is between man and beast.

ERAS.   Good advice.

DESID.   Next you must discipline your character in order to win self-control and to find delight in things productive of utility rather than pleasure. For what are in themselves honorable, even if somewhat painful at first, prove agreeable by becoming habitual. So it will come about that you will tire the tutor less and understand more easily by yourself; according to the saying of Isocrates, which should be painted in golden letters on the title page of your book: "If you are a lover of learning, you will learn much."

ERAS.   I'm quick enough at learning, but what's learned soon slips away.

DESID.   A jar with holes in it, you mean.

ERAS.   You're not far wrong. But what's the remedy?

DESID.   The chink must be stopped up to prevent leaks.

ERAS.   Stopped up with what?

DESID.   Not moss or plaster but industry. Whoever learns words without understanding the meaning soon forgets, for words, as Homer says, are "winged" and easily fly away unless held down by the weight of meaning. Make it your first task, therefore, to understand the matter thoroughly; next to review it and repeat it frequently to yourself; and in this respect your mind (as I remarked) must be disciplined so that whenever necessary it may be able to apply itself to thought. If one's mind is so wild that it can't be tamed in this way, it's unfit for learning.

ERAS.   How hard this is I understand only too well.

DESID.   One who is so giddy-minded that he can't concentrate on an idea is incapable of paying attention for long when somebody is speaking, or of fixing in memory what he's learned. A thing can be stamped on lead to stay; on water or quicksilver nothing can be stamped, since they are always fluid. But if you can subdue your nature in this respect, then, through constant association with learned men, whose daily conversation affords so much that is worth knowing, you'll learn a great deal with a minimum of effort.

ERAS.   True enough.

DESID.   For besides the table talk, besides the daily conversations, immediately after lunch you hear half a dozen witty sayings, selected from the best authors; and as many after dinner. Now just reckon how large a sum these amount to every month and year.

ERAS.   Splendid—if I could remember them!

DESID.   In addition, since you hear nothing but good Latin spoken, what's to prevent you from learning Latin within a few months, when uneducated boys learn French or Spanish in a very short time?

ERAS.   I'll follow your advice and see whether this nature can be broken to the yoke of the Muses.

DESID.   For my part, I know no other art of learning than hard work, devotion, and perseverance.

EDUCATION FOR SALVATION

AUTHOR:

Martin Luther (*1483–1546*)

WORK:

TO THE COUNCILMEN OF ALL CITIES IN GERMANY THAT THEY ESTABLISH AND MAINTAIN CHRISTIAN SCHOOLS (1524)

. . . It is a grave and important matter, and one which is of vital concern both to Christ and the world at large, that we take steps to help the youth. By so doing we will be taking steps to help also ourselves and everybody else. Bear in mind that such insidious, subtle, and crafty attacks of the devil must

From Walther I. Brandt (ed.), *Luther's Works,* Vol. 45 (Philadelphia: Muhlenberg Press, 1962), pp. 350–356, 367–369. Footnotes and Biblical reference annotations omitted. Specific work translated by Albert T. W. Steinhaeuser and revised by the editor. Reprinted by permission.

be met with great Christian determination. My dear sirs, if we have to spend such large sums every year on guns, roads, bridges, dams, and countless similar items to insure the temporal peace and prosperity of a city, why should not much more be devoted to the poor neglected youth—at least enough to engage one or two competent men to teach school?

Moreover, every citizen should be influenced by the following consideration. Formerly he was obliged to waste a great deal of money and property on indulgences, masses, vigils, endowments, bequests, anniversaries, mendicant friars, brotherhoods, pilgrimages, and similar nonsense. Now that he is, by the grace of God, rid of such pillage and compulsory giving, he ought henceforth, out of gratitude to God and for his glory, to contribute a part of that amount toward schools for the training of the poor children. That would be an excellent investment. If the light of the gospel had not dawned and set him free, he would have had to continue indefinitely giving up to the above-mentioned robbers ten times that sum and more, without hope of return. Know also that where there arise hindrances, objections, impediments, and opposition to this proposal, there the devil is surely at work, the devil who voiced no such objection when men gave their money for monasteries and masses, pouring it out in a veritable stream; for he senses that this kind of giving is not to his advantage. Let this, then, my dear sirs and friends, be the first consideration to influence you, namely, that herein we are fighting against the devil as the most dangerous and subtle enemy of all.

A second consideration is, as St. Paul says in II Corinthians 6, that we should not accept the grace of God in vain and neglect the time of salvation. Almighty God has indeed graciously visited us Germans and proclaimed a true year of jubilee. We have today the finest and most learned group of men, adorned with languages and all the arts, who could also render real service if only we would make use of them as instructors of the young people. Is it not evident that we are now able to prepare a boy in three years, so that at the age of fifteen or eighteen he will know more than all the universities and monasteries have known before? Indeed, what have men been learning till now in the universities and monasteries except to become asses, blockheads, and numbskulls? For twenty, even forty, years they pored over their books, and still failed to master either Latin or German, to say nothing of the scandalous and immoral life there in which many a fine young fellow was shamefully corrupted.

. . .

The third consideration is by far the most important of all, namely, the command of God, who through Moses urges and enjoins parents so often to instruct their children that Psalm 78 says: How earnestly he commanded our fathers to teach their children and to instruct their children's children. This is also evident in God's fourth commandment, in which the injunction that children shall obey their parents is so stern that he would even have rebellious children sentenced to death. Indeed, for what purpose do we older folks exist, other than to care for, instruct, and bring up the young? It is utterly impossible for these foolish young people to instruct and protect themselves. This is why God has entrusted them to us who are older and know from experience what is best for them. And God will hold us strictly accountable for them. This is also why Moses commands in Deuteronomy 32, "Ask your father and he will tell you; your elders, and they will show you."

.   .   .

Ah, you say, but all that is spoken to the parents; what business is it of councilmen and the authorities? Yes, that is true; but what if the parents fail to do their duty? Who then is to do it? Is it for this reason to be left undone, and the children neglected? How will the authorities and council then justify their position, that such matters are not their responsibility?

There are various reasons why parents neglect this duty. In the first place, there are some who lack the goodness and decency to do it, even if they had the ability. Instead, like the ostrich, they deal cruelly with their young. They are content to have laid the eggs and brought children into the world; beyond this they will do nothing more. But these children are supposed to live among us and with us in the community. How then can reason, and especially Christian charity, allow that they grow up uneducated, to poison and pollute the other children until at last the whole city is ruined, as happened in Sodom and Gomorrah, and Gibeah, and a number of other cities?

In the second place, the great majority of parents unfortunately are wholly unfitted for this task. They do not know how children should be brought up and taught, for they themselves have learned nothing but how to care for their bellies. It takes extraordinary people to bring children up right and teach them well.

In the third place, even if parents had the ability and desire to do it themselves, they have neither the time nor the opportunity for it, what with their other duties and the care of the household. Necessity compels us, therefore, to engage public schoolteachers for the children—unless each one were willing to engage his own private tutor. But that would be too heavy a burden for the common man, and many a promising boy would again be neglected on account of poverty. Besides, many parents die, leaving orphans, and if we do not know from experience how they are cared for by their guardians it should be quite clear from the fact that God calls himself Father of the fatherless, of those who are neglected by everyone else. Then too there are others who have no children of their own, and therefore take no interest in the training of children.

It therefore behooves the council and the authorities to devote the greatest care and attention to the young. Since the property, honor, and life of the whole city have been committed to their faithful keeping, they would be remiss in their duty before God and man if they did not seek its welfare and improvement day and night with all the means at their command. Now the welfare of a city does not consist solely in accumulating vast treasures, building mighty walls and magnificent buildings, and producing a goodly supply of guns and armor. Indeed, where such things are plentiful, and reckless fools get control of them, it is so much the worse and the city suffers even greater loss. A city's best and greatest welfare, safety, and strength consist rather in its having many able, learned, wise, honorable, and well-educated citizens. They can then readily gather, protect, and properly use treasure and all manner of property.

.   .   .

It is not necessary to repeat here that the temporal government is a divinely ordained estate (I have elsewhere treated this subject so fully that I trust no one has any doubt about it). The question is rather: How are we to get good and capable men into it? Here we are excelled and put to shame by the pagans of old, especially the Romans and the Greeks. Although they had no idea of whether this estate were pleasing to God or not, they were so earnest and diligent in educating and training their young boys and girls to fit them for the task, that when I call it to mind I am forced to blush for us Christians, and especially for us Germans. We are such utter blockheads and beasts that we dare to say, "Pray, why have schools for people who are not going to become spiritual?" Yet we know, or at least we ought to know, how essential and beneficial it is—and pleasing to God—that a prince, lord, councilman, or other person in a position of authority be educated and qualified to perform the functions of his office as a Christian should.

Now if (as we have assumed) there were no souls, and there were no need at all of schools and languages for the sake of the Scriptures and of God, this one consideration alone would be sufficient to justify the establishment everywhere of the very best schools for both boys and girls, namely, that in order to maintain its temporal estate outwardly the world must have good and capable men and women, men able to rule over land and people, women able to manage the household and train children and servants aright. Now such men must come from our boys, and such women from our girls. Therefore, it is a matter of properly educating and training our boys and girls to that end. I have pointed out above that the common man is doing nothing about it; he is incapable of it, unwilling, and ignorant of what to do. Princes and lords ought to be doing it, but they must needs be sleigh riding, drinking, and parading about in masquerades. They are burdened with high and important functions in cellar, kitchen, and bedroom. And the few who might want to do it must stand in fear of the rest lest they be taken for fools or heretics. Therefore, dear councilmen, it rests with you alone; you have a better authority and occasion to do it than princes and lords.

But, you say, everyone may teach his sons and daughters himself, or at least train them in proper discipline. Answer: Yes, we can readily see what such teaching and training amount to. Even when the training is done to perfection and succeeds, the net result is little more than a certain enforced outward respectability; underneath, they are nothing but the same old blockheads, unable to converse intelligently on any subject, or to assist or counsel anyone. But if children were instructed and trained in schools, or wherever learned and well-trained schoolmasters and schoolmistresses were available to teach the languages, the other arts, and history, they would then hear of the doings and sayings of the entire world, and how things went with various cities, kingdoms, princes, men, and women. Thus, they could in a short time set before themselves as in a mirror the character, life, counsels, and purposes—successful and unsuccessful—of the whole world from the beginning; on the basis of which they could then draw the proper inferences and in the fear of God take their own place in the stream of human events. In addition, they could gain from history the knowledge and understanding of what to seek and what to avoid in this outward life, and be able to advise and direct others accordingly. The training we undertake at home, apart from such schools, is intended to make us wise through our own experience. Before that can be accomplished we will be dead a hundred times over, and will have acted rashly throughout our mortal life, for it takes a long time to acquire personal experience.

THE EDUCATION
OF BOYS

AUTHOR:

Michel de Montaigne (1533–1592)

WORK:

ESSAYS (1580)

. . . The most difficult and important branch of human knowledge appears to be that which treats of the rearing and education of children.

In agriculture the operations which precede the planting and the planting itself, are certain and easy; but as soon as that which is planted comes to life, there are many and difficult ways of cultivating it. So it is with human beings: little industry is needed in the planting, but as soon as they are born, we are charged with a great variety of cares, accompanied by a plenitude of troubles and fears, in training and bringing them up.

The display of their inclinations at that early age is so slight and obscure, the promises are so uncertain and misleading, that it is hard to ground any positive conjecture upon them. Look at Cimon, look at Themistocles and a

From *The Essays of Montaigne,* Vol. I, trans. E. J. Trechmann (London: Oxford University Press, 1927), pp. 146–150, 154, 156–157. Footnotes omitted. The essay herein abridged was dedicated to Madame Diane de Foix, Comtesse de Gurson. Reprinted by permission.

thousand others, how they belied their promise. The young of bears and dogs show their natural disposition, but men, being very soon influenced by customs, opinions, and laws, easily change or disguise their nature.

And yet it is difficult to force natural propensities. Whence it comes to pass that, by reason of having chosen the wrong path, we often labor in vain and expend much time in training children for a calling to which they cannot settle down. In this difficulty, however, my advice is to guide them ever to the best and most profitable things, and to pay little heed to those uncertain divinations and prognostics which we draw from their childish actions. It seems to me that Plato in his *Republic* gives too much authority to them.

Madame, knowledge is a great ornament and an instrument of wonderful utility, especially in persons raised to such a degree of fortune as you are. And in truth it is not rightly used in the hands of people of mean and base condition. It takes more pride in lending its aid in the conduct of wars, in the ruling of a nation, in negotiating the friendship of a prince or a foreign people, than in formulating a dialectical argument in pleading in an appeal, or in prescribing a box of pills. Wherefore, Madame, because I believe that you will not neglect this point in the education of your children, you who have tasted the sweets of it, and who come of a lettered race (for we still possess the writings of those ancient Counts of Foix, from whom Monsieur the Count your husband and yourself are descended; and François Monsieur de Candale your uncle every day brings forth others that will make this quality in your family known to many generations to come), I will acquaint you with one idea of mine on the subject that is at variance with common usage, and that is all that I am able in this matter to contribute to your service.

The charge of the governor whom you select for your son, upon the choice of whom depends the whole success of his education, will comprise several other important duties, but I will not touch upon them, being unable to make any valuable suggestions; and in this particular matter on which I presume to give him advice he will take it in so far as he approves of it. For a child of good family who seeks learning, not for gain (for so mean an object is unworthy of the grace and favor of the Muses, and besides, it looks to and depends on others), and not so much for external advantages as for his own good, to enrich and furnish himself within, since you would desire to turn out a man of parts rather than a scholar, I would have you be careful to choose as his director one with a well-made rather than a well-filled head, and to seek one who possesses both, but no so much learning as character and intelligence; and he should exercise his charge after a new method.

The usual way is to keep bawling into the pupil's ears as one pours water into a funnel, the pupil's business being merely to repeat what he has been told. I would have the tutor amend this method, and at the outset, in order to test the capacity of the mind he has charge of, he should put it on trial, making his pupil to taste of things, and to discern and choose them of his own accord, sometimes opening out the path to him, and sometimes leaving him to open it out to himself. I would not have him always to start the subject and monopolize the speaking, but to listen while the pupil speaks in his turn. Socrates and after him Arcesilaus first made their disciples speak, and then spoke to them. *The authority of the teachers is generally prejudicial to those who desire to learn* (Cicero).

It is well that he should make him trot before him, to judge his paces, and see how far he must step down and adapt himself to his powers. For want of this proportion we spoil all; and to be able to choose this and be guided by it in due measure, is one of the hardest tasks I know; and it is the mark of a lofty and very powerful mind to be able to fall in with the child's gait and to guide it. I walk with a surer and firmer step up hill than down.

When, according to our custom, a teacher undertakes, in one and the same lesson, and with one measure of guidance, to train many minds differing so largely in kind and capacity, it is no wonder if, in a whole multitude of children he hardly come upon two or three who can reap any real fruit from their teaching.

Let the tutor demand of him an account not only of the words of his lesson, but of their meaning and substance, and let him estimate the profit he has gained, not by the testimony of his memory, but of his life. Let him show what he has just learned from a hundred points of view, and adapt it to as many different subjects, to see if he has yet rightly taken it in and made it his own, taking stock of his progress according to Plato's disciplinary method. It is a sign of crudeness and indigestion to disgorge meat as it has been swallowed. The stomach has not performed its operation, unless it has altered the form and condition of what has been given to it to cook.

Our mind only works on trust, bound and compelled to follow the appetite of another's fancy, a slave and captive to the authority of his teaching. We have been so much subjected to leading-strings, that we no longer have the power of walking freely. Our vigor and liberty are extinct. *They never cease to be under guardianship* (Seneca).

At Pisa I had a private interview with a worthy man, but such an Aristotelian that the most universal of his dogmas was: "That the touchstone and measure of all sound opinions and of every truth is conformity to the teaching of Aristotle; that outside of that there is nothing but chimeras and foolishness; That he had seen all and said all." This proposition of his, through having been interpreted a little widely and unjustly, once brought him and for a long time kept him in great danger of the Inquisition at Rome.

We must let him pass everything through a sieve, and store nothing in his head on mere authority and trust. To him Aristotle's principles should be no more principles than those of the Stoics and Epicureans; let their various theories be put to him, and he will choose, if he is able; if not, he will remain in doubt. Only fools are certain and cocksure.

For doubting pleases me no less than knowing. (Dante)

For if he embraces the opinions of Xenophon and Plato by his own reasons, they will be no more theirs: they will be his. He who follows another follows nothing; he finds nothing, nay, he seeks nothing. *We are under no king; let each one look to himself* (Seneca). Let him know that he knows at least. He must imbibe their modes of thought, not learn their precepts. Let him boldly forget, if he likes, whence he has them, but he must be able to appropriate them. Truth and reason are common to every man, and belong no more to him who first gave them utterance than to him who repeats them after him. It is no more according to Plato than according to me, since he and I understand it and see it alike.

. . .

Let his conscience and his virtue shine forth in his speech, and be guided solely by reason. Make him understand that to confess the error he discovers in his own reasoning, though he himself alone perceive it, is a mark of judgment and honesty, which are the chief qualities he aims at; that obstinacy and contention are vulgar qualities, most apparent in the basest minds; that to correct oneself and change one's mind, and in the heat of ardor to abandon a weak position, is a sign of strong, rare, and philosophical qualities.

Let him be advised, when in company, to have his eyes everywhere, for I have found that the chief places are commonly seized upon by the least capable men, and that greatness of fortune is seldom combined with ability. I have observed that whilst at the high end of a table the conversation has turned upon the beauty of a tapestry or the flavor of a Malmsey wine, many witty things spoken at the other end have been lost to them.

He will sound the depths of every man; a neatherd, a mason, a passing stranger; he should utilize and borrow from each according to his wares, for everything is of use in the household; he will learn something even from the follies and weaknesses of others. By observing the graces and manners of each, he will plant in himself the seeds of emulation of the good, and contempt of the bad.

Suggest to his fancy an honest curiosity that will make him inquire into things; he should see everything uncommon in his surroundings: a building, a fountain, a man, the scene of an ancient battle, the passage of Caesar or of Charlemagne:

What land's adust with heat, what numb'd with snow,
And all the winds to Italy that blow. (Propertius)

He will inquire into the character, the resources and the alliances of this and that prince: things very pleasant to learn and very useful to know.

. . .

Mixing with society has a marvellous effect in clearing up a man's judgment. We are all compressed and heaped up within ourselves, and our sight is shortened to the length of our noses. Some one asked Socrates whence he was. He did not answer "Of Athens," but "Of the world." He, whose imagination was fuller and wider, embraced the universe as his city, extended his acquaintance, his society, and his affection over all mankind; he was not as we are, who look no further than our feet. When the vines in my village are nipped by the frost, my priest argues therefrom God's anger with the human race, and concludes that the Cannibals are already dying of thirst. Who is there that, seeing our civil wars, does not cry out that this machine, the world, is being overthrown, and that the day of judgment is seizing us by the throat, without calling to mind that many worse things have happened, and that, notwithstanding, ten thousand parts of the world are meanwhile having a merry time? For my part, considering the licence and impunity they enjoy, I wonder to see them so gentle and moderate. To one who feels the hail coming down on his head, the whole hemisphere seems to be in storm and tempest. And a Savoyard said that "if that fool of a French king had been well able to look after his own interest, he might have become steward to the household of my Duke." His imagination could picture nothing higher and greater than his own master. We are all unconsciously in this error, an error fraught with great consequence and harm. But whoever shall conjure up in his fancy, as in a picture, that great form of our mother Nature, in her full majesty; whoever reads in her face so universal and so constant a variety; whoever observes himself therein, and not only himself, but a whole kingdom, to be no bigger than a point made with a very delicate brush, he alone estimates things according to their true proportion.

This great world, which some yet multiply as a species under one genus, is the mirror wherein we are to behold ourselves, in order to know ourselves from the right point of view. In a word, I should wish it to be my pupil's book. So many ways of looking at things, so many sects, judgments, opinions, laws and customs, teach us to form a sound estimate of our own, and teach our judgment to discover its own imperfection and its natural feebleness; and that is no small apprenticeship. So many disturbances of State and changes in public fortune instruct us to make no great miracle of our own. So many names, so many victories and conquests buried in oblivion, render ridiculous the hope of eternalizing our name by the capture of half a score of *arquebusiers** or of a wretched hovel that is only known to those that took it. The

---

* *Editor's note:* Spanish musketeers.

pride and arrogance of so many foreign pomps and ceremonies, the inflated majesty of so many courts and grandeurs, assures and fortifies our eyes to bear, without blinking, the brilliance of ours. So many millions of men interred before our time, encourage us to have no fear of finding as good company in the other world; and so with the rest.

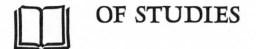

OF STUDIES

AUTHOR:

Francis Bacon (*1561–1626*)

WORK:

ESSAYS (1597)

Studies serve for delight, for ornament, and for ability. Their chief use for delight is in privateness and retiring; for ornament, is in discourse; and for ability is in the judgment and disposition of business. For expert men can execute, and perhaps judge of particulars, one by one; but the general counsels, and the plots and marshalling of affairs, come best from those that are learned. To spend too much time in studies is sloth; to use them too much for ornament is affectation; to make judgment wholly by their rules is the humor of a scholar. They perfect nature, and are perfected by experience; for natural abilities are like natural plants, that need pruning by study; and studies themselves do give forth directions too much at large, except they be bounded in by experience. Crafty men condemn studies; simple men admire them; and wise men use them: for they teach not their own use; but that is a wisdom without them and above them, won by observation. Read not to contradict and

From *The Essayes or Counsels Civill and Morall of Francis Bacon Lord Verulam* by Francis Bacon (London: J. M. Dent and Sons Ltd., 1906), pp. 150–151.

confute; nor to believe and take for granted; nor to find talk and discourse; but to weigh and consider. Some books are to be tasted, others to be swallowed, and some few to be chewed and digested: that is, some books are to be read only in parts; others to be read, but not curiously; and some few to be read wholly, and with diligence and attention. Some books also may be read by deputy, and extracts made of them by others; but that would be only in the less important arguments, and the meaner sort of books; else distilled books are like common distilled waters, flashy things. Reading maketh a full man; conference a ready man; and writing an exact man. And therefore, if a man write little, he had need have a great memory; if he confer little, he had need have a present wit; and if he read little, he had need have much cunning, to seem to know that he doth not. Histories make men wise; poets witty; the mathematics subtle; natural philosophy deep; moral grave; logic and rhetoric able to contend. *Abeunt studia in mores.* Nay, there is no stand or impediment in the wit, but may be wrought out by fit studies: like as diseases of the body may have appropriate exercises. Bowling is good for the stone and reins; shooting for the lungs and breast; gentle walking for the stomach; riding for the head; and the like. So if a man's wit be wandering, let him study the mathematics; for in demonstrations, if his wit be called away never so little, he must begin again: if his wit be not apt to distinguish or find differences, let him study the schoolmen; for they are *cymini sectores*: if he be not apt to beat over matters, and to call one thing to prove and illustrate another, let him study the lawyers' cases: so every defect of the mind may have a special receipt.

PLAN OF STUDIES
IN HIGHER EDUCATION

AUTHOR:

Society of Jesus (*the Jesuits*)

WORK:

RATIO STUDIORUM (1599)

LETTER OF TRANSMISSION OF THE
RATIO STUDIORUM OF 1599

The entire plan of our studies begun to be prepared fourteen years ago is now at length sent to the provinces finished and completely determined.

For although because of the great utility which it seemed it would afford to our studies, Very Reverend Father General had wished that it should be finished and put into use long ago, still up to the present time this could not well be done. For it was proper, in a matter so important and involved in so many difficulties, not to determine anything before the objections and the demands of the provinces should be carefully examined, so that as far as possible all might be satisfied and so that the work which hereafter ought to be put into practice by all should be more favorably received.

From Edward A. Fitzpatrick (ed.), *St. Ignatius and the Ratio Studiorum* (New York: McGraw-Hill Book Company, Inc., 1933), pp. 119–122, passim. Reprinted by permission.

Wherefore whatever in the beginning had been discussed and determined with great labor and carefulness concerning our whole plan of study by the six fathers deputed (for this purpose) has been sent to the provinces with this design, that our doctors and those skilled in such matters should weigh all things carefully and exactly so that if they should notice anything in this plan which was less suitable or which could be framed more suitably they should set this forth and also what their opinion was of the whole plan, giving the reasons for their opinion.

And when almost all the provinces had done this laboriously and carefully, and when everything which had been suggested or proposed by them was diligently gone over at Rome a second time by the principal doctors of the Roman College, and by three Fathers who for this purpose had remained at Rome, Very Reverend Father General with the Father's assistant carefully studied it and again sent this plan so modified to the whole Society, and commanded that it should be exactly observed by all.

Nevertheless, he warns all the provincials that since new plans acquired more solidity from experiment they should take note of and afterwards send to Rome whatever the daily practice of teaching should reveal in each province so that finally the finishing touch might be put to the work and the plan of our studies after so much and so long-continued discussion should be firmly established.

But since the provincials who came to the fifth general congregation brought with them whatever had been remarked from the daily use in their provinces to be less suitable, and since the majority preferred above all else greater brevity in this plan, the whole plan of studies was again carefully examined with considerable labor and having considered the weight of the reasons which were brought forward by the provinces, it was decided what should be firmly established and all things as far as possible were reduced to a shorter and more convenient method; and this was so done that we may rightly hope that this final labor of ours will be approved by all.

Wherefore, this plan of studies which is now sent ought to be observed in the future by all of ours, setting aside all other plans which heretofore had been sent for the sake of experiment, and the careful effort of our doctors should be fixed on this that what is prescribed in this final *Ratio* should be put into execution readily and cheerfully. And it will be so I readily persuade myself if all understand that our Reverend Father has this very much at heart.

Before the Superiors on whom especially this duty lies, Very Reverend Father General seriously and earnestly commands that they strive with as great zeal as possible that this matter which is so much commended in our *Constitutions*, and which it is believed will bring such rich advantages to all our students, be carried out by all readily and exactly.

Rome, January 8, 1599,
By Command of Very Reverend Father General,
JACOBUS DOMINICUS,
Secretary.

RATIO ATQUE INSTITUTIO STUDIORUM SOCIETATIS JESU

Rules for the Provincial

1. PURPOSE OF THE STUDIES OF THE SOCIETY

Since one of the principal functions of our Society is to transmit to those about us all of the schooling consistent with our Institute in such a way that they may be brought to a knowledge and love for our Creator and Redeemer, the Provincial shall realize that he must exert every effort to see to it that the manifold labor of our teaching achieves fully a result such as the grace of our vocation demands, a result such as fully corresponds to the manifold labor of our teaching.

2. GENERAL PREFECT OF STUDIES

Accordingly, he shall not only recommend this to the Rector but shall also give him as Prefect of Studies, or Chancellor, a man well versed in literature and science, who by his zeal and discretion shall be well qualified for the duties entrusted to him; it shall be the duty of the latter to be the general agent of the Rector in properly arranging the studies; and the professors and all Scholastics, both those in the same college and even those who may live in seminaries of boarders and students, and even the Prefects of Studies in the seminaries shall obey him with fitting humility in matters pertaining to studies.

3. PREFECT OF LOWER STUDIES, AND OF DISCIPLINE

But if, because of the extent and variety of the work of the school, one Prefect of Studies does not seem sufficient for supervising all of the classes, the Provincial shall appoint a second who, under direction of the general Prefect, shall take care of the lower studies; and if the situation requires, he shall appoint a third to preside over discipline.

4. METHOD OF SELECTING PROFESSORS

He shall consider ahead of time what professors are available for each department, noticing which seem more fitted to each subject, which are learned, industrious, and conscientious, advanced in their studies, and studious not only in daily lessons but also in other literary exercises.

.   .   .

16. REQUIREMENTS FOR PROFESSORS OF PHILOSOPHY

Professors of philosophy (unless pressing need demands otherwise) should not only have finished the course of theology but also have reviewed it for two years, so that their doctrine may be the more firmly established and serve theology the better. If there are any too prone to innovations, or too liberal in their views, they shall certainly be removed from the responsibility of teaching.

17. THE COURSE OF PHILOSOPHY

Let them complete the course in philosophy in three years, but not in a shorter time where ours are students; but where there are only extern students the matter is left to the judgment of the Provincial; but as far as possible one course is to be ended and another begun each year.

18. TIME FOR RHETORIC AND HUMANITIES

Although it is impossible to prescribe exactly the time to be devoted to the study of humanities and rhetoric, and it is for the Superior to decide how much each shall spend in these studies, at least none of our students shall pass on to philosophy until he has spent two years in rhetoric, unless his age or aptitude or something else is judged in the Lord to prevent it. But if any are endowed with natural aptitude for making progress, especially in these studies, it shall be decided whether it is worth while for them to spend a third year, so as to build a firmer foundation.

.   .   .

20. STUDENTS AND THE TIME FOR MATHEMATICS

In the second year of philosophy all the students of philosophy shall attend class in mathematics for three-quarters of an hour. If there are some, moreover, who are fitted and inclined towards these studies, let them be practiced in them in private lessons after the end of the course.

21. NUMBER OF LOWER CLASSES

1. There should not be more than five grades of lower studies (leaving out the ABC classes, for reasons stated in the fourth part of the *Constitution*), one of rhetoric, a second of humanities, and three of grammar.

2. WHY THEY SHOULD NOT BE COMBINED OR INCREASED IN NUMBER

These consist of five grades so properly related that they should by no means be combined or increased in number; then it will not be necessary to increase the number of ordinary professors; also the number of classes and grades will not require more time than is fitting for completing these lower studies.

3. TWO GRADES IN ONE CLASS

But if there are fewer than five classes, not even then should these five be altered but two grades may be arranged in one class, so that each rank will correspond to one of the five classes in the manner provided in the eighth rule for the Prefect of Lower Studies.

4. PREFERENCE FOR RETAINING THE HIGHER CLASSES

Care must be taken, whenever there are fewer classes, that the higher ones be retained as far as possible and the lower ones dropped.

5. INCREASING THE NUMBER OF CLASSES, BUT NOT GRADES

When we say that there should be no more than three classes of grammar, and no more than five classes of lower studies, we are referring not to the number of classes and teachers, but to the number of grades which we have just mentioned. For if the number of pupils is so great that one teacher is not sufficient, then the class may be divided, with the permission of the General, but in such a way that the same grade, the same lessons, the same method, and the same time for teaching shall be observed in both.

. . .

35. REGULARITY IN HOURS FOR CLASSES AND IN VACATIONS

He shall determine the hours at which classes shall begin and end throughout the year, and when they are to be varied at certain seasons of the year. When this has once been determined, it shall remain unchanged, so that the day of weekly vacation may not come earlier or later; and care shall be taken that the order of days for teaching and vacation be strictly observed.

36. VACATION

Just as earnestness is necessary in literary exercises, so is some vacation important; still, care must be taken that no new vacations be introduced, and that those which are prescribed be carefully observed. On this point, the following directions must be given.

37. GENERAL VACATIONS

The general yearly vacations of the upper classes should not be shorter than one month or longer than two. Rhetoric, unless the custom of the university requires something else, will have one month vacation, humanities three weeks, the higher grammar class two weeks, and the other classes one week.

.   .   .

Rules for the Rector

1. CONCERN FOR STUDIES

Since the Society takes up the work of colleges and universities in order that the members of our Order may be instructed in learning and in all matters pertaining to the helping of souls and may communicate to their neighbors the things which they have learned, the Rector, after looking to their religious and moral training, which ought to be of utmost importance, shall strive to bring about the end which our Society proposed to itself in undertaking the work of teaching.

2. AUTHORITY OF THE PREFECT

In directing studies, the Rector shall have a Prefect of Studies as his assistant; he shall bestow upon him all authority which he considers necessary to the functioning of his office.

3. PRESENCE AT LITERARY EXERCISES

The Rector shall manage and arrange his other duties so that he will be able to foster and improve literary exercises. He shall occasionally visit classes, even the lower ones; he shall frequently be present at both the public and private disputations of the theology and philosophy students, and shall notice if anything hinders the desired results of these exercises, and the reason for any such hindrance.

4. FORBIDDING OCCUPATIONS OF PUPILS

In order that they may realize the great importance of these functions, he shall not permit any students to be absent from disputations or reviews; accordingly he shall forbid any occupations of the pupils which may interfere with their studies.

. . .

8. USE OF LATIN

He shall see to it that the use of Latin is diligently preserved among the Scholastics; there shall be no exception from this rule of speaking Latin except on days of vacation and in hours of recreation, unless in some localities it seems good to the Provincial that the practice of speaking Latin be retained even at these times. He shall also see to it that when those of the Order who have not yet finished their studies write to other members of the Order, they shall write in Latin. Moreover, two or three times a year, when some celebration is held, such as at the recommencement of studies or the renewal of vows, both the philosophy and theology students shall prepare and post verses.

9. ACADEMY FOR THE PREPARATION OF TEACHERS

Lest the teachers of the lower classes come to their task too little prepared, the Rector of the college from which the teachers of the humanities and grammar are taken shall appoint someone thoroughly experienced in teaching. Those who are next to be teachers should toward the end of their course meet with him for an hour three times a week and should in turn give prelections, dictate, write, correct, and perform the other duties of a good teacher.

. . .

13. TRAGEDIES AND COMEDIES

The subject of tragedies and comedies which must not be given except in Latin and on very rare occasions, ought to be sacred and pious, and nothing should be introduced between the acts which is not in Latin and is not becoming; nor is a feminine role nor feminine attire to be introduced.

14. PRIZES

Premiums can be distributed publicly once a year provided it is done at the expense of prominent men and this expense ought to be moderate in proportion to the number of students and the nature of the college. And honorable mention is to be made of those who provide the expenses in the distribution of the prizes. Moreover, great care is to be taken that the scholars while they are preparing themselves for such an event do not suffer any moral or intellectual loss.

.   .   .

Common Rules for all Professors of Higher Faculties

1. PURPOSE

The special duty of a teacher shall be to move his hearers, both within class and out, as opportunity offers, to a reverence and love of God and of the virtues which are pleasing in His sight, and to pursue all their studies to that end.

.   .   .

9. DICTATION

If anyone can teach without dictating, yet in such a way that the pupils can easily tell what ought to be written down, it is preferable for him not to dictate. Certainly teachers who dictate should not pause after every word, but speak for a single breath and then, if necessary, repeat the words; they should not dictate the entire thesis and then explain it, but dictate and explain in turn.

10. REFERRING STUDENTS TO BOOKS

If the teacher brings forward material from books which are easily available, he shall explain rather than dictate; rather, he shall refer the students to those books which treat the matter in hand accurately and in detail.

11. REPETITIONS IN CLASS

After the lecture let him remain in the classroom or near the classroom for at least a quarter of an hour so that the students may approach him to ask questions, so that he may sometimes ask an account of the lectures, and so that the lectures may be repeated.

. . .

Rules of the Professor of Scholastic Theology

1. DUTY

He shall realize that it is his duty to join a well-founded subtlety in disputation with an orthodox faith and devotion in such a way that the former shall especially serve the latter.

2. FOLLOWING ST. THOMAS

All members of our Order shall follow the teaching of St. Thomas in scholastic theology, and consider him as their special teacher; they shall center all their efforts in him so that their pupils may esteem him as highly as possible. However, they should realize that they are not confined to him so closely that they are never permitted to depart from him in any matter, since even those who especially profess to be Thomists occasionally depart from him, and it would not befit the members of our Order to be bound to St. Thomas more tightly than the Thomists themselves.

. . .

Rules for the Professor of Philosophy

1. PURPOSE

Since the arts and the natural sciences prepare the mind for theology and help to a perfect knowledge and use of it and of themselves aid in reaching this end, the instructor, seeking in all things sincerely the honor and glory of God, shall so treat them as to prepare his hearers and especially ours for theology and stir them up greatly to the knowledge of their Creator.

2. HOW FAR ARISTOTLE IS TO BE FOLLOWED

In matters of any importance let him not depart from Aristotle unless something occurs which is foreign to the doctrine which academies everywhere approve of; much more if it is opposed to the orthodox faith, and if there are any arguments of this or any other philosopher against the faith, he will endeavor earnestly to refute them according to the Lateran Council.

3. AUTHORS HOSTILE TO CHRISTIANITY

He shall not read without careful selection or bring into class interpreters of Aristotle who are out of harmony with the Christian religion and he will take care that his students do not become influenced by them.

. . .

Rules for the Professor of Mathematics

1. WHAT AUTHORS ARE TO BE EXPLAINED, AND AT WHAT TIME AND TO WHAT STUDENTS

Let him explain in class to the students of physics for about three-quarters of an hour the elements of Euclid in which explanations, after they have become somewhat familiar during two months, let him add something of geography or of the sphere or other matters which students are glad to listen to, and this along with Euclid either on the same day or on alternate days.

2. PROBLEMS

And let him arrange that every month or every other month some one of the students before a large gathering of students of philosophy and theology has some famous mathematical problem to work out and afterwards, if it seems well, to defend his solution.

3. REPETITION

Once a month and generally on Saturday in place of the lecture, let the principal problems which have been explained during that month be publicly repeated.

. . .

Rules for the Prefect of Lower Studies

1. PURPOSE

Let him realize that he was chosen for this office that he might by all industry and effort aid the Rector in ruling and governing our schools in such a way that those who attend may progress no less in uprightness of life than in the liberal arts.

.   .   .

5. A SINGLE PLAN OF TEACHING

Let him take great care that new teachers carefully retain the method of teaching of their predecessors, and other customs not foreign to our plan, thereby giving outsiders less justification for condemning our frequent change of teachers.

6. VISITING THE CLASSES

At least every fifteenth day let him visit each teacher: let him see whether he devotes sufficient time and effort to Christian doctrine, whether he makes sufficient progress in performing the daily task and reviewing it; and finally whether he conducts himself properly and in a praiseworthy fashion in all matters.

.   .   .

14. WRITTEN EXAMINATIONS

Once a year, or oftener if need be, an examination in prose must be written by all the classes; also one in verse must be written by the highest class of grammar and that of humanities, and, if it seems good, one in Greek, allowing an interval of some days.

.   .   .

25. THE UNSUITABLE AND IGNORANT

If anyone is clearly unfit to make the grade, let there be no room for entreaty. If anyone is scarcely able, but still it seems that he should be advanced because of age, the time he has been in the same class, or some other reason; in such a case, unless something prevents, if the master approves his industry but little, let him be sent back to a lower class, but his name not added to the list. If there are some who are ignorant and it is not fitting to promote them, and no gain is to be expected in their own class, let them on consultation with the

Rector be allowed no place at all, and let their parents or guardians be civilly notified to this effect.

. . .

Rules for the Writing of Examinations

1. ALL PUPILS TO BE PRESENT AT THE WRITING

Let all understand on the very day of writing that if anyone is absent, unless he is detained by serious causes, no consideration will be had for him in the examination.

2. TIME OF WRITING

They must come on time to the class so that they may receive accurately the topic for writing and anything which the Prefect may explain, either in person or through his agent, and may finish everything before the end of the class. For when silence is demanded, no one may be permitted to speak with anyone, not even the Prefect himself or whomever he has appointed in his place.

3. PREPARATION

The pupils should come equipped with books and other things necessary for writing, so that they need not ask anything of anyone while writing.

4. FORM

The papers should be up to the standard of each class, clearly written and according to the words of the theme and the prescribed methods; if it is doubtfully written it will be considered wrong; if words are omitted or perhaps changed to avoid difficulty, it will be counted an error.

5. CARE CONCERNING THOSE WHO SIT TOGETHER

Let care be taken concerning those who sit together; for if perchance two compositions are found to be similar or identical, each must be held in suspicion; since it is not possible to find which one cribbed from the other.

PART 2

THE EARLY MODERN PERIOD

(1600 – 1800)

THE SOCIAL
CONTEXT

THE seventeenth and eighteenth centuries were marked
by many new dimensions in social, political, and economic change. This period
saw the beginnings of modern capitalism; the development of the Industrial
Revolution; advancing nationalism; efforts toward representative government
in many countries; the spread of Protestantism; the growth of scientism and
rationalism and, later, romanticism; the development in the New World of
colonies of major European powers—progress, change, and, of course, re-
trenchment. At the beginning of the period Jamestown was yet unfounded;
at the end of the period the United States appeared in the list of nations. And
by 1800, the basis for a distinctly American system of education was being
developed.

In Europe, the defeat of the Armada toward the end of the sixteenth
century had diminished the power and affluence of Spain. England and other
European powers, such as the Low Countries, emerged during the 1700s as
leaders in commerce, political influence and colonization. Toward the end of
the period, the French and American Revolutions altered established forms of
government and provided models for social change that would be looked to
by other peoples in the 1900s.

Mercantilism, closely allied to developing nationalism, encouraged the
expansion of trade and called for the acquisition of colonies so that European
powers could obtain raw materials and markets in which to sell domestically
produced goods. The great colonial empires of such countries as England,
France, and Holland resulted. By the end of the century, especially in England, the start of the modern industrial system was underway.

Religious dissension which had begun with the Reformation continued
throughout the period 1600–1800. In Germany, the Thirty Years' War
between Catholics and Lutherans devastated the land and retarded social and
economic progress for decades. In England the Stuarts and Protestants, especially the Puritans, collided. In France, the conflict was between Catholic and
Huguenot. In the American Colonies various denominations established

control of portions of the new land and were patently hostile to others than themselves. Different denominations developed their own educational systems in order to preserve in the populace the tenets of their accepted faiths and to guarantee the continued existence of their particular social orders.

This was a time of expansion in scientific knowledge. The late Renaissance produced men whose investigations and conjectures advanced contemporary knowledge of the physical world. It was during this period that scholarly and scientific societies were founded—e.g., the Royal Society in England and the Academy in Berlin. These became centers and sponsors of higher learning for many specialized areas of study. In the late eighteenth century, the American Philosophical Society was formed in Philadelphia. Its emphasis was both scholarly and productive. Among papers presented during 1786, for instance, were: "Franklin's Description of an Urn Stove," "Rush's Paper on Martin's Cancer Powder," and "Ewing's Method of Calculating the Size of the Earth." Fuller utilization of the printing press enabled scholars and laymen to communicate with and inform one another. For the first time in history, books in relative abundance, textbooks included, were available to more than a small minority of the population. Also by this time there was virtually full use of the vernacular both in print and in speech.

Along with science, advances were made in the arts and in philosophy. Shakespeare produced many of his greatest plays early in the seventeenth century. Realism and Cartesian rationalism offered a different framework for viewing the structure of knowledge and the world in which man existed. This was a time of social reformers—men who proposed new schemes for organizing society. Characteristic of the formulations of utopists like Bacon, Campanella and Andrea was the emphasis placed on the public importance of knowledge and education. The seventeenth century reflects the genius of such men as Cromwell, Pascal, Descartes, Harvey, and Comenius. A century later they were followed by Locke, Newton, Priestly, Kant, Rousseau, Diderot, Franklin, Jefferson, and Voltaire, to name but some.

Educational changes during the seventeenth and eighteenth centuries were slow to come. As an example, Latin, though still demanded, was by now of little value to a majority of those studying it; long before the seventeenth century it had begun to lose way as the language of learning, and the vernacular was increasingly the language both of literature and commerce. Attendance at Latin schools fell off, but since the alternative often was no schooling at all, the result often was a decrease in learning. Tradition, long in developing, is long too in disappearing.

In areas of Europe a state system of vernacular schools was urged, but little response was given. Trade schools were proposed yet few were started, and apprenticeship remained the common method of vocational preparation. Throughout the seventeenth and eighteenth centuries, most people received little or no formal education. The accent was aristocratic; Voltaire called for the enlightenment of the select, as centuries before him Plato and Quintilian had held this to be the imperative. Rousseau also denied that the poor needed education. Why should laborers, farmers, and artisans need formal schooling? An assumption underlying such views was that the social system would remain largely unchanged. During the seventeenth and eighteenth centuries, in most of Europe (Germany provided somewhat of an exception) there was not much more, perhaps even less, general opportunity for education than had existed in Athens or in Rome.

Rousseau's call for a return to a more simple life was a protest against contemporary social conventions and specious values. Curricula were content-centered and instructor-ruled. Little attention was paid to the child, to his development or his individual needs. Some efforts toward educating children of the lower classes were made, however, especially for children of the very poor. In England, the Sunday school movement began toward the end of the eighteenth century, providing a measure of learning in religion, of training in morality, and of elementary knowledge of reading and writing for lower-class children, who often spent a long week in physical labor.

During these centuries, universities in Protestant countries often were instruments for promoting loyalty to and training in the state-sponsored theology. In Catholic countries, seminaries were replacing universities as training centers for the clergy. State intrusion in curriculum and administration was common; in fact, it was more common than during much of the Middle Ages. Leibnitz refused to accept a chair in any university, contending that all were unworthy of serious consideration and discouraging of liberal study or independent investigation. For those who could afford it, travel—not university attendance—was considered an acceptable method of crowning one's education. Toward 1700, there was a partial revival of university life and a restoration of the more traditional functions and aims of universities.

The period 1600–1800 in France was the time of the *Ancien Regime,* and education perpetuated the status quo. In effect, education was often quite informal, more a period of play and social convention than an organized attempt at the presentation of knowledge or the acquiring of skill. Children of the nobility attended school, while the masses remained uneducated. Though the National Convention (1792–95) suppressed clerical schools, and reform legislation established some public elementary and secondary schools, these measures were relatively ineffective. In 1799, Napoleon organized a state system of education which emphasized uniformity and centralization. The teaching privileges of the Church were restored.

The French Revolution asserted man's general rights and, by implication, his right to education. It paved the way for nineteenth-century political and social developments, but not without provoking attempts at counteraction by those who feared the consequences of too much freedom, too much discussion, too much liberation of mind and spirit. Tight state control of public education, such as existed, persisted throughout most of the mainland European countries.

In Germany, Luther had called for a basic education for all, rich or poor, in state-supported and -controlled schools, and as early as 1619 his proposal was enacted into law in Weimar. In 1717, Frederick William I ordered that all children attend school where schools existed. In 1763, Frederick the Great laid down broad guidelines upon which Prussian systems of education were to be based. Included were the requirement that children of ages 5–14 must attend school and the principle that provision was to be made for the poor. Yet schools were rather few and far between, despite the requirement of general attendance. In practice, control of the schools rested with the clergy. The interest of Frederick the Great was in the education of leaders more than in the general raising of educational standards for the entire populace.[1] A result of this interest was reformation of the old knightly academies and the classical gymnasiums and their increased attendance by sons of the wealthy.

There was much difference in quality between schools attended by the masses and those attended by the nobility—difference both in degree and in kind, most noticeable perhaps in the quality of instructors. In Germany during the seventeenth and eighteenth centuries, as elsewhere in Europe, a two-track system of education existed: those of noble birth or fortunate circumstance had considerable opportunity for education, either by formal schooling or tutoring; the rest were fortunate to acquire the rudiments. But the foundations for universal education were established, and Germany (Prussia) was well ahead of other major European nations in this respect.

The second English Reformation (seventeenth century) might have led to an educational revival, but instead the activities of opposing denominational parties prevented establishment of anything like a concerted attempt to provide widespread education. A series of laws enacted during the sixteenth century and brought together in the laws of 1597–98 resulted in the famous English Poor Law of 1601. This act, passed during the reign of Elizabeth, was notable educationally and socially for several reasons:

it called for compulsory care of the poor as a State obligation,

it required compulsory apprenticeship of children of the indigent of both sexes, to learn a trade,

---

[1] More than altruism, though this was present, prompted the educational concern of the German rulers. If all children could become more obedient and of better moral character through schooling, a public and, for the state, protective service would be rendered.

it stated the obligation of masters to train apprentices and it required overseers to provide materials necessary to learning the trade and its basic requirements, which could include educational training of a rudimentary sort,

it provided compulsory taxation for the above purposes from persons of means and provided further for a sharing of costs among parishes when necessary.

The law influenced later legislation, both in England and the colonies. It pronounced the duty of the State to intervene for the benefit of the citizen, to insist that he be provided for, and, by the next step, that he be educated.

During the eighteenth century, a system of charity schools was begun in London and surrounding towns. About 1700, the Society for the Promotion of Christian Knowledge was established; it then founded catechetical schools for educating the poor in reading, writing, and the principles of religion. To accomplish the same aims in the colonies and territories, a related organization, the Society for the Propagation of the Gospel in Foreign Parts, was formed; this organization remained active in America until the close of the Revolution. Both these agencies were privately endowed. Sunday schools, which began about 1775 for children employed during the week and for certain adults, originally were charity schools. Later some of them developed into more formal schools in which tuition was charged.

Toward the close of the eighteenth century, monitorial schools were founded. In these schools, students of older ages or greater attainment were used to instruct younger students, under the supervision of a master or teacher. This practice became very popular because of its assumed efficiency and its low cost of operation, and it was hailed as a great step forward in education. The system soon spread to America. In Philadelphia in 1819 there were ten monitorial schools, each with one teacher in charge and with an average of nearly 300 pupils per school. Such schools pioneered some of the practices still prevalent in group education.

From Europe, the American colonists inherited both educational traditions and practices. Early education was considered a function of the church, and control of education was ecclesiastical. In 1642, in Massachusetts, a law was passed charging parents and guardians with the responsibility for providing sufficient education for their children or wards in order that they might learn the principles of religion and the colony's capital laws. The first school legislation in the colonies was passed in Massachusetts in 1647. It required towns of 50 householders or more to appoint a master to teach reading and writing to those who requested this instruction, and towns of 100 or more households to set up a grammar school to prepare youth for the university and particularly for the ministry.

From England came the precedent for the poor laws established by many American colonies—laws dealing with the training and protection of certain

classes of children. Illustrative of the provisions and scope of these enactments was the Massachusetts Bay Law of 1648, which read in part:

> It is . . . ordered that the selectmen of every town . . . shall have a vigi-
> lant eye over their brethren and neighbors, to see . . . first that none . . .
> shall suffer so much barbarism in any of their families as not to endeavor to
> teach by themselves or others, their children and apprentices so much learn-
> ing as may enable them perfectly to read the English tongue, and knowledge
> of the capital laws . . . Also that all masters of families do once a week
> . . . catechize their children and servants in the grounds and principles of
> religion, . . . And further that all parents and masters do breed and bring
> up their children and apprentices in some honest lawful calling, labor or
> employment . . . profitable for themselves, and the commonwealth if they
> will not or cannot train them up in learning to fit them for higher employ-
> ments.

An emphasis on religious training and on moral education marked the schools
of the colonies as well as the schools of the Post-Revolutionary period.

Dame schools appeared early in the colonies, as did evening schools, to
accommodate children who worked throughout the day. At best, their curricula included Bible reading, spelling, grammar, a bit of arithmetic, and
prayer. Single elementary schools were formed in the eighteenth century by
combining reading and writing schools and dame schools. Latin grammar
schools were formed in most colonies, particularly in New England. These
were quite exclusive and tuition was charged; college preparation was their
aim. Their curricula included Greek, Latin, Testament history and writings,
English, and mathematics.

In all schools, particularly in lower schools, materials were meager and
methods relatively inefficient. Texts used in America before the eighteenth
century were generally English in origin, e.g., the *New England Primer*.
Curriculum was quite static and teachers were poorly prepared. Schools increasingly became private as the eighteenth century progressed. Colleges were
established by philanthropy, with the preparation of ministers their initial
aim. Of the first ten colleges founded in the colonies, nine were denominational.

These centuries in America were times characterized by hard work, by
domestic-rural social organization, and by class structures inherited from the
Old World (early Harvard graduates were listed by social rank). The Church
permeated all aspects of life in the New England and Middle Colonies during
the seventeenth century and decreasingly through the eighteenth century. In
the South, less emphasis was placed on religion, and correspondingly, less
emphasis was placed on education.

As the colonists advanced the frontier and as localism became a prevalent
social and political arrangement, education reflected these changes. Near-

random establishment of schools took place. Gradually, toward 1800, district schools became fairly common in population centers. Overall, however, the eighteenth century witnessed a decline in schools and in schooling. Reasons for this decline included a decrease in religious zeal, population dispersion, decentralization of government to areas away from the Atlantic seaboard, individualism, localism, and lack of central support and financing. As in Europe, universal attendance was yet to come and the period of significant educational change was ahead, not at hand.

THE
EDUCATIONAL
ISSUES

IN the period 1600–1800, two figures stand out clearly for the thoroughness and impact of their conjectures on the process of education and its relationship to the nature of reality, man, and knowledge. These two were Comenius and Rousseau, the former a Moravian bishop who scanned the entire educational landscape and arrived at conclusions more acceptable to the world of the nineteenth century than that of the seventeenth, the latter a French social philosopher whose educational theories fed directly into the mainstream of the basic pedagogical principles underlying much of twentieth-century practice.

Both men founded their educational premises upon the Aristotelian positions concerning the natural development and actualization of human potentialities. This so-called "seed theory" of human development occupies the central position in Comenius's primary work, *The Great Didactic* (p. 107). Comenius here sets forth the rationale and methodology for a realistic approach to the education of the young, an approach for leading the individual toward maximum attainment in knowledge, virtue, and piety. Attention is given to all facets of the learner—to his intellect, his social and emotional development, and to his spirituality. Comenius devotes full attention to such matters as the readiness factor, positive reinforcement, encouragement of individual inquiry, and provision of experiences allied with the learners' interests and needs. On these matters the ideas of Comenius are as vital today as they ever were.

Rousseau (p. 132), to an even greater degree than Comenius, focuses upon the individual learner as a unique entity who should be allowed to flower rather than be imposed upon and molded by external forces, such as parents, teachers, and society. For Rousseau, man is naturally good, while society and its institutions are by their artificial natures misleading and corrupting. The greatest disservice that can be done to children is to force upon them rationalistic, abstract knowledge for which they have no immediate use. Education should allow the child to develop toward self-sufficiency—to grow naturally, to learn naturally, to react to life with joy and spontaneity, to develop his creative potentialities. Rousseau's is a romanticized conception of education, one which demands a maximal contact with nature during the formative years and an isolation from formal studies until the learner's dawning of reason (at approximately age twelve). Yet, given as he is to rhapsodizing about the simple and basic goodness of *la vie naturelle,* Rousseau's message is a clear indictment of the over-formalized and often sterile schooling prevalent in his time.

Other stirrings in educational theory and practice gave evidence of the continuing turn toward a more realistic education geared to the practical needs of men and to the expanding, more democratic societies in which they lived. Representative of the intellectual and social climates of the seventeenth and eighteenth centuries are the English poet and essayist Milton, the English philosopher Locke, the Italian schoolmaster Vico, the German philosopher Kant, and the American scientist-philosopher-statesman Franklin.

Milton, in his essay on education (p. 115), signals the advent of a new conception of liberal education—an education which concentrates upon "solid" and "sensible" things useful to the individual. He reflects the growing scientism of his age, as well as basic Aristotelian precepts, in his insistence upon education which builds from the concrete to the understanding of general principles and abstract ideas. He decries the wastefulness of the then-traditional scholastic and meaningless studies. A more explicit application of scientific procedure and instruments to the teaching-learning process is explained and promoted by Vico (p. 124). This study provides a further example of increasing attention to the specifics of subject-matter selection, methodology, and technology which marked educational developments in these centuries.

The primacy of character education predominates the pedagogical positions of both Locke (p. 119) and Kant (p. 141). Each sees the necessity for early attention to the "imprinting" or "implanting" of moral virtues into the developing individual. Without such a foundation, they contend, all other educational values will go unrealized. Ethical training obtained from proper exemplars and open discussion of moral problems forms the basis for complete manhood.

The expanding sense of obligation for the full nurturing of the learner within the context of societal needs is manifest in the thinking of Benjamin Franklin. His proposal for a uniquely American education format, as embodied in his founding of the Academy in Philadelphia (p. 126), is addressed to the meeting of this obligation. He proposes a very practical curriculum, one which went far beyond the college-preparation goals of the then-existent Latin Grammar Schools, a curriculum which was designed to meet the needs of the growing mercantile class in colonial America.

In the earliest phases of American educational development there were manifestations, primarily in the forms of detailed proposals and legislative actions, of earlier theories, formulations, and viewpoints. Martin Luther's call for a publicly supported school system to insure that all people would be able to read and understand the teachings of the Bible was translated into law shortly after the very beginnings of the colonial enterprises (p. 161). Education for the salvation of the soul was viewed as a goal of great practical value, particularly by the Massachusetts colonists.

In the seventeenth century Comenius had held out the hope that a truly democratic education could be achieved, an education available to everyone, regardless of social class or circumstance. Jefferson's proposal to the Virginia legislature (p. 143), although defeated, signals the growing intensity of concern for the establishment of well-organized school systems which would make possible the providing of at least a rudimentary education for all. Jefferson saw education as absolutely necessary for the population of a democracy; how else could an enlightened citizenry be formed? Noah Webster, seizing on the spirit of the new republic, sought the highest priority for the establishment of a solid and effective American public school system—a system not based upon European models but designed to serve and sustain recently won democratic freedoms. His essay (p. 154) calls for the printing and distribution of American history books and of books which would provide their readers with practical knowledge—of ethics, law, government, and economics.

From these early proposals and actions there emerged certain patterns which were to make distinctive imprints on the fabric of American education. The first pattern is one which formed from a reluctance to import European models of educational organization and practice, a pattern which leads, over the course of a century, to a basically pragmatic-experimental foundation for twentieth-century schooling in America. Secondly, and also in contrast to most foreign systems, there emerged a tri-level development in American education—a colonial-based tradition of local control of public schools, a post-Revolution movement toward the assurances of unity and consistency through state organization, and a manifestation of federal interest in educational development shown as early as the passing of the Northwest Ordinances (p. 164). Thirdly, against a colonial background of close educational alliance between Church and State, the statesmen of the new republic moved firmly toward separating these two bodies. The Constitution (p. 166) attests to this, and Madison's "Remonstrance" (p. 148) stands as one of the most lucid statements on the subject.

Thus were developed many of the educational issues to be argued, expanded, and clarified through the nineteenth century and, indeed, up to the present day—the issue of curricular objectives and their relationship to local, state, and national needs and goals; the issue of federal involvement in all levels of the educational system; and the issue of Church-State separation in educational affairs and the concomitant move toward secularization of the schools.

INDEX OF
BASIC ISSUES

THE EARLY MODERN PERIOD

(1600 – 1800)

MAJOR THOUGHTS

NATURE, THE GUIDE TO EDUCATIONAL GROWTH

AUTHOR:

John Amos Comenius (*1592–1670*)

WORK:

THE GREAT DIDACTIC (1657)

GREETINGS TO THE READER

1. Didactic signifies the art of teaching. Several men of ability, taking pity on the Sisyphus-labor of schools, have lately endeavored to find out some such Art, but with unequal skill and unequal success.

2. Some merely wished to give assistance towards learning some language or other with greater ease. Others found ways of imparting this or that science or art with greater speed. Others suggested improvements of various kinds; but almost all proceeded by means of unconnected precepts, gleaned from a superficial experience, that is to say, *a posteriori*.

From *The Great Didactic of John Amos Comenius,* translated by M. W. Keatinge (London: A & C Black, 1907), abridged. Reprinted by permission.

3. We venture to promise a GREAT DIDACTIC, that is to say, the whole art of teaching all things to all men, and indeed of teaching them with certainty, so that the result cannot fail to follow; further, of teaching them pleasantly, that is to say, without annoyance or aversion on the part of teacher or pupil, but rather with the greatest enjoyment for both; further of teaching them thoroughly, not superficially and showily, but in such a manner as to lead to true knowledge, to gentle morals, and to the deepest piety. Lastly, we wish to prove all this *a priori,* that is to say, *from the unalterable nature of the matter itself,* drawing off, as from a living source, the constantly flowing runlets, and bringing them together again into one concentrated stream, that we may lay the foundations of the universal art of founding universal schools.

. . .

CHAPTER I. MAN IS THE HIGHEST, THE MOST ABSOLUTE, AND THE MOST EXCELLENT OF THINGS CREATED

CHAPTER II. THE ULTIMATE END OF MAN IS BEYOND THIS LIFE

CHAPTER III. THIS LIFE IS BUT A PREPARATION FOR ETERNITY

CHAPTER IV. THERE ARE THREE STAGES IN THE PREPARATION FOR ETERNITY: TO KNOW ONESELF (AND WITH ONESELF ALL THINGS); TO RULE ONESELF; AND TO DIRECT ONESELF TO GOD

CHAPTER V. THE SEEDS OF THESE THREE (LEARNING, VIRTUE, AND PIETY) ARE NATURALLY IMPLANTED IN US

CHAPTER VI. IF A MAN IS TO BE PRODUCED, IT IS NECESSARY THAT HE BE FORMED BY EDUCATION

CHAPTER VII. A MAN CAN MOST EASILY BE FORMED IN EARLY YOUTH, AND CANNOT BE FORMED PROPERLY EXCEPT AT THIS AGE

CHAPTER VIII. THE YOUNG MUST BE EDUCATED IN COMMON, AND FOR THIS SCHOOLS ARE NECESSARY

CHAPTER IX. ALL THE YOUNG OF BOTH SEXES SHOULD BE SENT TO SCHOOL

CHAPTER X. THE INSTRUCTION GIVEN IN SCHOOLS SHOULD BE UNIVERSAL

CHAPTER XI. HITHERTO THERE HAVE BEEN NO PERFECT SCHOOLS

CHAPTER XII. IT IS POSSIBLE TO REFORM SCHOOLS

1. To cure deep-seated maladies is difficult and often well-nigh impossible. But if any one offer an efficacious remedy, does the sick man reject his services? Does he not rather wish to obtain aid as quickly as possible, and especially if he think that the physician is guided not by mere opinion but by

solid reason? We, at any rate, in this our undertaking, have reached the point at which we must make plain (i) what we actually promise, and (ii) on what principles we intend to proceed.

2. We promise, then, such a system of education that

(i.) All the young shall be educated (except those to whom God has denied understanding).

(ii.) And in all those subjects which are able to make a man wise, virtuous, and pious.

(iii.) That the process of education, being a preparation for life, shall be completed before maturity is reached.

(iv.) That this education shall be conducted without blows, rigor, or compulsion, as gently and pleasantly as possible, and in the most natural manner (just as a living body increases in size without any straining or forcible extension of the limbs; since if food, care, and exercise are properly supplied, the body grows and becomes strong, gradually, imperceptibly, and of its own accord. In the same way I maintain that nutriment, care, and exercise, prudently supplied to the mind, lead it naturally to wisdom, virtue, and piety).

(v.) That the education given shall be not false but real, not superficial but thorough; that is to say, that the rational animal, man, shall be guided, not by the intellects of other men, but by his own; shall not merely read the opinions of others and grasp their meaning or commit them to memory and repeat them, but shall himself penetrate to the root of things and acquire the habit of genuinely understanding and making use of what he learns.

(vi.) That this education shall not be laborious but very easy. The class instruction shall last only four hours each day, and shall be conducted in such a manner that one master may teach hundreds of pupils at the same time, with ten times as little trouble as is now expended on the teaching of one.

3. But who will have faith in these things before he see them? It is a well-known peculiarity of men that before a remarkable discovery is made they wonder how it can be possible, while after its achievement they are surprised that it was not discovered before. . . .

9. It would be easy for me to appeal to results as the most trustworthy witnesses (such confidence do I place in my God). But since I am writing this, not for the unlearned crowd, but for men of education, I must give demonstrative proof that it is possible to imbue all the young with knowl-edge, virtue, and piety, and to do so without that unpleasantness and difficulty continually experienced by the teachers, no less than by the learners, under the old system.

10. The one and sufficient demonstration is this: That each individual creature not only suffers itself to be easily led in the direction which its nature

finds congenial, but is actually impelled toward the desired goal, and suffers pain if any obstacle be interposed.

12. Since then, as we saw in chap. v., the seeds of knowledge, of virtue, and of piety exist in all men (with the exception of monstrosities), it follows of necessity that they need nothing but a gentle impulse and prudent guidance.

13. But, it is objected, it is not out of every piece of wood that a Mercury can be carved. I answer: But out of every human being, if he be not utterly corrupt, a man can be formed.

18. This is a suitable place in which to make a few remarks about differences of character. Some men are sharp, others dull; some soft and yielding, others hard and unbending; some eager after knowledge, others more anxious to acquire mechanical skill. From these three pairs of contradictory characters we get in all six distinct divisions.

19. In the first division must be placed those who are sharp-witted, anxious to learn, and easily influenced. These, more than all others, are suited for instruction. . . .

20. Others are sharp-witted, but inclined to be slow and lazy. These must be urged on.

21. In the third place we have those who are sharp-witted and anxious to learn, but who at the same time are perverse and refractory. These are usually a great source of difficulty in schools, and for the most part are given up in despair. If treated in the right way, however, they frequently develop into the greatest men. . . .

22. In the fourth place we have those who are flexible and anxious to learn, but who at the same time are slow and heavy. These can follow in the footsteps of the last-mentioned. But to render this possible the teacher must meet their weak natures half-way, must lay no heavy burden on them, must not demand anything excessive, but rather have patience, help them, strengthen them, and set them straight, that they may not be disheartened Though such pupils take longer to come to maturity, they will probably last all the better, like fruit that ripens late. And, just as the impression of a seal made in lead lasts a long time, though hard to make, so these men have more stable characters than those who are more gifted, and do not easily forget what they have once learned. At school, therefore, they should be given every opportunity.

23. The fifth type are those who are weak-minded and at the same time lazy and idle. With these also a great improvement can be made, provided they are not obstinate. But great skill and patience are necessary.

24. Finally, we have those whose intellects are weak and whose dispositions are perverse and wicked as well. These seldom come to any good. But, as

it is certain that nature always provides some antidote for pernicious things, and that barren trees can be rendered fruitful if properly transplanted, we ought not to give up all hope, but should see if the perverseness, at least, cannot be combated and got rid of. . . .

26. The . . . following reasons show that all the young, though of such different dispositions, may be instructed and educated by the same method.

27. Firstly: For all men the goal is the same, namely, knowledge, virtue, and piety.

28. Secondly: All men, though their dispositions may differ, possess the same human nature and are endowed with the same organs of sense and of reason.

29. Thirdly: The differences of character are caused by nothing more than a superfluity or a lack of some of the elements in the natural harmony, just as bodily diseases are nothing but abnormal states of wetness or dryness, of heat or cold.

CHAPTER XIII. THE BASIS OF SCHOOL REFORM MUST BE EXACT ORDER IN ALL THINGS

1. We find on investigation that the principle which really holds together the fabric of this world of ours, down to its smallest detail, is none other than order; that is to say, the proper division of what comes before and what comes after, of the superior and the subordinate, of the large and the small, of the similar and dissimilar, according to place, time, number, size, and weight, so that each may fulfil its function well. Order, therefore, has been called the soul of affairs. For everything that is well ordered preserves its position and its strength as long as it maintains its order; it is when it ceases to do so that it grows weak, totters, and falls. This may be seen clearly in instances taken from nature and from art.

.   .   .

14. What is the hidden power that brings this to pass? Nothing but the all-ruling force of order; that is to say, the force derived from arranging all the parts concerned according to their number, size, and importance, and in such a manner that each one shall perform its own proper function as well as work harmoniously with and assist the other parts whose action is necessary to produce the desired result; that is to say, the size of each part must fit properly into those which surround it; and the general laws that regulate the equal distribution of force to the several parts must be observed. In such a case all the processes are more exact than in a living body controlled by one mind. But

if any part get out of position, crack, break, become loose or bent, though it be the smallest wheel, the most insignificant axle, or the tiniest screw, the whole machine stops still or at least goes wrong, and thus shows us plainly that everything depends on the harmonious working of the parts.

15. The art of teaching, therefore, demands nothing more than the skilful arrangement of time, of the subjects taught, and of the method. As soon as we have succeeded in finding the proper method it will be no harder to teach schoolboys, in any number desired, than with the help of the printing-press to cover a thousand sheets daily with the neatest writing, or with Archimedes' machine to move houses, towers, and immense weight, or to cross the ocean in a ship, and journey to the New World. The whole process, too, will be as free from friction as is the movement of a clock whose motive power is supplied by the weights. It will be as pleasant to see education carried out on my plan as to look at an automatic machine of this kind, and the process will be as free from failure as are these mechanical contrivances, when skilfully made.

16. Let us therefore endeavor, in the name of the Almighty, to organize schools in such a way that in these points they may bear the greatest resemblance to a clock which is put together with the greatest skill, and is cunningly chased with the most delicate of tools.

. . .

CHAPTER XX. THE METHOD OF THE SCIENCES, SPECIFICALLY

16. (ii.) Whatever is taught should be taught as being of practical application in every-day life and of some definite use. . . .

17. (iii.) Whatever is taught should be taught straightforwardly and not in a complicated manner. . . .

18. (iv.) Whatever is taught must be taught with reference to its true nature and its origin; that is to say, through its causes. . . .

19. (v.) If anything is to be learned, its general principles must first be explained. Its details may then be considered, and not till then. . . .

20. (vi.) All the parts of an object, even the smallest, and without a single exception, must be learned with reference to their order, their position, and their connection with one another. . . .

21. (vii.) All things must be taught in due succession, and not more than one thing should be taught at one time. . . .

22. (viii.) We should not leave any subject until it is thoroughly understood. . . .

23. (ix.) Stress should be laid on the differences which exist between things, in order that what knowledge of them is acquired may be clear and distinct. . . .

. . .

CHAPTER XXIII. THE METHOD OF MORALS

3. The art of shaping the morals is based upon the following sixteen fundamental rules:

(i.) All the virtues, without exception, should be implanted in the young.

4. (ii.) Those virtues which are called cardinal should be first instilled; these are prudence, temperance, fortitude, and justice. . . .

5. (iii.) Prudence must be acquired by receiving good instruction, and by learning the real differences that exist between things, and the relative value of those things. . . .

6. (iv.) Boys should be taught to observe temperance in eating and in drinking, in sleeping and in waking, in work and in play, in talking and in keeping silence, throughout the whole period of their instruction. . . .

7. (v.) Fortitude should be learned by the subduing of self; that is to say, by repressing the desire to play at the wrong time or beyond the proper time, and by bridling impatience, discontent, and anger. . . .

8. (vi.) The young should learn to practice justice by hurting no man, by giving each his due, by avoiding falsehood and deceit, and by being obliging and agreeable. . . .

9. (vii.) The kinds of fortitude that are especially necessary to the young are frankness and endurance of toil.

10. (viii.) Frankness is acquired by constant intercourse with worthy people, and by behaving, while in their presence, in accordance with the precepts that have been given. . . .

11. (ix.) Boys will learn to endure toil if they are continually occupied, either with work or with play. . . .

12. (x.) The cognate virtue of justice, or promptness and willingness to serve others, must be diligently cultivated in the young. . . .

13. (xi.) Virtue must be inculcated at a very early stage before vice gets possession of the mind. . . .

14. (xii.) The virtues are learned by constantly doing what is right. . . .

15. (xiii.) Examples of well-ordered lives, in the persons of their parents, nurses, tutors, and school-fellows, must continually be set before children. . . .

16. (xiv.) But, in addition to examples, precepts and rules of conduct must be given. . . .

17. (xv.) Children must be very carefully guarded from bad society, lest they be infected by it. . . .

18. (xvi.) Since it is impossible for us to be so watchful that nothing evil can find an entrance, stern discipline is necessary to keep evil tendencies in check. . . .

THE NEW LIBERAL EDUCATION

AUTHOR:

John Milton (*1608–1674*)

WORK:

OF EDUCATION (1664)

The end then of Learning is to repair the ruines of our first Parents by regaining to know God aright, and out of that knowledge to love him, to imitate him, to be like him, as we may the neerest by possessing our souls of true vertue, which being united to the heavenly grace of faith makes up the highest perfection. But because our understanding cannot in this body found it self but on sensible things, nor arrive so clearly to the knowledge of God and things invisible, as by orderly conning over the visible and inferior creature, the same method is necessarily to be follow'd in all discreet teaching. And seeing every Nation affords not experience and tradition enough for all kind of Learning, therefore we are chiefly taught the Languages of those people who have at any time been most industrious after Wisdom; so that Language is but the Instrument conveying to us things usefull to be known.

From *Of Education* by John Milton, ed. Allan Abbott, in *The Works of John Milton,* Volume IV (New York: Columbia University Press, 1931), pp. 277–282. Reprinted by permission.

And though a Linguist should pride himself to have all the Tongues that *Babel* cleft the world into, yet, if he have not studied the solid things in them as well as the Words & Lexicons, he were nothing so much to be esteem'd a learned man, as any Yeoman or Tradesman competently wise in his Mother Dialect only. Hence appear the many mistakes which have made Learning generally so unpleasing and so unsuccessful; first we do amiss to spend seven or eight years meerly in scraping together so much miserable Latine and Greek, as might be learnt otherwise easily and delightfully in one year. And that which casts our proficiency therein so much behind, is our time lost partly in too oft idle vacancies given both to Schools and Universities, partly in a preposterous exaction, forcing the empty wits of Children to compose Theams, Verses and Orations, which are the acts of ripest judgment and the final work of a head fill'd by long reading and observing, with elegant maxims, and copious invention. These are not matters to be wrung from poor striplings, like blood out of the Nose, or the plucking of untimely fruit: besides the ill habit which they get of wretched barbarizing against the Latin and Greek *idiom,* with their untutor'd *Anglicisms,* odious to be read, yet not to be avoided without a well continu'd and judicious conversing among pure Authors digested, which they scarce taste, whereas, if after some preparatory grounds of speech by their certain forms got into memory, they were led to the praxis thereof in some chosen short book lesson'd throughly to them, they might then forthwith proceed to learn the substance of good things, and Arts in due order, which would bring the whole language quickly into their power. This I take to be the most rational and most profitable way of learning Languages, and whereby we may best hope to give account to God of our youth spent herein: And for the usual method of teaching Arts, I deem it to be an old errour of Universities not yet well recover'd from the Scholastick grossness of barbarous ages, that in stead of beginning with Arts most easie, and those be such as are most obvious to the sence, they present their young unmatriculated Novices at first comming with the most intellective abstractions of Logick and Metaphysicks: So that they having but newly left those Grammatick flats and shallows where they stuck unreasonably to learn a few words with lamentable construction, and now on the sudden transported under another climate to be lost and turmoil'd with their unballasted wits in fadomless and unquiet deeps of controversie, do for the most part grow into hatred and contempt of Learning, mockt and deluded all this while with ragged Notions and Babblements, while they expected worthy and delightful knowledge; till poverty or youthful years call them importunately their several wayes, and hasten them with the sway of friends either to an ambitious and mercenary, or ignorantly zealous Divinity; Some allur'd to the trade of Law, grounding their purposes not on the prudent and heavenly contemplation of justice and equity which was never taught them, but on the promising and pleasing thoughts of litigious terms, fat contentions, and flowing fees; others betake them to State affairs, with souls so unprincipl'd in vertue, and true generous breeding, that flattery, and Court shifts and tyrannous Aphorisms appear to them the highest points of wisdom; instilling their barren hearts with a conscientious slavery, if, as I rather think, it be not fain'd. Others lastly of a more delicious and airie spirit, retire themselves knowing no better, to the enjoyments of ease and luxury, living out their daies in feast and jollity; which indeed is the wisest and the safest course of all these, unless they were with more integrity undertaken. And these are the fruits of mispending our prime youth at the Schools and Universities as we do, either in learning meer words or such things chiefly, as were better unlearnt.

I shall detain you no longer in the demonstration of what we should not do, but strait conduct ye to a hill side, where I will point ye out the right path of a vertuous and noble Education; laborious indeed at the first ascent, but else so smooth, so green, so full of goodly prospect, and melodious sounds on every side, that the Harp of *Orpheus* was not more charming. I doubt not but ye shall have more adoe to drive our dullest and laziest youth, our stocks and stubbs from the infinite desire of such a happy nurture, then we have now to hale and drag our choisest and hopefullest Wits to that asinine feast of sowthistles and brambles which is commonly set before them, as all the food and entertainment of their tenderest and most docible age. I call therefore a compleat and generous Education that which fits a man to perform justly, skilfully and magnanimously all the offices both private and publick of Peace and War. And how all this may be done between twelve, and one and twenty, less time then is now bestow'd in pure trifling at Grammar and *Sophistry,* is to be thus order'd.

First to find out a spatious house and ground about it fit for an *Academy,* and big enough to lodge a hundred and fifty persons, whereof twenty or thereabout may be attendants, all under the government of one, who shall be thought of desert sufficient, and ability either to do all, or wisely to direct, and oversee it done. This place should be at once both School and University, not needing a remove to any other house of Scholership, except it be some peculiar Colledge of Law, or Physick, where they mean to be practitioners, but as for those general studies which take up all our time from *Lilly* to the commencing, as they term it, Master of Art, it should be absolute. After this pattern, as many Edifices may be converted to this use, as shall be needful in every City throughout this Land, which would tend much to the encrease of Learning and Civility every where. This number, less or more thus collected, to the convenience of a foot Company, or interchangeably two Troops of Cavalry, should divide their daies work into three parts, as it lies orderly. Their Studies, their Exercise, and their Diet.

For their Studies, First they should begin with the chief and necessary rules of some good Grammar, either that now us'd, or any better: and while this is doing, their speech is to be fashion'd to a distinct and clear pronunciation, as near as may be to the *Italian*, especially in the Vowels. For we *Englishmen* being far Northerly, do not open our mouths in the cold air, wide enough to grace a Southern Tongue; but are observ'd by all other Nations to speak exceeding close and inward: So that to smatter Latine with an English mouth, is as ill a hearing as Law-French. Next to make them expert in the usefullest points of Grammar, and withall to season them, and win them early to the love of vertue and true labour, ere any flattering seducement, or vain principle seise them wandering, some easie and delightful Book of Education would be read to them; whereof the Greeks have store, as *Cebes, Plutarch,* and other Socratic discourses. But in Latin we have none of classic authority extant, except the two or three first Books of *Quintilian,* and some select pieces elsewhere. But here the main skill and groundwork will be, to temper them such Lectures and Explanations upon every opportunity, as may lead and draw them in willing obedience, enflam'd with the study of Learning, and the admiration of Vertue; stirr'd up with high hopes of living to be brave men, and worthy Patriots, dear to God, and famous to all ages. That they may despise and scorn all their childish, and ill-taught qualities, to delight in manly, and liberal Exercises: which he who hath the Art, and proper Eloquence to catch them with, what with mild and effectual perswasions, and what with the intimation of some fear, if need be, but chiefly by his own example, might in a short space gain them to an incredible diligence and courage: infusing into their young brests such an ingenuous and noble ardor, as would not fail to make many of them renowned and matchless men. At the same time, some other hour of the day, might be taught them the rules of Arithmetick, and soon after the Elements of Geometry even playing, as the old manner was. After evening repast, till bed-time their thoughts will be best taken up in the easie grounds of Religion, and the story of Scripture.

EDUCATION
OF THE GENTLEMAN

AUTHOR:

John Locke (*1632–1704*)

WORK:

SOME THOUGHTS
CONCERNING EDUCATION
(1693)

The well educating of their children is so much the duty and concern of parents, and the welfare and prosperity of the nation so much depends on it, that I would have everyone lay it seriously to heart; and after having well examined and distinguished what fancy, custom or reason advises in the case, set his helping hand to promote everywhere that way of training up youth, with regard to their several conditions, which is the easiest, shortest and likeliest to produce virtuous, useful and able men in their distinct callings; though that most to be taken care of is the gentleman's calling. For if those of

From John Locke, *Some Thoughts Concerning Education,* ed. F. W. Garforth (Woodbury, N.Y.: Barron's Educational Series, Inc., 1964), pp. 25–26, 122–127, 129–130. Copyright by Heinemann Educational Books Ltd., London, England. Reprinted by permission.

that rank are by their education once set right, they will quickly bring all the rest into order.

A sound mind in a sound body is a short but full description of a happy state in this world. He that has these two has little more to wish for; and he that wants either of them will be but little the better for anything else. Men's happiness or misery is most part of their own making. He whose mind directs not wisely will never take the right way; and he whose body is crazy and feeble will never be able to advance in it. I confess there are some men's constitutions of body and mind so vigorous and well framed by nature that they need not much assistance from others; but by the strength of their natural genius they are from their cradles carried towards what is excellent, and by the privilege of their happy constitutions are able to do wonders. But examples of this kind are but few; and I think I may say that of all the men we meet with nine parts of ten are what they are, good or evil, useful or not, by their education. 'Tis that which makes the great difference in mankind. The little or almost insensible impressions on our tender infancies have very important and lasting consequences; and there 'tis, as in the fountains of some rivers, where a gentle application of the hand turns the flexible waters in channels that make them take quite contrary courses; and by this direction given them at first in the source they receive different tendencies and arrive at last at very remote and distant places.

. . .

That which every gentleman (that takes any care of his education) desires for his son, besides the estate he leaves him, is contained, I suppose, in these four things, virtue, wisdom, breeding and learning. I will not trouble myself whether these names do not some of them sometimes stand for the same thing, or really include one another. It serves my turn here to follow the popular use of these words, which, I presume, is clear enough to make me be understood, and I hope there will be no difficulty to comprehend my meaning.

I place virtue as the first and most necessary of those endowments that belong to a man or a gentleman, as absolutely requisite to make him valued and beloved by others, acceptable or tolerable to himself. Without that, I think, he will be happy neither in this nor the other world.

As the foundation of this there ought very early to be imprinted on his mind a true notion of God, as of the independent Supreme Being, Author and Maker of all things, from whom we receive all our good, who loves us and gives us all things. And consequent to this, instil into him a love and reverence of this Supreme Being. This is enough to begin with, without going to explain this matter any farther, for fear lest, by talking too early to him of spirits and being unseasonably forward to make him understand the incomprehensible nature of that Infinite Being, his head be either filled with false or perplexed with unintelligible notions of him. Let him only be told upon occasion that God made and governs all things, hears and sees everything, and does all manner of good to those that love and obey him; you will find that, being told of such a God, other thoughts will be apt to rise up fast enough in his mind about him, which, as you observe them to have any mistakes, you must set right. And I think it would be better if men generally rested in such an idea of God, without being too curious in their notions about a Being which all must acknowledge incomprehensible; whereby many, who have not strength and clearness of thought to distinguish between what they can and what they cannot know, run themselves in superstition or atheism, making God like themselves or, because they cannot comprehend anything else, none at all. And I am apt to think the keeping children constantly morning and evening to acts of devotion to God, as to their Maker, Preserver and Benefactor, in some plain and short form of prayer suitable to their age and capacity will be of much more use to them in religion, knowledge and virtue than to distract their thoughts with curious enquiries into his inscrutable essence and being.

Having laid the foundations of virtue in a true notion of God, such as the creed wisely teaches, as far as his age is capable, and by accustoming him to pray to him, the next thing to be taken care of is to keep him exactly to speaking of truth and by all the ways imaginable inclining him to be good-natured. Let him know that twenty faults are sooner to be forgiven than the straining of truth to cover anyone by an excuse. And to teach him betimes to love and be good-natured to others is to lay early the true foundation of an honest man; all injustice generally springing from too great love of ourselves and too little of others.

Wisdom I take in the popular acceptation for a man's managing his business ably and with foresight in this world. This is the product of a good natural temper, application of mind and experience together, and so above the reach of children. The greatest thing that in them can be done towards it is to hinder them as much as may be from cunning, which, being the ape of wisdom, is the most distant from it that can be. . . . Cunning is only the want of understanding, which, because it cannot compass its ends by direct ways, would do it by a trick and circumvention; and the mischief of it is, a cunning trick helps but once, but hinders ever after. No cover was ever made so big or so fine as to hide itself; nobody was ever so cunning as to conceal their being so; and when they are once discovered, everybody is shy, everybody distrustful of crafty men; and all the world forwardly join to oppose and defeat them, whilst the open, fair, wise man has everybody to make way for him and goes directly to his business. To accustom a child to have true notions of things and not to be satisfied till he has them, to raise his mind to great and worthy thoughts and to keep him at a distance from falsehood and cunning, which has always a broad mixture of falsehood in it, is the fittest preparation of a child for wisdom. The rest, which is to be learned from time, experience and observation and an acquaintance with men, their tempers and designs, is not to be expected in the ignorance and inadvertency of childhood or the inconsiderate heat and unwariness of youth. All that can be done towards it during this unripe age is, as I have said, to accustom them to truth and sincerity, to a submission to reason and, as much as may be, to reflection on their own actions.

The next good quality belonging to a gentleman is good breeding. There are two sorts of ill breeding, the one a sheepish bashfulness, and the other a misbecoming negligence and disrespect in our carriage; both which are avoided by duly observing this one rule, not to think meanly of ourselves and not to think meanly of others.

The first part of this rule must not be understood in opposition to humility but to assurance. We ought not to think so well of ourselves as to stand upon our own value and assume to ourselves a preference before others because of any advantage we may imagine we have over them, but modestly to take what is offered when it is our due. But yet we ought to think so well of ourselves as to perform those actions which are incumbent on and expected of us without discomposure or disorder in whose presence soever we are, keeping that respect and distance which is due to everyone's rank and quality. There is often in people, especially children, a clownish shamefacedness before strangers or those above them; they are confounded in their thoughts, words and looks, and so lose themselves in that confusion as not to be able to do anything, or at least not to do it with that freedom and gracefulness which pleases and makes them acceptable. The only cure for this, as for any other miscarriage, is by use to introduce the contrary habit. But since we cannot accustom ourselves to converse with strangers and persons of quality without being in their company, nothing can cure this part of ill breeding but change and variety of company and that of persons above us.

As the before-mentioned consists in too great a concern how to behave ourselves towards others, so the other part of ill breeding lies in the appearance of too little care of pleasing or showing respect to those we have to do with. To avoid this, these two things are requisite: first, a disposition of the mind not to offend others; and secondly, the most acceptable and agreeable way of expressing that disposition. From the one men are called civil; from the other well-fashioned. The latter of these is that decency and gracefulness of looks, voice, words, motions, gestures and of all the whole outward demeanor, which takes in company and makes those with whom we may converse easy and well pleased. This is, as it were, the language whereby that internal civility of the mind is expressed; which, as other languages are, being very much governed by the fashion and custom of every country, must, in the rules and practice of it, be learned chiefly from observation and the carriage of those who are allowed to be exactly well-bred. The other part, which lies deeper than the outside, is that general good will and regard for all people, which makes anyone have a care not to show in his carriage any contempt, disrespect or neglect of them, but to express, according to the fashion and way of that country, a respect and value for them according to their rank and condition. It is a disposition of mind that shows itself in the carriage, whereby a man avoids making anyone uneasy in conversation. . . .

You will wonder, perhaps, that I put learning last, especially if I tell you I think it the least part. This may seem strange in the mouth of a bookish man; and this making usually the chief, if not only, bustle and stir about children, this being almost that alone which is thought on when people talk of education, makes it the greater paradox. When I consider what ado is made about a little Latin and Greek, how many years are spent in it and what a noise and business it makes to no purpose, I can hardly forbear thinking that the parents of children still live in fear of the schoolmaster's rod, which they look on as the only instrument of education, as a language or two to be its whole business. How else is it possible that a child should be chained to the oar seven, eight or ten of the best years of his life to get a language or two which, I think, might be had at a great deal cheaper rate of pains and time, and be learned almost in playing?

Forgive me, therefore, if I say I cannot with patience think that a young gentleman should be put into the herd and be driven with a whip and scourge, as if he were to run the gauntlet through the several classes *ad capiendum ingenii cultum*. What then, say you, would you not have him write and read? . . . Not so, not so fast, I beseech you. Reading and writing and learning I allow to be necessary, but yet not the chief business. I imagine you would think him a very foolish fellow that shall not value a virtuous or a wise man infinitely before a great scholar. Not but that I think learning a great help to both in well-disposed minds; but yet it must be confessed also that in others not so disposed it helps them only to be the more foolish or worse men. I say this that when you consider the breeding of your son and are looking out for a schoolmaster or a tutor, you would not have (as is usual) Latin and logic only in your thoughts. Learning must be had, but in the second place, as subservient only to greater qualities. Seek out somebody that may know how discreetly to frame his manners; place him in hands where you may, as much as possible, secure his innocence, cherish and nurse up the good, and gently correct and weed out any bad inclinations and settle in him good habits. This is the main point, and this being provided for, learning may be had into the bargain, and that, as I think, at a very easy rate by methods that may be thought on.

THE NEW METHODOLOGY

AUTHOR:

Giambattista Vico (*1668–1744*)

WORK:

ON THE STUDY METHODS OF OUR TIME (1709)

My goal . . . is to indicate in what respect our study methods are superior to those of the Ancients; to discover in what they are inferior, and how we may remedy this inferiority.

For our purpose we must, if not separate, at least set up a distinction between new arts, sciences, and inventions on one hand, and new *instruments* and aids to knowledge on the other. The former are the constituent material of learning; the latter are the way and the means, precisely the subject of our discourse.

Every study method may be said to be made up of three things: instruments, complementary aids, and the aim envisaged. The instruments presuppose and include a systematic, orderly manner of proceeding; the apprentice

From Giambattista Vico: *On the Study Methods of Our Time,* translated by Elio Gianturco, copyright © 1965, by The Bobbs-Merrill Company, Inc., reprinted by permission of the Liberal Arts Press Division of The Bobbs-Merrill Company, Inc.

who, after suitable training, undertakes the task of mastering a certain art or science, should approach it in an appropriate and well-ordered fashion. Instruments are antecedent to the task of learning; complementary aids and procedures are concomitant with that task. As for the aim envisaged, although its attainment is subsequent to the process of learning, it should never be lost sight of by the learner, neither at the beginning nor during the entire learning process.

. . .

Some of the new instruments of science are, themselves, sciences; others are arts; still others, products of either art or nature. Modern philosophical "critique" is the common instrument of all our sciences and arts. The instrument of geometry is "analysis"; that of physics, geometry, plus the geometrical method (and, in a certain sense, modern mechanics). The instrument of medicine is chemistry and its offshoot, pharmacological chemistry. The instrument of anatomy is the microscope; that of astronomy, the telescope; that of geography, the mariner's needle.

As for "complementary aids," I include among them the orderly reduction to systematic rules, of a number of subjects which the Ancients were wont to entrust to practical common sense. Complementary aids are also works of literature and of the fine arts whose excellence designates them as patterns of perfection; the types used in the printing; and universities as institutions of learning.

In view of the easy accessibility, usefulness and value of the complementary aids, our study methods seem, beyond any doubt, to be better and more correct than those of the Ancients, whether in regard to facility, or to utility, or to merit.

As for the aim of all kinds of intellectual pursuits: one only is kept in view, one is pursued, one is honored by all: Truth.

A PRACTICAL CURRICULUM

AUTHOR:

Benjamin Franklin (*1706–1790*)

WORK:

PROPOSALS RELATING TO THE EDUCATION OF YOUTH IN PENNSYLVANIA (1749)

The good Education of Youth has been esteemed by wise Men in all Ages, as the surest Foundation of the Happiness both of private Families and of Commonwealths. Almost all Governments have therefore made it a principal Object of their Attention, to establish and endow with proper Revenues, such Seminaries of Learning, as might supply the succeeding Age with Men qualified to serve the Publick with Honour to themselves, and to their Country.

Many of the first Settlers of these Provinces were Men who had received a good Education in Europe, and to their Wisdom and good Management we

From *The Writings of Benjamin Franklin,* edited by Albert Henry Smyth, Volume II (New York: The Macmillan Company, 1907), pp. 388–389, 390–396.

owe much of our present Prosperity. But their Hands were full, and they could not do all Things. The present Race are not thought to be generally of equal Ability: For though the *American* Youth are allow'd not to want Capacity; yet the best Capacities require Cultivation, it being truly with them, as with the best Ground, which unless well tilled and sowed with profitable Seed, produces only ranker Weeds.

That we may obtain the Advantages arising from an Increase of Knowledge, and prevent as much as may be the mischievous Consequences that would attend a general Ignorance among us, the following *Hints* are offered towards forming a Plan for the Education of the Youth of Pennsylvania, viz.

It is propos'd

THAT some Persons of Leisure and publick Spirit apply for a CHARTER, by which they may be incorporated, with Power to erect an ACADEMY for the Education of Youth, to govern the same, provide Masters, make Rules, receive Donations, purchase Lands, etc., and to add to their Number, from Time to Time such other Persons as they shall judge suitable.

That the Members of the Corporation make it their Pleasure, and in some Degree their Business, to visit the Academy often, encourage and countenance the Youth, countenance and assist the Masters, and by all Means in their Power advance the Usefulness and Reputation of the Design; that they look on the Students as in some Sort their Children, treat them with Familiarity and Affection, and, when they have behav'd well, and gone through their Studies, and are to enter the World, zealously unite, and make all the Interest that can be made to establish them, whether in Business, Offices, Marriages, or any other Thing for their Advantage, preferably to all other Persons whatsoever even of equal Merit.

. . .

That a House be provided for the ACADEMY, if not in the Town, not many Miles from it; the Situation high and dry, and if it may be, not far from a River, having a Garden, Orchard, Meadow, and a Field or two.

That the House be furnished with a Library (if in the Country, if in the Town, the Town Libraries may serve) with Maps of all Countries, Globes, some mathematical Instruments, and Apparatus for Experiments in Natural Philosophy, and for Mechanics; Prints, of all Kinds, Prospects, Building, Machines, &c.

That the Rector by a Man of good Understanding, good Morals, diligent and patient, learn'd in the Languages and Sciences, and a correct pure Speaker and Writer of the *English* Tongue; to have such Tutors under him as shall be necessary.

That the boarding Scholars diet together, plainly, temperately, and frugally.

That, to keep them in Health, and to strengthen and render active their Bodies, they be frequently exercis'd in Running, Leaping, Wrestling, and Swimming, &c.

That they have peculiar Habits to distinguish them from other Youth, if the Academy be in or near the Town: for this, among other Reasons, that their Behaviour may be the better observed.

As to their STUDIES, it would be well if they could be taught *every Thing* that is useful, and *every Thing* that is ornamental: But Art is long, and their Time is short. It is therefore propos'd that they learn those Things that are likely to be *most useful* and *most ornamental*. Regard being had to the several Professions for which they are intended.

All should be taught to write a *fair Hand,* and swift, as that is useful to All. And with it may be learnt something of *Drawing,* by Imitation of Prints, and some of the first Principles of Perspective.

Arithmetick, Accounts, and some of the first Principles of *Geometry* and *Astronomy.*

The *English* Language might be taught by Grammar; in which some of our best Writers, as *Tillotson, Addison, Pope, Algernoon Sidney, Cato's Letters,* &c., should be Classicks: the *Stiles* principally to be cultivated, being the *clear* and the *concise*. Reading should also be taught, and pronouncing, properly, distinctly, emphatically; not with an even Tone, which *under-does,* nor a theatrical, which *over-does* Nature.

To form their Stile they should be put on Writing Letters to each other, making Abstracts of what they read; or writing the same Things in their own Words; telling or writing Stories lately read, in their own Expressions. All to be revis'd and corrected by the Tutor, who should give his Reasons, and explain the Force and Import of Words, &c.

To form their Pronunciation, they may be put on making Declamations, repeating Speeches, deliverying Orations, &c.; The Tutor assisting at the Rehearsals, teaching, advising, correcting their Accent, &c.

But if History be made a constant Part of their Reading, such as the Translations of the *Greek* and *Roman* Historians, and the modern Histories of ancient *Greece* and *Rome,* &c. may not almost all Kinds of useful Knowledge be that Way introduc'd to Advantage, and with Pleasure to the Student? As

GEOGRAPHY, by reading with Maps, and being required to point out the Places *where* the greatest Actions were done, to give their old and new Names, with the Bounds, Situation, Extent of the Countries concern'd, &c.

CHRONOLOGY, by the Help of *Helvicus* or some other Writer of the Kind, who will enable them to tell *when* those Events happened; what Princes were Contemporaries, what States or famous Men flourish'd about that Time, &c. The several principal Epochas to be first well fix'd in their Memories.

ANTIENT CUSTOMS, religious and civil, being frequently mentioned in History, will give Occasion for explaining them; in which the Prints of Medals, Basso-Relievos, and antient Monuments will greatly assist.

MORALITY, by descanting and making continual Observations on the Causes of the Rise or Fall of any Man's Character, Fortune, Power &c. mention'd in History; the Advantages of Temperance, Order, Frugality, Industry, Perseverence &c. &c. Indeed the general natural Tendency of Reading good History must be, to fix in the Minds of Youth deep Impressions of the Beauty and Usefulness of Virtue of all Kinds, Publick Spirit, Fortitude, &c.

History will show the wonderful Effects of ORATORY, in governing, turning and leading great Bodies of Mankind, Armies, Cities, Nations. When the Minds of Youth are struck with Admiration at this, then is the Time to give them the Principles of that Art, which they will study with Taste and Application. Then they may be made acquainted with the best Models among the antients, their Beauties being particularly pointed out to them. Modern Political Oratory being chiefly performed by the Pen and Press, its Advantages over the Antient in some Respects are to be shown; as that its Effects are more extensive, more lasting, &c.

History will also afford frequent Opportunities of showing the Necessity of a *Publick Religion,* from its Usefulness to the Publick; the Advantage of a Religious Character among private Persons; the Mischiefs of Superstition, &c. and the Excellency of the CHRISTIAN RELIGION above all others antient or modern.

History will also give Occasion to expatiate on the Advantage of Civil Orders and Constitutions; how Men and their Properties are protected by joining in Societies and establishing Government; their Industry encouraged and rewarded, Arts invented, and Life made more comfortable: The Advantages of *Liberty,* Mischiefs of *Licentiousness,* Benefits arising from good Laws and a due Execution of Justice, &c. Thus may the first Principles of sound *Politicks* be fix'd in the Minds of Youth.

On *Historical* Occasions, Questions of Right and Wrong, Justice and Injustice, will naturally arise, and may be put to Youth, which they may debate in Conversation and in Writing. When they ardently desire Victory, for the Sake of the Praise attending it, they will begin to feel the Want, and be sensible of the Use of *Logic,* or the Art of Reasoning to *discover* Truth, and of Arguing to *defend* it, and *convince* Adversaries. This would be the Time to acquaint them with the Principles of that Art. Grotius, Puffendorff, and some other writers of the same Kind, may be used on these Occasions to decide their Disputes. Publick Disputes warm the Imagination, whet the Industry, and strengthen the natural Abilities.

When Youth are told, that the Great Men whose Lives and Actions they read in History, spoke two of the best Languages that ever were, the most expressive, copious, beautiful; and that the finest Writings, the most correct Compositions, the most perfect Productions of human Wit and Wisdom, are in those Languages, which have endured Ages, and will endure while there are Men; that no Translation can do them Justice, or give the Pleasure found in Reading the Originals; that those Languages contain all Science; that one of them is become almost universal, being the Language of Learned Men in all Countries; that to understand them is a distinguishing Ornament, &c. they may be thereby made desirous of learning those Languages, and their Industry sharpen'd in the Acquisition of them. All intended for Divinity, should be taught the *Latin* and *Greek*; for Physick, the *Latin, Greek, and French*; for Law, the *Latin* and *French*; Merchants, the *French, German, and Spanish*: And though all should not be compell'd to learn *Latin, Greek,* or the modern foreign Languages; yet none that have an ardent Desire to learn them should be refused; their *English,* Arithmetick and other Studies absolutely necessary, being at the same Time not neglected.

If the new *Universal History* were also read, it would give a *connected* Idea of human Affairs, so far as it goes, which should be follow'd by the best modern Histories, particularly of our Mother Country; then of these Colonies; which should be accompanied with Observations on their Rise, Encrease, Use to *Great Britain,* Encouragements, Discouragements, etc. the Means to make them flourish, secure their Liberties, &c.

With the History of Men, Times, and Nations, should be read at proper Hours or Days, some of the best *Histories of Nature* which would not only be delightful to Youth, and furnish them with Matter for their Letters, &c. as well as other History; but afterwards of great Use to them, whether they are Merchants, Handicrafts, or Divines; enabling the first the better to understand many Commodities, Drugs, &c; the second to improve his Trade or Handicraft by new Mixtures, Materials, &c., and the last to adorn his Discourses by beautiful Comparisons, and strengthen them by new Proofs of Divine Providence. The Conversation of all will be improved by it, as Occasions frequently occur of making Natural Observations, which are instructive, agreeable, and entertaining in almost all Companies. *Natural History* will also afford Opportunities of introducing many Observations, relating to the Preservation of Health, which may be afterwards of great Use. *Arbuthnot* on Air and *Aliment, Sanctorius* on Perspiration, *Lemery* on Foods, and some others, may now be read, and a very little Explanation will make them sufficiently intelligible to Youth.

While they are reading Natural History, might not a little *Gardening,*

Planting, Grafting, Inoculating, etc., be taught and practised; and now and then Excursions made to the neighbouring Plantations of the best Farmers, their Methods observ'd and reason'd upon for the Information of Youth? The Improvement of Agriculture being useful to all, and Skill in it no Disparagement to any.

The History of *Commerce,* of the Invention of Arts, Rise of Manufactures, Progress of Trade, Change of its Seats, with the Reasons, Causes, &c., may also be made entertaining to Youth, and will be useful to all. And this, with the Accounts in other History of the prodigious Force and Effect of Engines and Machines used in War, will naturally introduce a Desire to be instructed in *Mechanicks,* and to be inform'd of the Principles of that Art by which weak Men perform such Wonders, Labour is sav'd, Manufactures expedited, &c. This will be the Time to show them Prints of antient and modern Machines, to explain them, to let them be copied, and to give Lectures in Mechanical Philosophy.

With the whole should be constantly inculcated and cultivated, that *Benignity of Mind,* which shows itself in *searching for* and *seizing* every opportunity *to serve* and *to oblige*; and is the Foundation of what is called GOOD BREEDING; highly useful to the Possessor, and most agreeable to all.

The Idea of what is *true Merit* should also be often presented to Youth, explain'd and impress'd on their Minds, as consisting in an *Inclination* join'd with an *Ability* to serve Mankind, one's Country, Friends and Family; which *Ability* is (with the Blessing of God) to be acquir'd or greatly encreas'd by *true Learning*; and should indeed be the great *Aim* and *End* of all Learning.

THE LEARNER AS STARTING POINT

AUTHOR:

Jean Jacques Rousseau (*1712–1778*)

WORK:

EMILE (1762)

God makes all things good; man meddles with them and they become evil. He forces one soil to yield the products of another, one tree to bear another's fruit. He confuses and confounds time, place, and natural conditions. He mutilates his dog, his horse, and his slave. He destroys and defaces all things; he loves all that is deformed and monstrous; he will have nothing as nature made it, not even man himself, who must learn his paces like a saddle-horse, and be shaped to his master's taste like the trees in his garden.

Yet things would be worse without this education, and mankind cannot be made by halves. Under existing conditions a man left to himself from birth would be more of a monster than the rest. Prejudice, authority, necessity, example, all the social conditions into which we are plunged, would stifle nature in him and put nothing in her place. She would be like a sapling

From the book *Emile; or, Education* by Jean Jacques Rousseau. Translated by Barbara Foxley. Everyman's Library Edition. Reprinted by permission of E. P. Dutton & Co., Inc., and J. M. Dent & Sons Ltd.

chance sown in the midst of the highway, bent hither and thither and soon crushed by the passers-by.

. . .

We are born weak, we need strength; helpless, we need aid; foolish, we need reason. All that we lack at birth, all that we need when we come to man's estate, is the gift of education.

This education comes to us from nature, from men, or from things. The inner growth of our organs and faculties is the education of nature, the use we learn to make of this growth is the education of men, what we gain by our experience of our surroundings is the education of things.

Thus we are each taught by three masters. If their teaching conflicts, the scholar is ill-educated and will never be at peace with himself; if their teaching agrees, he goes straight to his goal, he lives at peace with himself, he is well-educated.

Now of these three factors in education nature is wholly beyond our control, things are only partly in our power; the education of men is the only one controlled by us; and even here our power is largely illusory, for who can hope to direct every word and deed of all with whom the child has to do.

Viewed as an art, the success of education is almost impossible, since the essential conditions of success are beyond our control. Our efforts may bring us within sight of the goal, but fortune must favor us if we are to reach it.

What is this goal? As we have just shown, it is the goal of nature. Since all three modes of education must work together, the two that we can control must follow the lead of that which is beyond our control. Perhaps this word *nature* has too vague a meaning. Let us try to define it.

Nature, we are told, is merely habit. What does that mean? Are there not habits formed under compulsion, habits which never stifle nature? Such, for example, are the habits of plants trained horizontally. The plant keeps its artificial shape, but the sap has not changed its course, and any new growth the plant may make will be vertical. It is the same with a man's disposition; while the conditions remain the same, habits, even the least natural of them, hold good; but change the conditions, habits vanish, nature reasserts herself. Education itself is but habit, for are there not people who forget or lose their education and others who keep it? Whence comes this difference? If the term *nature* is to be restricted to habits conformable to nature we need say no more.

We are born sensitive and from our birth onward we are affected in various ways by our environment. As soon as we become conscious of our sensations we tend to seek or shun the things that cause them, at first because they are pleasant or unpleasant, then because they suit us or not, and at last because of judgments formed by means of the ideas of happiness and goodness which reason gives us. These tendencies gain strength and permanence with the growth of reason, but hindered by our habits they are more or less warped by our prejudices. Before this change they are what I call "nature" within us.

Everything should therefore be brought into harmony with these natural tendencies, and that might well be if our three modes of education merely differed from one another; but what can be done when they conflict, when instead of training man for himself you try to train him for others? Harmony becomes impossible. Forced to combat either nature or society, you must make your choice between the man and the citizen, you cannot train both.

.   .   .

As I said before, man's education begins at birth; before he can speak or understand he is learning. Experience precedes instruction; when he recognizes his nurse he has learnt much. The knowledge of the most ignorant man would surprise us if we had followed his course from birth to the present time. If all human knowledge were divided into two parts, one common to all, the other peculiar to the learned, the latter would seem very small compared with the former. But we scarcely heed this general experience, because it is acquired before the age of reason. Moreover, knowledge only attracts attention by its rarity, as in algebraic equations common factors count for nothing. . . .

The only habit the child should be allowed to contract is that of having no habits; let him be carried on either arm, let him be accustomed to offer either hand, to use one or other indifferently; let him not want to eat, sleep, or do anything at fixed hours, nor be unable to be left alone by day or night. Prepare the way for his control of his liberty and the use of his strength by leaving his body its natural habit, by making him capable of lasting self-control, of doing all that he wills when his will is formed.

.   .   .

As the child grows it gains strength and becomes less restless and unquiet and more independent. Soul and body become better balanced and nature no longer asks for more movement than is required for self-preservation. But the love of power does not die with the need that aroused it; power arouses and flatters self-love, and habit strengthens it; thus caprice follows upon need, and the first seeds of prejudice and obstinacy are sown.

FIRST MAXIM

Far from being too strong, children are not strong enough for all the claims of nature. Give them full use of such strength as they have; they will not abuse it.

SECOND MAXIM

Help them and supply the experience and strength they lack whenever the need is of the body.

THIRD MAXIM

In the help you give them confine yourself to what is really needful, without granting anything to caprice or unreason; for they will not be tormented by caprice if you do not call it into existence, seeing it is no part of nature.

FOURTH MAXIM

Study carefully their speech and gestures, so that at an age when they are incapable of deceit you may discriminate between those desires which come from nature and those which spring from perversity.

The spirit of these rules is to give children more real liberty and less power, to let them do more for themselves and demand less of others; so that by teaching them from the first to confine their wishes within the limits of their powers they will scarcely feel the want of whatever is not in their power.

. . .

What is to be thought, therefore, of that cruel education which sacrifices the present to an uncertain future, that burdens a child with all sorts of restrictions and begins by making him miserable in order to prepare him for some far-off happiness which he may never enjoy? Even if I considered that education wise in its aims, how could I view without indignation those poor wretches subjected to an intolerable slavery and condemned like galley-slaves to endless toil, with no certainty that they will gain anything by it? The age of harmless mirth is spent in tears, punishments, threats, and slavery. You torment the poor thing for his good; you fail to see that you are calling Death to snatch him from these gloomy surroundings. Who can say how many children fall victims to the excessive care of their fathers and mothers? They are happy to escape from this cruelty; this is all that they gain from the ills they are forced to endure: they die without regretting, having known nothing of life but its sorrows.

Men, be kind to your fellow-men; this is your first duty, kind to every age and station, kind to all that is not foreign to humanity. What wisdom can you find that is greater than kindness? Love childhood, indulge its sports, its pleasures, its delightful instincts. Who has not sometimes regretted that age when laughter was ever on the lips, and when the heart was ever at peace? Why rob these innocents of the joys which pass so quickly, of that precious gift which they cannot abuse? Why fill with bitterness the fleeting days of early childhood, days which will no more return for them than for you? Fathers, can you tell when death will call your children to him? Do not lay up sorrow for yourselves by robbing them of the short span which nature has allotted to them. As soon as they are aware of the joy of life, let them rejoice in it, so that whenever God calls them they may not die without having tasted the joy of life.

. . .

Oh, man! live your own life and you will no longer be wretched. Keep to your appointed place in the order of nature and nothing can tear you from it. Do not kick against the stern law of necessity, nor waste in vain resistance the strength bestowed on you by heaven, not to prolong or extend your existence, but to preserve it so far and so long as heaven pleases. Your freedom and your power extend as far and no further than your natural strength; anything more is but slavery, deceit, and trickery. Power itself is servile when it depends upon public opinion; for you are dependent on the prejudices of others when you rule them by means of those prejudices. To lead them as you will, they must be led as they will. They have only to change their way of thinking and you are forced to change your course of action. Those who approach you need only contrive to sway the opinions of those you rule, or of the favorite by whom you are ruled, or those of your own family or theirs. Had you the genius of Themistocles, viziers, courtiers, priests, soldiers, servants, babblers, the very children themselves, would lead you like a child in the midst of your legions. Whatever you do, your actual authority can never extend beyond your own powers. As soon as you are obliged to see with another's eyes you must will what he wills. You say with pride, "My people are my subjects." Granted, but what are you? The subject of your ministers. And your ministers, what are they? The subjects of their clerks, their mistresses, the servants of their servants. Grasp all, usurp all, and then pour out your silver with both hands; set up your batteries, raise the gallows and the wheel; make laws, issue proclamations, multiply your spies, your soldiers, your hangmen, your prisons, and your chains. Poor little men, what good does it do you? You will be no better served, you will be none the less robbed and deceived, you will be no nearer absolute power. You will say continually, "It is our will," and you will continually do the will of others.

There is only one man who gets his own way—he who can get it single-handed; therefore freedom, not power, is the greatest good. That man is truly free who desires what he is able to perform, and does what he desires. This is my fundamental maxim. Apply it to childhood, and all the rules of education spring from it.

Society has enfeebled man, not merely by robbing him of the right to his own strength, but still more by making his strength insufficient for his needs. This is why his desires increase in proportion to his weakness; and this is why the child is weaker than the man. If a man is strong and a child is weak it is not because the strength of the one is absolutely greater than the strength of the other, but because the one can naturally provide for himself and the other cannot. Thus the man will have more desires and the child more caprices, a word which means, I take it, desires which are not true needs, desires which can only be satisfied with the help of others.

I have already given the reason for this state of weakness. Parental affection is nature's provision against it; but parental affection may be carried to excess, it may be wanting, or it may be ill applied. Parents who live under our ordinary social conditions bring their child into these conditions too soon. By increasing his needs they do not relieve his weakness; they rather increase it. They further increase it by demanding of him what nature does not demand, by subjecting to their will what little strength he has to further his own wishes, by making slaves of themselves or of him instead of recognizing that mutual dependence which should result from his weakness or their affection.

The wise man can keep his own place; but the child who does not know what his place is, is unable to keep it. There are a thousand ways out of it, and it is the business of those who have charge of the child to keep him in his place, and this is no easy task. He should be neither beast nor man, but a child. He must feel his weakness, but not suffer through it; he must be dependent, but he must not obey; he must ask, not command. He is only subject to others because of his needs, and because they see better than he what he really needs, what may help or hinder his existence. No one, not even his father, has the right to bid the child do what is of no use to him.

. . .

Let us lay it down as an incontrovertible rule that the first impulses of nature are always right; there is no original sin in the human heart, the how and why of the entrance of every vice can be traced. The only natural passion is self-love or selfishness taken in a wider sense. This selfishness is good in itself and in relation to ourselves; and as the child has no necessary relations to other people he is naturally indifferent to them; his self-love only becomes good or bad by the use made of it and the relations established by its means. Until the time is ripe for the appearance of reason, that guide of selfishness, the main thing is that the child shall do nothing because you are watching him or listening to him; in a word, nothing because of other people, but only what nature asks of him; then he will never do wrong.

. . .

May I venture at this point to state the greatest, the most important, the most useful rule of education? It is: Do not save time, but lose it. I hope that every-day readers will excuse my paradoxes; you cannot avoid paradox if you think for yourself, and whatever you may say I would rather fall into paradox than into prejudice. The most dangerous period in human life lies between birth and the age of twelve. It is the time when errors and vices spring up, while as yet there is no means to destroy them; when the means of destruction are ready, the roots have gone too deep to be pulled up. If the infant sprang at one bound from its mother's breast to the age of reason, the present type of education would be quite suitable, but its natural growth calls for quite a different training. The mind should be left undisturbed till its faculties have developed; for while it is blind it cannot see the torch you offer it, nor can it follow through the vast expanse of ideas a path so faintly traced by reason that the best eyes can scarcely follow it.

Therefore the education of the earliest years should be merely negative. It consists, not in teaching virtue or truth, but in preserving the heart from vice and from the spirit of error. If only you could let well alone, and get others to follow your example; if you could bring your scholar to the age of twelve strong and healthy, but unable to tell his right hand from his left, the eyes of his understanding would be open to reason as soon as you began to teach him. Free from prejudices and free from habits, there would be nothing in him to counteract the effects of your labors. In your hands he would soon become the wisest of men; by doing nothing to begin with, you would end with a prodigy of education.

Reverse the usual practice and you will almost always do right. Fathers and teachers who want to make the child, not a child but a man of learning, think it never too soon to scold, correct, reprove, threaten, bribe, teach, and reason. Do better than they; be reasonable, and do not reason with your pupil, more especially do not try to make him approve what he dislikes; for if reason is always connected with disagreeable matters, you make it distasteful to him, you discredit it at an early age in a mind not yet ready to understand it. Exercise his body, his limbs, his senses, his strength, but keep his mind idle as long as you can. Distrust all opinions which appear before the judgment to discriminate between them. Restrain and ward off strange impressions; and to prevent the birth of evil do not hasten to do well, for goodness is only possible when enlightened by reason. Regard all delays as so much time gained; you have achieved much, you approach the boundary without loss.

Leave childhood to ripen in your children. In a word, beware of giving anything they need to-day if it can be deferred without danger to to-morrow.

.   .   .

Our island is this earth; and the most striking object we behold is the sun. As soon as we pass beyond our immediate surroundings, one or both of these must meet our eye. Thus the philosophy of most savage races is mainly directed to imaginary divisions of the earth or to the divinity of the sun.

What a sudden change you will say. Just now we were concerned with what touches ourselves, with our immediate environment, and all at once we are exploring the round world and leaping to the bounds of the universe. This change is the result of our growing strength and of the natural bent of the mind. While we were weak and feeble, self-preservation concentrated our attention on ourselves; now that we are strong and powerful, the desire for a wider sphere carries us beyond ourselves as far as our eyes can reach. But as the intellectual world is still unknown to us, our thoughts are bounded by the visible horizon, and our understanding only develops within the limits of our vision.

Let us transform our sensations into ideas, but do not let us jump all at once from the objects of sense to objects of thought. The latter are attained by means of the former. Let the senses be the only guide for the first workings of reason. No book but the world, no teaching but that of fact. The child who reads ceases to think, he only reads. He is acquiring words not knowledge.

Teach your scholar to observe the phenomena of nature; you will soon rouse his curiosity, but if you would have it grow, do not be in too great a hurry to satisfy this curiosity. Put the problems before him and let him solve them himself. Let him know nothing because you have told him, but because he has learnt it for himself. Let him not be taught science, let him discover it. If ever you substitute authority for reason, he will cease to reason; he will be a mere plaything of other people's thoughts.

.   .   .

"What is the use of that?" In future this is the sacred formula, the formula by which he and I test every action of our lives. This is the question with which I invariably answer all his questions; it serves to check the stream of foolish and tiresome questions with which children weary those about them. These incessant questions produce no result, and their object is rather to get a hold over you than to gain any real advantage. A pupil, who has been really taught only to want to know what is useful, questions like Socrates; he never asks a question without a reason for it, for he knows he will be required to give his reason before he gets an answer.

See what a powerful instrument I have put into your hands for use with your pupil. As he does not know the reason for anything you can reduce him to silence almost at will; and what advantages do your knowledge and experience give you to show him the usefulness of what you suggest. For, make no mistake about it, when you put this question to him, you are teaching him to put it to you, and you must expect that whatever you suggest to him in the future he will follow your own example and ask, "What is the use of this?"

THE TEACHING OF MORALITY

AUTHOR:

Immanuel Kant (*1724–1804*)

WORK:

ON BASEDOW'S PHILANTHROPIN (1778) AND DOCTRINE OF METHODS FROM "CRITIQUE OF PRACTICAL REASON" (1778)

The defects and inexpediency of many old school methods have become so evident that nothing but ancient tradition can protect them. Ask any man who is expert in his profession whether he got his skill at school or through his own labor and practice? Moral culture was left to parents and private tutors, unless motionless sitting on school-benches and the learning by heart of uncomprehended moral maxims is described as moral virtue. The whole

From Gabrielle Rabel, *Kant* (London: Oxford University Press, 1963), pp. 101–102, 204–205. Reprinted by permission.

school tuition was directed to breeding scholars. The future professor and the future craftsman or soldier, they all begin equally by learning Latin. If a boy knew more Latin than his fellow pupils, he was raised above others who might excel him in acute judgment, and misled into an unfounded and most pernicious pride. Care was taken neither of the intellect nor of the body of the children. Hardening of the body is very necessary, a self-indulgence in our time sends so many prematurely to the grave. Such discipline, however, was not achieved, except by frequently cruel beatings.

.   .   .

The term "method" is here used to describe the manner in which the moral law can be effectively introduced into human minds. In order to bring a mind which is either not yet formed or has run wild, into the track of moral goodness, allurements and threats are permitted. But as soon as this machinery has had some effect, pure moral motives must be introduced. As this method has never been practiced hitherto, we cannot prove its success, but we can show how receptive the human heart is for moral motives.

If you pay attention to the conversation in mixed company consisting of scholars and intellectuals as well as of businessmen and womenfolk, you will notice that, next to stories and jokes, arguing is most popular. And whenever there is a discussion of the moral value of some action by which a character is to be judged, even persons who otherwise are easily bored by arguments join in the fray with liveliness. Some become suddenly most subtle in minimizing the purity of the intentions and hence the degree of virtue or rendering it at least suspect. Often we see the character of the judges shine through. Some are especially bent on defending dead people against accusations and vindicating the moral value of the person attacked, others are extremely rigorous in their judgments. I do not know why the educators of youth have not put this propensity for enjoying a subtle examination of human motives to good use, why they did not search the biographies of ancient and recent times for suitable illustrations of dutiful behaviour. Even children take pleasure in such discussions, and while treating them as a game, their moral sense could be trained and refined. Only I wish they would be spared the so-called noble super-meritorious feats in which sentimental romancers revel. Melting, softish feelings or high-flying enthusiasms wither the soul instead of making it strong. What children need is an earnest representation of simple duty illustrated by examples.

A STATE PLAN
FOR PUBLIC EDUCATION

AUTHOR:

Thomas Jefferson (1743–1826)

WORK:

"A BILL
FOR THE MORE GENERAL
DIFFUSION OF
KNOWLEDGE" (1779)

Whereas it appeareth that however certain forms of government are better calculated than others to protect individuals in the free exercise of their natural rights, and are at the same time themselves better guarded against degeneracy, yet experience hath shewn, that even under the best forms, those entrusted with power have, in time, and by slow operations, perverted it into tyranny; and it is believed that the most effectual means of preventing this would be, to illuminate, as far as practicable, the minds of the people at large, and more especially to give them knowledge of those facts, which history

From *The Works of Thomas Jefferson,* collected and edited by Paul Leicester Ford, Volume II, Federal Edition (New York: G. P. Putnam's Sons, 1904), pp. 414–426, abridged.

exhibiteth, that, possessed thereby of the experience of other ages and countries, they may be enabled to know ambition under all its shapes, and prompt to exert their natural powers to defeat its purposes. And whereas it is generally true that that people will be happiest whose laws are best, and are best administered, and that laws will be wisely formed, and honestly administered, in proportion as those who form and administer them are wise and honest; whence it becomes expedient for promoting the publick happiness that those persons, whom nature hath endowed with genius and virtue, should be rendered by liberal education worthy to receive, and able to guard the sacred deposit of the rights and liberties of their fellow citizens, and that they should be called to that charge without regard to wealth, birth or other accidental condition or circumstance; but the indigence of the greater number disabling them from so educating, at their own expence, those of their children whom nature hath fitly formed and disposed to become useful instruments for the public, it is better that such should be sought for and educated at the common expence of all, than that the happiness of all should be confided to the weak or wicked:

Be it therefore enacted by the General Assembly, that in every county within this commonwealth, there shall be chosen annually, by the electors qualified to vote for Delegates, three of the most honest and able men of their county, to be called the Aldermen of the county; and that the election of the said Aldermen shall be held at the same time and place, before the same persons, and notified and conducted in the same manner as by law is directed for the annual election of Delegates for the county.

. . .

The said Aldermen . . . shall meet at the court-house of their county, and proceed to divide their said county into hundreds, . . . regulating the size of the said hundreds, according to the best of their discretion, so as that they may contain a convenient number of children to make up a school, and be of such convenient size that all the children within each hundred may daily attend the school to be established therein, distinguishing each hundred by a particular name; which division, with the names of the several hundreds, shall be returned to the court of the county and be entered of record, and shall remain unaltered until the increase or decrease of inhabitants shall render an alteration necessary, in the opinion of any succeeding Aldermen, and also in the opinion of the court of the county.

The electors aforesaid residing within every hundred shall meet on the third Monday in October after the first election of Aldermen, at such place, within their hundred, as the said Aldermen shall direct, notice thereof being previously given to them by such person residing within the hundred as the said Aldermen shall require who is hereby enjoined to obey such requisition, on pain of being punished by amercement and imprisonment. The electors being so assembled shall choose the most convenient place within their hundred for building a school-house. . . . The said Aldermen shall forthwith proceed to have a school-house built at the said place, and shall see that the same be kept in repair, and, when necessary that it be rebuilt; but whenever they shall think necessary that it be rebuilt, they shall give notice as before directed, to the electors of the hundred to meet at the said school-house, on such day as they shall appoint, to determine by vote, in the manner before directed, whether it shall be rebuilt at the same, or what other place in the hundred.

At every of these schools shall be taught reading, writing, and common arithmetick, and the books which shall be used therein for instructing the children to read shall be such as will at the same time make them acquainted with Graecian, Roman, English, and American history. At these schools all the free children, male and female, resident within the respective hundred, shall be intitled to receive tuition gratis, for the term of three years, and as much longer, at their private expence, as their parents, guardians or friends, shall think proper.

Over every ten of these schools (or such other number nearest thereto, as the number of hundreds in the county will admit, without fractional divisions) an overseer shall be appointed annually by the Aldermen at their first meeting, eminent for his learning, integrity, and fidelity to the commonwealth, whose business and duty it shall be, from time to time, to appoint a teacher to each school, who shall give assurance of fidelity to the commonwealth, and to remove him as he shall see cause; to visit every school once in every half year at the least; to examine the scholars; see that any general plan of reading and instruction recommended by the visiters of William and Mary College shall be observed; and to superintend the conduct of the teacher in every thing relative to his school.

Every teacher shall receive a salary . . . which, with the expences of building and repairing the school-houses, shall be provided in such manner as other county expences are by law directed to be provided and shall also have his diet, lodging, and washing found him, to be levied in like manner, save only that such levy shall be on the inhabitants of each hundred for the board of their own teacher only.

And in order that grammar schools may be rendered convenient to the youth in every part of the commonwealth, Be it farther enacted, that on the first Monday in November, after the first appointment of overseers for the hundred schools, . . . the said overseers appointed for the schools . . . shall fix on such place in some one of the counties in their district as shall be most proper for situating a grammar school-house, endeavouring that the situation be as central as may be to the inhabitants of the said counties, that it be furnished with good water, convenient to plentiful supplies of provision and fuel, and more than all things that it be healthy. . . .

The said overseers shall forthwith proceed to have a house of brick or stone, for the said grammar school, with necessary offices, built on the said lands, which grammar school-house shall contain a room for the school, a hall to dine in, four rooms for a master and usher, and ten or twelve lodging rooms for the scholars.

To each of the said grammar schools shall be allowed out of the public treasury, the sum of   pounds,* out of which shall be paid by the Treasurer, on warrant from the Auditors, to the proprietors or tenants of the lands located, the value of their several interests as fixed by the jury, and the balance thereof shall be delivered to the said overseers to defray the expence of the said buildings.

In these grammar schools shall be taught the Latin and Greek languages, English grammar, geography, and the higher part of numerical arithmetick, to wit, vulgar and decimal fractions, and the extraction of the square and cube roots.

A visiter from each county constituting the district shall be appointed, by the overseers, for the county, in the month of October annually, either from their own body or from their county at large, which visiters or the greater part of them, . . . shall have power to choose their own Rector, who shall call and preside at future meetings, to employ from time to time a master, and if necessary, an usher, for the said school, to remove them at their will, and to settle the price of tuition to be paid by the scholars. They shall also visit the school twice in every year at the least, either together or separately at their discretion, examine the scholars, and see that any general plan of instruction recommended by the visiters of William and Mary College shall be observed. The said masters and ushers, before they enter on the execution of their office, shall give assurance of fidelity to the commonwealth.

A steward shall be employed, and removed at will by the master, on such wages as the visiters shall direct; which steward shall see to the procuring provisions, fuel, servants for cooking, waiting, house cleaning, washing, mending, and gardening on the most reasonable terms; the expence of which, together with the steward's wages, shall be divided equally among all the scholars boarding either on the public or private expence. And the part of those who are on private expence, and also the price of their tuitions due to the master or usher, shall be paid quarterly by the respective scholars, their parents, or guardians, and shall be recoverable if withheld, together with costs, on motion in any Court of Record, . . .

---

* Editor's note: number missing in original.

Every overseer of the hundred schools shall, in the month of September annually, after the most diligent and impartial examination and enquiry, appoint from among the boys who shall have been two years at the least at some one of the schools under his superintendence, and whose parents are too poor to give them farther education, some one of the best and most promising genius and disposition, to proceed to the grammar school of his district; which appointment shall be made . . . in the presence of the Aldermen, . . .

Every boy so appointed shall be authorised to proceed to the grammar school of his district, there to be educated and boarded during such time as is hereafter limited; and his quota of the expences of the house together with a compensation to the master or usher for his tuition, at the rate of twenty dollars by the year, shall be paid by the Treasurer quarterly on warrant from the Auditors.

A visitation shall be held, for the purpose of probation, annually at the said grammar school . . . at which one third of the boys sent thither by appointment of the said overseers, and who shall have been there one year only, shall be discontinued as public foundationers, being those who, on the most diligent examination and enquiry, shall be thought to be of the least promising genius and disposition; and of those who shall have been there two years, all shall be discontinued, save one only the best in genius and disposition, who shall be at liberty to continue there four years longer on the public foundation, and shall thence forward be deemed a senior.

The visiters . . . after diligent examination and enquiry as before directed, shall chuse one among the said seniors, of the best learning and most hopeful genius and disposition, who shall be authorised by them to proceed to William and Mary College, there to be educated, boarded, and clothed three years; the expence of which annually shall be paid by the Treasurer on warrant from the Auditors.

THE RELIGIOUS FACTOR

AUTHOR:

James Madison (1751–1836)

WORK:

"A MEMORIAL AND REMONSTRANCE (TO THE GENERAL ASSEMBLY OF THE COMMONWEALTH OF VIRGINIA) (1785)

We the subscribers, citizens of the said Commonwealth, having taken into serious consideration a Bill printed by order of the last session of General Assembly, entitled "A Bill establishing a provision for Teachers of the Christian Religion," and conceiving that the same, if finally armed with the sanctions of a law, will be a dangerous abuse of power, are bound as faithful members of a free state to remonstrate against it, and to declare the reasons by which we are determined. We remonstrate against the said Bill—

From *Letters and Other Writings of James Madison,* Volume I. Published by order of Congress (Philadelphia: J. B. Lippincott & Co., 1865), pp. 162–169, abridged.

1. Because we hold it for a fundamental and undeniable truth, "that Religion, or the duty which we owe to our Creator, and the manner of discharging it, can be directed only by reason and conviction, not by force or violence." The Religion, then, of every man must be left to the conviction and conscience of every man; and it is the right of every man to exercise it, as these may dictate. This right is in its nature an unalienable right. It is unalienable, because the opinions of men, depending only on the evidence contemplated by their own minds, cannot follow the dictates of other men. It is unalienable, also, because what is here a right towards men is a duty towards the Creator. It is the duty of every man to render to the Creator such homage, and such only, as he believes to be acceptable to him. This duty is precedent, both in order of time and in degree of obligation, to the claims of Civil society. Before any man can be considered as a member of Civil Society, he must be considered as a subject of the Governor of the Universe; and if a member of Civil Society who enters into any subordinate Association must always do it with a reservation of his duty to the General Authority, much more must every man who becomes a member of any particular Civil Society do it with a saving of his allegiance to the Universal Sovereign. We maintain, therefore, that in matters of Religion no man's right is abridged by the institution of Civil Society, and that Religion is wholly exempt from its cognizance. True it is, that no other rule exists by which any question which may divide a Society can be ultimately determined than the will of the majority; but it is also true that the majority may trespass on the rights of the minority.

2. Because, if Religion be exempt from the authority of the Society at large, still less can it be subject to that of the Legislative Body. The latter are but the creatures and viceregents of the former. Their jurisdiction is both derivative and limited. It is limited with regard to the co-ordinate departments; more necessarily is it limited with regard to the constituents. The preservation of a free Government requires, not merely that the metes and bounds which separate each department of power be invariably maintained, but more especially that neither of them be suffered to overleap the great Barrier which defends the rights of the people. The rulers who are guilty of such an encroachment exceed the commission from which they derive their authority, and are Tyrants. The people who submit to it are governed by laws made neither by themselves nor by an authority derived from them, and are slaves.

3. Because it is proper to take alarm at the first experiment on our liberties. We hold this prudent jealousy to be the first duty of citizens, and one of the noblest characteristics of the late Revolution. The freemen of America did not wait till usurped power had strengthened itself by exercise, and entangled the question in precedents. They saw all the consequences in the principle, and they avoided the consequences by denying the principle. We revere this lesson too much soon to forget it. Who does not see that the same

authority which can establish Christianity, in exclusion of all other Religions, may establish, with the same ease, any particular sect of Christians, in exclusion of all other sects? that the same authority which can force a citizen to contribute three pence only of his property for the support of any one establishment, may force him to conform to any other establishment in all cases whatsoever?

4. Because the Bill violates that equality which ought to be the basis of every law, and which is more indispensable in proportion as the validity or expediency of any law is more liable to be impeached. "If all men are by nature equally free and independent" all men are to be considered as entering into Society on equal conditions; as relinquishing no more, and therefore retaining no less, one than another, of their natural rights. Above all, are they to be considered as retaining an *"equal* title to the free exercise of Religion according to the dictates of conscience." Whilst we assert for ourselves a freedom to embrace, to profess, and to observe, the Religion which we believe to be of divine origin, we cannot deny an equal freedom to them whose minds have not yet yielded to the evidence which has convinced us. If this freedom be abused, it is an offence against God, not against man. To God, therefore, not to man, must an account of it be rendered. As the Bill violates equality by subjecting some to peculiar burdens, so it violates the same principle by granting to others peculiar exemptions. . . .

5. Because the Bill implies, either that the civil Magistrate is a competent Judge of Religious truths, or that he may employ Religion as an engine of civil policy. The first is an arrogant pretension, falsified by the contradictory opinions of Rulers in all ages, and throughout the world; the second, an unhallowed perversion of the means of salvation.

6. Because the establishment proposed by the Bill is not requisite for the support of the Christian Religion. To say that it is, is a contradiction of the Christian Religion itself, for every page of it disavows a dependence on the powers of this world. It is a contradiction to fact, for it is known that this Religion both existed and flourished, not only without the support of human laws, but in spite of every opposition from them; and not only during the period of miraculous aid, but long after it had been left to its own evidence and the ordinary care of providence. Nay, it is a contradiction in terms; for a Religion not invented by human policy must have pre-existed and been supported before it was established by human policy. It is, moreover, to weaken in those who profess this Religion a pious confidence in its innate excellence and the patronage of its Author; and to foster in those who still reject it a suspicion that its friends are too conscious of its fallacies to trust it to its own merits.

7. Because experience witnesseth that ecclesiastical establishments, instead of maintaining the purity and efficacy of Religion, have had a contrary

operation. During almost fifteen Centuries has the legal establishment of Christianity been on trial. What have been its fruits? More or less, in all places, pride and indolence in the Clergy; ignorance and servility in the laity; in both, superstition, bigotry, and persecution. Enquire of the Teachers of Christianity for the ages in which it appeared in its greatest lustre; those of every Sect point to the ages prior to its incorporation with civil policy. Propose a restoration of this primitive state, in which its Teachers depended on the voluntary rewards of their flocks; many of them predict its downfall. On which side ought their testimony to have greatest weight; when for or when against their interest?

8. Because the establishment in question is not necessary for the support of Civil Government. If it be urged as necessary for the support of Civil Government only as it is a means of supporting Religion, and it be not necessary for the latter purpose, it cannot be necessary for the former. If Religion be not within the cognizance of Civil Government, how can its legal establishment be necessary to Civil Government? What influence, in fact, have ecclesiastical establishments had on Civil Society? In some instances they have been seen to erect a spiritual tyranny on the ruins of the civil authority; in many instances they have been seen upholding the thrones of political tyranny; in no instance have they been seen the guardians of the liberties of the people. Rulers who wished to subvert the public liberty may have found an established Clergy convenient auxiliaries. A just Government, instituted to secure and perpetuate it, needs them not. Such a Government will be best supported by protecting every citizen in the enjoyment of his Religion with the same equal hand which protects his person and his property; by neither invading the equal rights of any Sect, nor suffering any sect to invade those of another.

9. Because the proposed establishment is a departure from that generous policy which, offering an Asylum to the persecuted and oppressed of every Nation and Religion, promised a lustre to our country, and an accession to the number of its citizens. What a melancholy mark is the Bill of sudden degeneracy! Instead of holding forth an Asylum to the persecuted, it is itself a signal of persecution. It degrades from the equal rank of Citizens all those whose opinions in Religion do not bend to those of the Legislative authority. . . .

10. Because it will have a like tendency to banish our citizens. The allurements presented by other situations are every day thinning their number. To superadd a fresh motive to emigration by revoking the liberty which they now enjoy would be the same species of folly which has dishonoured and depopulated flourishing kingdoms.

11. Because it will destroy that moderation and harmony which the forbearance of our laws to intermeddle with Religion has produced among its

several Sects. Torrents of blood have been spilt in the old world in consequence of vain attempts of the secular arm to extinguish Religious discord by proscribing all differences in Religious opinion. Time has at length revealed the true remedy. Every relaxation of narrow and rigorous policy, wherever it has been tried, has been found to assuage the disease. The American theatre has exhibited proofs that equal and complete liberty, if it does not wholly eradicate it, sufficiently destroys its malignant influence on the health and prosperity of the State. If, with the salutary effects of this system under our own eyes, we begin to contract the bounds of Religious freedom, we know no name which will too severely reproach our folly. At least, let warning be taken at the first fruits of the threatened innovation. The very appearance of the Bill has transformed "that Christian forbearance, love, and charity," which of late mutually prevailed, into animosities and jealousies, which may not soon be appeased. What mischiefs may not be dreaded, should this enemy to the public quiet be armed with the force of a law?

12. Because the policy of the Bill is adverse to the diffusion of the light of Christianity. The first wish of those who enjoy this precious gift ought to be, that it may be imparted to the whole race of mankind. Compare the number of those who have as yet received it with the number still remaining under the dominion of false Religions, and how small is the former! Does the policy of the Bill tend to lessen the disproportion? No; it at once discourages those who are strangers to the light of revelation from coming into the Region of it, and countenances by example the nations who continue in darkness in shutting out those who might convey it to them. Instead of levelling, as far as possible, every obstacle to the victorious progress of truth, the Bill, with an ignoble and unchristian timidity, would circumscribe it with a wall of defence against the encroachments of error.

13. Because attempts to enforce, by legal sanctions, acts obnoxious to so great a proportion of citizens, tend to enervate the laws in general, and to slacken the bands of Society. If it be difficult to execute any law which is not generally deemed necessary or salutary, what must be the case where it is deemed invalid and dangerous? And what may be the effect of so striking an example of impotency in the Government on its general authority?

14. Because a measure of such singular magnitude and delicacy ought not to be imposed without the clearest evidence that it is called for by a majority of citizens; and no satisfactory method is yet proposed by which the voice of the majority in this case may be determined, or its influence secured. . . .

15. Because, finally, "the equal right of every Citizen to the free exercise of his Religion, according to the dictates of conscience," is held by the same tenure with all our other rights. If we recur to its origin, it is equally the gift of nature; if we weigh its importance, it cannot be less dear to us; if we

consult the Declaration of those rights "which pertain to the good people of Virginia as the basis and foundation of Government," it is enumerated with equal solemnity, or rather with studied emphasis. Either, then, we must say, that the will of the Legislature is the only measure of their authority, and that in the plenitude of that authority they may sweep away all our fundamental rights, or that they are bound to leave this particular right untouched and sacred. Either we must say, that they may controul the freedom of the press, may abolish the trial by jury, may swallow up the Executive and Judiciary powers of the State; nay, that they may despoil us of our very right of suffrage, and erect themselves into an independent and hereditary Assembly; or we must say, that they have no authority to enact into a law the Bill under consideration.

We, the subscribers, say that the General Assembly of this Commonwealth have no such authority. And in order that no effort may be omitted on our part against so dangerous an usurpation, we oppose to it this remonstrance; earnestly praying, as we are in duty bound, that the Supreme Lawgiver of the Universe, by illuminating those to whom it is addressed, may, on the one hand, turn their councils from every act which would affront his holy prerogative, or violate the trust committed to them; and on the other, guide them into every measure which may be worthy of his blessing, redound to their own praise, and establish more firmly the liberties, the prosperity, and the happiness of the Commonwealth.

THE PRIMACY
OF EDUCATION

AUTHOR:

Noah Webster (*1758–1843*)

WORK:

ON THE EDUCATION
OF YOUTH IN AMERICA
(1787–1788)

Our legislators frame laws for the suppression of vice and immorality; our divines thunder, from the pulpit, the terrors of infinite wrath, against the vices that stain the characters of men. And do laws and preaching effect a reformation of manners? Experience would not give a very favorable answer to this inquiry. The reason is obvious; the attempts are directed to the wrong objects. . . .

The only practicable method to reform mankind, is to begin with children; to banish, if possible, from their company, every low bred, drunken, immoral character. Virtue and vice will not grow together in a great degree, but they will grow where they are planted, and when one has taken root, it is

From *A Collection of Essays and Fugitive Writings* by Noah Webster (Boston: I. Thomas and E. T. Andrews, 1790), pp. 1–37, abridged.

not easily supplanted by the other. The great art of correcting mankind, therefore, consists in prepossessing the mind with good principles.

For this reason society requires that the education of youth should be watched with the most scrupulous attention. Education, in a great measure, forms the moral characters of men, and morals are the basis of government. Education should therefore be the first care of a legislature; not merely the institution of schools, but the furnishing of them with the best men for teachers. A good system of education should be the first article in the code of political regulations; for it is much easier to introduce and establish an effectual system for preserving morals, than to correct, by penal statutes, the ill effects of a bad system. I am so fully persuaded of this, that I shall almost adore that great man, who shall change our practice and opinions, and make it respectable for the first and best men to super-intend the education of youth.

Another defect in our schools, which, since the revolution, is become inexcusable, is the want of proper books. The collections which are now used consist of essays that respect foreign and ancient nations. The minds of youth are perpetually led to the history of Greece and Rome or to Great Britain; boys are consistently repeating the declamations of Demosthenes and Cicero, or debates upon some political question in the British Parliament. These are excellent specimens of good sense, polished style and perfect oratory; but they are not interesting to children. They cannot be very useful, except to young gentlemen who want them as models of reasoning and eloquence, in the pulpit or at the bar.

But every child in America should be acquainted with his own country. He should read books that furnish him with ideas that will be useful to him in life and practice. As soon as he opens his lips, he should rehearse the history of his own country; he should lisp the praise of liberty, and of those illustrious heroes and statesmen, who have wrought a revolution in her favor.

A selection of essays, respecting the settlement and geography of America; the history of the late revolution and of the most remarkable characters and events that distinguished it, and a compendium of the principles of the federal and provincial governments, should be the principal schoolbook in the United States. These are interesting objects to every man; they call home the minds of youth and fix them upon the interests of their own country, and they assist in forming attachments to it, as well as in enlarging the understanding.

"It is observed by the great Montesquieu, that the laws of education ought to be relative to the principles of the government."

In despotic governments, the people should have little or no education, except what tends to inspire them with a servile fear. Information is fatal to despotism.

In monarchies, education should be partial, and adapted to the rank of each class of citizens. But "in a republican government," says the same writer, "the whole power of education is required." Here every class of people should *know* and *love* the laws. This knowledge should be diffused by means of schools and newspapers; and an attachment to the laws may be formed by early impressions upon the mind.

Two regulations are essential to the continuance of republican governments: 1. Such a distribution of lands and such principles of descent and alienation, as shall give every citizen a power of acquiring what his industry merits. 2. Such a system of education as gives every citizen an opportunity of acquiring knowledge and fitting himself for places of trust. These are fundamental articles; the *sine qua non* of the existence of the American republics.

Hence the absurdity of our copying the manners and adopting the institutions of monarchies.

In several states, we find laws passed, establishing provision for colleges and academies, where people of property may educate their sons; but no provision made for instructing the poorer rank of people, even in reading and writing. Yet in these same states, every citizen who is worth a few shillings annually, is entitled to vote for legislators. This appears to me a most glaring solecism in government. The constitutions are *republican,* and the laws of education are *monarchical.* The *former* extend civil rights to every honest industrious man; the *latter* deprive a proportion of the citizens of a most valuable privilege.

In our American republics, where government is in the hands of the people, knowledge should be universally diffused by means of public schools. Of such consequence is it to society, that the people who make laws should be well informed, that I conceive no legislature can be justified in neglecting proper establishments for this purpose.

When I speak of a diffusion of knowledge, I do not mean merely a knowledge of spelling books, and the New Testament. An acquaintance with ethics, and with the general principles of law, commerce, money and government, is necessary for the yeomanry of a republican state. This acquaintance they might obtain by means of books calculated for schools, and read by the children, during the winter months, and by the circulation of public papers.

. . .

Every small district should be furnished with a school, at least four months in a year; when boys are not otherwise employed. This school should be kept by the most reputable and well informed man in the district. Here children should be taught the usual branches of learning; submission to superiors and to laws; the moral or social duties; the history and transactions of their own country; the principles of liberty and government. Here the rough manners of the wilderness should be softened, and the principles of virtue and good behavior inculcated. The *virtues* of men are of more consequence to society than their *abilities*; and for this reason, the heart should be cultivated with more assiduity than the head.

Such a general system of education is neither impracticable nor difficult; and excepting the formation of a federal government that shall be efficient and permanent, it demands the first attention of American patriots. Until such a system shall be adopted and pursued; until the statesman and Divine shall unite their efforts in forming the human mind, rather than in lopping its excrescences, after it has been neglected; until legislators discover that the only way to make good citizens and subjects, is to nourish them from infancy; and until parents shall be convinced that the *worst* of men are not the proper teachers to make the *best*; mankind cannot know to what a degree of perfection society and government may be carried. America affords the fairest opportunities for making the experiment, and opens the most encouraging prospect of success.

THE EARLY MODERN PERIOD
(1600-1800)
SIGNIFICANT ACTIONS

COLONIAL
EDUCATION
LEGISLATION

THE MASSACHUSETTS SCHOOL LAW OF 1642

This court, taking into consideration the great neglect of many parents and masters in training up their children in learning and labor and other employments which may be profitable to the common wealth, do hereupon order and decree that in every town the chosen men appointed for managing the prudential affairs of the same shall henceforth stand charged with the care of the redress of this evil, so as they shall be sufficiently punished by fines for the neglect thereof, upon presentment of the grand jury, or other information or complaint in any court within this jurisdiction; and for this end they, or the greater number of them, shall have power to take account from time to time of all parents and masters, and of their children, especially of their ability to read and understand the principles of religion and the capital laws of this country, and to impose fines upon such as shall refuse to render such accounts to them when they shall be required; and they shall have power, with consent of any court or the magistrate, to put forth apprentices the children of such as they shall [find] not to be able and fit to employ and bring them up. They

Modernized version of the original found in *Records of the Governor and Company of Massachusetts Bay in New England,* printed by order of the legislature, ed. Nathaniel B. Shurtleff (Boston: William White, Printer to the Commonwealth, 1853), pp. 6–7 of Volume II.

shall take . . . that boys and girls be not suffered to converse together, so as may occasion any wanton, dishonest, or immodest behavior; and for their better performance of this trust committed to them, they may divide the town amongst them, appointing to every of the said townsmen a certain number of families to have special oversight of. . . .

THE MASSACHUSETTS SCHOOL LAW OF 1647

It being one chief project of the old deluder, Satan, to keep men from the knowledge of the Scriptures, as in former times by keeping them in an unknown tongue, so in these latter times by persuading them from the use of tongues that so at least the true sense and meaning of the original might be clouded by false glosses of saint-seeming deceivers, that learning may not be buried in the grave of our fathers in the church and commonwealth, the Lord assisting our endeavors,

It is therefore ordered, that every township in this jurisdiction, after the Lord hath increased them to the number of fifty householders, shall then forthwith appoint one within their town to teach all such children as shall resort to him to write and read, whose wages shall be paid either by the parents or masters of such children, or by the inhabitants in general, by way of supply, as the major part of those that order the prudentials of the town shall appoint; provided, those that send their children be not oppressed by paying much more than they can have them taught for in other towns; and it is further ordered, that where any town shall increase to the number of one hundred families or householders they shall set up a grammar school, the master thereof being able to instruct youth so far as they may be fitted for the university; provided, that if any town neglect the performance hereof above one year, that every such town shall pay five pounds to the next school till they shall perform this order.

THE VIRGINIA APPRENTICESHIP LAWS

The Law of 1643

The guardians and overseers of all orphants shall carefully keep and preserve such estates as shall be committed to their trusts either by order of court or

Modernized version of the original found in *Records of the Governor and Company of Massachusetts Bay in New England,* printed by order of the legislature, ed. Nathaniel B. Shurtleff (Boston: William White, Printer to the Commonwealth, 1853), p. 203 of Volume II.
From *Statutes at Large of Virginia,* ed. William Waller Hening, p. 260 of Volume I and p. 298 of Volume II, n.d.

otherwise. And shall likewise render an exact accompt once everie year to the commissioners of the several county courts, respectively, of the said estates and of the increase and improvement, who are hereby to keep an exact register thereof. And all overseers and guardians of such orphants are enjoyned by authority aforesaid to educate and instruct them according to their best endeavors in Christian religion and in the rudiments of learning and to provide for their necessaries according to the competents of their estate.

The Law of 1672

That the justices of the peace in every county doe put the laws of England against vagrants, idlers, and dissolute persons, in strict execution, and the respective county courts shall and are hereby empowered and authorized to place out all the children whose parents are not able to bring them up apprentices to tradesmen, the males till one and twenty years of age and the females to other necessary employment till eighteen years of age and no longer, and the church wardens of every parish shall [be] strictly enjoyned by the courts to give them an account at their Orphans Courts of all such children within their parish.

EARLIEST
FEDERAL PROVISIONS
FOR EDUCATION

THE LAND ORDINANCE OF 1785

"An Ordinance for ascertaining the mode of disposing of Lands in the Western Territory"

Be it ordained by the United States in Congress assembled, that the territory ceded by individual States to the United States, which has been purchased of the Indian inhabitants, shall be disposed of in the following manner:

A surveyor from each state shall be appointed by Congress, or a committee of the States, who shall take an Oath for the faithful discharge of his duty, before the Geographer of the United States, who is hereby empowered and directed to administer the same; and the like oath shall be administered to each chain carrier, by the surveyor under whom he acts.

. . .

The Surveyors, as they are respectively qualified, shall proceed to divide the said territory into townships of six miles square, by lines running due north and south, and other crossing these at right angles, . . .

From *Journals of the Continental Congress,* from the original records in the Library of Congress, ed. J. C. Fitzpatrick, Vol. XXVIII (Washington, D.C.: U.S. Government Printing Office, 1933), p. 375–376, 378.

The first line, running north and south as aforesaid, shall begin on the river Ohio, at a point that shall be found to be due north from the western termination of a line, which has been run as the southern boundary of the state of Pennsylvania; and the first line, running east and west, shall begin at the same point, and shall extend throughout the whole territory.

. . .

There shall be reserved for the United States out of every township, the four lots, being numbered 8, 11, 26, 29, and out of every fractional part of a township, so many lots of the same numbers as shall be found thereon, for future sale. There shall be reserved the lot N 16, of every township, for the maintenance of public schools, within the said township. . . .

THE NORTHWEST ORDINANCE OF 1787

"An Ordinance for the government of the territory of the United States northwest of the river Ohio"

Be it ordained by the United States in Congress assembled, that the said territory, for the purposes of temporary government, be one district, subject, however, to be divided into two districts, as future circumstances may, in the opinion of Congress, make it expedient.

. . .

It is hereby ordained and declared, by the authority aforesaid, that the following articles shall be considered as articles of compact, between the original States and the people and States in the said territory, and forever remain unalterable, unless by common consent, to wit:

Article I

No person, demeaning himself in a peaceable and orderly manner, shall ever be molested on account of his mode of worship, or religious sentiments, in the said territory.

. . .

Article III

Religion, morality, and knowledge being necessary to good government and the happiness of mankind, schools and the means of education shall forever be encouraged. . . .

The Federal and State Constitutions, Colonial Charters, and Other Organic Laws, compiled and edited under the Act of Congress of June 30, 1906 by Francis Newton Thorpe (Washington, D.C.: Government Printing Office, 1909), p. 957, 960–961 of Volume II.

THE CONSTITUTION
OF THE UNITED STATES

AMENDMENT I (ADOPTED DECEMBER 15, 1791)

Congress shall make no law respecting an establishment of religion, or prohibiting the free exercise thereof; or abridging the freedom of speech, or of the press; or the right of the people peaceably to assemble, and to petition the government for a redress of grievances.

AMENDMENT X (ADOPTED DECEMBER 15, 1791)

The powers not delegated to the United States by the Constitution, nor prohibited by it to the states, are reserved to the states respectively, or to the people.

AMENDMENT XIV (ADOPTED 1868)

Section 1.　All persons born or naturalized in the United States and subject to the jurisdiction thereof are citizens of the United States and of the state wherein they reside. No state shall make or enforce any law which shall abridge the privileges or immunities of citizens of the United States; nor shall any state deprive any person of life, liberty, or property, without due process of law; nor deny to any person within its jurisdiction the equal protection of the laws. . . .

Section 5.　The Congress shall have power to enforce, by appropriate legislation, the provisions of this article.

PART 3

THE MODERN PERIOD
(1800-1900)

THE SOCIAL
CONTEXT

THE nineteenth century was a time of rapid change; traditions in politics and social organization were modified in nearly every European country and in America, and technical and scientific advances occurred at a pace unknown before. The Industrial Revolution entered its second phase and spread across Europe. A simultaneous revolution in agriculture took place, by the mechanization of farming. As the efficiency of agriculture increased, an exodus from farm to city began and has continued into the present century. Yet though there was much change and many advances, this, like previous centuries, was marked for the masses of people by continuing problems of poverty, sickness, and lack of educational opportunity —problems with which the present century is still quite familiar.

The nineteenth century was a time of war and of nation building, of revolution and of retrenchments by existing regimes. While the population of Europe and the United States was doubling, hardly a country escaped war, revolution, or civil conflict; if it did not become involved directly, it was affected by its neighbor's turmoils. The Napoleonic Wars, the Crimean War, the Austro-Prussian War, the Franco-Prussian War—these among others ravaged many lands. All the while, new nations or new political structures in existing nations appeared. Belgium, Greece, Italy, and Germany joined the list of independent countries before the century's end. In France, the range of political rule extended from empire to a near constitutional democracy. Probably the most significant change in the rank of continental European powers was the ascendency of Germany and the relative decline of France during the late 1800s. By 1900, the United States had joined the major powers of the world.

The map of Europe was altered many times during the nineteenth century. New alliances formed as attempts to strike a balance of power were made by England, Germany, Austria, France and Russia. The Congress of Vienna redistributed the lands won by Napoleon's armies. The Congress of Berlin drew political lines in southeast Europe. In a late-century effort at establishing arbitration through international law, the Hague Conference was convened. Early in the period, the United States, in the Monroe Doctrine, set down its sentiments regarding foreign intrusion in its sphere of influence. The United States, like other powers of the day, resorted both to war and to internal conflict in order to assert its interests and maintain its lawful order—in the War of 1812, the Mexican War, the Spanish-American War, and the Civil War.

Socially and philosophically the nineteenth century was marked by increasing democracy in the rule of governments, though this advance was not everywhere equal or at any time easily obtained. Against existing forms of political and social rule new proposals were formulated. Socialism in its many versions was proposed in a variety of settings—in England, in Germany, in France and in Russia. About mid-century the *Communist Manifesto* was published by Marx and Engels. Earlier the doctrine of utilitarianism was espoused by such political philosophers as James Mill and John Stuart Mill. Toward the end of the century the philosophic position called pragmatism was advanced by American philosophers. The concept of evolution was evolved by Darwin, and an attempt to relate this concept to the social order was worked out by Herbert Spencer. Different views of society and of political organization carried with them suggestions for reconstituting existing institutions, including education.

A fuller interest in the rational control of human life and of society through improvement of the person was displayed. Underlying this interest was the development of more democratic forms of government accompanied by greater social and economic expectations for the members of society. To be effective, modern governments needed enlightened citizens, so went the argument, and education was seen as the most appropriate means to this end. Equality in society and equality of opportunity, whether real or promised, suggested equality of opportunity for self-improvement. This in turn demanded education for the many, not just for the privileged.

During the 1800s what had begun as limited private or public education of the poor was developed into the general education of the many at the elementary level. However, it must be noted that legislation is one thing and implementation another. By 1900 there was no country in Europe or America that provided elementary schooling for all its eligible children. Certainly no country saw more than a small minority of its young men and women attending secondary school. Still the century is notable as the era in which the concept and practice of universal elementary education now became a near reality.

Formal education assumed a variety of shapes: state-supported public schools, state-supported private and parochial schools, private schools, the beginnings of technical institutes and trade schools; private and public colleges and universities, professional schools; preparatory schools, and still others. The education of girls, a side concern throughout preceding centuries, was sponsored in many countries. Public support for elementary education—and in some instances for secondary education—was accepted by the end of the century in much of Europe and in the United States. In some countries, for example France, a central agency was charged with administration and control of education; in other countries, for example the United States, control remained local or regional. The state replaced the Church as the dominant educational agency, though parochial schools endured and grew in number and in enrollment.

Among nineteenth-century advances in scientific thought and discovery were the germ theory of disease, the law of conservation of energy, the formulation of the laws of heredity, the discovery of the conditioned reflex, the revival and refinement of the atomic theory, the discovery of the X-ray, progress toward the explanation of light and magnetism, and the theory of evolution. This also was the century that saw economics, philosophy, and political science augmented by such specializations as sociology, anthropology, and psychology. The scientific approach to child study was established during the latter part of the century and it, assisted by psychology, provided the basis for the scientific approach to education.

Perhaps the most significant departure from previous approaches to learning and to investigation was the displacement of holistic theories that attempted to supply a grand design to the solution of major scientific and social problems. Instead, by the end of the century, the more common approach was to isolate a portion of a problem or investigation and work toward its solution. This is not to say that piecemeal approaches replaced attempts to deal with an entire issue; rather it is to note that increasing knowledge and research sophistication brought recognition that many enduring problems were much more complex than had been assumed and that multiple steps led to knowledge, not just one great leap.

Accompanying the advances in science were related gains in technology. This was the century that saw communications shrink the world with the invention of the telegraph, the telephone, and the wireless. The present age of fast and mass transportation was ushered in with the invention of the gasoline and the diesel engine and the development of railroads. The Bessemer process made steel the metal for myriad industrial and construction uses. The development of new metals and of synthetics to replace costly or rare natural materials was well advanced by the end of the century. Industry expanded and with this expansion came a concentration of population in manufacturing and trade centers. There followed the special social, health and economic problems that we see still today following close on the heels of massive population redistribution to urban areas. To support local manufacturing and to insure a steady supply of raw materials and an overseas marketing outlet, the major nations turned again to colonialism, this time to Africa and Asia. By 1900 there were fewer truly independent countries in all of Asia and Africa than in Europe.

In art, the nineteenth century saw both Romanticism and Realism come into full development and influence. Romanticism emphasized the intuitive, the mystical, the personal, the impressionistic, and the world of nature. Realism emphasized the factual, the natural and the concrete. Both movements affected educational thinking. Romanticism found its educational champions in Rousseau and his successors, who placed emphasis on the child as an individual and a creature of nature to be raised in accord with nature's dictates and the child's individual needs. Realism was more linked with the scientific approach to child study and with the training of teachers according to the demands imposed by social conditions, the nature of the students, and the required curriculum of the schools.

While the United States emerged from the nineteenth century as a distinct political and social society with many native institutions and artistic and technological features, nonetheless the influence of Europe on America remained considerable, especially in the early part of the century. European systems and philosophies of education helped direct American educational thinking and practice. American educators, for example Horace Mann, traveled abroad to view European education, and their impressions affected American practice. The writings of Pestalozzi, Froebel, Spencer, and Herbart were major influences in shaping aspects of American education, from the organization of the curriculum to the training of teachers. The immigration to America of tens of thousands of Europeans during the century was another factor in shaping American education; although since the bulk of these persons had received little education, this factor often tends to be overemphasized. It is necessary to remember that many Americans received their higher education abroad during the century, that at the beginning of the century a majority of American citizens had been born under another flag, and that for educational, artistic and philosophical models the Americans of the nineteenth century were wont to look abroad, at least for much of the century. There follows now, therefore, a very brief description of certain social and educational events of the nineteenth century in France, Germany (Prussia), and England. (The reader is urged to turn to the bibliography for suggested readings that provide discussion in depth.) Attention then will be re-directed to America.

. . .

The French Constitution of 1791 called for free elementary education, but aside from this declaration of intent little happened except that the control of education by the clergy was curtailed. Under Napoleon, education became centralized in one organization and a state monopoly was established. Later, in 1854, France was divided administratively into sixteen academies, each supervised by a director of education with inspectors responsible to him. In 1879, all Departments (administrative-political units) of France were directed to maintain training colleges for teachers. Minimum standards of attainment were assessed against teachers. Certification was introduced and certificates were regulated.[1]

In 1833 a law obliged communes to maintain schools and to pay their teachers. Towards mid-century, primary schools for girls were required of all communes with more than 500 population. These schools could be tuition-free if the commune so wished and would support them itself. In 1881, fees in all elementary schools and in training colleges were abolished by government action. In 1882, compulsory attendance at elementary school was required.

After Napoleon, the Restoration government returned the responsibility for teaching to the Church. Then, in 1886, a law required that only lay persons teach in the public schools, and religious instruction was replaced in the public schools by moral teaching, much against the wishes of the Church and a significant portion of the populace.

Like most European systems of this time, French education was divided into primary and secondary tracks. Secondary education was conceived as an entity unto itself and it extended from the first year of school until university. Those intending secondary education followed a different approach from that taken by the majority of students, and they undertook a notably different form and content of education. A system of elite training for the few accompanied the general, and lesser, education for others who were able to attain a measure of schooling.

During the nineteenth century, French education was strongly centralized and rigidly prescribed. A uniformity of curriculum was imposed with strict discipline the rule and adult authority the measure. This situation provided an interesting contrast: a relatively liberal philosophy of government and individual rights (stemming from the Revolution) coupled with a traditional centralization of authority within major social and political institutions.

The aims of education, at least of education at its best, reflected contemporary values of the society. The student was expected to achieve—insofar as he was able—rational judgment, expressiveness and fluency in the native language, an ability to deal with abstract and logical modes of thought, good taste, and above all, familiarity with and reverence for French culture and its

---

[1] The state of New York derived its administrative model for education, especially for post-elementary education, largely from France.

heritage. Training for life as a rational reflective citizen was the overall aim, not narrow preparation leading to a specific trade, profession or outlook. The tradition of humanistic and liberal education is seen to be still dominant and particularly appropriate for the elite.

Following defeat by Napoleon at the Battle of Jena, Prussia reorganized education. In 1807, education came under the Ministry of the Interior and von Humboldt was placed in charge. In 1810, state examination of teachers and state certification stopped the common practice of automatically allowing theological students to teach in the schools. This action upgraded the profession as a whole.

Prussia's rapidly became the notable system of European education and measurably influenced other systems, including that of the United States. Von Humboldt encouraged the introduction of Pestalozzi's experimental methods into teacher preparation institutions, hence into the elementary schools. School-leaving examinations were instituted. Local authorities in direct charge of education at the community level were named. Later, administrative divisions were formed and inspections were carried out by government officials.

The classification of schools was precise, and curricula were standardized, especially in secondary schools, where both the classical and the modern divisions were accepted but with the classical curriculum accorded more esteem.[2] After the founding of the Empire (1871), an educational argument raged over the relative merits of the classical and the modern curricula. In 1900, following much controversy, equality of privilege was accorded the different types of secondary schools, but faculties of theology and medicine still would not accept modern curriculum graduates. Despite the relative inflexibility of the system, some experimentation was possible and from this developed several significant advances in course offerings, organization, and methods of instruction.

During the nineteenth century, the Prussian system was state-controlled, though the state and Church cooperated closely and religion was taught in the schools. Schools were Catholic, Jewish or Evangelical (Lutheran) except in locations where creeds were so mixed or population so sparse as to make this

---

[2] In the classical secondary schools the accent was on the ancient languages, humanistic studies, religion, and on the theoretical aspects of such subjects as mathematics. Discipline of the mind was the aim. The curriculum was prescriptive and intended as preparation for high governmental and military posts and such professions as law, medicine, theology, and university teaching.

The modern schools accented contemporary languages, science, mathematics with a practical emphasis, and certain social studies. This preparation led to commerce, industry and common governmental posts. The modern curriculum was less esteemed than the classical curriculum, though it was hardly less prescriptive.

With considerable accuracy the description given applies to the secondary divisions of curriculum in France of the time and, later, England.

arrangement impracticable. Teachers were hired according to their religious faith and the clergy inspected the teaching of religion in the schools. Though education was compulsory by the middle of the century, it was hardly universal; for many areas lacked schools and teachers.

In Prussia, a strong centralized government produced a strong and centralized educational system through the cooperation of Church and state, with the state ascendant. The aim of the system was to produce, as efficiently as possible, trained, pious and obedient citizens to work toward the strengthening of national goals—in industry, in war, and in government. In so structuring the system, those who planned and implemented its programs derived support from the traditional attitudes of the populace: loyalty to the state, acceptance of authority, and thoroughness and detail in application of effort.[3] Rulers who desired education for the masses did so not so much from a desire to instill liberal inclinations and views in their subjects but rather to educate them to the furthering of the goals of the ruling class.

The efficiency of the Prussian educational system attracted attention from outside the country. Visitors and observers from France, England, and the United States, among other nations, urged their countrymen to put into practice much of what they had seen in Prussia. The effectiveness of the system, but not necessarily its aims, influenced educational practice in many other countries.

In England through much of the nineteenth century, support of schools was private or denominational. In 1832, the Whig government granted a modest sum of money for support of education; this became the basis of subsequent appropriations by Parliament. Misgivings were held, however, by supporters of private and denominational schools about such support. Certain inspections and controls were attached to governmental support and this was viewed in some quarters as unwarranted government trespass into traditionally private activity. Gradually, denominational schools other than those of the Anglican Church were subsidized and a system of public-private support was established. Grants-in-aid were made for normal school construction and maintenance, in cooperation with private agencies. As the century progressed, agreements were reached concerning the teaching of religion in the various schools (though somewhat of an over-simplification, the term "local option" would describe the results of these agreements).

Commissions and enquiries marked the latter part of the nineteenth century in English education. In 1858, the Newcastle Commission was formed to look into the condition of popular education and to suggest ways to extend proper elementary education to all classes. The Commission noted that about 2,500,000 children attended some form of day school—about one child

---

[3] Cf. The discussion of Spartan education preceding the selections of Part I.

in seven—and that only about half those attending were in publicly supported schools. Less than half those attending at all were in schools open to some sort of inspection, and but two-fifths of all students attended schools receiving an annual grant. As a whole, the Commission was against free and compulsory education, largely because of expected religious difficulties. A result of the Commission's inquiry was institution of payment by results. If, upon examination, fundamentals of knowledge were known by the child, the school received a grant which could be twice as much per capita as the amount received under existing arrangements. The immediate effect of this payment-by-payment policy was a decrease in the Crown's appropriations to public education.

The Elementary Education Act of 1870 was intended ". . . to complete the voluntary system and to fill up gaps." Under its provisions:

(1) voluntary schools (sponsored by private agencies, largely denominational) and rate-supported schools were continued, each subsidized, but with voluntary schools remaining under private management;

(2) board schools (those publicly established in areas where inadequate facilities or none existed) could offer only undenominational religious instruction;

(3) transfer of voluntary schools from their sponsors to public support was made possible.

Growth in attendance was rapid and in 1876 a law was passed requiring universal attendance at elementary school, with certain exceptions. In 1880, this law was strengthened; in 1891 attendance became largely free of charge.

Additional legislation led to the forming of the Secondary Education Commission (1894), a Royal Commission chaired by James Bryce and directed to inquire into secondary education.[4] The Commission recommended that

(1) existing central authorities be combined and that an educational council be formed to advise the Minister of Education in certain professional matters;

(2) local authorities be established;

(3) there be formed a listing of teachers, to encourage both professional training and a system of school registration based on inspection and examination.

These provisions were made partially effective by the Balfour Act of 1902, which brought under one authority all responsibility for the schools.

---

[4] Cf. The report of the "Committee of Ten" (see the selections in this section of readings).

Throughout the century, attendance at secondary school was the exception not the rule and quite uncommon for the less well-to-do. Nor was elementary education universal throughout England (and Wales) at century's end.

As contrasted with France and Germany, England had no national system of education during the nineteenth century. Instead, a system of private education, mostly church-sponsored and having its origins (especially at the secondary level) in past centuries provided what educational opportunity existed for much of the century. Gradually, the government undertook support of education while allowing a great deal of local option and direction of the schools. Late in the century, public establishment of elementary schools went hand-in-hand with public assistance to denominational schools, though with some restrictions imposed on denominational schools in regard to curriculum and the teaching of doctrine. As in France, the education of the many differed substantially from that of the elite; the great English "public" secondary schools (e.g., Eton) provided the university candidates and trained the future occupants of positions of prestige and esteem in society. Others who attended school received a much inferior, and much more limited, education. Little formal education was seen as needed for work in a factory or in a mill—a common employment of children during this time—or on a farm.

Characteristics of English social and political life, as well as of tradition, were reflected in the schools. Freedom of discourse and action was illustrated by the freedom of private agencies to establish and maintain schools, but a strong middle class and increasing industrial prosperity combined to conserve, not to change, existing institutional arrangements including education.[5] Religious equality guaranteed equal opportunity to erect schools. State intervention was considered potentially harmful and was opposed, particularly by the Anglican Church. The church-state issue, though enduringly present throughout the century, was accommodated without the state's taking control of the schools, as in Germany.

England did not acutely feel the need for using the schools as an instrument of national aspiration. No wars had been fought on her soil during the century and she led, not lagged, the industrial world. Her educational system is explicable, then, in terms of tradition, contemporary events, social values and practices. As also illustrated in the description of French and German education, England, in the nineteenth century, demonstrated the response of a major social institution (education) to the social, historical and economic

---

[5] More often than not, the combination of social factors and forces promotes educational conservatism, retention of the status quo. It is against this condition that spokesmen represented in the selections in this volume often speak out. If the inertia is great, the measures proposed tend to be more dramatic than if the social arrangements are fluid or undergoing change that, in the spokesman's view, merely needs guidance into new channels.

conditions of the native culture and to the expectations of that segment of the population that formed opinions and controlled the economy.

. . .

The United States during the nineteenth century experienced many of the changes and advances that were occurring in Europe. Population increased dramatically over the previous century, due in considerable measure to massive immigrations to America from the Old World—from Germany, Ireland, England and other European countries. The population of the United States, which had been clustered among the Eastern Seaboard, spread west, first to the Midwest and eventually to the Pacific. By 1900, all but a few of the contiguous forty-eight states had been formed and had established their own local governments, institutions and educational arrangements.

Industrial growth and increase in trade were rapid during the 1800s. The United States soon became an extensive trader with the rest of the world and exports annually grew larger as industry and agriculture became more diversified and more abundant. The wealth of the nation grew enormously but unequally; by the end of the century legislation had been passed to prevent further disparity among the different classes and to provide some control over the power of corporations and other economic organizations.

Convinced early in the century that the form of government it had chosen would endure, the United States began to take on characteristic forms and institutions. Business, social organizations, technology, and, eventually, artistic forms developed that were different from European models and that served to identify American culture and society. Localism of government increased as the new land to the west was settled and as the population moved away from the compact and more densely populated East. One of the most distinct institutions that developed during the century was the form of education that became typically American and not a facsimile of European models.

In evaluating the growth and progress of America during the nineteenth century, it is easy to rhapsodize, especially if vis-à-vis comparisons are made with many of the European countries. In so doing, one forgets the outstanding accomplishments of European countries in many respects—political, economic, scientific, and artistic. And one ignores, against the many notable achievements of nineteenth-century America, issues and situations that developed in America during this period and that today cause much social unrest and continue to provoke continuing legislation in an attempt to correct their abuses—urbanization, still-existent class distinctions and racial distinctions that are wholly unwarranted, highly advanced technology and means of production but less advanced social and educational means for using these as wisely as might be the case, still-persistent religious quarrels, and a host of additional problems as plaguing as ever though their solution may seem closer at hand. There is no reason to recite a litany of current social problems here or to lay at the feet of the nineteenth century the blame for all of them, but it is advisable while considering the many advances made in the past century in America to recognize that along with them often came side effects that we contend with today and for the removal of which we increasingly and hopefully turn to education.

During the 1800s, American schools broadened their aims and their curricula. Schools increased greatly in number, and as the century passed, they received correspondent public support. By 1900, free public elementary education was a common legislative requirement and the battle over public support of secondary education had been won by its advocates. During this century literacy, moral training and mental discipline were supplemented by a number of other aims of education, including citizenship, vocational training, individual development and a much-expanding offering of courses in subject matter. Private schools, which had been predominant in the first part of the century, still flourished; but public schools had far overtaken them in number and, often, in quality.

Early in the century, Sunday schools (in which were taught such basic skills as reading and writing, as well as religion) were prevalent, a carry-over from the eighteenth century. For the first third of the century, monitorial schools were common, especially in population centers. These schools, adopted from England, used more advanced students to teach younger students, with an instructor supervising the efforts of the older students. The assumption was a time-honored one: what one knows or has mastered, he can teach. The economy of this method and its ability to handle large numbers of pupils provided its appeal.

About 1825, the fight for free schools was joined in earnest. Conventions of public school proponents were held; sponsoring societies and groups were formed, and campaigns were mounted. Eventually the goal was reached, after much effort and opposition and through the labors of such advocates as Horace Mann. By the end of the Civil War, the public system of education was well outlined, and state after state now made elementary education a requirement. Elementary schools varied greatly in their quality, their size, and their facilities. In cities and towns, schools of several hundred pupils and a dozen or more teachers were available and teachers were fairly well trained. In more remote areas, one-room schools were not infrequent, and the teacher, if trained at all, had a dearth of texts and inadequate facilities.

Academies were the prevailing secondary institutions for the first part of the nineteenth century. These schools, privately run, were broader in aim and in offerings than the more traditional Latin grammar schools, which had been founded during colonial times. The best of the academies offered not only the classical languages, mathematics, and traditional subjects but also such courses as geography and commercial studies. Some early public support of academies was provided but the thrust turned toward the establishment of public high schools, the first of which appeared in Boston in 1821. Originally, the public high school was college preparatory in purpose, but gradually it developed terminal education programs for those not intending to enter college.

As opposed to the common European model of the times, elementary public and secondary education in the United States was viewed as an open system, not a system of two degrees and kinds. Inevitably, however, social status and economic means had their effects; nor were the states equal in the opportunities for education they provided. A sharp distinction in the quality and degree of education available also existed between metropolitan and rural areas. Denominational schools continued to increase during the nineteenth century but they gave way to public schools, especially at the elementary level, in both the total and relative number of students enrolled.

By 1890, 27 states and territories had enacted compulsory-attendance laws; by 1918, all states had done so. During the century the greatest growth in attendance was in elementary education; enrollment was about 16,000,000 by 1900, when a majority of eligible students attended elementary school. But by 1900, only some ten percent of the eligible age group was attending secondary school.

Control and support of education during the century was state-local, not national, and management of the schools was local. Toward mid-century, the graded system was quite common, especially in urban areas. By late in the century, the usual pattern of organization was the eight-year elementary school followed by a four-year high school. As schools developed, so did organizational and administrative arrangements. By the time of the Civil War each state had a state superintendent of education or the equivalent. Professional management and control of the schools saw its beginning and development in America during the nineteenth century.

Financial support during most of the century was inadequate and varied. Such devices as lotteries, liquor taxes and the sale of Western lands were used to raise funds for the operation of public schools. Rate bills also were common. The prevailing sentiment well into the century was that support of education was a private or denominational concern. Early in the century, for instance, Pennsylvania provided public support only for pauper schools. But as an outgrowth of expectations of the populace, state constitutions eventually called for subsidized public education. The district system developed along with local control and the authorization for local taxation and administration. Concomitantly, state-level support was increased.

Methods of instruction changed slowly. Early in the century progress was made by adding grouping according to differential abilities and by encouraging classroom use of discussion. Efforts to individualize curriculum and teaching were made; here the works of Pestalozzi and the observations of those who visited his schools were factors in promoting change. The "object" method of instruction was introduced and widely used.

Training colleges for elementary teachers appeared; in 1820 the first such institution, a private one, was founded in Massachusetts. The first public normal school was created in the 1830s. By the Civil War a dozen such institutions existed and after the war they increased rapidly. A growing number of women entered teaching (in relative contrast to European systems); well before 1900 they outnumbered men teachers in the public schools. Two-year normal schools started developing into four-year training schools beginning late in the century; wholesale upgrading of these institutions took place, however, mostly after 1900. Toward the end of the century, the writings and proposals of the German philosopher-psychologist Herbart virtually controlled the methods of instruction and the training of teachers in preparatory institutions.

Professional educational organizations made their initial appearance in the nineteenth century. In 1857, the National Education Association was organized. Near the end of the century accrediting agencies appeared. Professional associations among the various disciplines also were formed and grew rapidly. Toward mid-century the United States Office of Education was founded by an act of Congress.

During this century, state universities and colleges were built and many new private or denominational colleges and universities were chartered. At the time of the American Revolution there had been but nine colleges in the country; by 1860 there were about 200. Early efforts were made to transform private colleges into state institutions but the decision of the Supreme Court in the Dartmouth case halted such attempts. Public institutions thereafter had to be financed from tax monies, and appropriate legislation was written and passed. By the Civil War, twenty states had founded state universities. After the war, all new states and a number of the older states founded public colleges and universities that since have developed into many of today's leading institutions of higher education. Gradually, articulation between colleges and secondary schools was accomplished and the "ladder" of education was framed. Still, in 1900 less than two percent of the age group attended college.

THE
EDUCATIONAL
ISSUES

THE nineteenth century produced in American education a slow-moving but certain adjustment in the bases for curricula and methodologies and in the relation between education and all levels of government. In selecting purposes for education and criteria upon which to base selection of subject matter, educators increasingly turned from philosophical justification to psychological theorizing and experimentation. Central to this change of emphasis was a movement away from seeking intrinsic values in the various subject matters and toward examination of subject matter and methodology in terms of their value to the learner as an individual. The century also marked the gradual disengagement from European models and the rise of the common school ideology, which has become a hallmark of democratic society.

Johann Heinrich Pestalozzi, a Swiss educator, was the century's earliest proponent of the "new" education, an education dependent upon the study of human development and the structuring of a psychology of learning and instruction. In his work (p. 189) Pestalozzi clearly reflects the Aristotelian underpinnings of his thought as he converts many of the powerful but sometimes vague insights of his predecessors Comenius and Rousseau into concrete practices. His method is one of utilizing that which is natural, of deemphasizing purely verbal learning, and of concentrating on the total development of the child. In much of his phraseology, here and in his other writings, one encounters ideas, such as "guiding and stimulating self-activity," "fitting tasks to ability levels," and "proceeding by doing, not by words," which quite clearly are precursors of the progressive approach of the twentieth century. Pestalozzi had a more direct influence on the course of education through the visits of many foreign educators to his schools in Germany and Switzerland. A number of teacher training institutions in the United States adopted the Pestalozzian approach during the second half of the century.

Friedrich Froebel, German educator and follower of Pestalozzian principles, turned full attention to the child, condemning the education of the time which was imposing and prescriptive and did not allow the learner to develop his full range of potentialities. Ideas put forth in his *The Education of Man* (p. 196), though at times quite mystical, exerted a great influence upon the course of early childhood education. His interest in human development, especially at the early stages of growth, led to his founding an experimental school and his establishing the first kindergarten, in 1839.

A contemporary of Pestalozzi and Froebel, Johann Friedrich Herbart (p. 205) added psychological sophistication to some of the basic ideas of Rousseau, although in his formalizations he focused on collective man rather than on the individual, thus departing from Pestalozzi and Froebel. His emphasis was on the teacher and on the process of instruction, and his views were adopted by numerous teacher training schools as the only proper pedagogical method.

The Pestalozzian spirit found further expression in America through the eloquent pen of Ralph Waldo Emerson (p. 227). His admonition that education must start from a fundamental respect for the noble nature of the developing individual and proceed slowly, if inefficiently, toward the natural unfolding of the individual's potential clearly reflects the enthusiasm and optimism of the evolving "new education" and was given substance and encouragement by the most notable social philosophers of the day.

The controversy between subject matter values and the needs of the learner was central to the developing educational "tone" of the nineteenth century. At first the argument raged primarily on the collegiate level, but by the end of the century it dominated the entire educational scene. The 1828 report of the Yale University faculty (p. 200) defined not only the curricular position of Yale but also stated the viewpoint held by most other colleges of the time regarding the properly elevated status of the traditional subjects and their relationship to other offerings. The report contrasts, however, with Charles William Eliot's inaugural address as president of Harvard (p. 231), some forty years later; and together they illustrate the two dominant positions about the education to be provided by institutions of higher learning in America. Eliot's position, advocating as it does the necessity of an elective system to ensure a truly liberal education, was not widely held by either his faculty or other college faculties of his day; yet it was more acceptable than it would have been several decades earlier.

The desire for commonality in college admissions requirements and the notable lack of correspondence among secondary schools in their offerings and standards prompted the National Education Association to sponsor an investigation of the curricula of secondary schools. The committee, chaired by Charles William Eliot, was composed of five college presidents, a college professor, two public high school principals, the headmaster of a private preparatory school, and the United States Commissioner of Education. The report of this Committee of Ten (p. 262), although recommending a liberalization and expansion of course sequences at the secondary level, rejected Eliot's preference for electives and took a conservative stance regarding the purposes of high school education, a stance that was not in accord with the "education for the common man" movement of the last half of the century. The report, completed in 1893, nevertheless provoked much debate that still is heard, and influenced secondary school curricula and college entrance standards for many years.

The problems involved in successfully blending subject matter and the needs of the learner were pondered by British social philosopher Herbert Spencer after the turn of the half-century, and by American educational and social philosopher John Dewey at the turn of the century. Spencer, borrowing from the evolutionary theory of Darwin and the social theory of Comte, states in his essay "What Knowledge Is of Most Worth?" (p. 216), that the major aim of education is learning to live morally and completely through the rational foresight of consequences. This position, along with his emphasis on inquiry, practicality, and usefulness, clearly places him in the same stream as the American pragmatist Dewey. Though cognizant of both individual and social needs, Spencer adheres more to intrinsic and extrinsic values in certain subject matters, leaving to Dewey the task of demonstrating that often the method of learning far outstrips the content values of the subject matter involved. For Spencer, the sciences were key to the most important curricular aims—the aims of self-preservation, self-support, and child-rearing proficiency.

This "education-for-total-living" concept received full amplification by John Dewey, primarily in his writing after 1900. In one of his earlier essays, "My Pedagogic Creed" (p. 235), however, he laid the groundwork for the later development of his educational ideas, ideas that were to provide a new frame of reference for schooling in America. Dewey viewed the school as a social institution wherein all Americans could learn that which is most germane to their individual development and that which would most result in the improvement of society itself. Dewey thus articulated fully what Horace Mann had sketched and struggled for a half century earlier during the infancy of the common school movement (p. 209).

The work of Mann in the state of Massachusetts and of Henry Barnard in Connecticut set the pattern for the flowering of state school systems and the realization of free public elementary education for all. The road to the accomplishment of this latter objective was paved by the decision of the Massachusetts legislature to institute a compulsory attendance law in 1852 (p. 251). On the secondary school level, the decision in the Kalamazoo Case in 1874

(p. 257), gave impetus to the inclusion of a high school education as part of the free-public-schooling program, although development at the secondary level was relatively slow until after 1900. On the college level, the passing of the Morrill Act (p. 253) by the United States Congress encouraged the establishment of public state colleges and universities and provided further testimony to the federal government's abiding interest in education. The founding in 1867 of the bureau which was to become the U.S. Office of Education (p. 255) was another manifestation of this interest. Developments in the twentieth century, particularly after World War II, were to add great strength to this federal office and crystallize the issue of whether federal interest and involvement leads to or necessitates federal control.

Other issues important in the twentieth century were foreseen during the nineteenth. The problem of governmental intervention in the affairs of a private institution was clarified by the 1819 U.S. Supreme Court decision in the Dartmouth College case (p. 247). Differential treatment of Negro citizens was raised in the *Plessy v. Ferguson* decision in 1896 (p. 268), which dealt with separate transportation facilities but carried implications for educational facilities as well. This, of course, was to become a dominant educational issue of the current century, but not until 1954 was the fundamental social viewpoint articulated in *Plessy v. Ferguson* judicially overturned.

INDEX OF
BASIC ISSUES

THE MODERN PERIOD
(1800-1900)
MAJOR THOUGHTS

PSYCHOLOGICAL STARTING POINTS

AUTHOR:

Johann Heinrich Pestalozzi (1746–1827)

WORK:

HOW GERTRUDE TEACHES HER CHILDREN (1801)
and "THE METHOD, A REPORT BY PESTALOZZI" (1828)

LETTER TO HEINRICH GESSNER ON
EXPERIMENTS AT STANZ AND
BURGDORF

. . . As I was obliged to give the children instruction, alone, and without help, I learned the art of teaching many together; and since I had no other means but loud speaking, the idea of making the learners draw, write, and work at the same time was naturally developed.

From *How Gertrude Teaches Her Children* and *An Account of the Method,* by Johann Heinrich Pestalozzi, second edition, ed. Ebenezer Cooke, translated by Luch E. Holland and Frances C. Turner (Syracuse, N.Y.: C. W. Bardeen, Publisher, 1898), pp. 43–44, 46, 56–60, 67–68, 316–317, 318–320, 325–326. Footnotes omitted.

The confusion of the repeating crowd led me to feel the need of keeping time, and beating time increased the impression made by the lesson. The utter ignorance of all made me stay long over the beginnings; and this led me to realize the high degree of inner power to be obtained by perfecting the first beginnings, and the result of a feeling of completeness and perfection in the lowest stage. I learned, as never before, the relation of the first steps in every kind of knowledge to its complete outline; and I felt, as never before, the immeasurable gaps that would bear witness in every succeeding stage of knowledge to confusion and want of perfection on these points.

The result of attending to this perfecting of the early stages far outran my expectations. It quickly developed in the children a consciousness of hitherto unknown power, and particularly a general sense of beauty and order. They felt their own power, and the tediousness of the ordinary school-tone vanished like a ghost from my rooms. They wished, tried, persevered, succeeded: and they laughed. Their tone was not that of learners: it was the tone of unknown powers awakened from sleep; of a heart and mind exalted with the feeling of what these powers could and would lead them to do.

Children taught children. They tried [to put into practice] what I told them to do, [and often came themselves on the track of the means of its execution, from many sides. This self-activity, which had developed itself in many ways in the beginning of learning, worked with great force on the birth and growth of the conviction in me, that all true, all educated instruction must be drawn out of the children themselves, and be born within them.] . . .

. . .

I learned from them—I must have been blind if I had not learned—to know the natural relation in which real knowledge stands to book-knowledge. I learned from them what a disadvantage this one-sided letter knowledge and entire reliance on words (which are only sound and noise when there is nothing behind them) must be. I saw what a hindrance this may be to the real power of observation (*Anschauung*), and the firm conception of the objects that surround us.

So far I got in Stanz. I felt my experiment had decided that it was possible to found popular instruction on psychological grounds, to lay true knowledge, gained by sense-impression at its foundation, and to tear away the mask of its superficial bombast. . . .

I adapted my teaching daily more to my sense of such laws; but I was not really aware of their principles, until the Executive Councillor Glayre, to whom I had tried to explain the sense of my works last summer, said to me, *"Vous voulez mechaniser l'education."*

[I understood very little French. I thought by these words, he meant to say I was seeking means of bringing education and instruction into psychologically ordered sequence; and, taking the words in this sense] he really hit the nail on the head, and according to my view, put the word in my mouth which showed me the essentials of my purpose and all the means thereto. Perhaps it would have been long before I had found it out, because I did not examine myself as I went along, but surrendered myself wholly to vague though vivid feelings, that indeed made my course certain but did not teach me to know it. I could not do otherwise. I have read no book for thirty years. I could and can read none. I had nothing more to say to abstract ideas. I lived solely upon convictions that were the result of countless, though, for the most part, forgotten intuitions.

So without knowing the principles on which I was working I began to dwell upon the nearness with which the objects I explained to the children were wont to touch their senses; and so, as I followed out the teaching from its beginning to its utmost end, I tried to investigate back to its very beginning the early history of the child who is to be taught, and was soon convinced that the first hour of its teaching is the hour of its birth. From the moment in which his mind can receive impressions from Nature, Nature teaches him. The new life itself is nothing but the just-awakened readiness to receive these impressions; it is only the awakening of the perfect physical buds that now aspire with all their power and all their impulses towards the development of their individuality. It is only the awakening of the now perfect animal that will and must become a man.

All instruction of man is then only the Art of helping Nature to develop in her own way; and this Art rests essentially on the relation and harmony between the impressions received by the child and the exact degree of his developed powers. It is also necessary in the impressions that are brought to the child by instruction that there should be a sequence, so that beginning and progress should keep pace with the beginning progress of the powers to be developed in the child. I soon saw that an inquiry into this sequence throughout the whole range of human knowledge, particularly those fundamental points from which the development of the human mind originates, must be the simple and only way ever to attain and to keep satisfactory school and instruction books, of every grade, suitable for our nature and our wants. I saw just as soon that in making these books the constituents of instruction must be separated according to the degree of the growing power of the child; and that in all matters of instruction, it is necessary to determine with the greatest accuracy which of these constituents is fit for each age of the child, in order on the one hand not to hold him back if he is ready; and on the other, not to load him and confuse him with anything for which he is not quite ready.

This was clear to me. The child must be brought to a high degree of knowledge both of things seen and of words before it is reasonable to teach him to spell or read. I was quite convinced that at their earliest age children need psychological training in gaining intelligent sense-impressions of all things. But since such training, without the help of art, is not to be thought of or expected of men as they are, the need of picture-books struck me perforce. These should precede the A B C books, in order to make those ideas that men express by words clear to the children [by means of well-chosen real objects, that either in reality, or in the form of well-made models and drawings, can be brought before their minds.]

A happy experiment confirmed my then unripe opinion in a striking way, [in spite of all the limitations of my means, and the error and one-sidedness in my experiments.] An anxious mother entrusted her hardly three-year-old child to my private teaching. I saw him for a time every day for an hour; and for a time felt the pulse of a method with him. I tried to teach him by letters, figures, and anything handy; that is, I aimed at giving him clear ideas and expressions by these means. I made him name correctly what he knew of anything—color, limbs, place, form, and number. I was obliged to put aside that first plague of youth, the miserable letters; he would have nothing but pictures and things.

He soon expressed himself clearly about the objects that lay within the limits of his knowledge. He found common illustrations in the street, the garden, and the room; and soon learned to pronounce the hardest names of plants and animals, and to compare objects quite unknown to him with those known, and to produce a clear sense-impression of them in himself. Although this experiment led to byeways, and worked for the strange and distant to the disadvantage of the present, it threw many-sided light on the means of quickening the child to his surroundings, and showing him the charm of self-activity in the extension of his powers.

. . .

By these tentative and erring measures, blending their course with the clearest views of my purpose, these first trials gradually developed in me clear principles about my actions; and while every day it became clearer to me that in the youngest years we must not reason with children, but must limit ourselves to the means of developing their minds:

1. By ever widening more and more the sphere of their sense-impressions.

2. By firmly, and without confusion, impressing upon them those sense-impressions that have been brought to their consciousness.

3. By giving them sufficient knowledge of language for all that Nature and the Art have brought or may in part bring to their consciousness.

While, as I say, these three points of view became clearer to me every day, just as a firm conviction gradually developed within me:

1. Of the need of picture books for early childhood.

2. Of the necessity of a sure and definite means of explaining these books.

3. Of the need of a guide to names, and knowledge of words founded upon these books and their explanations, with which the children should be thoroughly familiar before the time of spelling.

THE METHOD

The most essential point from which I start is this:

Sense-impression of Nature is the only true foundation of human instruction, because it is the only true foundation of human knowledge.

All that follows is the result of this sense-impression, and the process of abstraction from it. Hence in every case where this is imperfect, the result also will be neither certain, safe, nor positive; and in any case, where the sense-impression is inaccurate, deception and error follow.

I start from this point and ask: "What does Nature itself do in order to present the world truly to me, so far as it affects me? That is, by what means does she bring the sense-impressions of the most important things around me to a perfection that contents me?" And I find, she does this through my surroundings, my wants and my relations to others.

Through my surroundings she determines the kinds of sense-impressions I receive. Through my wants she stimulates my activities. Through my relations to others she widens my observation and raises it to insight and forethought. Through my surroundings, my wants, my relations to others, she lays the foundations of my knowledge, my work, and my right-doing.

.   .   .

But the gradations by which physical impressions on the senses become clear ideas reach the limits of the spontaneous working of the intellect, independent of the senses, along a course in harmony with the laws of the physical mechanism.

Imitation precedes hieroglyphics; hieroglyphics precede cultivated language, just as the individual name precedes the generic.

Further, it is only through this course, in harmony with the mechanism of the senses, that culture brings up before me the sea of confused phenomena (*Anschauung*) flowing one into another, first as definite sense-impressions, and from these forms clear concepts.

Thus all the Art (of teaching) men is essentially a result of physico-mechanical laws, the most important of which are following:

1. Bring all things essentially related to each other to that connection in your mind which they really have in Nature.

2. Subordinate all unessential things to essential, and especially subordinate the impression given by the Art to that given by Nature and reality.

3. Give to nothing a greater weight in your idea than it has in relation to your race in Nature.

4. Arrange all objects in the world according to their likeness.

5. Strengthen the impressions of important objects by allowing them to affect you through different senses.

6. In every subject try to arrange graduated steps of knowledge, in which every new idea shall be only a small, almost imperceptible addition to that earlier knowledge which has been deeply impressed and made unforgetable.

7. Learn to make the simple perfect before going on to the complex.

8. Recognize that as every physical ripening must be the result of the whole perfect fruit in all its parts, so every just judgment must be the result of a sense-impression, perfect in all its parts, of the object to be judged. Distrust the appearance of precocious ripeness as the apparent ripeness of a worm-eaten apple.

9. All physical effects are absolutely necessary; and this necessity is the result of the art of Nature, with which she unites the apparently heterogenous elements of her material into one whole for the achievement of her end. The Art, which imitates her, must try in the same way to raise the results at which it aims to a physical necessity, while it unites its elements into one whole for the achievement of its end.

10. The richness of its charm and the variety of its free play cause the results of physical necessity to bear the impress of freedom and independence. Here, too, the Art must imitate the course of Nature, and by the richness of its charm and the variety of its free play try to make its results bear the impress of freedom and independence.

11. Above all, learn the first law of the physical mechanism, the powerful, universal connection between its results and the proportion of nearness or distance between the object and our senses. Never forget that this physical nearness of distance of all objects around you has an immense effect in determining your positive sense-impressions, practical ability, and even virtue.

. . .

Before the child can utter a sound, a many-sided consciousness of all physical truths exists already within him, as a starting-point for the whole round of his experiences. For instance, he feels that the pebble and the tree have different properties; that wood differs from glass. To make this dim consciousness clear, speech is necessary. We must give him names for the various things he knows, as well as for their properties.

So we connect his speech with his knowledge, and extend his knowledge with his speech. This makes the consciousness of impressions which have touched his senses clearer to the child. And the common work of all instruction is to make this consciousness clear.

This may be done in two ways. Either we lead the children through knowledge of names to that of things, or else through knowledge of things to that of names. The second method is mine. I wish always to let sense-impression precede the word, and definite knowledge the judgment. I wish to make words and talk unimportant on the human mind, and to secure that preponderance due to the actual impressions of physical objects (*Anschauung*), that forms such a remarkable protection against mere noise and empty sound. From his very first development I wish to lead my child into the whole circle of Nature surrounding him; I would organize his learning to talk by a collection of natural products; I would teach him early to abstract all physical generalizations from separate physical facts, and teach him to express them in words; and I would everywhere substitute physical generalizations for those metaphysical generalizations with which we begin the instruction of our race. Not till after the foundation of human knowledge (sense-impressions of Nature) has been fairly laid and secure would I begin the dull, abstract work of studying from books.

THE LAW
OF SELF-ACTIVITY

AUTHOR:

Friedrich Froebel (*1782–1852*)

WORK:

THE EDUCATION
OF MAN (1826)

Education consists in leading man, as a thinking, intelligent being, growing into self-consciousness, to a pure and unsullied, conscious and free representation of the inner law of Divine Unity, and in teaching him ways and means thereto.

The knowledge of that eternal law, the insight into its origin, into its essence, into the totality, the connection, and intensity of its effects, the knowledge of life in its totality, constitute science, the science of life; and, referred by the self-conscious, thinking, intelligent being to representation and practice through and in himself, this becomes science of education.

The system of directions, derived from the knowledge and study of that law, to guide thinking, intelligent beings in the apprehension of their life-work and in the accomplishment of their destiny, is the theory of education.

From *The Education of Man* by Friedrich Froebel, translated by W. N. Hailmann (New York: D. Appleton and Company, 1887), pp. 2–11. Italics omitted.

The self-active application of this knowledge in the direct development and cultivation of rational beings toward the attainment of their destiny, is the practice of education.

The object of education is the realization of a faithful, pure, inviolate, and hence holy life.

Knowledge and application, consciousness and realization in life, united in the service of a faithful, pure, holy life, constitute the wisdom of life, pure wisdom.

To be wise is the highest aim of man, is the most exalted achievement of human self-determination.

To educate one's self and others, with consciousness, freedom, and self-determination, is a twofold achievement of wisdom: it began with the first appearance of man upon the earth; it was manifest with the first appearance of full self-consciousness in man; it begins now to proclaim itself as a necessary, universal requirement of humanity, and to be heard and heeded as such. With this achievement man enters upon the path which alone leads to life; which surely tends to the fulfillment of the inner, and thereby also to the fullfillment of the outer, requirement of humanity; which, through a faithful, pure, holy life, attains beatitude.

By education, then, the divine essence of man should be unfolded, brought out, lifted into consciousness, and man himself raised into free conscious obedience to the divine principle that lives in him, and to a free representation of this principle in his life.

Education, in instruction, should lead man to see and know the divine, spiritual, and eternal principle which animates surrounding nature, constitutes the essence of nature, and is permanently manifested in nature; and, in living reciprocity and united with training, it should express and demonstrate the fact that the same law rules both (the divine principle and nature), as it does nature and man.

Education as a whole, by means of instruction and training, should bring to man's consciousness, and render efficient in his life, the fact that man and nature proceed from God and are conditioned by him—that both have their being in God.

Education should lead and guide man to clearness concerning himself and in himself, to peace with nature, and to unity with God; hence, it should lift him to a knowledge of himself and of mankind, to a knowledge of God and of nature, and to the pure and holy life to which such knowledge leads.

In all these requirements, however, education is based on considerations of the innermost.

The inner essence of things is recognized by the innermost spirit (of man) in the outer and through outward manifestations. The inner being, the spirit, the divine essence of things and of man, is known by its outward manifestations. In accordance with this, all education, all instruction and training, all life as a free growth, start from the outer manifestations of man and things, and, proceeding from the outer, act upon the inner, and form its judgments concerning the inner. Nevertheless, education should not draw its inferences concerning the inner from the outer directly, for it lies in the nature of things that always in some relation inferences should be drawn inversely. Thus, the diversity and multiplicity in nature do not warrant the inference of multiplicity in the ultimate cause—a multiplicity of gods—nor does the unity of God warrant the inference of finality in nature; but, in both cases, the inference lies conversely from the diversity in natural developments.

The failure to apply this truth, or rather the continual sinning against it, the drawing of direct inferences concerning the inner life of childhood and youth from certain external manifestations of life, is the chief cause of antagonism and contention, of the frequent mistakes in life and education. This furnishes constant occasion for innumerable false judgments concerning the motives of the young, for numberless failures in the education of children, for endless misunderstanding between parent and child, for so much needless complaint and unseemly arraignment of children, for so many unreasonable demands made upon them. Therefore, this truth, in its application to parents, educators, and teachers, is of such great importance that they should strive to render themselves familiar with its application in its smallest details. This would bring into the relations between parents and children, pupils and educators, teacher and taught, a clearness, a constancy, a serenity which are now sought in vain: for the child that seems good outwardly often is not good inwardly, i.e., does not desire the good spontaneously, or from love, respect and appreciation; similarly, the outwardly rough, stubborn, self-willed child that seems outwardly not good, frequently is filled with the liveliest, most eager, strongest desire for spontaneous goodness in his actions; and the apparently inattentive boy frequently follows a certain fixed line of thought that withholds his attention from all external things.

Therefore, education in instruction and training, originally and in its first principles, should necessarily be passive, following (only guarding and protecting), not prescriptive, categorical, interfering.

Indeed, in its very essence, education should have these characteristics; for the undisturbed operation of the Divine Unity is necessarily good—can not be otherwise than good. This necessity implies that the young human being—as it were, still in process of creation—would seek, although still unconsciously, as a product of nature, yet decidedly and surely, that which is in itself best; and, moreover, in a form wholly adapted to his condition, as well as to his disposition, his powers, and means. . . .

We grant space and time to young plants and animals because we know that, in accordance with the laws that live in them, they will develop properly and grow well; young animals and plants are given rest, and arbitrary interference with their growth is avoided, because it is known that the opposite practice would disturb their pure unfolding and sound development; but the young human being is looked upon as a piece of wax, a lump of clay, which man can mold into what he pleases. O man, who roamest through garden and field, through meadow and grove, why dost thou close thy mind to the silent teaching of nature? Behold even the weed, which, grown up amid hindrances and constraint, scarcely yields an indication of inner law; behold it in nature, in field or garden, and see how perfectly it conforms to law—what a pure inner life it shows, harmonious in all parts and features: a beautiful sun, radiant star, it has burst from the earth! Thus, O parents, could your children, on whom you force in tender years forms and aims against their nature, and who, therefore, walk with you in morbid and unnatural deformity—thus could your children, too, unfold in beauty and develop in all-sided harmony!

. . .

Therefore, the purely categorical, mandatory, and prescriptive education of man is not in place before the advent of intelligent self-consciousness, of unity in life between God and man, of established harmony and community of life between father and son, disciple and master; for then only can truth be deduced and known from insight into the essential being of the whole and into the nature of the individual.

Before any disturbance and marring in the original wholeness of the pupil has been shown and fully determined in its origin and tendency, nothing, therefore, is left for us to do but to bring him into relations and surroundings in all respects adapted to him, reflecting his conduct as in a mirror, easily and promptly revealing to him its effects and consequences, readily disclosing to him and others his true condition, and affording a minimum of opportunities for injury from the outbreaks and consequences of his inner failings.

The prescriptive, interfering education, indeed, can be justified only on two grounds; either because it teaches the clear, living thought, self-evident truth, or because it holds up a life whose ideal value has been established in experience. But, where self-evident, living, absolute truth rules, the eternal principle itself reigns, as it were, and will on this account maintain a passive, following character. For the living thought, the eternal divine principle as such demands and requires free self-activity and self-determination on the part of man, the being created for freedom in the image of God.

CONSERVATISM IN HIGHER EDUCATION

AUTHORS:

Jeremiah Day (1773–1867)
James L. Kingsley (1778–1852)

WORK:

REPORT OF THE YALE FACULTY (1828)

What then is the appropriate object of a college? It is not necessary here to determine what it is which, in every case, entitles an institution to the *name* of a college. But if we have not greatly misapprehended the design of the patrons and guardians of this college, its object is to *lay the foundation* of a *superior education*: and this is to be done, at a period of life when a substitute must be provided for *parental superintendence*. The ground work of a thorough education must be broad, and deep, and solid. For a partial or superficial education, the support may be of looser materials, and more hastily laid.

From "Original Papers in relation to a Course of Liberal Education," *The American Journal of Science and Arts,* Vol. XV (January, 1829), abridged from pp. 300–303, 308, 312–314, 318–320, 323, 325, 330, 333–336.

The two great points to be gained in intellectual culture are the *discipline* and the *furniture* of the mind; expanding its powers, and storing it with knowledge. The former of these is, perhaps, the more important of the two. A commanding object, therefore, in a collegiate course, should be to call into daily and vigorous exercise the faculties of the student. Those branches of study should be prescribed, and those modes of instruction adopted, which are best calculated to teach the art of fixing the attention, directing the train of thought, analyzing a subject proposed for investigation; following, with accurate discrimination, the course of argument; balancing nicely the evidence presented to the judgment; awakening, elevating, and controlling the imagination; arranging, with skill, the treasures which memory gathers, rousing and guiding the powers of genius. All this is not to be effected by a light and hasty course of study; by reading a few books, hearing a few lectures, and spending some months at a literary institution. The habits of thinking are to be formed, by long continued and close application. . . .

. . . In the course of instruction in this college, it has been an object to maintain such a proportion between the different branches of literature and science, as to form in the student a proper *balance* of character. From the pure mathematics, he learns the art of demonstrative reasoning. In attending to the physical sciences, he becomes familiar with facts, with the process of induction, and the varieties of probable evidence. In ancient literature, he finds some of the most finished models of taste. By English reading, he learns the powers of the language in which he is to speak and write. By logic and mental philosophy, he is taught the art of thinking; by rhetoric and oratory, the art of speaking. By frequent exercise on written composition, he acquires copiousness and accuracy of expression. By extemporaneous discussion, he becomes prompt, and fluent, and animated. It is a point of high importance, that eloquence and solid learning should go together; that he who has accumulated the richest treasures of thought, should possess the highest powers of oratory. . . .

No one feature in a system of intellectual education is of greater moment than such an arrangement of duties and motives, as will most effectually throw the student upon the *resources of his own mind.* . . .

. . . We doubt whether the powers of the mind can be developed, in their fairest proportions, by studying languages alone, or mathematics alone, or natural or political science alone. As the bodily frame is brought to its highest perfection, not by one simple and uniform motion, but by a variety of exercises; so the mental faculties are expanded, and invigorated, and adapted to each other, by familiarity with different departments of science.

. . .

The course of instruction which is given to the undergraduates in the college, is not designed to include *professional* studies. Our object is not to teach that which is peculiar to any one of the professions; but to lay the foundation which is common to them all. There are separate schools for medicine, law, and theology, connected with the college, as well as in various parts of the country; which are open for the reception of all who are prepared to enter upon the appropriate studies of their several professions. With these, the academical course is not intended to interfere.

. . .

But why, it is asked, should *all* the students in a college be required to tread in the *same steps*? Why should not each one be allowed to select those branches of study which are most to his taste, which are best adapted to his peculiar talents, and which are most nearly connected with his intended profession? To this we answer, that our prescribed course contains those subjects only which ought to be understood, as we think, by every one who aims at a thorough education. They are not the peculiarities of any profession or art. These are to be learned in the professional and practical schools. But the principles of sciences are the common foundation of all high intellectual attainments. As in our primary schools, reading, writing, and arithmetic are taught to all, however different their prospects; so in a college, all should be instructed in those branches of knowledge, of which no one destined to the higher walks of life ought to be ignorant. . . .

. . .

If the view which we have thus far taken of the subject is correct, it will be seen, that the object of the system of instruction at this college, is not to give a *partial* education, consisting of a few branches only; nor, on the other hand, to give a *superficial* education, containing a smattering of almost every thing; nor to *finish* the details of either a professional or practical education; but to *commence a thorough* course, and to carry it as far as the time of residence here will allow. It is intended to occupy, to the best advantage, the four years immediately preceding the study of a profession, or of the operations which are peculiar to the higher mercantile, manufacturing, or agricultural establishments. . . .

. . .

. . . It is said that the public now demand, that the doors should be thrown open to all; that education ought to be so modified, and varied, as to adapt it to the exigencies of the country, and the prospects of different individuals; that the instruction given to those who are destined to be merchants, or manufacturers, or agriculturalists, should have a special reference to their respective professional pursuits.

The public are undoubtedly right, in demanding that there should be appropriate courses of education, accessible to all classes of youth. And we rejoice at the prospect of ample provision for this purpose, in the improvement of our academies, and the establishment of commercial high-schools, gymnasia, lycea, agricultural seminaries, &c. But do the public insist, that every college shall become a high-school, gymnasium, lyceum, and academy? Why should we interfere with these valuable institutions? Why wish to take their business out of their hands? . . .

. . . There is no magical influence in an act of incorporation, to give celebrity to a literary institution, which does not command respect for itself, by the elevated rank of its education. When the college has lost its hold on the public confidence, by depressing its standard of merit, by substituting a partial, for a thorough education, we may expect that it will be deserted by that class of persons who have hitherto been drawn here by high expectations and purposes. Even if we should *not* immediately suffer in point of *numbers,* yet we shall exchange the best portion of our students, for others of inferior aims and attainments.

.   .   .

Our republican form of government renders it highly important, that great numbers should enjoy the advantage of a thorough education. On the Eastern continent, the *few* who are destined to particular departments in political life, may be educated for the purpose; while the mass of the people are left in comparative ignorance. But in this country, where offices are accessible to all who are qualified for them, superior intellectual attainments ought not to be confined to any description of persons. *Merchants, manufacturers,* and *farmers,* as well as professional gentlemen, take their places in our public councils. A thorough education ought therefore to be extended to all these classes. It is not sufficient that they be men of sound judgment, who can decide correctly, and give a silent vote, on great national questions. Their influence upon the minds of others is needed; an influence to be produced by extent of knowledge, and the force of eloquence. . . .

.   .   .

The subject of inquiry now presented, is, whether the plan of instruction pursued in Yale College, is sufficiently accommodated to the present state of literature and science; and, especially, whether such a change is demanded as would leave out of this plan the study of the Greek and Roman classics, and make an acquaintance with ancient literature no longer necessary for a degree in the liberal arts. . . .

.   .   .

But the study of the classics is useful, not only as it lays the foundations of a correct taste, and furnishes the student with those elementary ideas which are found in the literature of modern times, and which he no where so well acquires as in their original sources; but also as the study itself forms the most effectual discipline of the mental faculties. This is a topic so often insisted on, that little need be said of it here. It must be obvious to the most cursory observer, that the classics afford materials to exercise talent of every degree, from the first opening of the youthful intellect to the period of its highest maturity. The range of classical study extends from the elements of language, to the most difficult questions arising from literary research and criticism. Every faculty of the mind is employed; not only the memory, judgment, and reasoning powers, but the taste and fancy are occupied and improved.

. . .

. . . To suppose the modern languages more practical than the ancient, to the great body of our students, because the former are now spoken in some parts of the world, is an obvious fallacy. The proper question is, what course of discipline affords the best mental culture, leads to the most thorough knowledge of our own literature, and lays the best foundation for professional study. The ancient languages have here a decided advantage. . . .

. . .

Such, then, being the value of ancient literature, both as respects the general estimation in which it is held in the literary world, and its intrinsic merits, if the college should confer degrees upon students for their attainments in modern literature only, it would be to declare *that* to be a liberal education, which the world will not acknowledge to deserve the name; and which those who shall receive degrees in this way, will soon find, is not what it is called. A liberal education, whatever course the college should adopt, would without doubt continue to be, what it long has been. Ancient literature is too deeply inwrought into the whole system of the modern literature of Europe to be so easily laid aside. The college ought not to presume upon its influence, nor to set itself up in any manner as a dictator. If it should pursue a course very different from that which the present state of literature demands; if it should confer its honors according to a rule which is not sanctioned by literary men, the faculty see nothing to expect for favoring such innovations, but that they will be considered visionaries in education, ignorant of its true design and objects, and unfit for their places. The ultimate consequence, it is not difficult to predict. The college would be distrusted by the public, and its reputation would be irrecoverably lost. . . .

INTEREST
AS AN INSTRUCTIONAL
AIM

AUTHOR:

Johann Friedrich Herbart (1776–1841)

WORK:

OUTLINES
OF EDUCATIONAL
DOCTRINE (1835)

The ultimate purpose of instruction is contained in the notion, virtue. But in order to realize the final aim, another and nearer one must be set up. We may term it, *many-sidedness of interest*. The word *interest* stands in general for that kind of mental activity which it is the business of instruction to incite. Mere information does not suffice; for this we think of as a supply or store of facts, which a person might possess or lack, and still remain the same being. But he who lays hold of his information and reaches out for more, takes an

From *Outlines of Educational Doctrine* by Johann Friedrich Herbart, translated by Alexis F. Lange and annotated by Charles deGarmo (New York: The Macmillan Company, 1901), pp. 44–49, 60–62, 69–71. Notes and paragraph numbers omitted.

interest in it. Since, however, this mental activity is varied, we need to add the further determination supplied by the term *many-sidedness.*

We may speak also of indirect as distinguished from direct interest. But a predominance of indirect interest tends to one-sidedness, if not to selfishness. The interest of the selfish man in anything extends only so far as he can see advantages or disadvantages to himself. In this respect the one-sided man approximates the selfish man, although the fact may escape his own observation; since he relates everything to the narrow sphere for which he lives and thinks. Here lies his intellectual power, and whatever does not interest him as means to his limited ends, becomes an impediment.

As regards the bearings of interest on virtue, we need to remember that many-sidedness of interest alone, even of direct interest such as instruction is to engender, is yet far from being identical with virtue itself; also that, conversely, the weaker the original mental activity, the less likelihood that virtue will be realized at all, not to speak of the variety of manifestation possible in action. Imbeciles cannot be virtuous. Virtue involves an awakening of mind.

Scattering no less than one-sidedness forms an antithesis to many-sidedness. Many-sidedness is to be the basis of virtue; but the latter is an attribute of personality, hence it is evident that the unity of self-consciousness must not be impaired. The business of instruction is to form the person on many sides, and accordingly to avoid a distracting or dissipating effect. And instruction has successfully avoided this in the case of one who with ease surveys his well-arranged knowledge *in all of its unifying relations* and holds it together as *his very own.*

. . .

INTEREST means self-activity. The demand for a many-sided interest is, therefore, a demand for many-sided self-activity. But not all self-activity, only the right degree of the right kind, is desirable; else lively children might very well be left to themselves. There would be no need of educating or even of governing them. It is the purpose of instruction to give the right *direction* to their thoughts and impulses, to incline these toward the morally good and true. Children are thus in a measure passive. But this passivity should by no means involve suppression of self-activity. It should, on the contrary, imply a stimulation of all that is best in the child.

At this point a psychological distinction becomes necessary, namely, that between designedly reproduced, or "given," and spontaneous representations. In recitations of what has been learned we have an example of the former; the latter appear in the games and fancies of children. A method of study that issues in mere reproduction leaves children largely in a passive state, for it crowds out for the time being the thoughts they would otherwise have had. In games, however, and in the free play of fancy, and accordingly also in that kind of instruction which finds an echo here, free activity predominates.

This distinction is not intended to affirm the existence of two compartments in which the ideas, separated once for all, would, of necessity, have to remain. Ideas that must by effort be raised into consciousness because they do not rise spontaneously, may become spontaneous by gradual strengthening. But this development we cannot count on unless instruction, advancing step by step, bring it about.

It is the teacher's business, while giving instruction, to observe whether the ideas of his pupils rise spontaneously or not. If they do, the pupils are said to be attentive; the lesson has won their interest. If not, attention is, indeed, not always wholly gone. It may, moreover, be enforced for a time before actual fatigue sets in. But doubt arises whether instruction can effect a future interest in the same subjects.

. . .

Instruction is to supplement that which has been gained already by experience and by intercourse with others; these foundations must exist when instruction begins. If they are wanting, they must be firmly established first. Any deficiency here means a loss to instruction, because the pupils lack the thoughts which they need in order to interpret the words of the teacher.

In the same way, knowledge derived from earlier lessons must be extended and deepened by subsequent instruction. This presupposes such an organization of the whole work of instruction that that which comes later shall always find present the earlier knowledge with which it is to be united.

Ordinarily, because their eyes are fixed solely on the facts to be learned, teachers concern themselves little with the ideas already possessed by the pupils. Consequently they make an effort in behalf of the necessary attention only when it is failing and progress is checked. Now they have recourse to voluntary attention, and to obtain this rely on inducements, or, more often, on reprimands and penalties. Indirect interest is thus substituted for direct interest, with the result that the resolution of the pupil to be attentive fails to effect energetic apprehension and realizes but little coherence. It wavers constantly, and often enough gives way to disgust.

In the most favorable case, if instruction is thorough, *i.e.,* scientific, a foundation of elementary knowledge is gradually laid sufficiently solid for later years to build on; in other words, out of the elementary knowledge an apperceiving mass is created in the mind of the pupil which will aid him in his future studies. There may be several of such masses; but each constitutes by itself its own kind of one-sided learning, and it is after all doubtful whether even here direct interest is implied. For there is small hope that this interest will be aroused in the youth when the years of boyhood have been devoted merely to the mastering of preliminary knowledge. The prospects of future station and calling are opening before him and the examinations are at hand.

THE COMMON SCHOOL MOVEMENT

AUTHOR:

Horace Mann (*1796–1859*)

WORK:

10TH AND 12TH ANNUAL REPORTS TO THE MASSACHUSETTS BOARD OF EDUCATION

(1846 and 1848)

FROM THE 10TH REPORT (1846):

I believe in the existence of a great, immutable principle of natural law, or natural ethics, a principle antecedent to all human institutions and incapable of being abrogated by any ordinances of man, a principle of divine origin, clearly legible in the ways of Providence as those ways are manifested in the order of nature and in the history of the race, which proves the *absolute right* of every human being that comes into the world to an education; and which,

From the 10th Annual Report, published in *The Common School Journal,* Vol. IX, No. 9, edited by Horace Mann (Boston: William B. Fowle, 1847); the 12th Annual Report, published separately from the *Journal* by Fowle in 1849.

of course, proves the correlative duty of every government to see that the means of that education are provided for all.

In regard to the application of this principle of natural law, that is, in regard to the extent of the education to be provided for all, at the public expense, some differences of opinion may fairly exist, under different political organizations; but under a republican government, it seems clear that the minimum of this education can never be less than such as is sufficient to qualify each citizen for the civil and social duties he will be called to discharge; such an education as teaches the individual the great laws of bodily health; as qualifies for the fulfilment of parental duties; as is indispensable for the civil functions of a witness or a juror; as is necessary for the voter in municipal affairs; and finally, for the faithful and conscientious discharge of all those duties which devolve upon the inheritor of a portion of the sovereignty of this great republic.

FROM THE 12TH REPORT (1848):

The Capacities of Our Present School System to Improve
the Pecuniary Condition, and to Elevate the Intellectual
and Moral Character of the Commonwealth

Under the Providence of God, our means of education are the grand machinery by which the "raw material" of human nature can be worked up into inventors and discoverers, into skilled artisans and scientific farmers, into scholars and jurists, into the founders of benevolent institutions, and the great expounders of ethical and theological science. By means of early education, those embryos of talent may be quickened, which will solve the difficult problems of political and economical law; and by them, too, the genius may be kindled which will blaze forth in the Poets of Humanity. Our schools, far more than they have done, may supply the Presidents and Professors of Colleges, and Superintendents of Public Instruction, all over the land; and send, not only into our sister states, but across the Atlantic, the man of practical science, to superintend the construction of the great works of art. Here, too, may those judicial powers be developed and invigorated, which will make legal principles so clear and convincing as to prevent appeals to force; and, should the clouds of war ever lower over our country, some hero may be found, the nursling of our schools, and ready to become the leader of our armies, the best of all heroes, who will secure the glories of a peace, unstained by the magnificent murders of the battlefield. . . .

Without undervaluing any other human agency, it may be safely affirmed that the Common School, improved and energized, as it can easily be, may become the most effective and benignant of all the forces of civilization. Two reasons sustain this position. In the first place, there is a universality in its operation, which can be affirmed of no other institution whatever. If administered in the spirit of justice and conciliation, all the rising generation may be brought within the circle of its reformatory and elevating influences. And, in the second place, the materials upon which it operates are so pliant and ductile as to be susceptible of assuming a greater variety of forms than any other earthly work of the Creator. . . .

I proceed, then, in endeavoring to show how the true business of the schoolroom connects itself, and becomes identical, with the great interests of society. The former is the infant, immature state of those interests; the latter, their developed, adult state. As "the child is father to the man," so may the training of the schoolroom expand into the institutions and fortunes of the State.

Physical Education

In the worldly prosperity of mankind, Health and Strength are indispensable ingredients. . . .

My general conclusion, then, under this head, is, that it is the duty of all the governing minds in society, whether in office or out of it, to diffuse a knowledge of these beautiful and beneficient laws of health and life, throughout the length and breadth of the State; to popularize them; to make them, in the first place, the common acquisition of all, and, through education and custom, the common inheritance of all; so that the healthful habits naturally growing out of their observance, shall be inbred in the people; exemplified in the personal regimen of each individual; incorporated into the economy of every household; observable in all private dwellings, and in all public edifices, especially in those buildings which are erected by capitalists for the residence of their work-people, or for renting to the poorer classes; obeyed, by supplying cities with pure water; by providing public baths, public walks, and public squares; by rural cemeteries; by the drainage and sewerage of populous towns, and in whatever else may promote the general salubrity of the atmosphere; in fine, by a religious observance of all those sanitary regulations with which modern science has blessed the world.

For this thorough diffusion of sanitary intelligence, the Common School is the only agency. . . .

Intellectual Education, a Means of Removing Poverty, and Securing Abundance

Another cardinal object which the government of Massachusetts, and all the influential men in the State should propose to themselves, is the physical well-being of all the people; the sufficiency, comfort, competence, of every individual, in regard to food, raiment, and shelter. And these necessaries and conveniences of life should be obtained by each individual for himself, or by each family for themselves, rather than accepted from the hand of charity, or extorted by poor-laws. . . .

According to the European theory, men are divided into classes—some to toil and earn, others to seize and enjoy. According to the Massachusetts theory, all are to have an equal chance for earning, and equal security in the enjoyment of what they earn. The latter tends to equality of condition; the former to the grossest inequalities. Tried by any Christian standard of morals, or even by any of the better sort of heathen standards, can any one hesitate, for a moment, in declaring which of the two will produce the greater amount of human welfare; and which, therefore, is the more comfortable to the Divine will? . . .

I suppose it to be the universal sentiment of all those who mingle any ingredient of benevolence with their notions on Political Economy, that vast and overshadowing private fortunes are among the greatest dangers to which the happiness of the people in a republic can be subjected. Such fortunes would create a feudalism of a new kind; but one more oppressive and unrelenting than that of the Middle Ages. The feudal lords in England, and on the continent, never held their retainers in a more abject condition of servitude, than the great majority of foreign manufacturers and capitalists hold their operatives and laborers at the present day. The means employed are different, but the similarity in results is striking. What force did then, money does now. . . . The baron prescribed his own terms to his retainers; those terms were peremptory, and the serf must submit or perish. The British manufacturer or farmer prescribes the rate of wages he will give to his workpeople; he reduces these wages under whatever pretext he pleases; and they too have no alternative but submission or starvation. In some respects, indeed, the condition of the modern dependent is more forlorn than that of the corresponding serf class in former times. Some attributes of the patriarchal relation did spring up between the lord and his lieges, to soften the harsh relations subsisting between them. Hence came some oversight of the condition of children, some relief in sickness, some protection and support in the decrepitude of age. But only in instances comparatively few, have kindly offices smoothed the rugged relation between British Capital and British Labor. The children of the work-people are abandoned to their fate; and, notwithstanding the privations they suffer, and the dangers they threaten, no power in the realm has yet been able to secure them an education; and when the adult laborer is prostrated by sickness, or eventually worn out by toil and age, the poorhouse, which has all along been his destination, becomes his destiny.

. . .

Now, surely, nothing but Universal Education can counter-work this tendency to the domination of capital and the servility of labor. If one class possesses all the wealth and the education, while the residue of society is ignorant and poor, it matters not by what name the relation between them may be called; the latter, in fact and in truth, will be the servile dependents and subjects of the former. But if education be equably diffused, it will draw property after it, by the strongest of all attractions; for such a thing never did happen, and never can happen, as that an intelligent and practical body of men should be permanently poor. . . .

Education, then, beyond all other devices of human origin, is the great equalizer of the conditions of men—the balance-wheel of the social machinery. I do not here mean that it so elevates the moral nature as to make men disdain and abhor the oppression of their fellow-men. This idea pertains to another of its attributes. But I mean that it gives each man the independence and the means, by which he can resist the selfishness of other men. . . .

. . .

For the creation of wealth, then—for the existence of a wealthy people and a wealthy nation—intelligence is the grand condition. The number of improvers will increase, as the intellectual constituency, if I may so call it, increases. In former times, and in most parts of the world even at the present day, not one man in a million has ever had such a development of mind, as made it possible for him to become a contributor to art or science. Let this development precede, and contributions, numberless, and of inestimable value, will be sure to follow. That Political Economy, therefore, which busies itself about capital and labor, supply and demand, interest and rents, favorable and unfavorable balances of trade; but leaves out of account the element of a wide-spread mental development, is nought but stupendous folly. The greatest of all the arts in political economy is to change a consumer into a producer; and the next greatest is to increase the producing power—an end to be directly attained, by increasing his intelligence. . . .

Political Education

. . . Such being the rule established by common consent, and such the practice, observed with fidelity under it, it will come to be universally understood, that political proselytism is no function of the school; but that all indoctrination into matters of controversy between hostile political parties is to be elsewhere sought for, and elsewhere imparted. Thus, may all the children of the Commonwealth receive instruction in the great essentials of political knowledge, in those elementary ideas without which they will never be able to investigate more recondite and debatable questions; thus, will the only practicable method be adopted for discovering new truths, and for discarding, instead of perpetuating, old errors; and thus, too, will that pernicious race of intolerant zealots, whose whole faith may be summed up in two articles, that they, themselves, are always infallibly right, and that all dissenters are certainly wrong, be extinguished, not by violence, nor by proscription, but by the more copious inflowing of the light of truth.

Moral Education

Moral education is a primal necessity of social existence. The unrestrained passions of men are not only homicidal, but suicidal; and a community without a conscience would soon extinguish itself. . . .

. . .

But to all doubters, disbelievers, or despairers, in human progress, it may still be said, there is one experiment which has never yet been tried. It is an experiment which, even before its inception, offers the highest authority for its ultimate success. Its formula is intelligible to all; and it is as legible as though written in starry letters on an azure sky. It is expressed in these few and simple words: *"Train up a child in the way he should go, and when he is old he will not depart from it."* This declaration is positive. If the conditions are complied with, it makes no provision for a failure. Though pertaining to morals, yet, if the terms of the direction are observed, there is no more reason to doubt the result, than there would be in an optical or a chemical experiment.

But this experiment has never yet been tried. Education has never yet been brought to bear with one hundredth part of its potential force, upon the natures of children, and, through them, upon the character of men, and of the race. In all the attempts to reform mankind which have hitherto been made, whether by changing the frame of government, by aggravating or softening the severity of the penal code, or by substitution a government-created, for a God-created religion; in all these attempts, the infantile and youthful mind, its amenability to influences, and the enduring and self-operating character of the influences it receives, have been almost wholly unrecognized. Here, is a new agency, whose powers are but just beginning to be understood, and whose mighty energies, hitherto, have been but feebly invoked; and yet, from our experience, limited and imperfect as it is, we do know that, far beyond any other earthly instrumentality, it is comprehensive and decisive. . . .

Religious Education

. . . If, then, a government would recognize and protect the rights of religious freedom, it must abstain from subjugating the capacities of its children to any legal standard of religious faith, with as great fidelity as it abstains from controlling the opinions of men. It must meet the unquestionable fact, that the old spirit of religious domination is adopting new measures to accomplish its work—measures, which, if successful, will be as fatal to the liberties of mankind, as those which were practiced in by-gone days of violence and terror. These new measures are aimed at children instead of men. They propose to supersede the necessity of subduing free thought, *in the mind of the adult,* by forestalling the development of any capacity of free thought, *in the mind of the child.* They expect to find it easier to subdue the free agency of children, by binding them in fetters of bigotry, than to subdue the free agency of men, by binding them in fetters of iron. For this purpose, some are attempting to deprive children of their right to labor, and, of course, of their daily bread, unless they will attend a government school, and receive its sectarian instruction. Some are attempting to withhold all means, even of secular education, from the poor, and thus punish them with ignorance, unless, with the secular knowledge which they desire, they will accept theological knowledge which they condemn. Others, still, are striving to break down all free Public School systems, where they exist, and to prevent their establishment, where they do not exist, in the hope, that on the downfall of these, their system will succeed. The sovereign antidote against these machinations is Free Schools for all, and the right of every parent to determine the religious education of his children.

WHAT KNOWLEDGE IS OF MOST WORTH?

AUTHOR:

Herbert Spencer (*1820–1903*)

WORK:

EDUCATION— INTELLECTUAL, MORAL AND PHYSICAL (1860)

. . . Every one in contending for the worth of any particular order of information does so by showing its bearing upon some part of life. In reply to the question—"Of what use is it?" the mathematician, linguist, naturalist, or philosopher, explains the way in which his learning beneficially influences action—saves from evil or secures good—conduces to happiness. When the teacher of writing has pointed out how great an aid writing is to success in business—that is, to the obtainment of sustenance—that is, to satisfactory living; he is held to have proved his case. And when the collector of dead facts (say a numismatist) fails to make clear any appreciable effects which these facts can produce on human welfare, he is obliged to admit that they are

From *Education—Intellectual, Moral and Physical* by Herbert Spencer (New York: A. L. Burt, Publisher, 1900), pp. 15–22, 30–32, 41–42, 44–46, 51–54, 55–57, 62–66, 89–91.

comparatively valueless. All then, either directly or by implication, appeal to this as the ultimate test.

How to live?—that is the essential question for us. Not how to live in the mere material sense only, but in the widest sense. The general problem which comprehends every special problem is—the right ruling of conduct in all directions under all circumstances. In what way to treat the body; in what way to treat the mind; in what way to manage our affairs; in what way to bring up a family; in what way to behave as a citizen; in what way to utilize those sources of happiness which nature supplies—how to use all our faculties to the greatest advantage of ourselves and others—how to live completely? And this being the great thing needful for us to learn, is, by consequence, the great thing which education has to teach. To prepare us for complete living is the function which education has to discharge; and the only rational mode of judging of an educational course is, to judge in what degree it discharges such function.

This test, never used in its entirety, but rarely even partially used, and used then in a vague, half conscious way, has to be applied consciously, methodically, and throughout all cases. It behooves us to set before ourselves, and ever to keep clearly in view, complete living as the end to be achieved; so that in bringing up our children we may choose subjects and methods of instruction, with deliberate reference to this end. Not only ought we to cease from the mere unthinking adoption of the current fashion in education, which has no better warrant than any other fashion; but we must also rise above that rude, empirical style of judging displayed by those more intelligent people who do bestow some care in overseeing the cultivation of their children's minds. It must not suffice simply to *think* that such or such information will be useful in after life, or that this kind of knowledge is of more practical value than that; but we must seek out some process of estimating their respective values, so that as far as possible we may positively *know* which are most deserving of attention.

Doubtless the task is difficult—perhaps never to be more than approximately achieved. But, considering the vastness of the interests at stake, its difficulty is no reason for pusillanimously passing it by; but rather for devoting every energy to its mastery. And if we only proceed systematically, we may very soon get at results of no small moment.

Our first step must obviously be to classify, in the order of their importance, the leading kinds of activity which constitute human life. They may be naturally arranged into: 1. Those activities which directly minister to self-preservation; 2. Those activities which, by securing the necessaries of life, indirectly minister to self-preservation; 3. Those activities which have for their end the rearing and discipline of offspring; 4. Those activities which are involved in the maintenance of proper social and political relations; 5. Those miscellaneous activities which fill up the leisure part of life, devoted to the gratification of the tastes and feelings.

That these stand in something like their true order of subordination, it needs no long consideration to show. The actions and precautions by which, from moment to moment, we secure personal safety, must clearly take precedence of all others. Could there be a man, ignorant as an infant of surrounding objects and movements, or how to guide himself among them, he would pretty certainly lose his life the first time he went into the street; notwithstanding any amount of learning he might have on other matters. And as entire ignorance in all other directions would be less promptly fatal than entire ignorance in this direction, it must be admitted that knowledge immediately conducive to self-preservation is of primary importance.

That next after direct self-preservation comes the indirect self-preservation which consists in acquiring the means of living, none will question. That a man's industrial functions must be considered before his parental ones, is manifest from the fact that, speaking generally, the discharge of the parental functions is made possible only by the previous discharge of the industrial ones. The power of self-maintenance necessarily preceding the power of maintaining offspring, it follows that knowledge needful for self-maintenance has stronger claims than knowledge needful for family welfare—is second in value to none save knowledge needful for immediate self-preservation.

As the family comes before the State in order of time—as the bringing up of children is possible before the State exists, or when it has ceased to be, whereas the State is rendered possible only by the bringing up of children; it follows that the duties of the parent demand closer attention than those of the citizen. Or, to use a further argument—since the goodness of a society ultimately depends on the nature of its citizens; and since the nature of its citizens is more modifiable by early training than by anything else; we must conclude that the welfare of the family underlies the welfare of society. And hence knowledge directly conducing to the first, must take precedence of knowledge directly conducing to the last.

Those various forms of pleasurable occupation which fill up the leisure left by graver occupations—the enjoyments of music, poetry, painting, etc.— manifestly imply a pre-existing society. Not only is a considerable development of them impossible without a long-established social union; but their very subject-matter consists in great part of social sentiments and sympathies. Not only does society supply the conditions to their growth; but also the ideas and sentiments they expresss. And, consequently, that part of human conduct which constitutes good citizenship, is of more moment than that which goes out in accomplishments or exercise of the tastes; and, in education, preparation for the one must rank before preparation for the other.

Such then, we repeat, is something like the rational order of subordination: that education which prepares for direct self-preservation; that which prepares for indirect self-preservation; that which prepares for parenthood; that which prepares for citizenship; that which prepares for the miscellaneous refinements of life. We do not mean to say that these divisions are definitely separable. We do not deny that they are intricately entangled with each other, in such way that there can be no training for any that is not in some measure a training for all. Nor do we question that of each division there are portions more important than certain portions of the preceding divisions; that, for instance, a man of much skill in business but little other faculty, may fall further below the standard of complete living than one of but moderate ability in money-getting but great judgment as a parent; or that exhaustive information bearing on right social action, joined with entire want of general culture in literature and the fine arts, is less desirable than a more moderate share of the one joined with some of the other. But, after making due qualifications, there still remain these broadly-marked divisions; and it still continues substantially true that these divisions subordinate one another in the foregoing order, because the corresponding divisions of life make one another *possible* in that order.

Of course the ideal of education is—complete preparation in all these divisions. But failing this ideal, as in our phase of civilization every one must do more or less, the aim should be to maintain *a due proportion* between the degrees of preparation in each. Not exhaustive cultivation in any one, supremely important though it may be—not even an exclusive attention to the two, three, or four divisions of greatest importance; but an attention to all: greatest where the value is greatest; less where the value is less; least where the value is least. For the average man (not to forget the cases in which peculiar aptitude for some one department of knowledge, rightly makes pursuit of that one the bread-winning occupation)—for the average man, we say, the desideratum is, a training that approaches nearest to perfection in the things which most subserve complete living, and falls more and more below perfection in the things that have more and more remote bearings on complete living.

. . . .

. . . We infer that as vigorous health and its accompanying high spirits are larger elements of happiness than any other things whatever, the teaching how to maintain them is a teaching that yields in moment to no other whatever. And therefore we assert that such a course of physiology as is needful for the comprehension of its general truths, and their bearings on daily conduct, is an all-essential part of a rational education.

Strange that the assertion should need making! Stranger still that it should need defending! Yet are there not a few by whom such a proposition will be received with something approaching to derision. Men who would blush if caught saying Iphigénia instead of Iphigenía, or would resent as an insult any imputation of ignorance respecting the fabled labors of a fabled demigod, show not the slightest shame in confessing that they do not know where the Eustachian tubes are, what are the actions of the spinal cord, what is the normal rate of pulsation, or how the lungs are inflated. While anxious that their sons should be well up in the superstitions of two thousand years ago, they care not that they should be taught anything about the structure and functions of their own bodies—nay, even wish them not to be so taught. So overwhelming is the influence of established routine! So terribly in our education does the ornamental over-ride the useful!

We need not insist on the value of that knowledge which aids indirect self-preservation by facilitating the gaining of a livelihood. This is admitted by all; and, indeed, by the mass is perhaps too exclusively regarded as the end of education. But while every one is ready to endorse the abstract proposition that instruction fitting youths for the business of life is of high importance, or even to consider it of supreme importance; yet scarcely any inquire what instruction will so fit them. It is true that reading, writing, and arithmetic are taught with an intelligent appreciation of their uses. But when we have said this we have said nearly all. While the great bulk of what else is acquired has no bearing on the industrial activities, an immensity of information that has a direct bearing on the industrial activities is entirely passed over.

For, leaving out only some very small classes, what are all men employed in? They are employed in the production, preparation, and distribution of commodities. And on what does efficiency in the production, preparation, and distribution of commodities depend? It depends on the use of methods fitted to the respective natures of these commodities; it depends on an adequate acquaintance with their physical, chemical, or vital properties, as the case may be; that is, it depends on science. This order of knowledge which is in great part ignored in our school-courses, is the order of knowledge underlying the right performance of those processes by which civilized life is made possible. . . .

. . .

Thus, to all such as are occupied in the production, exchange, or distribution of commodities, acquaintance with science in some of its departments, is of fundamental importance. Each man who is immediately or remotely implicated in any form of industry (and few are not) has in some way to deal with the mathematical, physical, and chemical properties of things; perhaps, also, has a direct interest in biology; and certainly has in sociology. Whether he does or does not succeed well in that indirect self-preservation which we call getting a good livelihood, depends in a great degree on his knowledge of one or more of these sciences: not, it may be, a rational knowledge; but still a knowledge, though empirical. For what we call learning a business, really implies learning the science involved in it; though not perhaps under the name of science. And hence a grounding in science is of great importance, both because it prepares for all this, and because rational knowledge has an immense superiority over empirical knowledge. Moreover, not only is scientific culture requisite for each, that he may understand the *how* and the *why* of the things and processes with which he is concerned as maker or distributor; but it is often of much moment that he should understand the *how* and the *why* of various other things and processes. . . .

. . .

We come now to the third great division of human activities—a division for which no preparation whatever is made. If by some strange chance not a vestige of us descended to the remote future save a pile of our school-books or some college examination papers, we may imagine how puzzled an antiquary of the period would be on finding in them no sign that the learners were ever likely to be parents. "This must have been the *curriculum* for their celibates," we may fancy him concluding. "I perceive here an elaborate preparation for many things; especially for reading the books of extinct nations and of co-existing nations (from which indeed it seems clear that these people had very little worth reading in their own tongue); but I find no reference whatever to the bringing up of children. They could not have been so absurd as to omit all training for this gravest of responsibilities. Evidently then, this was the school-course of one of their monastic orders."

Seriously, is it not an astonishing fact, that though on the treatment of offspring depend their lives or deaths, and their moral welfare or ruin; yet not one word of instruction on the treatment of offspring is ever given to those who will by and by be parents? Is it not monstrous that the fate of a new generation should be left to the chances of unreasoning custom, impulse, fancy—joined with the suggestions of ignorant nurses and the prejudiced counsel of grandmothers? If a merchant commenced business without any knowledge of arithmetic and book-keeping, we should exclaim at his folly, and look for disastrous consequences. Or if, before studying anatomy, a man set up as a surgical operator, we should wonder at his audacity and pity his patients. But that parents should begin the difficult task of rearing children, without ever having given a thought to the principles—physical, moral, or intellectual—which ought to guide them, excites neither surprise at the actors nor pity for their victims.

. . .

. . . Under that common limited idea of education which confines it to knowledge gained from books, parents thrust primers into the hands of their little ones years too soon, to their great injury. Not recognizing the truth that the function of books is supplementary—that they form an indirect means to knowledge when direct means fail—a means of seeing through other men what you cannot see for yourself; teachers are eager to give second-hand facts in place of first-hand facts. Not perceiving the enormous value of that spontaneous education which goes on in early years—not perceiving that a child's restless observation, instead of being ignored or checked, should be diligently ministered to, and made as accurate and complete as possible; they insist on occupying its eyes and thoughts with things that are, for the time being, incomprehensible and repugnant. Possessed by a superstition which worships the symbols of knowledge instead of the knowledge itself, they do not see that only when his acquaintance with the objects and processes of the household, the streets, and the fields, is becoming tolerably exhaustive—only then should a child be introduced to the new sources of information which books supply: and this, not only because immediate cognition is of far greater value than mediate cognition; but also, because the words contained in books can be rightly interpreted into ideas, only in proportion to the antecedent experience of things. Observe next, that this formal instruction, far too soon commenced, is carried on with but little reference to the laws of mental development. Intellectual progress is of necessity from the concrete to the abstract. But regardless of this, highly abstract studies, such as grammar, which should come quite late, are begun quite early. Political geography, dead and uninteresting to a child, and which should be an appendage of sociological studies, is commenced betimes; while physical geography, comprehensible and comparatively attractive to a child, is in great part passed over. Nearly every subject dealt with is arranged in abnormal order: definitions and rules and principles being put first, instead of being disclosed, as they are in the order of nature, through the study of cases. And then, pervading the whole, is the vicious system of rote learning—a system of sacrificing the spirit to the letter. See the results. What with perceptions unnaturally dulled by early thwarting, and a coerced attention to books—what with the mental confusion produced by teaching subjects before they can be understood, and in each of them giving generalizations before the facts of which they are the generalizations—what with making the pupil a mere passive recipient of others' ideas, and not in the least leading him to be an active inquirer or self-instructor—and what with taxing the faculties to excess; there are very few minds that become as efficient as they might be. Examinations being once passed, books are laid aside; the greater part of what has been acquired, being unorganized, soon drops out of recollection; what remains is mostly inert— the art of applying knowledge not having been cultivated; and there is but little power either of accurate observation or independent thinking. To all which add, that while much of the information gained is of relatively small value, an immense mass of information of transcendent value is entirely passed over.

Thus we find the facts to be such as might have been inferred *a priori*. The training of children—physical, moral, and intellectual—is dreadfully defective. And in great measure it is so because parents are devoid of that knowledge by which this training can alone be rightly guided. What is to be expected when one of the most intricate of problems is undertaken by those who have given scarcely a thought to the principles on which its solution depends? . . .

Thus we see that for regulating the third great division of human activities, a knowledge of the laws of life is the one thing needful. Some acquaintance with the first principles of physiology and the elementary truths of psychology, is indispensable for the right bringing up of children. We doubt not that many will read this assertion with a smile. That parents in general should be expected to acquire a knowledge of subjects so abstruse will seem to them an absurdity. And if we proposed that an exhaustive knowledge of these subjects should be obtained by all fathers and mothers, the absurdity would indeed be glaring enough. But we do not. General principles only, accompanied by such illustrations as may be needed to make them understood, would suffice. And these might be readily taught—if not rationally, then dogmatically. Be this as it may, however, here are the indisputable facts: that the development of children in mind and body follows certain laws; that unless these laws are in some degree conformed to by parents, death is inevitable; that unless they are in a great degree conformed to, there must result serious physical and mental defects; and that only when they are completely conformed to, can a perfect maturity be reached. Judge, then, whether all who may one day be parents, should not strive with some anxiety to learn what these laws are.

From the parental functions let us pass now to the functions of the citizen. We have here to inquire what knowledge fits a man for the discharge of these functions. It cannot be alleged that the need for knowledge fitting him for these functions is wholly overlooked; for our school-courses contain certain studies, which, nominally at least, bear upon political and social duties. Of these the only one that occupies a prominent place is History.

But, as already hinted, the information commonly given under this head, is almost valueless for purposes of guidance. Scarcely any of the facts set down in our school-histories, and very few of those contained in the more elaborate works written for adults, illustrate the right principles of political action. The biographies of monarchs (and our children learn little else) throw scarcely any light upon the science of society. Familiarity with court intrigues, plots, usurpations, or the like, and with all the personalities accompanying them, aids very little in elucidating the causes of national progress. We read of some squabble for power, that it led to a pitched battle; that such and such were the names of the generals and their leading subordinates; that they had each so many thousand infantry and cavalry, and so many cannon; that they arranged their forces in this and that order; that they manoeuvred, attacked, and fell back in certain ways; that at this part of the day such disasters were sustained, and at that such advantages gained; that in one particular movement some leading officer fell, while in another a certain regiment was decimated; that after all the changing fortunes of the fight, the victory was gained by this or that army; and that so many were killed and wounded on each side, and so many captured by the conquerors. And now, out of the accumulated details making up the narrative, say which it is that helps you in deciding on your conduct as a citizen. . . .

. . . The only history that is of practical value is what may be called Descriptive Sociology. And the highest office which the historian can discharge, is that of so narrating the lives of nations, as to furnish materials for a Comparative Sociology; and for the subsequent determination of the ultimate laws to which social phenomena conform.

But now mark, that even supposing an adequate stock of this truly valuable historical knowledge has been acquired, it is of comparatively little use without the key. And the key is to be found only in Science. In the absence of the generalizations of biology and psychology, rational interpretation of social phenomena is impossible. Only in proportion as men draw certain rude, empirical inferences respecting human nature, are they enabled to understand even the simplest facts of social life: as, for instance, the relation between supply and demand. And if the most elementary truths of sociology cannot be reached until some knowledge is obtained of how men generally think, feel, and act under given circumstances; then it is manifest that there can be nothing like a wide comprehension of sociology, unless through a competent acquaintance with man in all his faculties, bodily, and mental. Consider the matter in the abstract, and this conclusion is self-evident. Thus: Society is made up of individuals; all that is done in society is done by the combined actions of individuals; and therefore, in individual actions only can be found the solutions of social phenomena. But the actions of individuals depend on the laws of their natures; and their actions cannot be understood until these laws are understood. These laws, however, when reduced to their simplest expressions, prove to be corollaries from the laws of body and mind in general. Hence it follows, that biology and psychology are indispensable as interpreters of sociology. Or, to state the conclusions still more simply: all social phenomena of life—are the most complex manifestations of life—must conform to the laws of life—and can be understood only when the laws of life are understood. Thus, then, for the regulation of this fourth division of human activities, we are, as before, dependent on Science. Of the knowledge commonly imparted in educational courses, very little is of service for guiding a man in his conduct as a citizen. Only a small part of the history he reads is of practical value; and of this small part he is not prepared to make proper use. He lacks not only the materials for, but the very conception of, descriptive sociology; and he also lacks those generalizations of the organic sciences, without which even descriptive sociology can give him but small aid.

And now we come to that remaining division of human life which includes the relaxations and amusements filling leisure hours. After considering what training best fits for self-preservation, for the obtainment of sustenance, for the discharge of parental duties, and for the regulation of social and political conduct; we have now to consider what training best fits for the miscellaneous ends not included in these—for the enjoyment of Nature, of Literature, and of the Fine Arts, in all their forms. Postponing them as we do to things that bear more vitally upon human welfare; and bringing everything, as we have, to the test of actual value; it will perhaps be inferred that we are inclined to slight these less essential things. No greater mistake could be made, however. We yield to none in the value we attach to aesthetic culture and its pleasures. Without painting, sculpture, music, poetry, and the emotions produced by natural beauty of every kind, life would lose half its charm. So far from regarding the training and gratification of the tastes as unimportant, we believe that in time to come they will occupy a much larger share of human life than now. When the forces of Nature have been fully conquered to man's use—when the means of production have been brought to perfection—when labor has been economized to the highest degree—when education has been so systematized that a preparation for the more essential activities may be made with comparative rapidity—and when, consequently, there is a great increase of spare time; then will the beautiful, both in Art and Nature, rightly fill a large space in the minds of all.

But it is one thing to approve of aesthetic culture as largely conducive to human happiness; and another thing to admit that it is a fundamental requisite to human happiness. However important it may be, it must yield precedence to those kinds of culture which bear directly upon daily duties. As before hinted, literature and the fine arts are made possible by those activities which make individual and social life possible; and manifestly, that which is made possible, must be postponed to that which makes it possible. . . .

.   .   .

Thus to the question we set out with—What knowledge is of most worth?—the uniform reply is—Science. This is the verdict on all the counts. For direct self-preservation, or the maintenance of life and health, the all-important knowledge is—Science. For that indirect self-preservation, which we call gaining a livelihood, the knowledge of greatest value is—Science. For the due discharge of parental functions, the proper guidance is to be found only in—Science. For that interpretation of national life, past and present, without which the citizen cannot rightly regulate his conduct, the indispensable key is—Science. Alike for the most perfect production and highest enjoyment of art in all its forms, the needful preparation is still—Science. And for purposes of discipline—intellectual, moral, religious—the most efficient study is, once more—Science. The question which at first seemed so perplexed, has become, in the course of our inquiry, comparatively simple. We have not to estimate the degrees of importance of different orders of human activity, and different studies as severally fitting us for them; since we find that the study of Science, in its most comprehensive meaning, is the best preparation for all these orders of activity. We have not to decide between the claims of knowledge of great though conventional value, and knowledge of less though intrinsic value; seeing that the knowledge which proves to be of most value in all other respects, is intrinsically most valuable: its worth is not dependent upon opinion, but is as fixed as is the relation of man to the surrounding world. Necessary and eternal as are its truths, all Science concerns all mankind for all time. Equally at present and in the remotest future, must it be of incalculable importance for the regulation of their conduct, that men should understand the science of life, physical, mental, and social; and that they should understand all other science as a key to the science of life.

THE UNRESTRICTED SCOPE OF EDUCATION

AUTHOR:

Ralph Waldo Emerson (*1803–1882*)

WORK:

EDUCATION, FROM "LECTURES AND BIOGRAPHICAL SKETCHES"
(1864)

It is ominous, a presumption of crime, that this word Education has so cold, so hopeless a sound. A treatise on education, a convention for education, a lecture, a system, affects us with slight paralysis and a certain yawning of the jaws. We are not encouraged when the law touches it with its fingers. Education should be as broad as man. Whatever elements are in him that should foster and demonstrate. If he be dexterous, his tuition should make it appear; if he be capable of dividing men by the trenchant sword of his thought, education should unsheathe and sharpen it; if he is one to cement society by

From *Lectures and Biographical Sketches* by Ralph Waldo Emerson, Vol. X of *The Complete Works of Ralph Waldo Emerson*, introduction and notes by Edward Waldo Emerson (Boston and New York: Houghton Mifflin and Company, 1904), pp. 133–157 abridged.

his all-reconciling affinities, oh! hasten their action! If he is jovial, if he is mercurial, if he is great-hearted, a cunning artificer, a strong commander, a potent ally, ingenious, useful, elegant, witty, prophet, diviner—society has need of all these. The imagination must be addressed. Why always coast on the surface and never open the interior of Nature, not by science, which is surface still, but by poetry? Is not the Vast an element of the mind? Yet what teaching, what book of this day appeals to the Vast?

Our culture has truckled to the time—to the senses. It is not manworthy. If the vast and the spiritual are omitted, so are the practical and the moral. It does not make us brave or free. We teach boys to be such men as we are. We do not teach them to aspire to be all they can. We do not give them a training as if we believed in their noble nature. We scarce educate their bodies. We do not train the eye and the hand. We exercise their understandings to the apprehension and comparison of some facts, to a skill in numbers, in words; we aim to make accountants, attorneys, engineers; but not to make able, earnest, great-hearted men. The great object of Education should be commensurate with the object of life. It should be a moral one; to teach self-trust: to inspire the youthful man with an interest in himself; with a curiosity touching his own nature; to acquaint him with the resources of his mind, and to teach him that there is all his strength, and to inflame him with a piety towards the Grand Mind in which he lives. Thus would education conspire with the Divine Providence. A man is a little thing whilst he works by and for himself, but, when he gives voice to the rules of love and justice, is godlike, his word is current in all countries; and all men, though his enemies, are made his friends and obey it as their own.

In affirming that the moral nature of man is the predominant element and should therefore be mainly consulted in the arrangements of a school, I am very far from wishing that it should swallow up all the other instincts and faculties of man. It should be enthroned in his mind, but if it monopolize the man he is not yet sound, he does not yet know his wealth. He is in danger of becoming merely devout, and wearisome through the monotony of his thought. It is not less necessary that the intellectual and the active faculties should be nourished and matured. . . .

I call our system a system of despair, and I find all the correction, all the revolution that is needed and that the best spirits of this age promise, in one word, in Hope. Nature, when she sends a new mind into the world, fills it beforehand with a desire for that which she wishes it to know and do. Let us wait and see what is this new creation, of what new organ the great Spirit had need when it incarnated this new Will. . . . I suffer whenever I see that common sight of a parent or senior imposing his opinion and way of thinking and being on a young soul to which they are totally unfit. Cannot we let people be themselves, and enjoy life in their own way? . . .

I believe that our own experience instructs us that the secret of Education lies in respecting the pupil. It is not for you to choose what he shall know, what he shall do. It is chosen and foreordained, and he only holds the key to his own secret. By your tampering and thwarting and too much governing he may be hindered from his end and kept out of his own. Respect the child. Wait and see the new product of Nature. Nature loves analogies, but not repetitions. Respect the child. Be not too much his parent. Trespass not on his solitude.

But I hear the outcry which replies to this suggestion: Would you verily throw up the reins of public and private discipline; would you leave the young child to the mad career of his own passions and whimsies, and call this anarchy a respect for the child's nature? I answer, Respect the child, respect him to the end, but also respect yourself. Be the companion of his thought, the friend of his friendship, the lover of his virtue—but no kinsman of his sin. Let him find you so true to yourself that you are the irreconcilable hater of his vice and the imperturbable slighter of his trifling.

The two points in a boy's training are, to keep his *naturel* and train off all but that—to keep his *naturel,* but stop off his uproar, fooling and horse-play—keep his nature and arm it with knowledge in the very direction in which it points. Here are the two capital facts, Genius and Drill. The first is the inspiration in the well-born healthy child, the new perception he has of nature. Somewhat he sees in forms or hears in music or apprehends in mathematics, or believes practicable in mechanics or possible in political society, which no one else sees or hears or believes. This is the perpetual romance of new life, the invasion of God into the old dead world, when he sends into quiet houses a young soul with a thought which is not met, looking for something which is not there, but which ought to be there: the thought is dim but it is sure, and he casts about restless for means and masters to verify it; he makes wild attempts to explain himself and invoke the aid and consent of the bystanders. . . .

Nor are the two elements, enthusiasm and drill, incompatible. Accuracy is essential to beauty. The very definition of the intellect is Aristotle's: "that by which we know terms or boundaries." Give a boy accurate perceptions. Teach him the difference between the similar and the same. Make him call things by their right names. Pardon in him no blunder. Then he will give you solid satisfaction as long as he lives. It is better to teach the child arithmetic and Latin grammar than rhetoric or moral philosophy, because they require exactitude of performance; it is made certain that the lesson is mastered, and that power of performance is worth more than the knowledge. He can learn anything which is important to him now that the power to learn is secured: as mechanics say, when one has learned the use of tools, it is easy to work at a new craft.

. . .

But this function of opening and feeding the human mind is not to be fulfilled by any mechanical or military method; is not to be trusted to any skill less large than Nature itself. You must not neglect the form, but you must secure the essentials. It is curious how perverse and intermeddling we are, and what vast pains and cost we incur to do wrong. Whilst we all know in our own experience and apply natural methods in our own business, in education our common sense fails us, and we are continually trying costly machinery against nature, in patent schools and academies and in great colleges and universities.

The natural method forever confutes our experiments, and we must still come back to it. The whole theory of the school is on the nurse's or mother's knee. The child is as hot to learn as the mother is to impart. . . .

Our modes of Education aim to expedite, to save labor; to do for masses what cannot be done for masses, what must be done reverently, one by one: say rather, the whole world is needed for the tuition of each pupil. The advantages of this system of emulation and display are so prompt and obvious, it is such a time-saver, it is so energetic on slow and on bad natures, and is of so easy application, needing no sage or poet, but any tutor or schoolmaster in his first term can apply it, that it is not strange that this calomel of culture should be a popular medicine. On the other hand, total abstinence from this drug, and the adoption of simple discipline and the following of nature, involves at once immense claims on the time, the thoughts, on the life of the teacher. It requires time, use, insight, event, all the great lessons and assistances of God; and only to think of using it implies character and profoundness; to enter on this course of discipline is to be good and great. . . .

Now the correction of this quack practice is to import into Education the wisdom of life. Leave this military hurry and adopt the pace of Nature. Her secret is patience. . . .

Talk of Columbus and Newton! I tell you the child just born in yonder hovel is the beginning of a revolution as great as theirs. But you must have the believing and prophetic eye. Have the self-command you wish to inspire. Your teaching and discipline must have the reserve and taciturnity of Nature. Teach them to hold their tongues by holding your own. Say little; do not snarl; do not chide; but govern by the eye. See what they need, and that the right thing is done.

I confess myself utterly at a loss in suggesting particular reforms in our ways of teaching. No discretion that can be lodged with a school-committee, with the overseers or visitors of an academy, of a college, can at all avail to reach these difficulties and perplexities, but they solve themselves when we leave institutions and address individuals.

THE CHANGING FACE
OF HIGHER EDUCATION

AUTHOR:

Charles W. Eliot (*1834–1926*)

WORK:

INAUGURAL ADDRESS
AS PRESIDENT
OF HARVARD (1869)

Recent discussions have added pitifully little to the world's stock of wisdom about the staple of education. Who blows to-day such a ringing trumpet-call to the study of language as Luther blew? Hardly a significant word has been added in two centuries to Milton's description of the unprofitable way to study languages. Would any young American learn how to profit by travel, that foolish beginning but excellent sequel to education, he can find no apter advice than Bacon's. The practice of England and America is literally centuries behind the precept of the best thinkers upon education. A striking illustration may be found in the prevailing neglect of the systematic study of the English language. How lamentably true to-day are these words of Locke:

From *Educational Reform: Essays and Addresses* by Charles W. Eliot (New York: The Century Co., 1898), pp. 1–38, abridged.

"If any one among us have a facility or purity more than ordinary in his mother-tongue, it is owing to chance, or his genius, or anything rather than to his education or any care of his teacher."

The best result of the discussion which has raged so long about the relative educational value of the main branches of learning is the conviction that there is room for them all in a sound scheme, provided that right methods of teaching be employed. It is not because of the limitation of their faculties that boys of eighteen come to college, having mastered nothing but a few score pages of Latin and Greek, and the bare elements of mathematics. Not nature, but an unintelligent system of instruction from the primary school through the college, is responsible for the fact that many college graduates have so inadequate a conception of what is meant by scientific observation, reasoning, and proof. It is possible for the young to get actual experience of all the principal methods of thought. There is a method of thought in language, and a method in mathematics, and another of natural and physical science, and another of faith. With wise direction, even a child would drink at all these springs. The actual problem to be solved is not what to teach, but how to teach. . . . With good methods, we may confidently hope to give young men of twenty to twenty-five an accurate general knowledge of all the main subjects of human interest, besides a minute and thorough knowledge of the one subject which each may select as his principal occupation in life. To think this impossible is to despair of mankind; for unless a general acquaintance with many branches of knowledge, good so far as it goes, be attainable by great numbers of men, there can be no such thing as an intelligent public opinion; and in the modern world the intelligence of public opinion is the one indispensable condition of social progress.

. . .

. . . The very word "education" is a standing protest against dogmatic teaching. The notion that education consists in the authoritative inculcation of what the teacher deems true may be logical and appropriate in a convent, or a seminary for priests, but it is intolerable in universities and public schools, from primary to professional. The worthy fruit of academic culture is an open mind, trained to careful thinking, instructed in the methods of philosophic investigation, acquainted in a general way with the accumulated thought of past generations, and penetrated with humility. It is thus that the university in our day serves Christ and the church.

Only a few years ago, all students who graduated at this College passed through one uniform curriculum. Every man studied the same subjects in the same proportions, without regard to his natural bent or preference. The individual student had no choice of either subjects or teachers. This system is still the prevailing system among American colleges, and finds vigorous defenders. It has the merit of simplicity. So had the school methods of our grandfathers—one primer, one catechism, one rod for all children. On the whole, a single common course of studies, tolerably well selected to meet the average needs, seems to most Americans a very proper and natural thing, even for grown men.

As a people, we do not apply to mental activities the principle of division of labor; and we have but a halting faith in special training for high professional employments. The vulgar conceit that a Yankee can turn his hand to anything we insensibly carry into high places, where it is preposterous and criminal. . . .

In education, the individual traits of different minds have not been sufficiently attended to. Through all the period of boyhood the school studies should be representative; all the main fields of knowledge should be entered upon. But the young man of nineteen or twenty ought to know what he likes best and is most fit for. If his previous training has been sufficiently wide, he will know by that time whether he is most apt at language or philosophy or natural science or mathematics. If he feels no loves, he will at least have his hates. At that age the teacher may wisely abandon the school-dame's practice of giving a copy of nothing but zeros to the child who alleges that he cannot make that figure. When the revelation of his own peculiar taste and capacity comes to a young man, let him reverently give it welcome, thank God, and take courage. Thereafter he knows his way to happy, enthusiastic work, and, God willing, to usefulness and success. The civilization of a people may be inferred from the variety of its tools. There are thousands of years between the stone hatchet and the machine-shop. As tools multiply, each is more ingeniously adapted to its own exclusive purpose. So with the men that make the State. For the individual, concentration, and the highest development of his own peculiar faculty, is the only prudence. But for the State, it is variety, not uniformity, of intellectual product, which is needful.

These principles are the justification of the system of elective studies which has been gradually developed in this College during the past forty years. At present the Freshman year is the only one in which there is a fixed course prescribed for all. In the other three years, more than half the time allotted to study is filled with subjects chosen by each student from lists which comprise six studies in the Sophomore year, nine in the Junior year, and eleven in the Senior year. The range of elective studies is large, though there are some striking deficiencies. The liberty of choice of subject is wide, but yet has very rigid limits. There is a certain framework which must be filled; and about half the material of the filling is prescribed. The choice offered to the student does not lie between liberal studies and professional or utilitarian studies. All the studies which are open to him are liberal and disciplinary, not narrow or special. Under this system the College does not demand, it is true, one invariable set of studies of every candidate for the first degree in Arts; but its requisitions for this degree are nevertheless high and inflexible, being nothing less than four years devoted to liberal culture.

It has been alleged that the elective system must weaken the bond which unites members of the same class. This is true; but in view of another much more efficient cause of the diminution of class intimacy, the point is not very significant. The increased size of the college classes inevitably works a great change in this respect. One hundred and fifty young men cannot be so intimate with each other as fifty used to be. This increase is progressive. Taken in connection with the rising average age of the students, it would compel the adoption of methods of instruction different from the old, if there were no better motive for such change. The elective system fosters scholarship, because it gives free play to natural preferences and inborn aptitudes, makes possible enthusiasm for a chosen work, relieves the professor and the ardent disciple of the presence of a body of students who are compelled to an unwelcome task, and enlarges instruction by substituting many and various lessons given to small, lively classes, for a few lessons many times repeated to different sections of a numerous class. The College therefore proposes to persevere in its efforts to establish, improve, and extend the elective system.

THE DEWEYAN SYNTHESIS

AUTHOR:

John Dewey (*1859–1952*)

WORK:

MY PEDAGOGIC CREED (1897)

ARTICLE ONE—WHAT EDUCATION IS

I believe that all education proceeds by the participation of the individual in the social consciousness of the race. This process begins unconsciously almost at birth, and is continually shaping the individual's powers, saturating his consciousness, forming his habits, training his ideas, and arousing his feelings and emotions. Through this unconscious education the individual gradually comes to share in the intellectual and moral resources which humanity has succeeded in getting together. He becomes an inheritor of the funded capital of civilization. The most formal and technical education in the world cannot safely depart from this general process. It can only organize it or differentiate it in some particular direction.

The only true education comes through the stimulation of the child's powers by the demands of the social situations in which he finds himself. Through these demands he is stimulated to act as a member of a unity, to

From "My Pedagogic Creed" by John Dewey, *School Journal,* 54:77–80, January 16, 1897.

emerge from his original narrowness of action and feeling, and to conceive of himself from the standpoint of the welfare of the group to which he belongs. Through the responses which others make to his own activities he comes to know what these mean in social terms. The value which they have is reflected back into them. For instance, through the response which is made to the child's instinctive babblings the child comes to know what those babblings mean; they are transformed into articulate language, and thus the child is introduced into the consolidated wealth of ideas and emotions which are now summed up in language.

This educational process has two sides—one psychological and one sociological—and neither can be subordinated to the other, or neglected, without evil results following. Of these two sides, the psychological is the basis. The child's own instincts and powers furnish the material and give the starting point for all education. Save as the efforts of the educator connect with some activity which the child is carrying on of his own initiative independent of the educator, education becomes reduced to a pressure from without. It may, indeed, give certain external results, but cannot truly be called educative. Without insight into the psychological structure and activities of the individual, the educative process will, therefore, be haphazard and arbitrary. If it chances to coincide with the child's activity it will get a leverage; if it does not, it will result in friction, or disintegration, or arrest of the child-nature.

Knowledge of social conditions, of the present state of civilization, is necessary in order properly to interpret the child's powers. The child has his own instincts and tendencies, but we do not know what these mean until we can translate them into their social equivalents. We must be able to carry them back into a social past and see them as the inheritance of previous race activities. We must also be able to project them into the future to see what their outcome and end will be. In the illustration just used, it is the ability to see in the child's babblings the promise and potency of a future social intercourse and conversation which enables one to deal in the proper way with that instinct.

The psychological and social sides are organically related, and that education cannot be regarded as a compromise between the two, or a superimposition of one upon the other. We are told the psychological definition of education is barren and formal—that it gives us only the idea of a development of all the mental powers without giving us any idea of the use to which these powers are put. On the other hand, it is urged that the social definition of education, as getting adjusted to civilization, makes of it a forced and external process, and results in subordinating the freedom of the individual to a preconceived social and political status.

Each of these objections is true when urged against one side isolated from the other. In order to know what a power really is we must know what its end, use, or function is, and this we cannot know save as we conceive of the individual as active in social relationships. But, on the other hand, the only possible adjustment which we can give to the child under existing conditions is that which arises through putting him in complete possession of all his powers. With the advent of democracy and modern industrial conditions, it is impossible to foretell definitely just what civilization will be twenty years from now. Hence it is impossible to prepare the child for any precise set of conditions. To prepare him for the future life means to give him command of himself; it means so to train him that he will have the full and ready use of all his capacities; that his eye and ear and hand may be tools ready to command, that his judgment may be capable of grasping the conditions under which it has to work, and the executive forces be trained to act economically and efficiently. It is impossible to reach this sort of adjustment save as constant regard is had to the individual's own powers, tastes, and interests—that is, as education is continually converted into psychological terms.

In sum, I believe that the individual who is to be educated is a social individual, and that society is an organic union of individuals. If we eliminate the social factor from the child we are left only with an abstraction; if we eliminate the individual factor from society, we are left only with an inert and lifeless mass. Education, therefore, must begin with a psychological insight into the child's capacities, interests, and habits. It must be controlled at every point by reference to these same considerations. These powers, interests, and habits must be continually interpreted—we must know what they mean. They must be translated into terms of their social equivalents—into terms of what they are capable of in the way of social service.

ARTICLE TWO—WHAT THE SCHOOL IS

I believe that the school is primarily a social institution. Education being a social process, the school is simply that form of community life in which all those agencies are concentrated that will be most effective in bringing the child to share in the inherited resources of the race, and to use his own powers for social ends.

Education, therefore, is a process of living and not a preparation for future living.

The school must represent life, life as real and vital to the child as that which he carries on in the home, in the neighborhood, or on the playground.

That education which does not occur through forms of life, forms that are worth living for their own sake, is always a poor substitute for the genuine reality, and tends to cramp and to deaden.

The school, as an institution, should simplify existing social life; should reduce it, as it were, to an embryonic form. Existing life is so complex that the child cannot be brought into contact with it without either confusion or distraction; he is either overwhelmed by the multiplicity of activities which are going on, so that he loses his own power of orderly reaction, or he is so stimulated by these various activities that his powers are prematurely called into play and he becomes either unduly specialized or else disintegrated.

As such simplified social life, the school should grow gradually out of the home life; it should take up and continue the activities with which the child is already familiar in the home.

It should exhibit these activities to the child, and reproduce them in such ways that the child will gradually learn the meaning of them, and be capable of playing his own part in relation to them.

This is a psychological necessity, because it is the only way of securing continuity in the child's growth, the only way of giving a background of past experience to the new ideas given in school.

It is also a social necessity because the home is the form of social life in which the child has been nurtured and in connection with which he has had his moral training. It is the business of the school to deepen and extend his sense of the values bound up in his home life.

Much of present education fails because it neglects this fundamental principle of the school as a form of community life. It conceives the school as a place where certain information is to be given, where certain lessons are to be learned, or where certain habits are to be formed. The value of these is conceived as lying largely in the remote future; the child must do these things for the sake of something else he is to do; they are mere preparations. As a result they do not become a part of the life experience of the child and so are not truly educative.

The moral education centers upon this conception of the school as a mode of social life, that the best and deepest moral training is precisely that which one gets through having to enter into proper relations with others in a unity of work and thought. The present educational systems, so far as they destroy or neglect this unity, render it difficult or impossible to get any genuine, regular moral training.

The child should be stimulated and controlled in his work through the life of the community.

Under existing conditions far too much of the stimulus and control proceeds from the teacher, because of neglect of the idea of the school as a form of social life.

The teacher's place and work in the school is to be interpreted from this same basis. The teacher is not in the school to impose certain ideas or to form certain habits in the child, but is there as a member of the community to select the influences which shall affect the child and to assist him in properly responding to these influences.

The discipline of the school should proceed from the life of the school as a whole and not directly from the teacher.

The teacher's business is simply to determine, on the basis of larger experience and riper widsom, how the discipline of life shall come to the child.

All questions of the grading of the child and his promotion should be determined by reference to the same standard. Examinations are of use only so far as they test the child's fitness for social life and reveal the place in which he can be of the most service and where he can receive the most help.

ARTICLE THREE—THE SUBJECT MATTER OF EDUCATION

I believe that the social life of the child is the basis of concentration, or correlation, in all his training or growth. The social life gives the unconscious unity and the background of all his efforts and of all his attainments.

The subject matter of the school curriculum should mark a gradual differentiation out of the primitive unconscious unity of social life.

We violate the child's nature and render difficult the best ethical results by introducing the child too abruptly to a number of special studies, of reading, writing, geography, etc., out of relation to this social life.

The true center of correlation on the school subjects is not science, nor literature, nor history, nor geography, but the child's own social activities.

Education cannot be unified in the study of science, or so-called nature study, because apart from human activity, nature itself is not a unity; nature in itself is a number of diverse objects in space and time, and to attempt to make it the center of work by itself is to introduce a principle of radiation rather than one of concentration.

Literature is the reflex expression and interpretation of social experience; hence it must follow upon and not precede such experience. It, therefore, cannot be made the basis, although it may be made the summary of unification.

Once more, history is of educative value insofar as it presents phases of social life and growth. It must be controlled by reference to social life. When taken simply as history it is thrown into the distant past and becomes dead and inert. Taken as the record of man's social life and progress it becomes full of meaning. I believe, however, that it cannot be so taken excepting as the child is also introduced directly into social life.

The primary basis of education is in the child's powers at work along the same general constructive lines as those which have brought civilization into being.

The only way to make the child conscious of his social heritage is to enable him to perform those fundamental types of activity which make civilization what it is.

In the so-called expressive or constructive activities is the center of correlation.

This gives the standard for the place of cooking, sewing, manual training, etc., in the school.

They are not special studies which are to be introduced over and above a lot of others in the way of relaxation or relief, or as additional accomplishments. I believe rather that they represent, as types, fundamental forms of social activity; and that it is possible and desirable that the child's introduction into the more formal subjects of the curriculum be through the medium of these constructive activities.

The study of science is educational insofar as it brings out the materials and processes which make social life what it is.

One of the greatest difficulties in the present teaching of science is that the material is presented in purely objective form, or is treated as a new peculiar kind of experience which the child can add to that which he has already had. In reality, science is of value because it gives the ability to interpret and control the experience already had. It should be introduced, not as so much new subject matter, but as showing the factors already involved in previous experience and as furnishing tools by which that experience can be more easily and effectively regulated.

At present we lose much of the value of literature and language studies because of our elimination of the social element. Language is almost always treated in the books of pedagogy simply as the expression of thought. It is true that language is a logical instrument, but it is fundamentally and primarily a social instrument. Language is the device for communication; it is the tool through which one individual comes to share the ideas and feelings of others. When treated simply as a way of getting individual information, or as a means of showing off what one has learned, it loses its social motive and end.

There is, therefore, no succession of studies in the ideal school curriculum. If education is life, all life has, from the outset, a scientific aspect, an aspect of art and culture, and an aspect of communication. It cannot, therefore, be true that the proper studies for one grade are mere reading and writing, and that at a later grade, reading, or literature, or science, may be introduced. The progress is not in the succession of studies, but in the development of new attitudes towards, and new interests in, experience.

Education must be conceived as a continuing reconstruction of experience; the process and the goal of education are one and the same thing.

To set up any end outside of education, as furnishing its goal and standard, is to deprive the educational process of much of its meaning, and tends to make us rely upon false and external stimuli in dealing with the child.

ARTICLE FOUR—THE NATURE OF METHOD

I believe that the question of method is ultimately reducible to the question of the order of development of the child's powers and interests. The law for presenting and treating material is the law implicit within the child's own nature. Because this is so I believe the following statements are of supreme importance as determining the spirit in which education is carried on.

The active side precedes the passive in the development of the child nature; expression comes before conscious impression; the muscular development precedes the sensory; movements come before conscious sensations; I believe that consciousness is essentially motor or impulsive; that conscious states tend to project themselves in action.

The neglect of this principle is the cause of a large part of the waste of time and strength in school work. The child is thrown into a passive, receptive, or absorbing attitude. The conditions are such that he is not permitted to follow the law of his nature; the result is friction and waste.

Ideas also result from action and devolve for the sake of the better control of action. What we term reason is primarily the law of order or effective action. To attempt to develop the reasoning powers, the powers of judgment, without reference to the selection and arrangement of means in action, is the fundamental fallacy in our present methods of dealing with this matter. As a result we present the child with arbitrary symbols. Symbols are a necessity in mental development, but they have their place as tools for economizing effort; presented by themselves they are a mass of meaningless and arbitrary ideas imposed from without.

The image is the great instrument of instruction. What a child gets out of any subject presented to him is simply the images which he himself forms with regard to it.

If nine-tenths of the energy at present directed towards making the child learn certain things were spent in seeing to it that the child was forming proper images, the work of instruction would be indefinitely facilitated.

Much of the time and attention now given to the preparation and presentation of lessons might be more wisely and profitably expended in training the child's power of imagery and in seeing to it that he was continually forming definite vivid and growing images of the various subjects with which he comes in contact in his experience.

Interests are the signs and symptoms of growing power. I believe that they represent dawning capacities. Accordingly the constant and careful observation of interests is of the utmost importance for the educator.

These interests are to be observed as showing the state of development which the child has reached.

They prophesy the stage upon which he is about to enter.

Only through the continual and sympathetic observation of childhood's interests can the adult enter into the child's life and see what it is ready for, and upon what material it could work most readily and fruitfully.

These interests are neither to be humored nor repressed. To repress interest is to substitute the adult for the child, and so to weaken intellectual curiosity and alertness, to suppress initiative, and to deaden interest. To humor the interests is to substitute the transient for the permanent. The interest is always the sign of some power below; the important thing is to discover this power. To humor the interest is to fail to penetrate below the surface, and its sure result is to substitute caprice and whim for genuine interest.

The emotions are the reflex of actions.

To endeavor to stimulate or arouse the emotions apart from their corresponding activities is to introduce an unhealthy and morbid state of mind.

If we can only secure right habits of action and thought, with reference to the good, the true, and the beautiful, the emotions will for the most part take care of themselves.

Next to deadness and dullness, formalism and routine, our education is threatened with no greater evil than sentimentalism.

This sentimentalism is the necessary result of the attempt to divorce feeling from action.

ARTICLE FIVE—THE SCHOOL AND SOCIAL PROGRESS

I believe that education is the fundamental method of social progress and reform.

All reforms which rest simply upon the enactment of law, or the threatening of certain penalties, or upon changes in mechanical or outward arrangements, are transitory and futile.

Education is a regulation of the process of coming to share in the social consciousness; and the adjustment of individual activity on the basis of this social consciousness is the only sure method of social reconstruction.

This conception has due regard for both the individualistic and socialistic ideals. It is duly individual because it recognizes that this right character is not to be formed by merely individual precept, example, or exhortation, but rather by the influence of a certain form of institutional or community life upon the individual, and that the social organism through the school, as its organ, may determine ethical results.

In the ideal school we have the reconciliation of the individualistic and the institutional ideals.

The community's duty to education is, therefore, its paramount moral duty. By law and punishment, by social agitation and discussion, society can regulate and form itself in a more or less haphazard and chance way. But through education society can formulate its own purposes, can organize its own means and resources, and thus shape itself with definiteness and economy in the direction in which it wishes to move.

When society once recognizes the possibilities in this direction, and the obligations which these possibilities impose, it is impossible to conceive of the resources of time, attention, and money which will be put at the disposal of the educator.

It is the business of everyone interested in education to insist upon the school as the primary and most effective interest of social progress and reform in order that society may be awakened to realize what school stands for, and aroused to the necessity of endowing the educator with sufficient equipment properly to perform his task.

Education thus conceived marks the most perfect and intimate union of science and art conceivable in human experience.

The art of thus giving shape to human powers and adapting them to social service is the supreme art; one calling into its service the best of artists; no insight, sympathy, tact, executive power, is too great for such service.

With the growth of psychological service, giving added insight into individual structure and laws of growth; and with growth of social science, adding to our knowledge of the right organization of individuals, all scientific resources can be utilized for the purposes of education.

When science and art thus join hands the most commanding motive for human action will be reached, the most genuine springs of human conduct aroused, and the best service that human nature is capable of guaranteed.

The teacher is engaged, not simply in the training of individuals, but in the formation of the proper social life.

Every teacher should realize the dignity of his calling; he is a social servant set apart for the maintenance of proper social order and the securing of the right social growth.

In this way the teacher always is the prophet of the true God and the usherer in of the true kingdom of God.

THE MODERN PERIOD
(*1800-1900*)

SIGNIFICANT ACTIONS

THE DARTMOUTH
COLLEGE CASE

The Trustees of Dartmouth College v.
Woodward (1819)

. . . This court can be insensible neither to the magnitude nor delicacy of this question. The validity of a legislative act is to be examined, and the opinion of the highest law tribunal of a state is to be revised; an opinion which carries with it intrinsic evidence of the diligence, of the ability, and the integrity with which it was formed. On more than one occasion this court has expressed the cautious circumspection with which it approaches the consideration of such questions; and has declared that, in no doubtful case, would it pronounce a legislative act to be contrary to the constitution. But the American people have said, in the constitution of the United States, that "no state shall pass any bill of attainder, ex post facto law, or law impairing the obligation of contracts." In the same instrument they have also said, "that the judicial power shall extend to all cases in law and equity arising under this constitution." . . .

It can require no argument to prove that the circumstances of this case constitute a contract. An application is made to the crown for a charter to incorporate a religious and literary institution. In the application it is stated

From *Reports of Cases Argued and Decided in the Supreme Court of the United States,* Book IV, Wheaton, Vol. 4 (518–715) (Newark: The Lawyers' Co-operative Publishing Co., 1882), pp. 629–678.

that large contributions have been made for the object, which will be conferred on the corporation as soon as it shall be conveyed. Surely in this transaction every ingredient of a complete and legitimate contract is to be found.

The points for consideration are, 1. Is this contract protected by the Constitution of the United States? 2. Is it impaired by the acts under which the defendant holds?

. . .

The parties in this case differ less on general principles, less on the true construction of the constitution in the abstract, than on the application of those principles to this case, and on the true construction of the charter of 1769. This is the point on which the cause essentially depends. If the act of incorporation be a grant of political power, if it create a civil institution to be employed in the administration of the government, or if the funds of the college be public property, or if the state of New Hampshire, as a government, be alone interested in its transactions, the subject is one in which the legislature of the state may act according to its own judgment, unrestrained by any limitation of its power imposed by the constitution of the United States.

But if this be a private eleemosynary institution, endowed with a capacity to take property for objects unconnected with government, whose funds are bestowed by individuals on the faith of the charter; if the donors have stipulated for the future disposition and management of those funds in the manner prescribed by themselves, there may be more difficulty in the case, although neither the persons who have made these stipulations nor those for whose benefit they were made, should be parties to the cause. Those who are no longer interested in the property, may yet retain such an interest in the preservation of their own arrangements as to have a right to insist that those arrangements shall be held sacred. Or, if they have themselves disappeared, it becomes a subject of serious and anxious inquiry, whether those whom they have legally empowered to represent them forever may not assert all the rights which they possessed, while in being; whether, if they be without personal representatives who may feel injured by a violation of the compact, the trustees be not so completely their representatives, in the eye of the law, as to stand in their place, not only as respects the government of the college, but also as respects the maintenance of the college charter.

It becomes, then, the duty of the court most seriously to examine this charter, and to ascertain its true character. . . .

. . .

From this review of the charter, it appears that Dartmouth College is an eleemosynary institution, incorporated for the purpose of perpetuating the application of the bounty of the donors, to the specified objects of that bounty; that its trustees or governors were originally named by the founder, and invested with the power of perpetuating themselves; that they are not public officers, nor is it a civil institution, participating in the administration of government; but a charity school, or a seminary of education, incorporated for the preservation of its property, and the perpetual application of that property to the objects of its creation. . . .

This is plainly a contract to which the donors, the trustees, and the crown (to whose rights and obligations New Hampshire succeeds), were the original parties. It is a contract made on a valuable consideration. It is a contract for the security and disposition of property. It is a contract, on the faith of which real and personal estate has been conveyed to the corporation. It is then a contract within the letter of the constitution, and within its spirit also, unless the fact that the property is invested by the donors in trustees for the promotion of religion and education, for the benefit of persons who are perpetually changing, though the objects remain the same, shall create a particular exception, taking this case out of the prohibition contained in the constitution.

It is more than possible that the preservation of rights of this description was not particularly in the view of the framers of the constitution when the clause under consideration was introduced into that instrument. It is probable that interferences of more frequent recurrence, to which the temptation was stronger, and of which the mischief was more extensive, constituted the great motive for imposing this restriction on the state legislatures. But although a particular and a rare case may not, in itself, be of sufficient magnitude to induce a rule, yet it must be governed by the rule, when established, unless some plain and strong reason for excluding it can be given. It is not enough to say that this particular case was not in the mind of the convention when the article was framed, nor of the American people when it was adopted. It is necessary to go farther, and to say that, had this particular case been suggested, the language would have been so varied, as to exclude it, or it would have been made a special exception. The case being within the words of the rule, must be within its operation likewise, unless there be something in the literal construction so obviously absurd, or mischievous, or repugnant to the general spirit of the instrument, as to justify those who expound the constitution in making it an exception.

. . .

Almost all eleemosynary corporations, those which are created for the promotion of religion, of charity, or of education, are of the same character. The law of this case is the law of all. . . .

The opinion of the court, after mature deliberation, is, that this is a contract, the obligation of which cannot be impaired without violating the constitution of the United States. This opinion appears to us to be equally supported by reason, and by the former decisions of this court.

.   .   .

The obligations . . . which were created by the charter to Dartmouth College, were the same in the new that they had been in the old government. The power of the government was also the same. A repeal of this charter at any time prior to the adoption of the present constitution of the United States, would have been an extraordinary and unprecedented act of power, but one which could have been contested only by the restrictions upon the legislature, to be found in the constitution of the state. But the constitution of the United States has imposed this additional limitation, that the legislature of a state shall pass no act "impairing the obligation of contracts."

.   .   .

It results from this opinion, that the acts of the legislature of New Hampshire, which are stated in the special verdict found in this cause, are repugnant to the constitution of the United States; and that the judgment on this special verdict ought to have been for the plaintiffs. The judgment of the State Court must therefore be reversed.

FIRST COMPULSORY
SCHOOL ATTENDANCE LAW

An Act Concerning the Attendance of Children
at School (1852)

*Be it enacted by the Senate and House of Representatives in General Court
assembled, and by the authority of the same, as follows:*

Sect. 1.   Every person who shall have any child under his control,
between the ages of eight and fourteen years, shall send such child to some
public school within the town or city in which he resides, during at least
twelve weeks, if the public schools within such town or city shall be so long
kept, in each and every year during which such child shall be under his
control, six weeks of which shall be consecutive.

Sect. 2.   Every person who shall violate the provisions of the first section
of this act shall forfeit, to the use of such town or city, a sum not exceeding
twenty dollars, to be recovered by complaint or indictment.

Sect. 3.   It shall be the duty of the school committee in the several towns
or cities to inquire into all cases of violation of the first section of this act, and
to ascertain of the persons violating the same, the reasons, if any, for such
violation, and they shall report such cases, together with such reasons, if any,
to the town or city in their annual report; but they shall not report any cases
such as are provided for by the fourth section of this act.

From *Acts and Resolves Passed by the General Court of Massachusetts in the Year
1852*, pp. 170–171.

Sect. 4. If, upon inquiry by the school committee, it shall appear, or if upon the trial of any complaint or indictment under this act it shall appear, that such child has attended some school, not in the town or city in which he resides, for the time required by this act, or has been otherwise furnished with the means of education for a like period of time, or has already acquired those branches of learning which are taught in common schools, or if it shall appear that his bodily or mental condition has been such as to prevent his attendance at school, or his acquisition of learning for such a period of time, or that the person having control of such child, is not able, by reason of poverty, to send such child to school, or to furnish him with the means of education, then such person shall be held not to have violated the provisions of this act.

Sect. 5. It shall be the duty of the treasurer of the town or city to prosecute all violations of this act.

THE MORRILL ACT
OF 1862

An Act donating Public Lands to the several
States and Territories which may provide
Colleges for the Benefit of Agriculture and
the Mechanic Arts

*Be it enacted by the Senate and House of Representatives of the United States
of America in Congress assembled,* That there be granted to the several States,
for the purposes hereinafter mentioned, an amount of public land, to be
apportioned to each State a quantity equal to thirty thousand acres for each
senator and representative in Congress to which the States are respectively
entitled by the apportionment under the census of eighteen hundred and
sixty. . . .

. . .

Sec. 4. And be it further enacted, That all moneys derived from the
sale of the lands aforesaid by the States to which the lands are apportioned,
and from the sales of land scrip hereinbefore provided for, shall be invested
in stocks of the United States, or of the States, or some other safe stocks,
yielding not less than five per centum upon the par value of said stocks; and
that the moneys so invested shall constitute a perpetual fund, the capital of

From *The Statutes at Large of the United States,* Vol. XII (37th Congress), pp. 503–505.

which shall remain forever undiminished, (except so far as may be provided in section fifth of this act,) and the interest of which shall be inviolably appropriated, by each State which may take and claim the benefit of this act, to the endowment, support, and maintenance of at least one college where the leading object shall be, without excluding other scientific and classical studies, and including military tactics, to teach such branches of learning as are related to agriculture and the mechanic arts, in such manner as the legislatures of the States may respectively prescribe, in order to promote the liberal and practical education of the industrial classes in the several pursuits and professions in life.

Sec. 5.   And be it further enacted, That the grant of land and land scrip hereby authorized shall be made on the following conditions, to which . . . the previous assent of the several States shall be signified by legislative acts:

First. . . . A sum, not exceeding ten per centum upon the amount received by any State under the provisions of this act, may be expended for the purchase of lands for sites or experimental farms, whenever authorized by the respective legislatures of said States.

. . .

Third. Any State which may take and claim the benefit of the provisions of this act shall provide, within five years, at least not less than one college, as described in the fourth section of this act, or the grant to such State shall cease; and said State shall be bound to pay the United States the amount received of any lands previously sold, and that the title to purchasers under the State shall be valid.

Fourth. An annual report shall be made regarding the progress of each college, recording any improvements and experiments made, with their cost and results, and such other matters, including State industrial and economical statistics, as may be supposed useful; one copy of which shall be transmitted by mail free, by each, to all the other colleges which may be endowed under the provisions of this act, and also one copy to the Secretary of the Interior.

FOUNDING
OF THE U.S. OFFICE
OF EDUCATION

An Act To Establish a Department of Education
(Approved March 2, 1867)

Be it enacted by the Senate and House of Representatives of the United States of America in Congress assembled, That there shall be established, at the city of Washington, a department of education, for the purpose of collecting such statistics and facts as shall show the condition and progress of education in the several States and Territories, and of diffusing such information respecting the organization and management of schools and school systems, and methods of teaching, as shall aid the people of the United States in the establishment and maintenance of efficient school systems, and otherwise promote the cause of education throughout the country.

Sec. 2.   And be it further enacted, That there shall be appointed by the President, by and with the advice and consent of the Senate, a Commissioner of Education, who shall be intrusted with the management of the department herein established, and who shall receive a salary of $4,000 per annum, and who shall have authority to appoint 1 chief clerk of his department, who shall receive a salary of $2,000 per annum, 1 clerk who shall receive a salary of

From HR No. 276, 2nd Session, 39th Congress (1866–1867), *Congressional Globe*, Vol. 147, p. 199 of Appendix.

$1,800 per annum, and 1 clerk who shall receive a salary of $1,600 per annum, which said clerks shall be subject to the appointing and removing powers of the Commissioner of Education.

Sec. 3. And be it further enacted, That it shall be the duty of the Commissioner of Education to present annually to Congress a report embodying the results of his investigations and labors, together with a statement of such facts and recommendations as will, in his judgment, subserve the purpose for which this department is established. In the first report made by the Commissioner of Education under this act, there shall be presented a statement of the several grants of land made by Congress to promote education, and the manner in which these several trusts have been managed, the amount of funds arising therefrom, and the annual proceeds of the same, as far as the same can be determined.

Sec. 4. And be it further enacted, That the Commissioner of Public Buildings is hereby authorized and directed to furnish proper offices for the use of the department herein established.

THE KALAMAZOO CASE

Michigan State Supreme Court Decision (1874)

COOLEY, J.:

The bill in this case is filed to restrain the collection of such portion of the school taxes assessed against complainants for the year 1872, as have been voted for the support of the high school in that village, and for the payment of the salary of the superintendent. While, nominally, this is the end sought to be attained by the bill, the real purpose of the suit is wider and vastly more comprehensive than this brief statement would indicate, inasmuch as it seeks a judicial determination of the right of school authorities, in what are called union school districts of the state, to levy taxes upon the general public for the support of what in this state are known as high schools, and to make free by such taxation the instruction of children in other languages than the English. The bill is consequently, of no small interest to all the people of the state; and to a large number of very flourishing schools, it is of the very highest interest, as their prosperity and usefulness, in a large degree, depend upon the method in which they are supported, so that a blow at this method seems a blow at the schools themselves. . . .

The complainants rely upon two objections to the taxes in question, one of which is general, and the other applies only to the authority or action of this particular district. The general objection has already been indicated; the

From Charles E. Stuart *et al. v.* School District No. 1 of the Village of Kalamazoo, 30 *Michigan Reports* (1874–1875), pp. 69–84.

particular objection is that, even conceding that other districts in the state may have authority under special charters or laws, or by the adoption of general statutes, to levy taxes for the support of high schools in which foreign and dead languages shall be taught, yet this district has no such power, because the special legislation for its benefit, which was had in 1859, was invalid for want of compliance with the constitution in the forms of enactment, and it has never adopted the general law . . . by taking a vote of the district to establish a union school in accordance with its provisions, . . .

Whether this particular objection would have been worthy of serious consideration had it been made sooner, we must, after this lapse of time, wholly decline to consider. This district existed *de facto,* and we suppose *de jure,* also, for we are not informed to the contrary, when the legislation of 1859 was had, and from that time to the present it has assumed to possess and exercise all the franchises which are now brought in question, and there has since been a steady concurrence of action on the part of its people in the election of officers, in the levy of large taxes, and in the employment of teachers for the support of a high school. The state has aquiesced in this assumption of authority, and it has never, so far as we are advised, been questioned by any one until, after thirteen years user, three individual tax payers, out of some thousands, in a suit instituted on their own behalf, and to which the public authorities give no countenance, come forward in this collateral manner and ask us to annul the franchises. . . . If every municipality must be subject to be called into court at any time to defend its original organization and its franchises at the will of any dissatisfied citizen who may feel disposed to question them, and subject to dissolution, perhaps, or to be crippled in authority and powers if defects appear, however complete and formal may have been the recognition of its rights and privileges, on the part alike of the state and of its citizens, it may very justly be said that few of our municipalities can be entirely certain of the ground they stand upon, and that any single person, however honestly inclined, if disposed to be litigious, or over technical and precise, may have it in his power in many cases to cause infinite trouble, embarrassment and mischief.

. . .

The more general question which the record presents we shall endeavor to state in our own language, but so as to make it stand out distinctly as a naked question of law, disconnected from all considerations of policy or expediency; in which light alone are we at liberty to consider it. It is, as we understand it, that there is no authority in this state to make the high schools free by taxation levied on the people at large. The argument is that while there may be no constitutional provision expressly prohibiting such taxation, the general course of legislation in the state and the general understanding of the people have been such as to require us to regard the instruction in the classics and in living modern languages in these schools as in the nature not of practical and therefore necessary instruction for the benefit of the people at large, but rather as accomplishments for the few, to be sought after in the main by those best able to pay for them, and to be paid for by those who seek them, and not by general tax. And not only has this been the general state policy, but this higher learning of itself, when supplied by the state, is so far a matter of private concern to those who receive it that the courts ought to declare it incompetent to supply it wholly at the public expense. This is in substance, as we understand it, the position of the complainants in this suit.

. . .

It is not disputed that the dissemination of knowledge by means of schools has been a prominent object from the first, and we allude to the provision of the ordinance of 1787 on that subject, and to the donation of lands by congress for the purpose, . . .

Thus stood the law when the constitution of 1835 was adopted. The article on education in that instrument contained the following provisions:

"2. The legislature shall encourage by all suitable means the promotion of intellectual, scientific and agricultural improvement. . . .

"3. The legislature shall provide for a system of common schools, . . ."

. . . Two things are specially noticeable in these provisions: *first,* that they contemplated provision by the state for a complete system of instruction, beginning with that of the primary school and ending with that of the university; *second,* that while the legislature was required to make provisions for district schools for at least three months in each year, no restriction was imposed upon its power to establish schools intermediate to the common district school and the university, and we find nothing to indicate an intent to limit their discretion as to the class or grade of schools to which the proceeds of school lands might be devoted, or as to the range of studies or grade of instruction which might be provided for in the district schools.

. . .

The system adopted by the legislature, and which embraced a university and branches, and a common or primary school in every school district of the state, was put into successful operation, and so continued, with one important exception, until the adoption of the constitution of 1850. The exception relates to the branches of the university, which the funds of the university did not warrant keeping up, and which were consequently abandoned. Private schools to some extent took their place; but when the convention met to frame a constitution in 1850, there were already in existence, in a number of the leading towns, schools belonging to the general public system, which were furnishing instruction which fitted young men for the university. These schools for the most part had been organized under special laws, which, while leaving the primary school laws in general applicable, gave the districts a larger board of officers and larger powers of taxation for buildings and the payment of teachers. As the establishment and support of such schools were optional with the people, they encountered in some localities considerable opposition, which, however, is believed to have been always overcome, and the authority of the districts to provide instruction in the languages in these union schools was not, so far as we are aware, seriously contested. . . .

It now becomes important to see whether the constitutional convention and the people, in 1850, did any thing to undo what previously had been accomplished towards furnishing high schools as a part of the primary school system. The convention certainly did nothing to that end. On the contrary, they demonstrated in the most unmistakable manner that they cherished no such desire or purpose. . . .

The instrument submitted by the convention to the people and adopted by them provided for the establishment of free schools in every school district for at least three months in each year, and for the university. By the aid of these we have every reason to believe the people expected a complete collegiate education might be obtained. The branches of the university had ceased to exist; the university had no preparatory department, and it must either have been understood that young men were to be prepared for the university in the common schools, or else that they should go abroad for the purpose, or be prepared in private schools. Private schools adapted to the purpose were almost unknown in the state, and comparatively a very few persons were at that time of sufficient pecuniary ability to educate their children abroad. The inference seems irresistible that the people expected the tendency towards the establishment of high schools in the primary school districts would continue until every locality capable of supporting one was supplied. . . .

If these facts do not demonstrate clearly and conclusively a general state policy, beginning in 1817 and continuing until after the adoption of the present constitution, in the direction of free schools in which education, and at their option the elements of classical education, might be brought within the reach of all the children of the state, then, as it seems to us, nothing can demonstrate it. We might follow the subject further, and show that the subsequent legislation has all concurred with this policy, but it would be a waste of time and labor. We content ourselves with the statement that neither in our state policy, in our constitution, or in our laws, do we find the primary school districts restricted in the branches of knowledge which their officers may cause to be taught, or the grade of instruction that may be given, if their voters consent in regular form to bear the expense and raise the taxes for the purpose.

Having reached this conclusion, we shall spend no time upon the objection that the district in question had no authority to appoint a superintendent of schools, and that the duties of superintendency should be performed by the district board. We think the power to make the appointment was incident to the full control which by law the board had over the schools of the district, and that the board and the people of the district have been wisely left by the legislature to follow their own judgment in the premises.

It follows that the decree dismissing the bill was right, and should be affirmed.

The other justices concurred.

INVESTIGATION
OF SECONDARY
SCHOOL STUDIES

Report of the Committee of Ten (Submitted
December 4, 1893)

. . . The committee of ten, after a preliminary discussion on November 9, decided on November 10 to organize conferences on the following subjects: (1) Latin; (2) Greek; (3) English; (4) other modern languages; (5) mathematics; (6) physics, astronomy, and chemistry; (7) natural history (biology, including botany, zoology, and physiology); (8) history, civil government, and political economy; (9) geography (physical geography, geology, and meteorology). They also decided that each conference should consist of ten members. They then proceeded to select the members of each of these conferences, having regard in the selection to the scholarship and experience of the gentlemen named, to the fair division of the members between colleges on the one hand and schools on the other, and to the proper geographical distribution of the total membership. . . .

All the conferences sat for three days. Their discussions were frank, earnest, and thorough; but in every conference an extraordinary unity of opinion was arrived at. . . .

From *The Executive Documents of the House of Representatives*, 2nd Session, 53rd Congress (1893–1894) (Washington: Government Printing Office, 1895), pp. 1415 ff.

. . . The conferences which found their tasks the most difficult were the conferences on physics, astronomy, and chemistry; natural history; history, civil government, and political economy; and geography; and these four conferences make the longest and most elaborate reports, for the reason that these subjects are to-day more imperfectly dealt with in primary and secondary schools than are the subjects of the first five conferences. The experts who met to confer together concerning the teaching of the last four subjects in the list of conferences all felt the need of setting forth in an ample way what ought to be taught, in what order, and by what method. They ardently desired to have their respective subjects made equal to Latin, Greek, and mathematics in weight and influence in the schools; but they know that educational tradition was adverse to this desire, and that many teachers and directors of education felt no confidence in these subjects as disciplinary material. Hence the length and elaboration of these reports. In less degree, the conferences on English and other modern languages felt the same difficulties, these subjects being relatively new as substantial elements in school programmes.

. . .

It might have been expected that every conference would have demanded for its subject a larger proportion of time than is now commonly assigned to it in primary and secondary schools; but, as a matter of fact, the reports are noteworthy for their moderation in this respect, especially the reports on the old and well-established subjects. The Latin conference declares that "in view of the just demand for more and better work in several other subjects of the preparatory course, it seemed clear to the conference that no increase in the quantity of the preparation in Latin should be asked for." Among the votes passed by the Greek conference will be noticed the following: "That in making the following recommendations this conference desires that the average age at which pupils now enter college should be lowered rather than raised; and the conference urges that no addition be made in the advanced requirements in Greek for admission to college." The mathematical conference recommends that the course in arithmetic in elementary schools should be abridged, and recommends only a moderate assignment of time to algebra and geometry. The conference on geography says of the present assignment of time to geography in primary and secondary schools that "it is the judgment of the conference that too much time is given to the subject in proportion to the results secured. It is not their judgment that more time is given to the subject than it merits, but that either more should be accomplished or less time taken to attain it."

Anyone who reads these nine reports consecutively will be struck with the fact that all these bodies of experts desire to have the elements of their several subjects taught earlier than they now are, and that the conferences on all the subjects except the languages desire to have given in the elementary schools what may be called perspective views, or broad surveys, of their respective subjects—expecting that in later years of the school course parts of these same subjects will be taken up with more amplitude and detail. The conferences on Latin, Greek, and the modern languages agree in desiring to have the study of foreign languages begin at a much earlier age than now— the Latin conference suggesting by a reference to European usage that Latin be begun from three to five years earlier than it commonly is now. The conference on mathematics wish to have given in elementary schools not only a general survey of arithmetic, but also the elements of algebra, and concrete geometry in connection with drawing. The conference on physics, chemistry, and astronomy urge that nature studies should constitute an important part of the elementary school course from the very beginning. The conference on natural history wish the elements of botany and zoology to be taught in the primary schools. The conference on history wish the systematic study of history to begin as early as the tenth year of age, and the first two years of study to be devoted to mythology and to biography for the illustration of general history as well as of American history. Finally, the conference on geography recommend that the earlier course treat broadly of the earth, its environment and inhabitants, extending freely into fields which in later years of study are recognized as belonging to separate sciences.

. . .

If anyone feels dismayed at the number and variety of the subjects to be opened to children of tender age, let him observe that while these nine conferences desire each their own subject to be brought into the courses of elementary schools, they all agree that these different subjects should be correlated and associated one with another by the programme and by the actual teaching. . . .

. . . The committee of ten unanimously agree with the conferences. Ninety-eight teachers, intimately concerned either with the actual work of American secondary schools, or with the results of that work as they appear in students who come to college, unanimously declare that every subject which is taught at all in a secondary school should be taught in the same way and to the same extent to every pupil so long as he pursues it, no matter what the probable destination of the pupil may be, or at what point his education is to cease. . . .

Persons who read all the appended reports will observe the frequent occurrence of the statement that, in order to introduce the changes recommended, teachers more highly trained will be needed in both the elementary and the secondary schools. . . . The committee believe that the conferences have carried out wisely the desire of the committee, in that they have recommended improvements which, though great and seldom to be made at once and simultaneously, are by no means unattainable. The existing agencies for giving instruction to teachers already in service are numerous; and the normal schools and the colleges are capable of making prompt and successful efforts to supply the better trained and equipped teachers for whom the reports of the conferences call.

. . .

. . . The suggestions of the conferences presuppose that all the pupils of like intelligence and maturity in any subject study it in the same way and to the same extent, so long as they study it at all, this being a point on which all the conferences insist strongly. No provision is made, therefore, for teaching Latin or algebra or history to one portion of a class four times a week, and to another portion of the same class only thrice or twice a week. Such provisions are very common in American schools, but the recommendations of the conferences, if put into effect, would do away with all expenditures of this sort.

. . .

. . . If every subject studied at all is to be studied thoroughly and consecutively, every subject must receive an adequate time allotment. If every subject is to provide a substantial mental training, it must have a time allotment sufficient to produce that fruit. Finally, since selection must be exercised by or on behalf of the individual pupil, all the subjects between which choice is allowed should be approximately equivalent to each other in seriousness, dignity, and efficacy. Therefore they should have approximately equal time allotments. The conferences have abundantly shown how every subject which they recommend can be made a serious subject of instruction, well fitted to train the pupil's powers of observation, expression, and reasoning. It remains for makers of school programmes to give every subject the chance of developing a good training capacity by giving it an adequate time allotment.

. . .

. . . The committee present the following working programmes,[1] which they recommend for trial wherever the secondary school period is limited to four years. . . .

. . .

---

[1] Editors' note: The four programs were: *Classical* (3 foreign languages, one of which could be modern, e.g., French or German); *Latin-Scientific* (2 languages, one of which could be modern); *Modern Languages* (2 languages, both modern); and *English* (1 language, ancient or modern).

The most striking differences in the four programmes will be found, as is intimated in the headings, in the relative amounts of time given to foreign languages. In the classical programme the foreign languages get a large share of time; in the English programme a small share. In compensation, English and history are more developed in the English programme than in the classical.

.   .   .

Although the committee thought it expedient to include among the four programmes one which included neither Latin nor Greek, and one which included only one foreign language (which might be either ancient or modern), they desired to affirm explicitly their unanimous opinion that, under existing conditions in the United States as to the training of teachers and the provision of necessary means of instruction, the two programmes called respectively modern languages and English must in practice be distinctly inferior to the other two.

.   .   .

The secondary schools of the United States, taken as a whole, do not exist for the purpose of preparing boys and girls for colleges. Only an insignificant percentage of the graduates of these schools go to colleges or scientific schools. Their main function is to prepare for the duties of life that small proportion of all the children in the country—a proportion small in number, but very important to the welfare of the nation—who show themselves able to profit by an education prolonged to the eighteenth year, and whose parents are able to support them while they remain so long at school. There are, to be sure, a few private or endowed secondary schools in the country which make it their principal object to prepare students for colleges and universities, but the number of these schools is relatively small. A secondary school programme intended for national use must therefore be made for those children whose education is not to be pursued beyond the secondary school. The preparation of a few pupils for college or scientific school should in the ordinary secondary school be the incidental and not the principal object. At the same time, it is obviously desirable that the colleges and scientific schools should be accessible to all boys or girls who have completed creditably the secondary school course. Their parents often do not decide for them, four years before the college age, that they shall go to college, and they themselves may not, perhaps, feel the desire to continue their education until near the end of their school course. In order that any successful graduate of a good secondary school should be free to present himself at the gates of the college or scientific school of his choice, it is necessary that the colleges and scientific schools of the country should accept for admission to appropriate courses of their instruction the attainments of any youth who has passed creditably through a good secondary school course, no matter to what group of subjects he may have mainly devoted himself in the secondary school. As secondary school courses are now too often arranged, this is not a reasonable request to prefer to the colleges and scientific schools, because the pupil may now go through a secondary school course of a very feeble and scrappy nature—studying a little of many subjects and not much of any one, getting, perhaps, a little information in a variety of fields, but nothing which can be called a thorough training.

Now the recommendations of the nine conferences, if well carried out, might fairly be held to make all the main subjects taught in the secondary schools of equal rank for the purposes of admission to college or scientific school. They would all be taught consecutively and thoroughly, and would all be carried on in the same spirit; they would all be used for training the powers of observation, memory, expression, and reasoning; and they would all be good to that end, although differing among themselves in quality and substance. . . . But the committee are of the opinion that the satisfactory completion of any one of the four years' courses of study embodied in the foregoing programmes should admit to corresponding courses of study in colleges and scientific schools. They believe that this close articulation between the secondary schools and the higher institutions would be advantageous alike for the schools, the colleges, and the country.

. . .

The committee also wish to call attention to the service which schools of law, medicine, engineering, and technology, whether connected with universities or not, can render to secondary education by arranging their requirements for admission, as regards selection and range of subjects, in conformity with the courses of study recommended by the committee. By bringing their entrance requirements into close relation with any or all of the programmes recommended for secondary schools, these professional schools can give valuable support to high schools, academies, and preparatory schools.

THE PLESSY
VERSUS FERGUSON
DECISION

Homer Adolph Plessy v. John H. Ferguson
(May 18, 1896)

This case turns upon the constitutionality of an act of the general assembly of the state of Louisiana, passed in 1890, providing for separate railway carriages for the white and colored races. . . .

The information filed in the criminal district court charged in substance that Plessy, being a passenger between two stations within the state of Louisiana, was assigned by officers of the company to the coach used for the race to which he belonged, but he insisted upon going into a coach used by the race to which he did not belong. . . .

The petition for the writ of prohibition averred that petitioner was seven-eighths Caucasian and one-eighth African blood; that the mixture of colored blood was not discernible in him, and that he was entitled to every right, privilege, and immunity secured to citizens of the United States of the white race; and that, upon such theory, he took possession of a vacant seat in a coach where passengers of the white race were accommodated, and was ordered by the conductor to vacate said coach and take a seat in another assigned to persons of the colored race, and having refused to comply with such demand

From 163 U.S. 537, *United States Supreme Court Reports* (Rochester, N.Y.: The Lawyers' Cooperative Publishing Co., 1897), pp. 256–265.

he was forcibly ejected with the aid of a police officer, and imprisoned in the parish jail to answer a charge of having violated the above act.

The constitutionality of this act is attacked upon the ground that it conflicts both with the 13th Amendment of the Constitution, abolishing slavery, and the 14th Amendment, which prohibits certain restrictive legislation on the part of the states.

. . . That it does not conflict with the 13th Amendment, which abolished slavery and involuntary servitude, except as a punishment for crime, is too clear for argument. . . .

A statute which implies merely a legal distinction between the white and colored races—a distinction which is founded in the color of the two races, and which must always exist so long as white men are distinguished from the other race by color—has no tendency to destroy the legal equality of the two races, or re-establish a state of involuntary servitude. Indeed, we do not understand that the 13th Amendment is strenuously relied upon by the plaintiff in error in this connection.

. . . By the 14th Amendment, all persons born or naturalized in the United States, and subject to the jurisdiction thereof, are made citizens of the United States and of the state wherein they reside; and the states are forbidden from making or enforcing any law which shall abridge the privileges or immunities of citizens of the United States, or shall deprive any person of life, liberty, or property without due process of law, or deny to any person within their jurisdiction the equal protection of the laws.

. . .

The object of the amendment was undoubtedly to enforce the absolute equality of the two races before the law, but in the nature of things it could not have been intended to abolish distinctions based upon color, or to enforce social, as distinguished from political, equality, or a commingling of the two races upon terms unsatisfactory to either. Laws permitting, and even requiring their separation in places where they are liable to be brought into contact do not necessarily imply the inferiority of either race to the other, and have been generally, if not universally, recognized as within the competency of the state legislatures in the exercise of their police power. The most common instance of this is connected with the establishment of separate schools for white and colored children, which have been held to be a valid exercise of the legislative power even by courts of states where the political rights of the colored race have been longest and most earnestly enforced.

. . .

The distinction between laws interfering with the political equality of the Negro and those requiring the separation of the two races in schools, theaters, and railway carriages, has been frequently drawn by this court. . . .

It is claimed by the plaintiff in error that, in any mixed community, the reputation of belonging to the dominant race, in this instance the white race, is *property,* in the same sense that a right of action, or of inheritance, is property. Conceding this to be so, for the purposes of this case, we are unable to see how this statute deprives him of, or in any way affects his right to, such property. If he be a white man and assigned to a colored coach, he may have his action for damages against the company for being deprived of his so-called property. Upon the other hand, if he be a colored man and be so assigned, he has been deprived of no property, since he is not lawfully entitled to the reputation of being a white man.

. . . The reply to all this is that every exercise of the police power must be reasonable, and extend only to such laws as are enacted in good faith for the promotion of the public good, and not for the annoyance or oppression of a particular class. . . .

So far, then, as a conflict with the 14th Amendment is concerned, the case reduces itself to the question whether the statute of Louisiana is a reasonable regulation, and with respect to this there must necessarily be a large discretion on the part of the legislature. In determining the question of reasonableness it is at liberty to act with reference to the established usages, customs, and traditions of the people, and with a view to the promotion of their comfort, and the preservation of the public peace and good order. Gauged by this standard, we cannot say that a law which authorizes or even requires the separation of the two races in public conveyances is unreasonable or more obnoxious to the 14th Amendment than the acts of Congress requiring separate schools for colored children in the District of Columbia, the constitutionality of which does not seem to have been questioned, or the corresponding acts of state legislatures.

We consider the underlying fallacy of the plaintiff's argument to consist in the assumption that the enforced separation of the two races stamps the colored race with a badge of inferiority. If this be so, it is not by reason of anything found in the act, but solely because the colored race chooses to put that construction upon it. The argument necessarily assumes that if, as has been more than once the case, and is not unlikely to be so again, the colored race should become the dominant power in the state legislature, and should enact a law in precisely similar terms, it would thereby relegate the white race to an inferior position. We imagine that the white race, at least, would not acquiesce in this assumption. The argument also assumes that social prejudices may be overcome by legislation, and that equal rights cannot be secured to the Negro except by an enforced commingling of the two races. We cannot accept this proposition. If the two races are to meet on terms of social equality, it must be the result of natural affinities, a mutual appreciation of each other's merits and a voluntary consent of individuals. . . . Legislation is powerless to eradicate racial instincts or to abolish distinctions based upon physical differences, and the attempt to do so can only result in accentuating the difficulties of the present situation. If the civil and political rights of both races be equal, one cannot be inferior to the other civilly or politically. If one race be inferior to the other socially, the Constitution of the United States cannot put them upon the same plane.

.   .   .

The judgment of the court below is therefore affirmed.

PART 4

THE CONTEMPORARY PERIOD
(20th Century)

THE SOCIAL
CONTEXT

THROUGH distance, the encouraging advances made during the nineteenth century in government, science, and social progress make the 1800s seem near utopian when compared with such twentieth century events as two World Wars, rebellions and revolutions by the score, population explosions, rampant nationalism and communism, social and educational ferment, and the development of weapons that stagger the imagination. The present century presents a paradox: considerable social, economic, and scientific advances accompanied by continuing social unrest. It probably would not surprise Plato to learn that while man circles the earth in outer space he looks down upon war in one country and in an adjacent land sees simultaneous attempts to improve living standards and social and economic opportunity for the citizens, or that the positions of the two countries might well have been reversed in less than a decade's time. Certainly Plato would discover that many of the social, political, and educational issues with which he dealt have not been resolved and that some of them have hardly changed their appearance in intervening centuries.

A listing of social upheavals and wars since 1900 would require several pages. As a result of treaties, especially after the two World Wars, political maps of Europe, Asia, and Africa changed dramatically. Countries such as Serbia no longer exist. Former countries such as Poland have been restored. The colonial possessions of the major powers have diminished, in many instances totally; and in their place are new political entities, some of which emerged nearly ready to join modern industrial society, while others would be hard pressed to endure in the world of the eighteenth century. The United Nations now includes as members well over 100 separate countries, and the list increases yearly. Nationalism has marked the twentieth century as strongly as it stamped any previous age. New countries have discarded former political and social conventions in order to develop their own characteristic forms and structures. At the same time, advances in communication and transportation make countries more interdependent than ever before, and nowhere is this more recognizable than in the effort of nearly all countries to advance standards of living and increase national strength through education.

New alliances have appeared during this century and earnest but relatively fruitless attempts at world government have been made. Following various coalitions that existed before and during World War I, the League of Nations was established, as an outgrowth of a world weary with war, and in sequence to earlier attempts, such as the Hague Conferences, to deal with international problems. The League failed in its over-all purpose but not without achieving some successes, although power politics played more of a part in decisions than did democratic discussion. Like the League, the United Nations, which was formed after World War II, now tries to deal with the same types of problems but is similarly handicapped by the nationalistic and pluralistic aims of many of its members. Still it provides a forum for discussion and has been partially effective in attempts to maintain peace and encourage prosperity in various parts of the world. Certain of its organizations, especially UNESCO, offer both information and assistance to a host of countries to improve their social, educational and economic conditions.

The United States has become more involved in world affairs since the close of World War II. It has carried much of the post-World War II burden of restructuring the economies of European nations. With programs of international and special assistance, it has helped a variety of nations in their problems with agriculture, finance, education, public health, and the like. Through membership in alliances like NATO, the United States has helped guarantee the continued independence of a number of countries against foreign aggrandizement or internal unrest. This position is a reversal of that taken prior to World War II; before then the United States existed in relative isolation from the rest of the world, except for its economic involvement through trade and investment. Not the least of the ventures that the United States has undertaken involves educational programs in foreign lands, and during this century American education has become one of the models followed by other nations.

The twentieth century has seen virtually every conceivable form of government. In England the first political administration by the Labour Party held office. In France, governments have come and gone, displaying a range of forms from coalition to near-autocracy. Germany has been governed by both the Weimar Republic and the Nazis, and similar patterns were seen in Italy. Japan has experienced a totalitarian regime and a modified democracy. In Russia, monarchy gave way to communist rule—despotic under Stalin, somewhat more representative under his successors. Military dictators and cabals have ruled a number of countries. Elsewhere, trusteeships and mandates have held political power. In the United States, the two-party system has endured, but there have been times when one party was nearly supreme and other times when third parties exerted considerable influence. American government has reflected social demands and pressures as characterized by "The New Deal," "The Fair Deal," and "The Great Society."

The century has seen more industrial and scientific progress each successive decade than ever before. Discoveries and new technologies have been many, and breathtaking in their speed of arrival. But current national budgets typically include defense spending as their largest item; in some instances this item is larger than the total budget for all other concerns; and much of the present technological and scientific advance has resulted from research and production for war.

Major discoveries in physics, chemistry, biology and other fields are far too numerous to relate. Along with advances made in traditional fields has come the development of new areas of research and study in both the physical and social sciences—e.g., biochemistry, biophysics, social psychology. A person entering college today can obtain a degree in fields that did not appear in catalogue listings when he was born. Automation is rapidly making its imprint on contemporary culture and is bringing both solutions to existing needs and new problems—e.g., personal and economic displacement and re-allocation.

Economic growth has been staggering. The gross national product of most modern countries has doubled several times during the century, and the quantity of goods and services increases each decade. But there have been setbacks: the Depression of the 1930s produced mass unemployment and caused major changes in forms of government and political parties. Today most modern governments attempt a variety of controls to fend off dramatic economic setbacks, yet depressions are not a thing of the past; and economic hardship, even in advanced countries, continually reappears. The plight of underdeveloped countries is great; more people starve today than in the nineteenth century, and it is agreed that a majority of mankind is underfed and undernourished.

The population explosion imperils millions of lives. The growth rate of areas such as India and Central America has reduced the standard of living in many parts of these regions, despite efforts by local governments and outside assistance. At such base levels of subsistence there is little opportunity for funds to be diverted into general education and social welfare programs. It is estimated that half the world's children do not attend school, and that a majority of the rest receive unsatisfactory schooling. Millions of persons do not have educational opportunities beyond a rudimentary level; in no country is education yet equally available to even the most able candidates.

The separation of church and state in matters of public education is still an issue in Europe and America. By World War I the state controlled public education in practically every modern nation. In a period of increased taxation and rising expenses, the existence of private schools below the university level (and even at this level, in many cases) is hazardous. Though denominational schools continue to be opened, much concern is expressed over how long their supporters will be able or willing to contribute to a dual system of education. A major contemporary educational question concerns federal assistance to parochial schools.

Social protest has taken on new forms in this century. Though revolutions and uprisings continue, pacific demonstrations are frequently encountered. The ballot box, the organized march, the use of communication mechanisms, and what might be called passive resistance are commonly employed to show dissatisfaction with present institutions and programs. True both in western Europe and in the United States, this is notable because of the involvement of the younger members of society. Young persons are especially concerned with education: with quality, aims, methods, and materials. The unrest of minorities is more visible and more vocal. Though attempts are being made to relieve former injustices, many persons see these attempts as too little and too late. Self-determination and more proportional aid are demanded. "Black Power" is more than a slogan in the United States; it is a call for both autonomy and redress—in economics, society and education. A focus of this situation is the metropolitan school systems—e.g., New York City, Chicago, Philadelphia.

This introductory commentary will contain no special mention of European systems of education, and no commentary on specific European countries or their twentieth-century social and cultural events. This is not to suggest that American education in the present century has been unaware of or uninterested in happenings elsewhere. The origins of many of the following selections deny this. But more so than ever before, contemporary American education builds on its own past, on its developing cultural patterns and social expectations. Indeed, since 1900, and particularly since World War II, the United States has been an exporter of educational thought, innovations, and programs, more than it has been an importer.

The most accurate word to describe American education since the turn of the century, particularly in the past several decades, is enormity. More students are attending school than ever before, and they are attending school longer.[1] Budgets for education total in the billions; some state budgets for education now are greater than the annual federal budget was in the previous century. The same is true of texts, teachers, facilities, administrators and special service personnel, curricular offerings, auxiliary activities and so on.

---

[1] Even so it is estimated that by 1985 one-third of our adults will not have a high school diploma.

The following figures[2] provide an overview of the contemporary educational scene in the United States:

Schools: app. 89,000 elementary
          31,000 secondary
          2,400 community colleges, colleges, universities

Students:	K–8th grade, app.	32,000,000	(public school)
		5,000,000	(non public school)
	9th–12th grade, app.	13,000,000	(public)
		1,500,000	(non public)
	College/university, app.	4,500,000	(public)
	(working toward degrees)	2,000,000	(non public)
Teachers:	Elementary, app.	1,100,000	(public)
		150,000	(non public)
	Secondary, app.	850,000	(public)
		100,000	(non public)
	College/university, app.	300,000	(public)
		200,000	(non public)

School Superintendents, app.	13,000
Principals/Supervisors, app.	113,000
College/University Presidents, app.	2,400
Senior Administrators, College, app.	82,000
School Board Members, app.	110,000
College/University Trustees, app.	25,000

The Total Annual Educational Exenditure: app. $60 billion.

An example will emphasize this order of magnitude: some selected statistics from the Chicago public school system as of 1965 show:

600,000 students in the kindergarten-to-junior-college program, with an annual increase of enrollment of up to 20,000;

21,000 teachers and several thousand administrators and special service personnel;

a budget of more than $300,000,000;

millions of textbooks with annual purchases exceeding 1,000,000;

250,000 hearing and vision tests administered annually.

More than one-fourth of our citizens attend school regularly; and if the figure includes all who take a course of some kind or other during the year, the fraction is closer to one-half, so much has adult education grown. These

---

[2] USOE/NEA estimates for 1968–69.

percentages apparently will continue to climb: one of three Americans is under the age of 14 and about half are under 20 years of age. Furthermore, an increasingly complex industrial and service society demands of adults that they look to education in some form as a life-long activity; the necessity for this is seen easily by examining the help-wanted columns of a metropolitan newspaper and by noting the types of jobs available and the requirements demanded.

At the beginning of this century somewhat less than 10 percent of the eligible age group graduated from secondary school; the current figure is about 75 percent. In 1900 it was the exceptional (at least numerically) young man or woman who attended college, but now nearly 40 percent of high school graduates enter a senior institution and about 25 percent graduate. Totally there are more college students today than there were high school students a few decades ago.

A major factor accounting for increased enrollments is extended legal dismissal ages. By 1960 all states required attendance to at least age 16 (though hardly all students in the required age bracket were enrolled), some to age 18.

Of late, the rapid development of the junior colleges has caused perhaps the most notable increase at any level of schooling; but at both ends of the educational ladder, increased attendance has been remarkable. Kindergartens now are found in a majority of today's metropolitan areas as well as in many less-populated regions. Adult education in its many forms touches tens of millions of persons each year, in community colleges, college extension programs, high school evening classes and by correspondence.

Such growth has strained the teacher-training capacity of colleges and universities to the breaking point and, inevitably, has resulted in emergency certification of thousands of teachers who do not meet the requirements of the various states and licensing agencies. A wide assortment of training programs has developed, with much accompanying debate over what constitutes the proper preparation for teaching. New and experimental programs for preparing teachers have appeared both as a result of the demand for greater teacher competence and from arguments over what method of preparation is most suitable and most fruitful. Nearly all states now require at least the B.A. degree for elementary teaching, and a number of states require that secondary teachers obtain a master's degree before full certification is granted. A significant change in teacher preparation has been the raising of standards requisite to certification, accompanied by more controls imposed by state agencies.

The annual sums of money necessary to finance the over-all educational enterprise have climbed into billions of dollars. Meanwhile, sources of support have changed; where once the community raised most of the funds necessary to maintain and expand the schools, now the state is a full-fledged partner, and sometimes the major partner, in support. As well, the federal government increasingly underwrites specific educational programs, and it is this particular support that has raised heated arguments. Should the federal government become involved in education, in the absence of any direct constitutional obligation to do so? If so, in what ways? With what restraints should it be charged? It is one thing, say those who fear federal involvement, for the government to grant land to the states for the general support of education, but quite another thing for the government to become involved with aspects of the curriculum. It seems clear, however, that federal involvement is sure to grow and to extend into additional areas of education—either through direct financial aid or through the enforcement of legislation aimed at equalizing opportunity.

Centralization of financial support has taken place alongside a continuation of local administration of the schools. Management of the schools still is the primary responsibility of local boards of education, within operating limits imposed by the states. Recently the number of school districts in the nation has decreased; in 1950 they numbered 75,000, but today the total is around 22,000. From such reduction, increased efficiency of operation has resulted and the curriculum has been strengthened, particularly in less populous areas.

The curriculum itself is much broadened since the turn of the century. Course listings in a typical metropolitan high school today far exceed the listing of courses offered a century ago in the typical college. The progressive emphasis on preparation for social living was reflected in curriculum changes during the period 1920–1940 especially. With society as a referent and potential occupations of the student in mind, curriculum makers introduced a variety of courses unknown to the nineteenth century.

Across the country today are found a wide array of programs and optional courses. Most high schools and junior high schools require a concentration in "basic" subjects, but this core can be augmented according to the choice of the student, the wishes of his parents, and the advice of school counselors. College entrance requirements control much of the curriculum for the college-bound student during grades 7–12, but for other students choices can be many and varied.

The nineteenth century saw the beginnings of "formal" educational research with the work of psychologists and physiologists in learning theory and child growth and development. From these beginnings, research in all aspects of education has grown. Virtually every area of education is subject to experimentation and inquiry. Learning occupies the attention of educational investigators. Curriculum and methods of instruction also are targets for study. The design of school buildings for optimum efficiency, the most productive organizational structures, the differential learning capacities of various groups, the social and personal variables that affect educational achievement—these and many more aspects of education are being explored by school personnel, by researchers in colleges and universities, and by investigators in government, foundations, and research laboratories. Reports stemming from this activity inundate libraries and research centers; for example, more than 4,000 studies in reading have been recorded within the past several decades. Such effort has developed much information that is helpful to the teacher and to the learner, some findings that are basic to our understanding of teaching and learning, and much too that apparently has little or no relevance to education. Progress has been made, but few final answers are yet in sight; and education in all its configurations is increasingly recognized as an extremely difficult, often intangible, process.

Until about 1950, little money from the federal government was available for educational research or for the support of special programs. Such assistance as existed provided for lunch programs, vocational training of particular kinds, and quite specialized support in the way of facilities and equipment. Assistance with research and curriculum came mainly from private foundations, e.g., Ford, Carnegie, Rockefeller. But since the 1950s, the federal government has increased grants to schools, districts, and colleges for work in curriculum, training projects and research. With some of these grants have come special stipulations concerning the expenditures of funds. Agencies like the Office of Economic Opportunity, the National Science Foundation, the Office of Education, the Bureau of Public Health and others now finance educational programs and allied research. Federal support of education for such activities presently exceeds the total support of private foundations. This is a relatively new pattern for the United States, but a relatively old one for many European countries. The primary issue, of course, is over the amount of control that the government should exert.

Today's educational dilemmas still include: what shall be taught and to whom? who shall control the curriculum? who shall support the schools and the various programs? are standards being lowered? what is needed not only for today's conditions of life but also for tomorrow's? are we abandoning traditional moral and spiritual values in our education? are the schools trespassing increasingly on the time-honored prerogatives of the home, the church, and the society's formal and informal organizations? are we holding our own, through the building of an educated citizenry, with other nations? what can we do to provide equal educational opportunities for all our citizens?

Former issues continue, with new conditions bringing them into focus. An example is the contemporary relationship of Church and State. The years since 1940 have witnessed more Supreme Court cases involving religion and the public schools than did the entire nineteenth century. But also, some issues of the past have disappeared. For example, it is accepted now that the state, or local authority, has the right, even the duty, to tax the citizenry for support of the schools, even beyond high school.

In the twentieth century, American education has faced a number of problems engendered by the great increase in numbers of educational clients to be served, by the shifting social trends of the years since 1900, by the expectations held for further progress, and, of course, by the lack of agreed-upon solutions to problems and issues of many types. The range of hope, promise, accomplishment—and, alike, of problems, issues, and debates—of education in this century in America is indicated by the selections which constitute the final section of this anthology.

THE
EDUCATIONAL
ISSUES

THE development of education in twentieth century America has been shaped by three primary forces: (1) a philosophical debate which has prompted a continuing examination of the purposes to be served by the schools and the methodologies to be used to meet those purposes, (2) psychological findings which have led to better definitions of appropriate relationships between teacher and student and between student and learning materials, and (3) a sociological climate which has attempted clarifications of the problems of public school secularization, desegregation of educational facilities, the control of education, and the role of the federal government in promoting educational opportunities.

The roots of the philosophical debate are found in the basic argument between those who believe in the intrinsic values of knowledge and those who believe in the instrumental values of knowledge. The former tend to reside philosophically in the idealist camp and to promote an education geared to intellectual development, the acknowledged artistic and scientific works of mankind, and the fostering of disciplined habits of character. The latter tend to reside in the pragmatist camp and to promote an education geared to social as well as intellectual development, useful knowledge from contemporary life, and the expansion of creative individual potentialities. The former are often labelled "traditional" by the latter. The latter are often called "anti-intellectual" by the former.

Although this basic argument has raged, in one form or another, since Plato's clash with the Sophists, it has reached a new peak in the United States since the turn of the current century. The idealistic and the pragmatic spirits are both deeply ingrained in American culture. Ralph Waldo Emerson, Bronson Alcott, and William T. Harris helped to hold the idealist position in ascendency through the later nineteenth century. William James and John Dewey brought the pragmatic sentiment to the forefront as the twentieth century was born.

The basic position of pragmatism was most concisely stated by James (p. 303), who characterized it as an attitude which focuses upon the results of actions and upon the efficiency of the methods employed in attaining those results. Dewey translated the tenets of this philosophy into an educational view which he felt fit the structure of American democracy and the social-psychological needs of the learner in a far more productive way than did the then-accepted patterns of education. Dewey's philosophy, usually referred to as experimentalism, was the driving influence behind the progressive education movement which became a dominant force in education, particularly at the elementary school level, and the source of a great deal of controversy. Dewey insisted that the student must be a more active agent in the learning process, and that education should allow and encourage the learner to solve problems through reflective and creative thinking and scientific inquiry. The product of Deweyan schooling should be a socially-adapted individual able to control himself and cope with his environment.

This point of view was given support by the British philosopher Alfred North Whitehead in his essay *The Aims of Education* (p. 325), one of the most widely read modern works on education. Further support came from George Counts who, however, saw Dewey as short-sighted in his delineation of the scope and power of education. In his controversial work *Dare the School Build a New Social Order* (p. 335), Counts depicts an educational system which would be the primary force in bringing about social reforms. Although his somewhat utopian philosophy of "reconstructionism" gained few adherents, its fundamental ideas are linked with recent tendencies toward greater governmental attention to education and increased usage of power by members of the teaching profession.

The influence of Dewey's pragmatic-democratic viewpoint was revealed quite clearly in the 1918 document *The Cardinal Principles of Secondary Education* (p. 460), which signaled a separation from the rigid curricular patterns of the past, including those recommended by the Committee of Ten, and called for a secondary school curriculum flexible enough to meet the social and educational needs of all American youth. This new curricular formulation also clearly reflected the earlier thinking of Horace Mann and Herbert Spencer in its content and emphasis.

Karl Jaspers (p. 330) contends that man is not solely a biological being, something explainable in physiological and scientific terms. Man's second nature is his culture built up through social experience and over time. Spirit, tradition, character—these shape the individual, are major determinants of the conditions of his existence, and indicate the true value of man. A developed human being aware of cultural and historical continuity and the brotherhood of man is the aim of education. An early existentialist, Jaspers sets forth the need for man's becoming aware of himself, his situation, and his potential through the developmental process of education.

Enthusiasm over the "new education" proposed by Dewey, which crystal-lized in the progressive movement in education, led to oversimplifications of his message and, particularly in the 1930s, to some exaggerated versions of his concepts of "felt needs," "permissiveness," and "problem solving," among others. Some of the extremes of the movement were criticized by Dewey himself, as can be witnessed in his 1938 examination of the old and new approaches, in his *Experience and Education* (p. 340).

The mark of "progressivism" upon American education was vociferously regretted by a number of learned critics in the 1950s and, indeed, is still lamented to the present day. Robert M. Hutchins and Arthur Bestor are representative of those who have taken issue with what are seen as the anti-intellectual tendencies of the progressive movement. Hutchins' analysis (p. 351) calls for the seeking of a firmer basis for all education, centering in the significant mental achievements of mankind and concentrating on the task of strengthening each student's ability to think for himself, to reason, and to understand. Bestor (p. 367) condemns contemporary education for its lack of standards, its proliferation of non-intellectual subject matter, and its lack of attention to those subjects which he feels are essential. A more middle-of-the-road position was concisely stated by the Harvard faculty's report on the status and content of general education (p. 464).

Two viewpoints which were directly or indirectly stimulated by Dewey's ideas were those of I. B. Berkson (p. 384) and Ashley Montagu (p. 379). Both deal with education in its relationship with the larger culture of com-munity and humanity, Berkson expressing hope for a rebirth of the idealist spirit and Montagu explaining the dire need for schooling which humanizes the individual.

Excellent analyses of the politics of modern American education can be found in the recent statements of David Riesman (p. 372), Myron Lieberman (p. 390), Admiral H. G. Rickover (p. 408), and James Bryant Conant (p. 413). Each examines the elements in the controlling powers behind public education which have tended to impede progress, regardless of the educational philosophy in effect.

Paralleling the debate regarding the overall purposes and methodologi-cal structures of education has been the development of somewhat conflicting psychologies of education, especially of learning. Although some of the lines of demarcation have been obliterated, the basic positions of the two major schools of psychology were enunciated early in the twentieth century by the connectionist E. L. Thorndike (p. 310) and the behaviorist John B. Watson (p. 316), with their emphasis on the elements of experience and their inter-relationship; and by the gestaltist Kurt Koffka (p. 321), with his emphasis on the organization of experience. More recent expansions upon and combinings of these fundamental viewpoints which have had an increasing effect upon educational practices and instructional materials are provided by Jean Piaget (p. 345), B. F. Skinner (p. 357), and Jerome Bruner (p. 398). Indeed the last two authors seem to be bridging the gap between educational psychology and educational philosophy as they place their theories in the largest possible context of meaning. To these advances can be added the psychology and philosophy of Dr. Maria Montessori (p. 307), which, though articulated early in the century, has enjoyed a rebirth in the United States in recent years.

Of at least equal importance to the studies made in educational theory and psychological findings have been clarifications of issues inherited from the preceding century: for instance, the many problems of church-state separation and the emotion-laden problem of providing equal educational opportunities for Negro Americans and other minority groups.

The relationship between the government and private schools was clarified in the Oregon Case decision by the Supreme Court of the United States (p. 423). The decision was a victory for preservation of the pluralistic tradition in American education. A number of other Supreme Court verdicts concerned with educational matters have added clarification to the interpretation of intent to separate Church and State, as set forth in the Constitution. Decisions in the Cochran case (p. 425), the Everson case (p. 427), the McCollum case (p. 433), and the Zorach case (p. 441), delimited the boundaries of governmental support of parochial educational enterprises and of religious instruction. In *Engel v. Vitale* (p. 451), and in *Murray v. Curlett* and *Abington v. Schempp* (p. 455), the Court defined the place of religious ceremonies in the public schools.

Basic statements on the provision of educational opportunities for Negroes were made by Booker T. Washington (p. 295) and W. E. B. DuBois (p. 300), early in the century. The more conservative Washington adhered to a position of compromise with the white power structure, suggesting that Negroes be given opportunities primarily in the fields of industrial and agricultural arts. The radical DuBois foreshadowed the activist movement which since has exerted great pressure in all aspects of the civil rights movement. A high point in this movement was reached in 1954 when the Supreme Court handed down its decision in the Brown desegreation case (p. 447), although this event by no means resolved the problem.

Another issue which has grown more visible in the twentieth century is that of increasing federal involvement in education. This involvement is felt through the many U.S. Supreme Court decisions bearing on education and through Congressional legislation, particularly during the past two decades.

Two of the major enactments of the 1950s were the forming of the National Science Foundation (p. 469) and the 1959 National Defense Education Act (p. 472), which has since been expanded. Both of these measures were geared to the national need for strengthening instruction in vital subject matter areas and for supporting research. Another national problem, that of unemployment, prompted the federal government to devise ways of attacking a basic ill behind the situation—unemployability. The result was the Economic Opportunity Act of 1964 (p. 474), with its provisions for such programs as the Job Corps, work-study opportunities, and adult education for illiterates.

In his message on education (p. 478), delivered on January 12, 1965, President Johnson reviewed the condition of the educational enterprise and made a series of recommendations which triggered a far-reaching federal program for the improvement of educational opportunities and facilities throughout the nation. Among the actions taken by the Congress were the Elementary and Secondary Education Act (p. 480), the National Arts and Humanities Foundation Act (p. 484), and the Higher Education Act (p. 487).[1] This legislation ushers in what may lead to a new phase in the development of American education.

In response to the increasing number of court actions involving (college) student discipline, a U.S. District Court in Missouri issued in 1968 a memorandum stating judicial standards of procedure and substance applicable to discipline cases in tax-supported colleges and universities. Intended for guidance, this memorandum seems likely to have far-reaching effect, for it is a specific statement dealing with an increasingly urgent issue in higher education in the United States (as well as abroad): the relative roles of higher educational institutions and the courts in regard to students—their rights, obligations, exemptions, and so on. The memorandum (p. 491) necessarily discusses such matters as the mutual concern of the college and the courts with

---

[1] Not included in the selections of this section are two pieces of legislation enacted in 1968 by the 90th Congress: (1) Public Law 90–575, "An Act To Amend the Higher Education Act of 1965, the National Defense Education Act of 1958, the National Vocational Student Loan Insurance Act of 1965, the Higher Education Facilities Act of 1963, and related Acts," and (2) Public Law 90–576, "An Act to amend the Vocational Education Act of 1963, and for other purposes."

P.L. 90–575, an omnibus higher education bill, extended several prior basic education laws and added certain new programs and provisions. This legislation in effect consolidated former legislative provisions, coordinated a number of existing programs and extended support for higher education into new curricular areas and to an increased constituency.

P.L. 90–576 will increase the involvement of colleges and universities in vocational education. This law recognized society's need for increased support of vocational training, the rapid expansion of technical knowledge and the parallel need for requisite skills, and the requirement that vocational-technical training keep apace of academic-professional education as a worthy and necessary goal of the overall educational enterprise. In effect P.L. 90–576 combines under a single act much of the vocational educational legislation enacted by Congress since its passage in 1917 of the Smith-Hughes Act (support for vocational training).

justice, the respective realms of the college and the courts, the aims and purposes of education, institutional rights, student rights, and societal expectations. It is interesting to note in the memorandum the many references to educational figures and groups both past and present, another example of both the longitudinal and the contemporary basis of educational discussion and involvement.

INDEX OF BASIC ISSUES

THE CONTEMPORARY PERIOD
(20th Century)

MAJOR THOUGHTS

THE CASE
FOR INDUSTRIAL
EDUCATION

AUTHOR:

Booker T. Washington (*1856–1915*)

WORK:

THE NEGRO
IN THE SOUTH (1907)

From Hampton and Tuskeegee and other large educational centers the idea of industrial education has spread throughout the South, and there are now scores of institutions that are giving this kind of training in a most effective and helpful manner; so that, in my opinion, the greatest thing that we have accomplished for the Negro race within the last twenty-five years has been to rid his mind of all idea of labor's being degrading. This has been no inconsiderable achievement. If I were asked to point out the greatest change accomplished for the Negro race, I would say that it was not a tangible, physical change, but a change of the spirit—the new idea of our people with respect to Negro labor.

From *The Negro in the South,* by Booker T. Washington and W. E. B. DuBois, the William Levi Bull Lectures for 1907 (Philadelphia: George W. Jacobs & Company, 1907), pp. 50–55, 59–62, 72–74.

Industrial education has had another value wherever it has been put into practice, that is in starting the Negro off in his new life in a natural, logical, sensible manner instead of allowing him to be led into temptation to begin life in an artificial atmosphere without any real foundation.

All races that have reached success and have influenced the world for righteousness have laid their foundation at one stage of their career in the intelligent and successful cultivation of the soil; that is, have begun their free life by coming into contact with earth and wood and stone and minerals. Any people that begins on a natural foundation of this kind, rises slowly but naturally and gradually in the world.

In my work at Tuskeegee and in what I have endeavored to accomplish in writing and in speaking before the public, I have always found it important to stick to nature as closely as possible, and the same policy should be followed with a race. If you will excuse my making a personal reference, just as often as I can when I am at home, I like to get my hoe and dig in my garden, to come into contact with real earth, or to touch my pigs and fowls. Whenever I want new material for an address or a magazine article, I follow the plan of getting away from the town with its artificial surroundings and getting back into the country, where I can sleep in a log cabin and eat the food of the farmer, go among the people at work on the plantations and hear them tell their experiences. I have gotten more material in this way than I have by reading books.

Many of these seemingly ignorant people, while not educated in the way that we consider education, have in reality a very high form of education—that which they have gotten out of contact with nature. Only a few days ago I heard one of these old farmers, who could neither read nor write, give a lesson before a Farmers' Institute that I shall never forget. The old man got up on the platform and began with this remark: "I'se had no chance to study science, but I'se been making some science for myself," and then he held up before the audience a stalk of cotton with only two bolls on it. He said he began his scientific work with that stalk. Then he held up a second stalk and showed how the following year he had improved the soil so that the stalk contained four bolls, and then he held up a third stalk and showed how he had improved the soil and method of cultivation until the stalk contained six bolls, and so he went through the whole process until he had demonstrated to his fellow farmers how he had made a single stalk of cotton produce twelve or fourteen bolls. At the close of the old man's address somebody in the audience asked what his name was. He replied, "When I didn't own no home and was in debt, they used to call me old Jim Hill, but now that I own a home and am out of debt, they call me 'Mr. James Hill.' "

In the previous chapter I referred to the practical benefit that could be achieved in foreign mission fields through economic and industrial development. Now that industrial education is understood and appreciated by the Negro in America, the question which has the most practical value to you and to me is what effect has this kind of development had upon the moral and religious life of the Negro right here in America since the race became free.

By reason of the difficulty in getting reliable and comprehensive statistics, it is not easy to answer this question with satisfaction, but I believe that enough facts can be given to show that economic and industrial development has wonderfully improved the moral and religious life of the Negro race in America, and that, just in proportion as any race progresses in this same direction, its moral and religious life will be strengthened and made more practical.

Let me first emphasize the fact that in order for the moral and religious life to be strengthened we must of necessity have industry, but along with industry there must be intelligence and refinement. Without these two elements combined, the moral and religious lives of the people are not very much helped.

.   .   .

It should always be borne in mind that, for any person of any race, literary education alone increases his want; and, if you increase these wants without at the same time training the individual in a manner to enable him to supply these increased wants, you have not always strengthened his moral and religious basis.

The same principle might be illustrated in connection with South Africa. In that country there are six millions of Negroes. Notwithstanding this fact, South Africa suffers today perhaps as never before for lack of labor. The natives have never been educated by contact with the white man in the same way as has been true of the American Negro. They have never been educated in the day school nor in the Sunday-school nor in the church, nor in the industrial school or college; hence their ambitions have never been awakened, their wants have not been increased, and they work perhaps two days out of the week and are in idleness during the remaining portion of the time. This view of the case I had confirmed in a conversation with a gentleman who had large interests in South Africa.

How different in the Southern part of the United States where we have eight millions of black people! Ask any man who has had practical experience in using the masses of these people as laborers and he will tell you that in proportion to their progress in the civilization of the world, it is difficult to find any set of men who will labor in a more satisfactory way. True, these people have not by any means reached perfection in this regard, but they have advanced on the whole much beyond the condition of the South Africans. The trained American Negro has learned to want the highest and best in our civilization, and as we go on giving him more education, increasing his industrial efficiency and his love of labor, he will soon get to the point where he will work six days out of each week.

But as to the result of industrial training. Following the example of the modern pedagogue, let me begin with that which I know most about, the Tuskeegee Institute. This institution employs one of its officers who spends a large part of his time in keeping in close contact with our graduates and former students. He visits them in their homes and in their places of employment and not only sees for himself what they are doing, but gets the testimony of their neighbors and employers, and I can state positively that not ten percent of the men and women who have graduated from Tuskeegee Institute or who have been there long enough to understand the spirit and methods of that institution can be found today in idleness in any part of the country. They are at work because they have learned the dignity and beauty and civilizing influence and, I might add, Christianizing power of labor; they have learned the degradation and demoralizing influence of idleness; they have learned to love labor for its own sake and are miserable unless they are at work. I consider labor one of the greatest boons which our Creator has conferred upon human beings.

Further, after making careful investigation, I am prepared to say that there is not a single man or woman who holds a diploma from the Tuskeegee Institute who can be found within the walls of any penitentiary in the United States.

. . .

May I add that, out of my own observation and experience in the heart of the South during the last twenty-five years, I have learned that the man of my race who has some regular occupation, who owns his farm, is a taxpayer and perhaps has a little money in the bank, is the most reliable and helpful man in the Sunday-school, in the church, and in all religious endeavor. The man who has gotten upon his feet in these directions is almost never charged with crime, but is the one who has the respect and the confidence of both races in his community.

I can give you no better idea of the tremendous advance which the Negro has made since he became free than to say that largely through the influence of industrial education the race has acquired ownership in land that is equal in area to the combined countries of Belgium and Holland. This, for a race starting in poverty and ignorance forty years ago, it seems to me, is a pretty good record.

I would not have you understand that I emphasize material possessions as the chief thing in life or as an object within itself. I emphasize economic growth because the civilization of the world teaches that the possession of a certain amount of material wealth indicates the ability of a race to exercise self-control, to plan today for tomorrow, to do without today in order that it may possess tomorrow. In other words, a race, like an individual, becomes highly civilized and useful in proportion as it learns to use the good things of this earth, not as an end, but as a means toward promoting its own moral and religious growth and the prosperity and happiness of the world. This is what I advocate for my race; it is what I would advocate for any race.

THE PLIGHT
OF THE NEGRO

AUTHOR:

W. E. B. DuBois (1868–1963)

WORK:

THE NEGRO IN THE SOUTH
(1907)

It was promised that disfranchisement would lead to more careful attention to the Negro's moral and economic advancement. It has on the contrary stripped them naked to their enemies; discriminating laws of all sorts have followed, the administration of other laws has become harsher and more unfair, school funds have been curtailed and education discouraged, and mobs and murder have gone on.

If the new policy has been a farce politically and socially, how much more has it failed as an economic cure-all! No sooner was it proclaimed from the house-tops than the rift in the lute appeared. "We do not want educated Negro artisans," cried the white artisans, and they enforced their demands by their votes and by mob violence. "We do not want to raise the Negro: we

From *The Negro in the South,* by Booker T. Washington and W. E. B. DuBois, the William Levi Bull Lectures for 1907 (Philadelphia: George W. Jacobs & Company, 1907), pp. 112–115, 119–121.

want to put him in his place and keep him there," cried the dominant forces of the South. Then those northerners who had lightly embraced the fair sounding program of limited labor training and disfranchisement found themselves grasping the air.

Not only this, but the South itself faced a puzzling paradox. The industrial revolution was demanding labor; it was demanding intelligent labor, while the supposed political and social exigencies of the situation called for ignorance and subserviency. It was an impossible contradiction and the South today knows it.

What is it that makes a successful laboring force? It is laborers of education and natural intelligence, reasonably satisfied with their conditions, inspired with certain ideals of life, and with a growing sense of self-respect and self-reliance. How is the caste system of the South influencing the Negro laborer? It is systematically restricting his development; it is restricting his education so that the public common schools of the South except in a few cities are worse this moment than they were twenty years ago; it is seeking to kill self-respect by putting upon the accident of color every mark of humiliation that it can invent; it is discouraging self-reliance by treating a class of men as wards and children; it is killing ambition by drawing a color line instead of a line of desert and accomplishment; and finally, through these things, it is encouraging crime, and by the unintelligent and brutal treatment of criminals, it is developing more crime.

This general attitude toward the main laboring class reflects itself less glaringly but as certainly in the treatment even of white laborers. So long as white labor must compete with black labor, it must approximate black labor conditions—long hours, small wages, child labor, labor of women, and even peonage. Moreover it can raise itself above black labor only by a legalized caste system which will cut off competition and this is what the South is straining every nerve to create.

. . .

It is becoming distinctly obvious to Negroes that today, in modern economic organization, the one thing that is giving the workman a chance is intelligence and political power, and that it is utterly impossible for a moment to suppose that the Negro in the South is going to hold his own in the new competition with immigrants if, on the one hand, the immigrant has access to the best schools of the community and has equal political power with other men to defend his rights and to assert his wishes, while, on the other hand, his black competitor is not only weighed down by past degradation, but has few or no schools and is disfranchised.

The question then as to what will happen in the South when immigration comes, is a very simple question. If the Negro is kept disfranchised and ignorant and if the new foreign immigrants are allowed address to the schools and given votes as they undoubtedly will be, then there can ensue only accentuated race hatred, the spread of poverty and disease among Negroes, the increase of crime, and the gradual murder of the eight millions of black men who live in the South except in so far as they escape North and bring their problems there as thousands will.

If on the contrary, with the coming of the immigrants to the South, there is given to the Negro equal educational opportunity and the chance to cast his vote like a man and be counted as a man in the councils of the county, city, state, and nation, then there will ensure that competition between men in the industrial world which, if it is not altogether just, is at least better than slavery and serfdom.

There of course could be strong argument that the nation owes the Negro something better than harsh industrial competition just after slavery, but the Negro does not ask the payment of debts that are dead. He is perfectly willing to come into competition with immigrants from any part of the world, to welcome them as human beings and as fellows in the struggle for life, to struggle with them and for them and for a greater South and a better nation. But the black man certainly has a right to ask, when he starts into this race, that he be allowed to start with hands untied and brain unclouded.

WHAT PRAGMATISM MEANS

AUTHOR:

William James (*1842–1910*)

WORK:

PRAGMATISM: A NEW NAME FOR SOME OLD WAYS OF THINKING (1907)

. . . The pragmatic method is primarily a method of settling metaphysical disputes that otherwise might be interminable. Is the world one or many? fated or free? material or spiritual? Here are notions either of which may or may not hold good of the world; and disputes over such notions are unending. The pragmatic method in such cases is to try to interpret each notion by tracing its respective practical consequences. What difference would it practically make to any one if this notion rather than that notion were true? If no practical difference whatever can be traced, then the alternatives mean prac-

From *Pragmatism: A New Name for Some Old Ways of Thinking* by William James (New York: Longmans, Green, and Co., 1907), from Lecture II, "What Pragmatism Means," pp. 45–46, 49–52, 53–55, 67–68.

tically the same thing, and all dispute is idle. Whenever a dispute is serious, we ought to be able to show some practical difference that must follow from one side or the other's being right.

. . .

It is astonishing to see how many philosophical disputes collapse into insignificance the moment you subject them to this simple test of tracing a concrete consequence. There can *be* no difference anywhere that doesn't *make* a difference elsewhere—no difference in abstract truth that doesn't express itself in a difference in concrete fact and in conduct consequent upon that fact, imposed on somebody, somehow, somewhere, and somewhen. The whole function of philosophy ought to be to find out what definite difference it will make to you and me, at definite instants of our life, if this world-formula or that world-formula be the true one.

There is absolutely nothing new in the pragmatic method. Socrates was an adept at it. Aristotle used it methodically. Locke, Berkeley, and Hume made momentous contributions to truth by its means. Shadworth Hodgson keeps insisting that realities are only what they are "known as." But these forerunners of pragmatism used it in fragments: they were preluders only. Not until in our time has it generalized itself, become conscious of a universal mission, pretended to a conquering destiny. I believe in that destiny, and I hope I may end by inspiring you with my belief.

Pragmatism represents a perfectly familiar attitude in philosophy, the empiricist attitude, but it represents it, as it seems to me, both in a more radical and in a less objectionable form than it has ever yet assumed. A pragmatist turns his back resolutely and once for all upon a lot of inveterate habits dear to professional philosophers. He turns away from abstraction and insufficiency, from verbal solutions, from bad *a priori* reasons, from fixed principles, closed systems, and pretended absolutes and origins. He turns towards action and towards power. That means the empiricist temper regnant and the rationalist temper sincerely given up. It means the open air and possibilities of nature, as against dogma, artificiality, and the pretence of finality in truth.

At the same time it does not stand for any special results. It is a method only. But the general triumph of that method would mean an enormous change in what I called in my last lecture the "temperament" of philosophy. Teachers of the ultra-rationalistic type would be frozen out, much as the courtier type is frozen out in republics, as the ultramontane type of priest is frozen out in protestant lands. Science and metaphysics would come much nearer together, would in fact work absolutely hand in hand.

. . .

Theories thus become instruments, not answers to enigmas, in which we can rest. We don't lie back upon them, we move forward, and, on occasion, make nature over again by their aid. Pragmatism unstiffens all our theories, limbers them up and sets each one at work. Being nothing essentially new, it harmonizes with many ancient philosophic tendencies. It agrees with nominalism for instance, in always appealing to particulars; with utilitarianism in emphasizing practical aspects; with positivism in its disdain for verbal solutions, useless questions and metaphysical abstractions.

All these, you see, are *anti-intellectualist* tendencies. Against rationalism as a pretension and a method pragmatism is fully armed and militant. But, at the outset, at least, it stands for no particular results. It has no dogmas, and no doctrines save its method. As the young Italian pragmatist Papini has well said, it lies in the midst of our theories, like a corridor in a hotel. Innumerable chambers open out of it. In one you may find a man writing an atheistic volume; in the next some one on his knees praying for faith and strength; in a third a chemist investigating a body's properties. In a fourth a system of idealistic metaphysics is being excogitated; in a fifth the impossibility of metaphysics is being shown. But they all own the corridor, and all must pass through it if they want a practicable way of getting into or out of their respective rooms.

No particular results then, so far, but only an attitude of orientation, is what the pragmatic method means. *The attitude of looking away from first things, principles, "categories," supposed necessities; and of looking towards last things, fruits, consequences, facts.*

. . .

. . . Pragmatism is uncomfortable away from facts. Rationalism is comfortable only in the presence of abstractions. This pragmatist talk about truths in the plural, about their utility and satisfactoriness, about the success with which they "work," etc., suggests to the typical intellectualist mind a sort of coarse lame second-rate makeshift article of truth. Such truths are not real truth. Such tests are merely subjective. As against this, objective truth must be something non-utilitarian, haughty, refined, remote, august, exalted. It must be an absolute correspondence of our thoughts with an equally absolute reality. It must be what we *ought* to think unconditionally. The conditioned ways in which we *do* think are so much irrelevance and matter for psychology. Down with psychology, up with logic, in all this question!

See the exquisite contrast of the types of mind! The pragmatist clings to facts and concreteness, observes truth at its work in particular cases, and generalizes. Truth, for him, becomes a class-name for all sorts of definite working-values in experience. For the rationalist it remains a pure abstraction, to the bare name of which we must defer. When the pragmatist undertakes to show in detail just *why* we must defer, the rationalist is unable to recognize the concretes from which his own abstraction is taken. He accuses us of denying truth; whereas we have only sought to trace exactly why people follow it and always ought to follow it. Your typical ultra-abstractionist fairly shudders at concreteness: other things equal, he positively prefers the pale and spectral. If the two universes were offered, he would always choose the skinny outline rather than the rich thicket of reality. It is so much purer, clearer, nobler.

THE PRIMACY
OF SENSORY
DEVELOPMENT

AUTHOR:

Maria Montessori (*1870–1952*)

WORK:

THE MONTESSORI
METHOD (1909)

Our aim in education in general is two-fold, biological and social. From the biological side we wish to help the natural development of the individual, from the social standpoint it is our aim to prepare the individual for the environment. Under this last head technical education may be considered as having a place, since it teaches the individual to make use of his surroundings. The education of the senses is most important from both these points of view. The development of the senses indeed precedes that of superior intellectual activity and the child between three and seven is in the period of formation.

We can, then, help the development of the senses while they are in this

From *The Montessori Method* by Maria Montessori, translated by Anne E. George (New York: Schocken Books, Inc., 1964), pp. 215–217, 218, 221–222, 223. George translation first published in New York by Frederick A. Stokes in 1912. Present edition contains an introduction by J. McV. Hunt. Reprinted by permission.

period. We may graduate and adapt the stimuli just as, for example, it is necessary to help the formation of language before it shall be completely developed.

All education of little children must be governed by this principle—to help the natural *psychic* and *physical development* of the child.

The other aim of education (that of adapting the individual to the environment) should be given more attention later on when the period of intense development is past.

These two phases of education are always interlaced, but one or the other has prevalence according to the age of the child. Now, the period of life between the ages of three and seven years covers a period of rapid physical development. It is the time for the formation of the sense activities as related to the intellect. The child in this age develops his senses. His attention is further attracted to the environment under the form of passive curiosity.

The stimuli, and not yet the reasons for things, attract his attention. This is, therefore, the time when we should methodically direct the sense stimuli, in such a way that the sensations which he receives shall develop in a rational way. This sense training will prepare the ordered foundation upon which he may build up a clear and strong mentality.

It is, besides all this, possible with the education of the senses to discover and eventually to correct defects which today pass unobserved in the school. Now the time comes when the defect manifests itself in an evident and irreparable inability to make use of the forces of life about him. (Such defects as deafness and nearsightedness.) This education, therefore, is physiological and prepares directly for intellectual education, perfecting the organs of sense, and the nerve-paths of projection and association.

But the other part of education, the adaptation of the individual to his environment, is indirectly touched. We prepare with our method the infancy of the *humanity of our time.* The men of the present civilization are preeminently observers of their environment because they must utilize to the greatest possible extent all the riches of this environment.

· · ·

The education of the senses makes men observers, and not only accomplishes the general work of adaptation to the present epoch of civilization, but also prepares them directly for practical life. We have had up to the present time, I believe, a most imperfect idea of what is necessary in the practical living of life. We have always started from ideas, and have *proceeded thence to motor activities;* thus, for example, the method of education has always been to teach intellectually, and then to have the child follow the principles he has been taught. In general, when we are teaching, we talk about the object which interests us, and then we try to lead the scholar, when he has understood, to perform some kind of work with the object itself; but often the scholar who has understood the idea finds great difficulty in the execution of the work which we give him, because we have left out of his education a factor of the utmost importance, namely, the perfecting of the senses. I may, perhaps, illustrate this statement with a few examples. We ask the cook to buy only "fresh fish." She understands the idea, and tries to follow it in her marketing, but, if the cook has not been trained to recognize through sight and smell the signs which indicate freshness in the fish, she will not know how to follow the order we have given her.

. . .

But very often sense education is most difficult for the adult, just as it is difficult for him to educate his hand when he wishes to become a pianist. It is necessary to begin the education of the senses in the formative period, if we wish to perfect this sense development with the education which is to follow. The education of the senses should be begun methodically in infancy, and should continue during the entire period of instruction which is to prepare the individual for life in society.

Aesthetic and moral education are closely related to this sensory education. Multiply the sensations, and develop the capacity of appreciating fine differences in stimuli, and we *refine* the sensibility and multiply man's pleasures.

Beauty lies in harmony, not in contrast; and harmony is refinement; therefore, there must be a fineness of the senses if we are to appreciate harmony. The aesthetic harmony of nature is lost upon him who has coarse senses. The world to him is narrow and barren. In life about us, there exist inexhaustible fonts of aesthetic enjoyment, before which men pass as insensible as the brutes seeking their enjoyment in those sensations which are crude and showy, since they are the only ones accessible to them.

. . .

. . . Indeed, when with *intellectual culture* we believe ourselves to have completed education, we have but made thinkers, whose tendency will be to live without the world. We have not made practical men. If, on the other hand, wishing through education to prepare for practical life, we limit ourselves to exercising the psychomotor phase, we lose sight of the chief end of education, which is to put man in direct communication with the external world.

THE LAWS OF LEARNING

AUTHOR:

Edward L. Thorndike (1874–1949)

WORK:

EDUCATIONAL PSYCHOLOGY: BRIEFER COURSE (1914)

The arts and sciences serve human welfare by helping man to change the world, including man himself, for the better. The word education refers especially to those elements of science and art which are concerned with changes in man himself. Wisdom and economy in improving man's wants and in making him better able to satisfy them depend upon knowledge—first, of what his nature is, apart from education, and second, of the laws which govern changes in it. It is the province of educational psychology to give such knowledge of the original nature of man and of the laws of modifiability or learning, in the case of intellect, character and skill.

A man's nature and the changes that take place in it may be described in

From *Educational Psychology: Briefer Course* by Edward L. Thorndike (New York: Teachers College, Columbia University, 1921), pp. 1–5, 69–71. Copyright 1914 by Edward L. Thorndike. Reprinted by permission.

terms of the responses—of thought, feeling, action and attitude—which he makes, and of the bonds by which these are connected with the situations which life offers. Any fact of intellect, character or skill means a tendency to respond in a certain way to a certain situation—involves a *situation* or state of affairs influencing the man, *a response* or state of affairs in the man, and a *connection* or bond whereby the latter is the result of the former.

ORIGINAL *VERSUS* LEARNED TENDENCIES

Any man possesses at the very start of his life—that is, at the moment when the ovum and spermatozoon which are to produce him have united—numerous well-defined tendencies to future behavior.[1] Between the situations which he will meet and the responses which he will make to them, pre-formed bonds exist. It is already determined by the constitution of these two germs, that under certain circumstances he will see and hear and feel and act in certain ways. His intellect and morals, as well as his bodily organs and movements, are in part the consequence of the nature of the embryo in the first moment of its life. What a man is and does throughout life is a result of whatever constitution he has at the start and of all the forces that act upon it before and after birth. I shall use the term "original nature" for the former and "environment" for the latter.

THE PROBLEMS OF ORIGINAL NATURE

Elementary psychology acquaints us with the fact that men are, apart from education, equipped with tendencies to feel and act in certain ways in certain circumstances—that the response to be made to a situation may be determined by man's inborn organization. It is, in fact, a general law that, other things being equal, the response to any situation will be that which is by original nature connected with that situation, or with some situation like it. Any neurone will, when stimulated, transmit the stimulus, other things being equal, to the neurone with which it is by inborn organization most closely connected. The basis of intellect and character is this fund of unlearned tendencies, this original arrangement of the neurones in the brain.

---

[1] Since the term, *behavior,* has acquired certain technical meanings in its use by psychologists, and since it will be frequently used in this book, the meaning which will be attached to it here should perhaps be stated. I use it to refer to those activities of thought, feeling, and conduct in the broadest sense which an animal—here, man— exhibits, which are omitted from discussion by the physics, chemistry and ordinary physiology of today, and which are referred by popular usage to intellect, character, skill and temperament. Behavior, then, is not contrasted with, but inclusive of, conscious life.

The original connections may develop at various dates and may exist for only limited times; their waxing and waning may be sudden or gradual. They are the starting point for all education or other human control. The aim of education is to perpetuate some of them, to eliminate some, and to modify or redirect others. They are perpetuated by providing the stimuli adequate to arouse them and give them exercise, and by associating satisfaction with their action. They are eliminated by withholding these stimuli so that they abort through disuse, or by associating discomfort with their action. They are redirected by substituting, in the *situation-connection-response* series, another response instead of the undesirable original one; or by attaching the response to another situation in connection with which it works less or no harm, or even positive good.

It is a first principle of education to utilize any individual's original nature as a means to changing him for the better—to produce in him the information, habits, powers, interests and ideals which are desirable.

The behavior of man in the family, in business, in the state, in religion, and in every other affair of life is rooted in his unlearned, original equipment of instincts and capacities. All schemes of improving human life must take account of man's original nature, most of all when their aim is to reverse or counteract it.

NAMES FOR ORIGINAL TENDENCIES

Three terms, *reflexes, instincts,* and *inborn capacities,* divide the work of naming these unlearned tendencies. When the tendency concerns a very definite and uniform response to a very simple sensory situation, and when the connection between the situation and the response is very hard to modify and is also very strong so that it is almost inevitable, the connection or response to which it leads is called a reflex. Thus the knee-jerk is a very definite and uniform response to the simple sense-stimulus of sudden hard pressure against a certain spot. It is hard to lessen, to increase, or otherwise control the movement, and, given the situation, the response almost always comes. When the response is more indefinite, the situation more complex, and the connection more modifiable, instinct becomes the customary term. Thus one's misery at being scorned is too indefinite a response to too complex a situation and is too easily modifiable to be called a reflex. When the tendency is to an extremely indefinite response or set of responses to a very complex situation, and when the connection's final degree of strength is commonly due to very large contributions from training, it has seemed more appropriate to replace reflex and instinct by some term like capacity, or tendency, or potentiality. Thus an original tendency to respond to the circumstances of school education by achievement in learning the arts and sciences is called the capacity for scholarship.

There is, of course, no gap between reflexes and instincts, or between instincts and the still less easily describable original tendencies. The fact is that original tendencies range with respect to the nature of the responses from such as are single, simple, definite, uniform within the individual and only slightly variable amongst individuals, to responses that are highly compound, complex, vague, and variable within one individual's life and amongst individuals. They range with respect to the nature of the situation from simple facts like temperature, oxygen or humidity, to very complex facts like "meeting suddenly and unexpectedly a large animal when in the dark without human companions," and include extra-bodily, bodily, and what would be commonly called purely mental, situations. They range with respect to the bond or connection from slight modifiability to great modifiability, and from very close likeness amongst individuals to fairly wide variability.

Much labor has been spent in trying to make hard and fast distinctions between reflexes and instincts and between instincts and these vaguer predispositions which are here called capacities. It is more useful and more scientific to avoid such distinctions in thought, since in fact there is a continuous gradation. . . .

It is a fact of original nature that certain states of affairs are satisfying to a man's neurones—are such as they do nothing to avoid, whereas other states of affairs are annoying to the neurones—stimulate them to do something until the annoying state of affairs gives way to a satisfying one which they do nothing to avoid. That is, reflexes, instincts and capacities (1) always take place in time, (2) sometimes produce or modify the inner conscious life of the animal whose they are, and (3) sometimes change the organism more or less permanently. The neurones which are concerned in them have roughly the original tendency (4) to do nothing different when their life processes are being facilitated and to make whatever changes are in their repertory when their life processes are disturbed.

The first and second of these general tendencies everyone properly takes for granted. No more need be said of them.

The third fact noted above refers to the capacity for permanent modifiability or "learning," which is, from the point of view of man's welfare, the most important fact in nature.

THE LAWS OF LEARNING

The Law of Use

To the situation, "a modifiable connection being made by him between a situation S and a response R," man responds originally, other things being equal, by an increase in the strength of that connection. By the strength of a connection is meant roughly the probability that it will be made when the situation recurs. Greater probability that a connection will be made means a greater probability for the same time, or an equal probability but for a longer time.[2] Thus, strengthening the connection between "being asked how many six and seven are" and "saying 'thirteen,' " may mean that the probability of that response during the next six days is eight out of ten instead of seven out of ten, or that the probability is seven out of ten for sixty days instead of for forty.

The Law of Disuse

To the situation, "a modifiable connection not being made by him between a situation S and a response R, during a length of time T," man responds originally, other things being equal, by a decrease in the strength of that connection.

The tendencies of use and disuse may be listed together under one name as the *Law of Exercise.*

As corollaries of the law of use we have the facts that the degree of strengthening of a connection will depend upon the vigor and duration as well as the frequency of its making. To think "6 + 7 = 13" attentively and for ten seconds will thus increase the strength of its bond more than to think of it lightly and for only half a second.

The Law of Effect

To the situation, "a modifiable connection being made by him between an S and an R and being accompanied or followed by a satisfying state of affairs" man responds, other things being equal, by an increase in the strength of that connection. To a connection similar, save that an *annoying* state of affairs goes with or follows it, man responds, other things being equal, by a decrease in the strength of the connection.

As a corollary to the law of effect we have the fact that the strengthening effect of satisfyingness varies with its intimacy with the bond in question as well as with the degree of satisfyingness. Such intimacy, or closeness of connection between the satisfying state of affairs and the bond it affects, may be due to close temporal sequence or to attentiveness to the situation and response. Other things being equal, the same degree of satisfyingness will act more strongly on a bond made two seconds previously than on one made two minutes previously—more strongly on a bond between a situation and a response attended to closely than on a bond equally remote in time in an unnoticed series.

---

[2] Certain additions and qualifications are necessary to make this definition adequate, but it will serve provisionally.

These tendencies for connections to grow strong by exercise and satisfying consequences and to grow weak by disuse and annoying consequences should, if importance were the measure of the space to be allotted to topics, preëmpt at least half of this inventory. As the features of man's original equipment whereby all the rest of that equipment is modified for use in a complex civilized world, they are of universal importance in education. They are the effective original forces in what has variously been called nurture, training, learning by experience, or intelligence.

THE PSYCHOLOGY
OF BEHAVIORISM

AUTHOR:

John B. Watson (1878–1958)

WORK:

BEHAVIORISM (1924)

THE OLD AND NEW PSYCHOLOGY CONTRASTED

Two opposed points of view are still dominant in American psychological thinking—introspective or subjective psychology, and behaviorism or objective psychology. Until the advent of behaviorism in 1912, introspective psychology completely dominated American university psychological life.

The conspicuous leaders of introspective psychology in the first decade of the twentieth century were E. B. Titchener of Cornell and William James of Harvard. The death of James in 1910 and the death of Titchener in 1927 left introspective psychology without emotional leadership. Although Titchener's psychology differed in many points from that of William James, their fundamental assumptions were the same. In the first place, both were of German origin. In the second place, and of more importance, both claimed that *consciousness is the subject matter of psychology.*

Behaviorism, on the contrary, holds that the subject matter of human psychology *is the behavior of the human being.* Behaviorism claims that consciousness is neither a definite nor a usable concept. The behaviorist, who has been trained always as an experimentalist, holds, further, that belief in the existence of consciousness goes back to the ancient days of superstition and magic.

The great mass of the people even today has not yet progressed very far away from savagery—it wants to believe in magic. The savage believes that incantations can bring rain, good crops, good hunting, that an unfriendly voodoo doctor can bring disaster to a person or to a whole tribe; that an enemy who has obtained a nail paring or a lock of your hair can cast a harmful spell over you and control your actions. There is always interest and news in magic. Almost every era has its new magic, black or white, and its new magician. Moses had his magic: he smote the rock and water gushed out. Christ had his magic: he turned water into wine and raised the dead to life. Coué had his magic word formula. Mrs. Eddy had a similar one.

Magic lives forever. As time goes on, all of these critically undigested, innumerably told tales get woven into the folk lore of the people. Folk lore in turn gets organized into religions. Religions get caught up into the political and economic network of the country. Then they are used as tools. The public is forced to accept all of the old wives' tales, and it passes them on as gospel to its children's children.

The extent to which most of us are shot through with a savage background is almost unbelievable. Few of us escape it. Not even a college education seems to correct it. If anything, it seems to strengthen it, since the colleges themselves are filled with instructors who have the same background. Some of our greatest biologists, physicists, and chemists, when outside of their laboratories, fall back upon folk lore which has become crystallized into religious concepts. These concepts—these heritages of a timid savage past— have made the emergence and growth of scientific psychology extremely difficult.

. . .

THE BEHAVIORIST'S PLATFORM

The behaviorist asks: Why don't we make what we can *observe* the real field of psychology? Let us limit ourselves to things that can be observed, and formulate laws concerning only those things. Now what can we observe? We can observe *behavior—what the organism does or says.* And let us point out at once: that *saying* is doing—that is, *behaving.* Speaking overtly or to ourselves (thinking) is just as objective a type of behavior as baseball.

The rule, or measuring rod, which the behaviorist puts in front of him always is: Can I describe this bit of behavior I see in terms of "stimulus and response"? By stimulus we mean any object in the general environment or any change in the tissues themselves due to the physiological condition of the animal, such as the change we get when we keep an animal from sex activity, when we keep it from feeding, when we keep it from building a nest. By response we mean anything the animal does—such as turning toward or away from a light, jumping at a sound, and more highly organized activities such as building a skyscraper, drawing plans, having babies, writing books, and the like.

.   .   .

DEFINITION OF BEHAVIORISM

Definitions are not as popular today as they once were. The definition of any one science, physics, for example, would necessarily include the definition of all other sciences. And the same is true of behaviorism. About all that we can do in the way of defining a science at the present time is to mark a ring around that part of the whole of natural science that we claim particularly as our own.

Behaviorism . . . is, then, a natural science that takes the whole field of human adjustments as its own. Its closest scientific companion is physiology. Indeed you may wonder, as we proceed, whether behaviorism can be differentiated from that science. It is different from physiology only in the grouping of its problems, not in fundamentals or in cental viewpoint. Physiology is particularly interested in the functioning of parts of the animal—for example, its digestive system, the circulatory system, the nervous system, the excretory systems, the mechanics of neural and muscular response. Behaviorism, on the other hand, while it is intensely interested in all of the functioning of these parts, is intrinsically interested in what the whole animal will do from morning to night and from night to morning.

The interest of the behaviorist in man's doings is more than the interest of the spectator—he wants to control man's reactions as physical scientists want to control and manipulate other natural phenomena. It is the business of behavioristic psychology to be able to predict and to control human activity. To do this it must gather scientific data by experimental methods. Only then can the trained behaviorist predict, given the stimulus, what reaction will take place; or, given the reaction, state what the situation or stimulus is that has caused the reaction.

.   .   .

The behaviorist has often been criticized for this emphasis upon response. Some psychologists seem to have the notion that the behaviorist is interested only in the recording of minute muscular responses. Nothing could be further from the truth. Let me emphasize again that the behaviorist is primarily interested in the behavior of the whole man. From morning to night he watches him perform his daily round of duties. If it is brick-laying, he would likely measure the number of bricks he can lay under different conditions, how long he can go without dropping from fatigue, how long it takes him to learn his trade, whether we can improve his efficiency or get him to do the same amount of work in a less period of time. In other words, the response the behaviorist is interested in is the commonsense answer to the question "what is he doing and why is he doing it?" Surely with this as a general statement, no one can distort the behaviorist's platform to such an extent that it can be claimed that the behaviorist is merely a muscle physiologist.

.   .   .

HOW TO STUDY PERSONALITY

In youth personality changes rapidly: Naturally if personality is but a cross section at any given age of the complete organization of an individual, you can see that this cross section must change at least slightly every day—but not too rapidly for us to get a fair picture from time to time. Personality changes most rapidly in youth when habit patterns are forming, maturing and changing. Between 15 and 18 a female changes from a child to a woman. At 15 she is but the playmate of boys and girls of her own age. At 18 she becomes a sex object to every man. After 30 personality changes very slowly owing to the fact . . . that by the time most individuals, unless constantly stimulated by a new environment, are pretty well settled into a humdrum way of living. Habit patterns become set. If you have an adequate picture of the average individual at 30 you will have it with few changes for the rest of that individual's life—as most lives are lived. A quacking, gossiping, neighbor-spying, disaster-enjoying woman of 30 will be, unless a miracle happens, the same at 40 and still the same at 60.

.   .   .

Assuming that we are all careful observers of personality, that we are pretty free from sensitive spots ourselves and are really seeking to get a true estimate of the personality of any given individual, what shall we do to gain this information? Here are a few ways of going about our quest:

(1) By studying the educational chart of the individual; (2) by studying the individual's achievement chart; (3) by using psychological tests; (4) by studying the spare time and recreation record of the individual; (5) by studying the emotional make-up of the individual under the practical situations of daily living. *There is no rapid way of studying the behavior or psychological make-up of individuals.* There are various psychological fakers in the field who believe there are such shortcuts but their methods are unproductive of any satisfactory results.

DEVELOPMENTAL
PSYCHOLOGY

AUTHOR:

Kurt Koffka (*1886–1941*)

WORK:

THE GROWTH
OF THE MIND (1924)

THE CONCEPT OF DEVELOPMENT
IN PSYCHOLOGY

When we set out to make a psychological study of the world in which we live, we continually come upon facts that can be understood only after we conceive them as products of evolution. For a long time psychological theory was dominated by the question: How much of any observed fact can be explained as a process of development? And even today no agreement has been reached between the rival theories of *empiricism* and *nativism,* the first of which emphasizes the influence of environment, and the second the influence of heredity. With this situation before us it is surprising to learn—though his-

From *The Growth of the Mind* by Kurt Koffka, translated by Robert M. Ogden, 2nd ed. (New York: Humanities Press), pp. 1–3, 16–18. First published in English by Routledge & Kegan Paul Ltd, London, in 1924. Reprinted by permission of Humanities Press and Routledge & Kegan Paul Ltd.

torically not difficult to understand—that psychology, and German psychology in particular, has made so little use of the general principles of development. Indeed, from the point of view of experience, the problem of development has been dealt with in a very specialized way, which is mechanistic rather than truly biological. This tendency seems, however, to be drawing to a close; for the need is now felt of introducing the facts of psychology into a larger sphere, embracing other facts of life, from which our science has already departed too far. We must therefore try to envisage the problems of mental growth as they really are; we must seek to understand the peculiarities of mental evolution, and must try to discover its laws.

In accomplishing this task we should not forget that the subject of a psychological investigation is usually the mature and cultured "West European" type of man; a living being—biologically considered—at the highest level of development. In the first place, we are dealing with the human being as opposed to the animal. Since Darwin's time, the conception of the descent of man has become common property, and we assume that what is valid in morphology and physiology must also have its significance in psychology. In the second place, we are dealing with representatives of a highly differentiated, as opposed to the members of a primitive, civilization. The world appears otherwise to us than it does to a Negro in Central Africa, and otherwise than it did to Homer. We speak a different language from either, and this difference is a fundamental one, inasmuch as a real translation of their words into our own is impossible, because the categories of thought are different. In the third place, we deal with the adult as opposed to the child, though each of us was once a child, and has become an adult only by having outgrown his childhood.

We must not forget, then, that without a comparative psychology, without animal, folk-, and child-psychology, the experimental psychology of the human adult is and must remain defective. For this reason the psychology of the human adult has not infrequently and in various respects been unable to define its problems correctly, to say nothing of arriving at serviceable hypotheses. For instance, the error has often been committed of trying to explain a fact by merely referring to its evolution, thus building up a theory of evolution instead of first investigating the facts by comparative methods. Whenever one has had a genetic problem to deal with, the danger has always been great that one would accept the old hypotheses and apply them to his new facts, instead of first giving his facts an unprejudiced consideration.

We might think that in child-psychology the process of development would be obvious to every one; for we know the end-product to be an adult, with whom experimental psychology can deal, and the growth of the adult can be traced continuously from infancy. Yet this procedure is not so simple as it might seem; for as a matter of fact there is no principle of mental development which we owe directly to child-psychology and, in so far as child-psychology makes use of any principles at all, they have originated either in experimental or in animal psychology. And yet there must be a genetic psychology; for the child-psychologist can follow the growth of a human being who in a relatively brief period of time changes from a simple inefficient individual into a highly complex and efficient man. It ought therefore to be possible to study this development in such a way that we can better understand the product, which is the human adult. Furthermore, if we could but understand this development, we should know more than we now know concerning the aims and methods of education.

This, therefore, is our problem: To discover the evolutionary principles of child-psychology. But although we must depend for assistance upon comparative psychology, we must not confine ourselves merely to transferring the principles of comparative psychology to our own field; instead, we must first test the value of these principles, and where necessary we must be ready to recast them.

. . .

A DENIAL OF THE BEHAVIORIST'S POINT OF VIEW

The behaviorist is right in denying the existence of conscious criteria wherever the method of experiential observation is inapplicable; but in spite of this we shall refuse to accept his position, for the simple reason that there is a consciousness, reports of which can only be made by the experiencing individual, and which is therefore not subject to the control of others. Science can not refuse to evaluate factual material of any sort that is placed at its disposal. Furthermore, what appear to be two cases of the same objective behavior may prove to be fundamentally different when the accompanying phenomena of consciousness are taken under consideration. A completely conscious action and an automatic action may seem to be identical, yet they may be widely different, while acts which are objectively quite different may be very similar when one considers the likeness of their attendant phenomena; and hence, were we to leave experiential observation out of account, we should often reach false conclusions. If the behaviorist answers that some natural-scientific method should be sought in investigating these differences, our rejoinder is that we are quite ready to leave that task to him; but at the same time the remark is permissible that it would never have occurred to him to search for such methods, had he not first become aware of these differences through his own conscious experience.

Finally, the bare fact that I am able to make a descriptive report is one of extraordinary significance. To me, it is at least as characteristic as that I breathe, or that I digest my food. A stick of wood can not do this, neither can an amoeba; and when I am dead I shall no longer be able to do it. Were I not able to make a descriptive report of my behavior, I should be unable to make any record of it at all. Paradoxically expressed, if one had only the capacity to make such responses as others can observe, no one would be able to observe anything.

It is therefore impossible to remove this aspect of behavior from science, not merely because of its immanent significance—since whatever we are, and of whatever we are proud, our culture, art, and religion, would otherwise be incomprehensible—but also because of the intimate connection which experience has with the objective side of behavior.

VITALITY AND MEANING IN EDUCATION

AUTHOR:

Alfred North Whitehead (*1861–1947*)

WORK:

THE AIMS OF EDUCATION AND OTHER ESSAYS (1929)

Culture is activity of thought, and receptiveness to beauty and humane feeling. Scraps of information have nothing to do with it. A merely well-informed man is the most useless bore on God's earth. What we should aim at producing is men who possess both culture and expert knowledge in some special direction. Their expert knowledge will give them the ground to start from, and their culture will lead them as deep as philosophy and as high as art. We have to remember that the valuable intellectual development is self-development, and that it mostly takes place between the ages of sixteen and thirty. . . .

In training a child to activity of thought, above all things we must beware of what I will call "inert ideas"—that is to say, ideas that are merely received into the mind without being utilised, or tested, or thrown into fresh combinations.

In the history of education, the most striking phenomenon is that schools of learning, which at one epoch are alive with a ferment of genius, in a succeeding generation exhibit merely pedantry and routine. The reason is, that they are overladen with inert ideas. Education with inert ideas is not only useless: it is, above all things, harmful—*Corruptio optimi, pessima.* Except at rare intervals of intellectual ferment, education in the past has been radically infected with inert ideas. That is the reason why uneducated clever women, who have seen much of the world, are in middle life so much the most cultured part of the community. They have been saved from this horrible burden of inert ideas. Every intellectual revolution which has ever stirred humanity into greatness has been a passionate protest against inert ideas. Then, alas, with pathetic ignorance of human psychology, it has proceeded by some educational scheme to bind humanity afresh with inert ideas of its own fashioning.

Let us now ask how in our system of education we are to guard against this mental dryrot. We enunciate two educational commandments, "Do not teach too many subjects," and again, "What you teach, teach thoroughly."

The result of teaching small parts of a large number of subjects is the passive reception of disconnected ideas, not illumined with any spark of vitality. Let the main ideas which are introduced into a child's education be few and important, and let them be thrown into every combination possible. The child should make them his own, and should understand their application here and now in the circumstances of his actual life. From the very beginning of his education, the child should experience the joy of discovery. The discovery which he has to make, is that general ideas give an understanding of that stream of events which pours through his life, which is his life. By understanding I mean more than a mere logical analysis, though that is included. I mean "understanding" in the sense in which it is used in the French proverb, "To understand all, is to forgive all." Pedants sneer at an education which is useful. But if education is not useful, what is it? Is it a talent, to be hidden away in a napkin? Of course, education should be useful, whatever your aim in life. It was useful to Saint Augustine and it was useful to Napoleon. It is useful, because understanding is useful.

. . .

I appeal to you, as practical teachers. With good discipline, it is always possible to pump into the minds of a class a certain quantity of inert knowledge. You take a text-book and make them learn it. So far, so good. The child then knows how to solve a quadratic equation. But what is the point of teaching the child to solve a quadratic equation? There is a traditional answer to this question. It runs thus: The mind is an instrument, you first sharpen it, and then use it; the acquisition of the power of solving a quadratic equation is part of the process of sharpening the mind. Now there is just enough truth in this answer to have made it live through the ages. But for all its half-truth, it embodies a radical error which bids fair to stifle the genius of the modern world. I do not know who was first responsible for this analogy of the mind to a dead instrument. For aught I know, it may have been one of the seven wise men of Greece, or a committee of the whole lot of them. Whoever was the originator, there can be no doubt of the authority which it has acquired by .he continuous approval bestowed upon it by eminent persons. But whatever its weight of authority, whatever the high approval which it can quote, I have no hesitation in denouncing it as one of the most fatal, erroneous, and dangerous conceptions ever introduced into the theory of education. The mind is never passive; it is a perpetual activity, delicate, receptive, responsive to stimulus. You cannot postpone its life until you have sharpened it. Whatever interest attaches to subject-matter must be worked here and now; whatever powers you are strengthening in the pupil, must be exercised here and now; whatever possibilities of mental life your teaching should impart, must be exhibited here and now. That is the golden rule of education, and a very difficult rule to follow.

The difficulty is just this: the apprehension of general ideas, intellectual habits of mind, and pleasurable interest in mental achievement can be evoked by no form of words, however accurately adjusted. All practical teachers know that education is a patient process of the mastery of details, minute by minute, hour by hour, day by day. There is no royal road to learning through an airy path of brilliant generalisations. There is a proverb about the difficulty of seeing the wood because of the trees. That difficulty is exactly the point which I am enforcing. The problem of education is to make the pupil see the wood by means of the trees.

The solution which I am urging, is to eradicate the fatal disconnection of subjects which kills the vitality of our modern curriculum. There is only one subject-matter for education, and that is Life in all its manifestations. Instead of this single unity, we offer children—Algebra, from which nothing follows; Geometry, from which nothing follows; Science, from which nothing follows; History, from which nothing follows; a Couple of Languages, never mastered; and lastly, most dreary of all, Literature, represented by plays of Shakespeare, with philological notes and short analyses of plot and character to be in substance committed to memory. Can such a list be said to represent Life, as it is known in the midst of the living of it? The best that can be said of it is, that it is a rapid table of contents which a deity might run over in his mind while he was thinking of creating a world, and had not yet determined how to put it together.

. . .

Again, there is not one course of study which merely gives general culture, and another which gives special knowledge. The subjects pursued for the sake of a general education are special subjects specially studied; and, on the other hand, one of the ways of encouraging general mental activity is to foster a special devotion. You may not divide the seamless coat of learning. What education has to impart is an intimate sense for the power of ideas, for the beauty of ideas, and for the structure of ideas, together with a particular body of knowledge which has peculiar reference to the life of the being possessing it.

The appreciation of the structure of ideas is that side of a cultured mind which can only grow under the influence of a special study. I mean that eye for the whole chess-board, for the bearing of one set of ideas on another. Nothing but a special study can give any appreciation for the exact formulation of general ideas, for their relations when formulated, for their service in the comprehension of life. A mind so disciplined should be both more abstract and more concrete. It has been trained in the comprehension of abstract thought and in the analysis of facts.

Finally, there should grow the most austere of all mental qualities; I mean the sense for style. It is an aesthetic sense, based on admiration for the direct attainment of a foreseen end, simply and without waste. Style in art, style in literature, style in science, style in logic, style in practical execution have fundamentally the same aesthetic qualities, namely, attainment and restraint. The love of a subject in itself and for itself, where it is not the sleepy pleasure of pacing a mental quarter-deck, is the love of style as manifested in that study.

Here we are brought back to the position from which we started, the utility of education. Style, in its finest sense, is the last acquirement of the educated mind; it is also the most useful. It pervades the whole being. The administrator with a sense for style hates waste; the engineer with a sense for style economises his material; the artisan with a sense for style prefers good work. Style is the ultimate morality of mind.

But above style, and above knowledge, there is something, a vague shape like fate above the Greek gods. That something is Power. Style is the fashioning of power, the restraining of power. But, after all, the power of attainment of the desired end is fundamental. The first thing is to get there. Do not bother about your style, but solve your problem, justify the ways of God to man, administer your province, or do whatever else is set before you.

Where, then, does style help? In this, with style the end is attained without side issues, without raising undesirable inflammations. With style you attain your end and nothing but your end. With style the effect of your activity is calculable, and foresight is the last gift of gods to men. With style your power is increased, for your mind is not distracted with irrelevancies, and you are more likely to attain your object. Now style is the exclusive privilege of the expert. Whoever heard of the style of an amateur painter, of the style of an amateur poet? Style is always the product of specialist study, the peculiar contribution of specialism to culture.

. . .

When one considers in its length and in its breadth the importance of this question of the education of a nation's young, the broken lives, the defeated hopes, the national failures, which result from the frivolous inertia with which it is treated, it is difficult to restrain within oneself a savage rage. In the conditions of modern life the rule is absolute, the race which does not value trained intelligence is doomed. Not all your heroism, not all your social charm, not all your wit, not all your victories on land or at sea, can move back the finger of fate. Today we maintain ourselves. Tomorrow science will have moved forward yet one more step, and there will be no appeal from the judgment which will then be pronounced on the uneducated.

We can be content with no less than the old summary of educational ideal which has been current at any time from the dawn of our civilization. The essence of education is that it be religious.

Pray, what is religious education?

A religious education is an education which inculcates duty and reverence. Duty arises from our potential control over the course of events. Where attainable knowledge could have changed the issue, ignorance has the guilt of vice. And the foundation of reverence is this perception, that the present holds within itself the complete sum of existence, backwards and forwards, that whole amplitude of time, which is eternity.

THE HUMAN SITUATION

AUTHOR:

Karl Jaspers (*1883–1969*)

WORK:

MAN IN THE MODERN AGE
(1930)

SIGNIFICANCE OF EDUCATION

Man is now what he is solely in virtue of biological inheritance, but also, and much more, thanks to what tradition makes him. Education is a process recapitulated in each individual. Through the working of the factual historical world in which the individual grows up, in conjunction with the purposive education to which he is subjected by parents and school, and in conjunction likewise with the influence of the various institutions of social life, to which, finally, there is super-added the effect of all that he hears and experiences—he acquires that which, elaborated by the activity of his own being, is known as his culture, which becomes for him, so to say, his second nature.

Culture brings the individual, by way of his own being, into cognizance

From *Man in the Modern Age* by Karl Jaspers, translated by Eden and Cedar Paul (Garden City, N.Y.: Anchor Books, Doubleday & Company, Inc., 1957), pp. 110–116. This version originally published by Routledge & Kegan Paul Ltd., London, in 1951.

of the whole. Instead of staying fixed in one particular place, he goes out into the world, so that, though his life be cast in narrow circumstances, it is still animated by contact with the lives of all. A man can become more decisively himself in proportion to the clarity and richness of the world with which his own reality becomes unified.

When the substance of the whole is unquestionably present, education, linked with stable forms, has a self-evident value. It denotes the earnestness with which each successive generation is absorbed into the spirit of the whole as the culture out of which experience, work, and action proceed. The personal achievement of the educator is, as such, barely conscious. He serves a cause without making experiments; swims in the stream of mankind in the making—a stream which, as a rule, has a regular and continuous flow.

But when the substance of the whole has become questionable and is in a state of disintegration, education, too, becomes insecure and disintegrated. No longer does it bring children into touch with the greatness of an all-embracing whole, but has vague and multifarious results. Disquiet prevails throughout the world. Feeling that they are slipping down into fathomless abysses, people recognize that everything turns on what can be made of the coming generation. They know that education will determine the human existence of the future, and that a decay of education would mean the decay of mankind. But education decays when, in the individual human beings who, at their maturity, have to bear responsibility, the historically transmitted substance has crumbled. Anxiety about this substance is tantamount to a consciousness that there is peril of its being absolutely lost. In such circumstances, a man will look backwards, and will have his children taught as absolute that which he himself no longer regards as such. Another will reject this historical tradition, and will have education carried on as if it had no relationship with time at all, and consisted only of training for technical skill, the acquisition of realist knowledge, and information that will enable a child to take up a position toward the contemporary world. Every one knows that he who molds children molds the future.

Symptomatic of the uneasiness of our own age concerning education is the intensity of pedagogical efforts in the absence of any unified ideas upon the subject, the superabundance of new books on education, the perpetual amplification of the didactic art. Nowadays the individual teacher is a more self-sacrificing person than ever before, and is nonetheless, because he is not sustained by a whole, practically impotent. Moreover, it seems as if the characteristic feature of our situation was the breaking-up of substantial education into an interminable pedagogic experiment, its decomposition into indifferent possibilities. The freedoms which men have wrung for themselves are being dissipated in the futile liberty of the null. One attempt is speedily abandoned in favor of another, the contents, aims, and methods of education being changed from moment to moment. An epoch which does not trust its own self is anxiously concerned about education as if in this domain something could once more be made out of Nothingness.

Characteristic is the part played by young people. When education is substantial because it proceeds from the spirit of a whole, youth is immature. It venerates, obeys, trusts, and does not claim validity as youth; for it is no more than preparatory and the possible mission of a future. But when things are in a state of dissolution, youth acquires a value *per se*. We actually turn to youth expecting it to supply us with what has been lost from the world. It is considered entitled to regard itself as an original source. Already our children are allowed to have a say in the ordering of the school. It seems as if young folk were demanding the right to produce for themselves what their teachers no longer possess. Just as the coming generations are burdened with the national debt of earlier days, so will they have to bear the consequences of our squandering of mental goods, which they will have to reacquire for themselves. Youth is endowed with a fictitious preponderance, and misses its purpose for the reason that man can only become man if he grows in the continuity of decades and is strictly guided into the right path by a succession of footsteps which he has to follow.

When, after such an education, in the medley of the indifferent and the chance-given, the adult has not succeeded in making his way into a world, but is left forsaken and becomes aware of the fact, there arises, as a sign of the times, a demand for adult education. Formerly, as far as grown-ups were concerned, there was only a question of the diffusion of knowledge into wider circles; the only problem was the possibility of popularization. Today the burning question is whether it will be possible, out of the sources of contemporary life, not to dilute the old culture, but to establish a new one in the community of popular educators, workers, employees, and peasants. Man in his forlornness is not merely to accommodate himself by comprehending reality, but is once more to belong to a community which, transcending occupation and party, will bring human beings together as such; men are once again to become a nation. Whatever doubts we may entertain as to the feasibility of adult education in this sense, we must not fail to recognize the serious importance of the proposed task. If all our old ideals are to be shattered upon the realities of the times, the attempt to rise superior to the situation may perhaps be foredoomed to failure, but the mere endeavor shows a vestige of human dignity. . . .

THE STATE AND EDUCATION

The State, in virtue of its power, is the guarantor of the extant form of mass-order.

The masses do not really know what they want. Mass-demands relate to average matters, as capable of being expressed in the crudest terms. When the demands of the masses determine the nature of education, the upshot is something of this kind. People want to learn what will be practically applicable in life: they want to keep in close contact with life, and understand (in this connexion) by "life" all that makes life easy and comfortable, not excepting the means of communication in the great cities; they want to cultivate individuality, denoting by this, on the one hand, utility (which they miscall "efficiency"), and, on the other hand, lack of discipline, this meaning a license to give rein to every inclination and to take pleasure in doing what all of like ways of thinking do (which they term "being natural"); they protest against the stringency of ideal aims, for these demand gradations of being instead of mere utility; they want individuals who can live together without friction, and they deny the possibility of essentially responsible human beings.

The State, being the framework in which the permanent education of all can be carried on, is concerned about the education of youth. For it is through education that the human beings are produced who will in due course have to sustain the State.

Today it would seem that two widely differing possibilities are open to the State.

On the one hand, it may leave education alone, may let the mass-demands take their own course, and may try, in conflict with them, to work out an aristocratic educational system of its own. In these circumstances it will dominate without any kind of unification or stability by means of its personal policy, which will result in a distribution of the leading educational positions among the dominant parties. Multiplicity of curricula and of educational experiments will be tolerated to the extent of utter disintegration, restricted only by this consideration, that nothing can be established which does not, in the long run, secure the support of a powerful political group. Here and there a school may thrive thanks to the personality of its headmaster, if he be allowed free choice in the appointment of his assistant masters. On the whole, however, the result will be that the teachers will all be at sixes and sevens, failing to understand one another, harnessed to mechanical curricula, in schools where no genuine community spirit prevails, but subject to guidance by empty rhetoric of one sort or another—nationalist, philosophical, or social. Continuity is rendered impossible by reciprocal interference. Everything is higgledy-piggledy, and there are continual changes. Children fail to receive the sincere, great, noble impressions which are able to influence character in a way that can never be forgotten. Immense demands are made upon the young as regards the acquisition of facts, so that immature minds are strained whilst no imprint is effected upon their real being. There is a lack of straightforward objectivity which, upon the foundation of a belief, would energetically resist the subjectivity of the individual capacity or incapacity. More is done to develop individuality than is desirable, and yet the teacher fails to achieve what he strives to achieve—namely, the formation of character. Torn hither and thither, the child finds, indeed, fragments of a tradition, but no world into which it can confidently enter.

If the alternative plan is followed, the State acquires control of education for the quiet but forcible molding of character in accordance with its own purposes. Then we have a unified education at the cost of paralysis of mental freedom. Basic opinions are inculcated with the fixity of religious dogmas, knowledge and accomplishments being drilled into the learner as ways of feeling and valuing. What the bolsheviks and the fascists respectively do in this field and what we learn of the decline of liberty in the United States, differ in respect of many points of detail—but, common to them all, is that human beings are turned out according to standardized types.

The masses are aware of this imposition of uniformity by the force of the State, and they are aware of an aimless multiplicity. But if education is once more to become what it was in its best days, namely the possibility, through historical continuity, of developing into a human being possessed of full selfhood, that can only ensue through a faith which, amid all necessary strictness in learning and practice, indirectly conveys a spiritual value.

No simple recipe can be given for this. Here the power of the State cannot create anything, but can only protect or destroy. It is the mental situation which imposes its demands when, contemplating the future, we become aware of the whole. Education will only be restored to its true level when the valuations of the masses are overridden by a distinction between teaching and discipline, between that which is comprehensible to all, and that which is attainable by an elite through a training of the inner being.

EDUCATION AND THE SOCIAL ORDER

AUTHOR:

George S. Counts (*1889–*   )

WORK:

DARE THE SCHOOL BUILD A NEW SOCIAL ORDER? (1932)

Like all simple and unsophisticated peoples we Americans have a sublime faith in education. Faced with any difficult problem of life we set our minds at rest sooner or later by the appeal to the school. We are convinced that education is the one unfailing remedy for every ill to which man is subject, whether it be vice, crime, war, poverty, riches, injustice, racketeering, political corruption, race hatred, class conflict, or just plain original sin. We even speak glibly and often about the general reconstruction of society through the school. We cling to this faith in spite of the fact that the very period in which our troubles have multiplied so rapidly has witnessed an unprecedented expansion of organized education. This would seem to suggest that our schools instead of directing the course of change, are themselves driven by the very forces that are transforming the rest of the social order.

The bare fact, however, that simple and unsophisticated peoples have unbounded faith in education does not mean that the faith is untenable. History shows that the intuitions of such folk may be nearer the truth than the weighty and carefully reasoned judgments of the learned and the wise. Under certain conditions education may be as beneficent and as powerful as we are wont to think. But if it is to be so, teachers must abandon much of their easy optimism, subject the concept of education to the most rigorous scrutiny, and be prepared to deal much more fundamentally, realistically, and positively with the American social situation than has been their habit in the past. Any individual or group that would aspire to lead society must be ready to pay the costs of leadership: to accept responsibility, to suffer calumny, to surrender security, to risk both reputation and fortune. If this price, or some important part of it, is not being paid, then the chances are that the claim to leadership is fraudulent. Society is never redeemed without effort, struggle, and sacrifice. Authentic leaders are never found breathing that rarefied atmosphere lying above the dust and smoke of battle. With regard to the past we always recognize the truth of this principle, but when we think of our own times we profess the belief that the ancient roles have been reversed and that now prophets of a new age receive their rewards among the living.

That the existing school is leading the way to a better social order is a thesis which few informed persons would care to defend. Except as it is forced to fight for its own life during times of depression, its course is too serene and untroubled. Only in the rarest of instances does it wage war on behalf of principle or ideal. Almost everywhere it is in the grip of conservative forces and is serving the cause of perpetuating ideas and institutions suited to an age that is gone. But there is one movement above the educational horizon which would seem to show promise of genuine and creative leadership. I refer to the Progressive Education movement. Surely in this union of two of the great faiths of the American people, the faith in progress and the faith in education, we have reason to hope for light and guidance. Here is a movement which would seem to be completely devoted to the promotion of social welfare through education.

Even a casual examination of the program and philosophy of the Progressive schools, however, raises many doubts in the mind. To be sure, these schools have a number of large achievements to their credit. They have focused attention squarely upon the child; they have recognized the fundamental importance of the interest of the learner; they have defended the thesis that activity lies at the root of all true education; they have conceived learning in terms of life situations and growth of character; they have championed the rights of the child as a free personality. Most of this is excellent, but in my judgment it is not enough. It constitutues too narrow a conception of the meaning of education; it brings into the picture but one-half of the landscape.

If an educational movement, or any other movement, calls itself progressive, it must have orientation; it must possess direction. The word itself implies moving forward, and moving forward can have little meaning in the absence of clearly defined purposes.

. . .

. . . An education that does not strive to promote the fullest and most thorough understanding of the world is not worthy of the name. Also there must be no deliberate distortion or suppression of facts to support any theory or point of view. On the other hand, I am prepared to defend the thesis that all education contains a large element of imposition, that in the very nature of the case this is inevitable, that the existence and evolution of society depend upon it, that it is consequently eminently desirable, and that the frank acceptance of this fact by the educator is a major professional obligation. . . .

. . . Any defensible educational program must be adjusted to a particular time and place, and the degree and nature of the imposition must vary with the social situation. Under ordinary conditions the process of living suffices in itself to hold society together, but when the forces of disintegration become sufficiently powerful it may well be that a fairly large measure of deliberate control is desirable and even essential to social survival. . . .

. . . My thesis is that complete impartiality is utterly impossible, that the school must shape attitudes, develop tastes, and even impose ideas. It is obvious that the whole of creation cannot be brought into the school. This means that some selection must be made of teachers, curricula, architecture, methods of teaching. And in the making of the selection the dice must always be weighted in favor of this or that. Here is a fundamental truth that cannot be brushed aside as irrelevant or unimportant; it constitutes the very essence of the matter under discussion. Nor can the reality be concealed beneath agreeable phrases. Professor Dewey states in his *Democracy and Education* that the school should provide a *purified* environment for the child. With this view I would certainly agree; probably no person reared in our society would favor the study of pornography in the schools. I am sure, however, that this means stacking the cards in favor of the particular systems of value which we may happen to possess. It is one of the truisms of the anthropologist that there are no maxims of purity on which all peoples would agree. Other vigorous opponents of imposition unblushingly advocate the "cultivation of democratic sentiments" in children or the promotion of child growth in the direction of "a better and richer life." The first represents definite acquiescence in imposition; the second, if it does not mean the same thing, means nothing. I believe firmly that democratic sentiments should be cultivated and that a better and richer life should be the outcome of education, but in neither case would I place responsibility on either God or the order of nature. I would merely contend that as educators we must make many choices involving the development of attitudes in boys and girls and that we should not be afraid to acknowledge the faith that is in us or mayhap the forces that compel us.

. . .

If we may now assume that the child will be imposed upon in some fashion by the various elements in his environment, the real question is not whether imposition will take place, but rather from what source it will come. If we were to answer this question in terms of the past, there could, I think, be but one answer: on all genuinely crucial matters the school follows the wishes of the groups or classes that actually rule society; on minor matters the school is sometimes allowed a certain measure of freedom. But the future may be unlike the past. Or perhaps I should say that teachers, if they could increase sufficiently their stock of courage, intelligence, and vision, might become a social force of some magnitude. About this eventuality I am not over sanguine, but a society lacking leadership as ours does, might even accept the guidance of teachers. Through powerful organizations they might at least reach the public conscience and come to exercise a larger measure of control over the schools than hitherto. They would then have to assume some responsibility for the more fundamental forms of imposition which, according to my argument, cannot be avoided.

That the teachers should deliberately reach for power and then make the most of their conquest is my firm conviction. To the extent that they are permitted to fashion the curriculum and the procedures of the school they will definitely and positively influence the social attitudes, ideals, and behavior of the coming generation. In doing this they should resort to no subterfuge or false modesty. They should say neither that they are merely teaching the truth nor that they are unwilling to wield power in their own right. The first position is false and the second is a confession of incompetence. It is my observation that the men and women who have affected the course of human events are those who have not hesitated to use the power that has come to them. Representing as they do, not the interests of the moment or of any special class, but rather the common and abiding interests of the people, teachers are under heavy social obligation to protect and further those interests. In this they occupy a relatively unique position in society. Also since the profession should embrace scientists and scholars of the highest rank, as well as teachers working at all levels of the educational system, it has at its disposal, as no other group, the knowledge and wisdom of the ages. It is scarcely thinkable that these men and women would ever act as selfishly or bungle as badly as have the so-called "practical" men of our generation—the politicians, the financiers, the industrialists. If all of these facts are taken into account, instead of shunning power, the profession should rather seek power and then strive to use that power fully and wisely and in the interests of the great masses of the people.

. . .

Our generation has the good or the ill fortune to live in an age when great decisions must be made. The American people, like most of the other peoples of the earth, have come to the parting of the ways; they can no longer trust entirely the inspiration which came to them when the Republic was young; they must decide afresh what they are to do with their talents. Favored above all other nations with the resources of nature and the material instrumentalities of civilization, they stand confused and irresolute before the future. They seem to lack the moral quality necessary to quicken, discipline, and give direction to their matchless energies. In a recent paper Professor Dewey has, in my judgment, correctly diagnosed our troubles: "the schools, like the nation," he says, "are in need of a central purpose which will create new enthusiasm and devotion, and which will unify and guide all intellectual plans."

This suggests, as we have already observed, that the educational problem is not wholly intellectual in nature. Our Progressive schools therefore cannot rest content with giving children an opportunity to study contemporary society in all aspects. This of course must be done, but I am convinced that they should go much farther. If the schools are to be really effective, they must become centers for the building, and not merely for the contemplation, of our civilization. This does not mean that we should endeavor to promote particular reforms through the educational system. We should, however, give to our children a vision of the possibilities which lie ahead and endeavor to enlist their loyalties and enthusiasms in the realization of the vision. Also our social institutions and practices, all of them, should be critically examined in the light of such a vision.

TRADITIONAL VS. PROGRESSIVE EDUCATION

AUTHOR:

John Dewey (*1859–1952*)

WORK:

EXPERIENCE AND EDUCATION (1938)

Mankind likes to think in terms of extreme opposites. It is given to formulating its beliefs in terms of *Either-Ors,* between which it recognizes no intermediate possibilities. When forced to recognize that the extremes cannot be acted upon, it is still inclined to hold that they are all right in theory but that when it comes to practical matters circumstances compel us to compromise. Educational philosophy is no exception. The history of educational theory is marked by opposition between the idea that education is development from within and that it is formation from without; that it is based upon natural

From *Experience and Education* by John Dewey, Kappa Delta Pi Lecture Series (New York: The Macmillan Company, 1938), pp. 1–11. Copyright 1938 by Kappa Delta Pi, An Honor Society in Education, Box A, West Lafayette, Indiana. Reprinted by permission.

endowments and that education is a process of overcoming natural inclination and substituting in its place habits acquired under external pressure.

At present, the opposition, so far as practical affairs of the school are concerned, tends to take the form of contrast between traditional and progressive education. If the underlying ideas of the former are formulated broadly, without the qualifications required for accurate statement, they are found to be about as follows: The subject-matter of education consists of bodies of information and of skills that have been worked out in the past; therefore, the chief business of the school is to transmit them to the new generation. In the past, there have also been developed standards and rules of conduct; moral training consists in forming habits of action in conformity with these rules and standards. Finally, the general pattern of school organization (by which I mean the relations of pupils to one another and to the teachers) constitutes the school a kind of institution sharply marked off from other social institutions. Call up in imagination the ordinary schoolroom, its time-schedule, schemes of classification, of examination and promotion, of rules of order, and I think you will grasp what is meant by "pattern of organization." If then you contrast this scene with what goes on in the family, for example, you will appreciate what is meant by the school being a kind of institution sharply marked off from any other form of social organization.

The three characteristics just mentioned fix the aims and methods of instruction and discipline. The main purpose or objective is to prepare the young for future responsibilities and for success in life, by means of acquisition of the organized bodies of information and prepared forms of skill which comprehend the material of instruction. Since the subject-matter as well as standards of proper conduct are handed down from the past, the attitude of pupils must, upon the whole, be one of docility, receptivity, and obedience. Books, especially textbooks, are the chief representatives of the lore and wisdom of the past, while teachers are the organs through which pupils are brought into effective connection with the material. Teachers are the agents through which knowledge and skills are communicated and rules of conduct enforced.

I have not made this brief summary for the purpose of criticizing the underlying philosophy. The rise of what is called new education and progressive schools is of itself a product of discontent with traditional education. In effect it is a criticism of the latter. When the implied criticism is made explicit it reads somewhat as follows: The traditional scheme is, in essence, one of imposition from above and from outside. It imposes adult standards, subject-matter, and methods upon those who are only growing slowly toward maturity. The gap is so great that the required subject-matter, the methods of learning and behaving are foreign to the existing capacities of the young.

They are beyond the reach of the experience the young learners already possess. Consequently, they must be imposed; even though good teachers will use devices of art to cover up the imposition so as to relieve it of obviously brutal features.

But the gulf between the mature or adult products and the experience and abilities of the young is so wide that the very situation forbids much active participation by pupils in the development of what is taught. Theirs is to do—and learn, as it was the part of the six hundred to do and die. Learning here means acquisition of what already is incorporated in books and in the heads of the elders. Moreover, that which is taught is thought of as essentially static. It is taught as a finished product, with little regard either to the ways in which it was originally built up or to changes that will surely occur in the future. It is to a large extent the cultural product of societies that assumed the future would be much like the past, and yet it is used as educational food in a society where change is the rule, not the exception.

If one attempts to formulate the philosophy of education implicit in the practices of the newer education, we may, I think, discover certain common principles amid the variety of progressive schools now existing. To imposition from above is opposed expression and cultivation of individuality; to external discipline is opposed free activity; to learning from texts and teachers, learning through experience; to acquisition of isolated skills and techniques by drill, is opposed acquisition of them as means of attaining ends which make direct vital appeal; to preparation for a more or less remote future is opposed making the most of the opportunities of present life; to static aims and materials is opposed acquaintance with a changing world.

Now, all principles by themselves are abstract. They become concrete only in the consequences which result from their application. Just because the principles set forth are so fundamental and far-reaching, everything depends upon the interpretation given them as they are put into practice in the school and the home. It is at this point that the reference made earlier to *Either-Or* philosophies becomes peculiarly pertinent. The general philosophy of the new education may be sound, and yet the difference in abstract principles will not decide the way in which the moral and intellectual preference involved shall be worked out in practice. There is always the danger in a new movement that in rejecting the aims and methods of that which it would supplant, it may develop its principles negatively rather than positively and constructively. Then it takes its clew in practice from that which is rejected instead of from the constructive development of its own philosophy.

I take it that the fundamental unity of the newer philosophy is found in the idea that there is an intimate and necessary relation between the processes of actual experience and education. If this be true, then a positive and constructive development of its own basic idea depends upon having a correct idea of experience. Take, for example, the question of organized subject-matter—which will be discussed in some detail later. The problem for progressive education is: What is the place and meaning of subject-matter and of organization *within* experience? How does subject-matter function? Is there anything inherent in experience which tends towards progressive organization of its contents? What results follow when the materials of experience are not progressively organized? A philosophy which proceeds on the basis of rejection, of sheer opposition, will neglect these questions. It will tend to suppose that because the old education was based on ready-made organization, therefore it suffices to reject the principle of organization *in toto,* instead of striving to discover what it means and how it is to be attained on the basis of experience. We might go through all the points of difference between the new and the old education and reach similar conclusions. When external control is rejected, the problem becomes that of finding the factors of control that are inherent within experience. When external authority is rejected, it does not follow that all authority should be rejected, but rather that there is need to search for a more effective source of authority. Because the older education imposed the knowledge, methods, and the rules of conduct of the mature person upon the young, it does not follow, except upon the basis of the extreme *Either-Or* philosophy, that the knowledge and skill of the mature person has no directive value for the experience of the immature. On the contrary, basing education upon personal experience may mean more multiplied and more intimate contacts between the mature and the immature than ever existed in the traditional school, and consequently more, rather than less, guidance by others. The problem, then, is: how these contacts can be established without violating the principle of learning through personal experience. The solution of this problem requires a well thought-out philosophy of the social factors that operate in the constitution of individual experience.

What is indicated in the foregoing remarks is that the general principles of the new education do not of themselves solve any of the problems of the actual or practical conduct and management of progressive schools. Rather, they set new problems which have to be worked out on the basis of a new philosophy of experience. The problems are not even recognized, to say nothing of being solved, when it is assumed that it suffices to reject the ideas and practices of the old education and then go to the opposite extreme. Yet I am sure that you will appreciate what is meant when I say that many of the newer schools tend to make little or nothing of organized subject-matter of study; to proceed as if any form of direction and guidance by adults were an invasion of individual freedom, and as if the idea that education should be concerned with the present and future meant that acquaintance with the past has little or no role to play in education. Without pressing these defects to the point of exaggeration, they at least illustrate what is meant by a theory and practice of education which proceeds negatively or by reaction against what has been current in education rather than by a positive and constructive development of purposes, methods, and subject-matter on the foundation of a theory of experience and its educational potentialities.

It is not too much to say that an educational philosophy which professes to be based on the idea of freedom may become as dogmatic as ever was the traditional education which is reacted against. For any theory and set of practices is dogmatic which is not based upon critical examination of its own underlying principles. Let us say that the new education emphasizes the freedom of the learner. Very well. A problem is now set. What does freedom mean and what are the conditions under which it is capable of realization? Let us say that the kind of external imposition which was so common in the traditional school limited rather than promoted the intellectual and moral development of the young. Again, very well. Recognition of this serious defect sets a problem. Just what is the role of the teacher and of books in promoting the educational development of the immature? Admit that traditional education employed as the subject-matter for study facts and ideas so bound up with the past as to give little help in dealing with the issues of the present and future. Very well. Now we have the problem of discovering the connection which actually exists *within* experience between the achievements of the past and the issues of the present. We have the problem of ascertaining how acquaintance with the past may be translated into a potent instrumentality for dealing effectively with the future. We may reject knowledge of the past as the *end* of education and thereby only emphasize its importance as a *means*. When we do that we have a problem that is new in the story of education: How shall the young become acquainted with the past in such a way that the acquaintance is a potent agent in appreciation of the living present?

SOCIAL FACTORS IN INTELLECTUAL DEVELOPMENT

AUTHOR:

Jean Piaget (*1896*–)

WORK:

THE PSYCHOLOGY OF INTELLIGENCE (1947)

The human being is immersed right from birth in a social environment which affects him just as much as his physical environment. Society, even more, in a sense, than the physical environment, changes the very structure of the individual, because it not only compels him to recognize facts, but also provides him with a ready-made system of signs, which modify his thought; it presents him with new values and it imposes on him an infinite series of obligations. It is therefore quite evident that social life affects intelligence through the three media of language (signs), the content of interaction (intellectual values) and rules imposed on thought (collective logical or prelogical norms).

From *The Psychology of Intelligence* by Jean Piaget, translated by Malcolm Piercy and D. E. Berlyne (London: Routledge & Kegan Paul Ltd., 1950), pp. 156–162. Footnotes omitted. Reprinted by permission.

Certainly, it is necessary for sociology to envisage society as a whole, even though this whole, which is quite distinct from the sum of the individuals composing it, is only the totality of relations or interaction between these individuals. Every relation between individuals (from two onwards) literally modifies them and therefore immediately constitutes a whole, so that the whole formed by society is not so much a thing, a being or a cause as a system of relations. But these relations are extremely numerous and complex, since, in fact, they constitute just as much a continuous plot in history, through the action of successive generations on each other, as a synchronous system of equilibrium at each moment of history. It is therefore legitimate to adopt statistical language and to speak of "society" as a coherent whole (in the same way as a *Gestalt* is the resultant of a statistical system of relations). But it is essential to remember the statistical nature of statements in sociological language, since to forget this would be to attribute a mythological sense to the words. In the sociology of thought it might even be asked whether it would not be better to replace the usual global language by an enumeration of the types of relation involved (types which, needless to say, are likewise statistical).

When we are concerned with psychology, on the other hand, i.e. when the unit of reference is the individual modified by social relations, rather than the complex or complexes of relations as such, it becomes quite wrong to content oneself with statistical terms, since these are too general. The "effect of social life" is a concept which is just as vague as that of "the effect of the physical environment" if it is not described in detail. From birth to adult life, the human being is subject, as nobody denies, to social pressures, but these pressures are of extremely varied types and are subject to a certain order of development. Just as the physical environment is not imposed on developing intelligence all at once or as a single entity, but in such a way that acquisitions can be followed step by step as a function of experience, and especially as a function of the kinds of assimilation or accommodation—varying greatly according to mental level—that govern these acquisitions, so the social environment gives rise to interactions between the developing individual and his fellow, interactions that differ greatly from one another and succeed one another according to definite laws. These types of interaction and these laws of succession are what the psychologist must carefully establish, lest he simplify the task to the extent of giving it up in favor of the problems of sociology. Now there is no longer any reason for conflict between this science and psychology once one recognizes the extent to which the structure of the individual is modified by these interactions; both of these two disciplines, therefore, stand to gain by an investigation that goes beyond a global analysis and undertakes to analyze relations.

THE SOCIALIZATION OF
INDIVIDUAL INTELLIGENCE

The interaction with his social environment in which the individual indulges varies widely in nature according to his level of development, and consequently in its turn it modifies the individual's mental structure in an equally varied manner.

During the sensori-motor period the infant is, of course, already subject to manifold social influences; people afford him the greatest pleasures known to his limited experience—from food to the warmth and affection which surrounds him—people gather round him, smile at him, amuse him, calm him; they inculcate habits and regular courses of conduct linked to signals and words; some behavior is already forbidden and he is scolded. In short, seen from without, the infant is in the midst of a multitide of relations which forerun the signs, values and rules of subsequent social life. But from the point of view of the subject himself, the social environment is still not essentially distinct from the physical environment, at least up to the fifth of the stages of sensori-motor intelligence that we have distinguished. The signs that are used to affect him are, as far as he is concerned, only indices or signals. The rules imposed on him are not yet obligations of conscience and he confuses them with the regularity characteristic of habit. As for people, they are seen as pictures like all the pictures which constitute reality, but they are particularly active, unpredictable and the source of the most intense feelings. The infant reacts to them in the same way as to objects, namely with gestures that happen to cause them to continue interesting actions, and with various cries, but there is still as yet no interchange of thought, since at this level the child does not know thought; nor, consequently, is there any profound modification of intellectual structures by the social life surrounding him.

With the acquisition of language, however, i.e. with the advent of the symbolic and intuitive periods, new social relations appear which enrich and transform the individual's thought. But in this context three points should be noted.

In the first place, the system of collective signs does not create the symbolic function, but naturally develops it to a degree that the individual by himself would never know. Nevertheless, the sign as such, conventional (arbitrary) and ready-made, is not an adequate medium of expression for the young child's thought; he is not satisfied with speaking, he must needs "play out" what he thinks and symbolize his ideas by means of gestures and objects, and represent things by imitation, drawing and construction. In short, from the point of view of expression itself, the child at the outset is still midway between the use of the collective sign and that of the individual symbol, both still being necessary, no doubt, but the second being much more so in the child than in the adult.

In the second place, language conveys to the individual an already prepared system of ideas, classifications, relations—in short, an inexhaustible stock of concepts which are reconstructed in each individual after the age-old pattern which previously molded earlier generations. But it goes without saying that the child begins by borrowing from this collection only as much as suits him, remaining disdainfully ignorant of everything that exceeds his mental level. And again, that which is borrowed is assimilated in accordance with his intellectual structure; a word intended to carry a general concept at first engenders only a half-individual, half-socialized pre-concept (the word "bird" thus evokes the familiar canary, etc.).

There remain, in the third place, the actual relations that the subject maintains with his fellows beings, i.e. "synchronous" relations, as opposed to the "diachronic" processes that influence the child's acquisition of language and the modes of thought that are associated with it. Now these synchronous relations are at first essential; when conversing with his family, the child will at every moment see his thoughts approved or contradicted, and he will discover a vast world of thought external to himself, which will instruct or impress him in various ways. From the point of view of intelligence (which is all that concerns us here), he will therefore be led to an ever more intensive exchange of intellectual values and will be forced to accept an ever-increasing number of obligatory truths (ready-made ideas and true norms of reasoning).

But here again we must not exaggerate or confuse capacities for assimilation as they appear in intuitive thought with the form they take at the operational level. In fact, as we have seen in connection with the adaptation of thought to the physical environment, intuitive thought, which is dominant up to the end of early childhood (7 years), is characterized by a disequilibrium, still unresolved, between assimilation and accommodation. An intuitive relation always results from a "centering" of thought depending on one's own action, as opposed to a "grouping" of all the relations involved; thus the equivalence between two series of objects is recognized only in relation to the act of making them correspond, and is lost as soon as this action is replaced by another. Intuitive thought, therefore, always evinces a distorting egocentricity, since the relation that is recognized is related to the subject's action and not decentralized into an objective system.

Conversely, and precisely because intuitive thought is from moment to moment "centered" on a given relation, it is phenomenalistic and grasps only the perceptual appearance of reality. It is therefore a prey to suggestion coming from immediate experience, which it copies and imitates instead of correcting. Now the reaction of intelligence at this level to the social environment is exactly parallel to its reaction to the physical environment, and this is self-evident, since the two kinds of experience are indistinguishable in reality.

For one thing, however dependent he may be on surrounding intellectual influences, the young child assimilates them in his own way. He reduces them to his point of view and therefore distorts them without realizing it, simply because he cannot yet distinguish his point of view from that of others through failure to co-ordinate or "group" the points of view. Thus, both on the social and physical plane, he is egocentric through ignorance of his own subjectivity. For example, he can show his right hand but confuses the right-left relationship in a partner facing him, since he cannot see another point of view, either socially or geometrically; similarly, we have noted how, in problems of perspective, he first attributes his own view of things to others; in questions involving time there are even cases where a young child, while stating that his father is much older than himself, believes him to have been born "after" himself, since he cannot "remember" what he did before! In short, intuitive centralization, as opposed to operational decentralization, is thus reinforced by an unconscious—and therefore all the more systematic—primacy of his own point of view. This intellectual egocentricity is in both cases nothing more than a lack of co-ordination, a failure to "group" relations with other individuals as well as with other objects. There is nothing here that is not perfectly natural; the primacy of one's own point of view, like intuitive centralization in accordance with the subject's own action, is merely the expression of an original failure to differentiate, of an assimilation that distorts because it is determined by the only point of view that is possible at first. Actually, such a failure to differentiate is inevitable, since the distinction between different points of view, as well as their co-ordination, requires the activity of intelligence.

But, because the initial egocentricity results from a simple lack of differentiation between *ego* and *alter,* the subject finds himself exposed during the very same period to all the suggestions and constraints of his fellows, and he accommodates himself without question, simply because he is not conscious of the private nature of his viewpoint (it thus frequently happens that young children do not realize that they are imitating, and believe that they have originated the behavior in question, just as they may attribute their own private ideas to others). That is why the period of maximum egocentricity in the course of development coincides with the maximum pressure from the examples and opinions of his fellows, and the combination of assimilation to the self and accommodation to surrounding models is just as explicable as that of the egocentricity and phenomenalism characterizing the first intuition of physical relations.

However, it is obvious that under these conditions (all of which involve the absence of "grouping") the coercions of other people would not be enough to engender a logic in the child's mind, even if the truths that they imposed were rational in content; repeating correct ideas, even if one believes that they originate from oneself, is not the same as reasoning correctly. On the contrary, in order to teach others to reason logically it is indispensable that there should be established between them and oneself those simultaneous relationships of differentiation and reciprocity which characterize the co-ordination of viewpoints.

In short, at the pre-operational levels, extending from the appearance of language to the age of about 7–8 years, the structures associated with the beginnings of thought preclude the formation of the co-operative social functions which are indispensable for logic to be formed. Oscillating between distorting egocentricity and passive acceptance of intellectual suggestion, the child is, therefore, not yet subject to a socialization of intelligence which could profoundly modify its mechanism.

THE BASIS
OF EDUCATION

AUTHOR:

Robert M. Hutchins (*1899–*   )

WORK:

THE CONFLICT
IN EDUCATION (1953)

The obvious failures of the doctrines of adaptation, immediate needs, social reform, and of the doctrine that we need no doctrine at all may suggest to us that we require a better definition of education. Let us concede that every society must have some system that attempts to adapt the young to their social and political environment. If the society is bad, in the sense, for example, in which the Nazi state was bad, the system will aim at the same bad ends. To the extent that it makes men bad in order that they may be tractable subjects of a bad state, the system may help to achieve the social ideals of the society. It may be what the society wants; it may even be what the society needs, if it is to perpetuate its form and accomplish its aims. In pragmatic terms, in terms of success in the society, it may be a "good" system.

But it seems to me clearer to say that, though it may be a system of training, or instruction, or adaptation, or meeting immediate needs, it is not a system of education. It seems clearer to say that the purpose of education is to improve men. Any system that tries to make them bad is not education, but something else. If, for example, democracy is the best form of society, a system that adapts the young to it will be an educational system. If despotism is a bad form of society, a system that adapts the young to it will not be an educational system, and the better it succeeds in adapting them the less educational it will be.

Every man has a function as a man. The function of a citizen or a subject may vary from society to society, and the system of training, or adaptation, or instruction, or meeting immediate needs may vary with it. But the function of a man as man is the same in every age and in every society, since it results from his nature as a man. The aim of an educational system is the same in every age and in every society where such a system can exist: it is to improve man as man.

If we are going to talk about improving men and societies, we have to believe that there is some difference between good and bad. This difference must not be, as the positivists think it is, merely conventional. We cannot tell this difference by any examination of the effectiveness of a given program as the pragmatists propose; the time required to estimate these effects is usually too long and the complexity of society is always too great for us to say that the consequences of a given program are altogether clear. We cannot discover the difference between good and bad by going to the laboratory, for men and societies are not laboratory animals. If we believe that there is no truth, there is no knowledge, and there are no values except those which are validated by laboratory experiment, we cannot talk about the improvement of men and societies, for we can have no standard of judging anything that takes place among men or in societies.

Society is to be improved, not by forcing a program of social reform down its throat, through the schools, or otherwise, but by the improvement of the individuals who compose it. As Plato said, "Governments reflect human nature. States are not made out of stone or wood, but out of the characters of their citizens: these turn the scale and draw everything after them." The individual is the heart of society.

To talk about making men better we must have some idea of what men are, because if we have none, we can have no idea of what is good or bad for them. If men are brutes like other animals, then there is no reason why they should not be treated like brutes by anybody who can gain power over them. And there is no reason why they should not be trained as brutes are trained. A sound philosophy in general suggests that men are rational, moral, and spiritual beings and that the improvement of men means the fullest development of their rational, moral, and spiritual powers. All men have these powers, and all men should develop them to the fullest extent.

Man is by nature free, and he is by nature social. To use his freedom rightly he needs discipline. To live in society he needs the moral virtues. Good moral and intellectual habits are required for the fullest development of the nature of man.

To develop fully as a social, political animal man needs participation in his own government. A benevolent despotism will not do. You cannot expect the slave to show the virtues of the free man unless you first set him free. Only democracy, in which all men rule and are ruled in turn for the good life of the whole community, can be an absolutely good form of government.

The community rests on the social nature of men. It requires communication among its members. They do not have to agree with one another; but they must be able to understand one another. And their philosophy in general must supply them with a common purpose and a common concept of man and society adequate to hold the community together. Civilization is the deliberate pursuit of a common ideal. The good society is not just a society we happen to like or to be used to. It is a community of good men.

Education deals with the development of the intellectual powers of men. Their moral and spiritual powers are the sphere of the family and the church. All three agencies must work in harmony; for, though a man has three aspects, he is still one man. But the schools cannot take over the role of the family and the church without promoting the atrophy of those institutions and failing in the task that is proper to the schools.

We cannot talk about the intellectual powers of men, though we can talk about training them, or amusing them, or adapting them, and meeting their immediate needs, unless our philosophy in general tells us that there is knowledge and that there is a difference between true and false. We must believe, too, that there are other means of obtaining knowledge than scientific experimentation. If knowledge can be sought only in the laboratory, many fields in which we thought we had knowledge will offer us nothing but opinion or superstition, and we shall be forced to conclude that we cannot know anything about the most important aspects of man and society. If we are to set about developing the intellectual powers of man through having them acquire knowledge of the most important subjects, we have to begin with the proposition that experimentation and empirical data will be of only limited use to us, contrary to the convictions of many American social scientists, and that philosophy, history, literature, and art give us knowledge, and significant knowledge, on the most significant issues.

If the object of education is the improvement of men, then any system of education that is without values is a contradiction in terms. A system that seeks bad values is bad. A system that denies the existence of values denies the

possibility of education. Relativism, scientism, skepticism, and anti-intellectualism, the four horsemen of the philosophical apocalypse, have produced
that chaos in education which will end in the disintegration of the West.

The prime object of education is to know what is good for man. It is to
know the goods in their order. There is a hierarchy of values. The task of
education is to help us understand it, establish it, and live by it. This Aristotle
had in mind when he said: "It is not the possessions but the desires of men
that must be equalized, and this is impossible unless they have a sufficient
education according to the nature of things."

Such an education is far removed from the triviality of that produced by
the doctrines of adaptation, of immediate needs, of social reform, or of the
doctrine of no doctrine at all. Such an education will not adapt the young to a
bad environment, but it will encourage them to make it good. It will not
overlook immediate needs, but it will place these needs in their proper relationship to more distant, less tangible, and more important goods. It will be
the only effective means of reforming society.

This is the education appropriate to free men. It is liberal education. If
all men are to be free, all men must have this education. It makes no difference how they are to earn their living or what their special interests or aptitudes may be. They can learn to make a living, and they can develop their
special interests and aptitudes, after they have laid the foundation of free and
responsible manhood through liberal education. It will not do to say that they
are incapable of such education. This claim is made by those who are too
indolent or unconvinced to make the effort to give such education to the
masses.

Nor will it do to say that there is not enough time to give everybody a
liberal education before he becomes a specialist. In America, at least, the
waste and frivolity of the educational system are so great that it would be
possible through getting rid of them to give every citizen a liberal education
and make him a qualified specialist, too, in less time than is now consumed in
turning out uneducated specialists.

A liberal education aims to develop the powers of understanding and
judgment. It is impossible that too many people can be educated in this sense,
because there cannot be too many people with understanding and judgment.
We hear a great deal today about the dangers that will come upon us through
the frustration of educated people who have got educated in the expectation
that education will get them a better job, and who then fail to get it. But
surely this depends on the representations that are made to the young about
what education is. If we allow them to believe that education will get them
better jobs and encourage them to get educated with this end in view, they are
entitled to a sense of frustration if, when they have got the education, they do
not get the jobs. But, if we say that they should be educated in order to be

men, and that everybody, whether he is a ditch-digger or a bank president, should have this education because he is a man, then the ditch-digger may still feel frustrated, but not because of his education.

Nor is it possible for a person to have too much liberal education, because it is impossible to have too much understanding and judgment. But it is possible to undertake too much in the name of liberal education in youth. The object of liberal education in youth is not to teach the young all they will ever need to know. It is to give them the habits, ideas, and techniques that they need to continue to educate themselves. Thus the object of formal institutional liberal education in youth is to prepare the young to educate themselves throughout their lives.

I would remind you of the impossibility of learning to understand and judge many of the most important things in youth. The judgment and understanding of practical affairs can amount to little in the absence of experience with practical affairs. Subjects that cannot be understood without experience should not be taught to those who are without experience. Or, if these subjects are taught to those who are without experience, it should be clear that these subjects can be taught only by way of introduction and that their value to the student depends on his continuing to study them as he acquires experience. The tragedy in America is that economics, ethics, politics, history, and literature are studied in youth, and seldom studied again. Therefore the graduates of American universities seldom understand them.

This pedagogical principle, that subjects requiring experience can be learned only by the experienced, leads to the conclusion that the most important branch of education is the education of adults. We sometimes seem to think of education as something like the mumps, measles, whooping-cough, or chicken-pox. If a person has had education in childhood, he need not, in fact he cannot, have it again. But the pedagogical principle that the most important things can be learned only in mature life is supported by a sound philosophy in general. Men are rational animals. They achieve their terrestrial felicity by the use of reason. And this means that they have to use it for their entire lives. To say that they should learn only in childhood would mean that they were human only in childhood.

And it would mean that they were unfit to be citizens of a republic. A republic, a true *res publica*, can maintain justice, peace, freedom, and order only by the exercise of intelligence. When we speak of the consent of the governed, we mean, since men are not angels who seek the truth intuitively and do not have to learn it, that every act of assent on the part of the governed is a product of learning. A republic is really a common educational life in process. So Montesquieu said that, whereas the principle of a monarchy was honor, and the principle of a tyranny was fear, the principle of a republic was education.

Hence the ideal republic is the republic of learning. It is the utopia by which all actual political republics are measured. The goal toward which we started with the Athenians twenty-five centuries ago is an unlimited republic of learning and a world-wide political republic mutually supporting each other.

All men are capable of learning. Learning does not stop as long as a man lives, unless his learning power atrophies because he does not use it. Political freedom cannot endure unless it is accompanied by provision for the un-limited acquisition of knowledge. Truth is not long retained in human affairs without continual learning and relearning. Peace is unlikely unless there are continuous, unlimited opportunities for learning and unless men continuously avail themselves of them. The world of law and justice for which we yearn, the world-wide political republic, cannot be realized without the world-wide republic of learning. The civilization we seek will be achieved when all men are citizens of the world republic of law and justice and of the republic of learning all their lives long.

A SCIENCE
OF BEHAVIOR

AUTHOR:

B. F. Skinner (1904–   )

WORK:

SCIENCE
AND HUMAN BEHAVIOR (1953)

The immediate tangible results of science make it easier to appraise than philosophy, poetry, art, or theology. As George Sarton has pointed out, science is unique in showing a cumulative progress. Newton explained his tremendous achievements by saying that he stood on the shoulders of giants. All scientists, whether giants or not, enable those who follow them to begin a little further along. This is not necessarily true elsewhere. Our contemporary writers, artists, and philosophers are not appreciably more effective than those of the golden age of Greece, yet the average high-school student understands much more of nature than the greatest of Greek scientists. A comparison of the effectiveness of Greek and modern science is scarcely worth making.

It is clear, then, that science "has something." It is a unique intellectual process which yields remarkable results. The danger is that its astonishing

357

accomplishments may conceal its true nature. This is especially important when we extend the methods of science to a new field. The basic characteristics of science are not restricted to any particular subject matter. When we study physics, chemistry, or biology, we study organized accumulations of information. These are not science itself but the products of science. We may not be able to use much of this material when we enter new territory. Nor should we allow ourselves to become enamored of instruments of research. We tend to think of the scientist in his observatory or laboratory, with his telescopes, microscopes, and cyclotrons. Instruments give us a dramatic picture of science in action. But although science could not have gone very far without the devices which improve our contact with the surrounding world, and although any advanced science would be helpless without them, they are not science itself. We should not be disturbed if familiar instruments are lacking in a new field. Nor is science to be identified with precise measurement or mathematical calculation. It is better to be exact than inexact, and much of modern science would be impossible without quantitative observations and without the mathematical tools needed to convert its reports into more general statements; but we may measure or be mathematical without being scientific at all, just as we may be scientific in an elementary way without these aids.

SOME IMPORTANT CHARACTERISTICS OF SCIENCE

Science is first of all a set of attitudes. It is a disposition to deal with the facts rather than with what someone has said about them. Rejection of authority was the theme of the revival of learning, when men dedicated themselves to the study of "nature, not books." Science rejects even its own authorities when they interfere with the observation of nature.

Science is a willingness to accept facts even when they are opposed to wishes. Thoughtful men have perhaps always known that we are likely to see things as we want to see them instead of as they are, but thanks to Sigmund Freud we are today much more clearly aware of "wishful thinking." The opposite of wishful thinking is intellectual honesty—an extremely important possession of the successful scientist. Scientists are by nature no more honest than other men but, as Bridgman has pointed out, the practice of science puts an exceptionally high premium on honesty. It is characteristic of science that any lack of honesty quickly brings disaster. Consider, for example, a scientist who conducts research to test a theory for which he is already well known. The result may confirm his theory, contradict it, or leave it in doubt. In spite of any inclination to the contrary, he must report a contradiction just as readily as a confirmation. If he does not, someone else will—in a matter of weeks or months or at most a few years—and this will be more damaging to his prestige than if he himself had reported it. Where right and wrong are not so easily or so quickly established, there is no similar pressure. In the long run, the issue is not so much one of personal prestige as of effective procedure. Scientists have simply found that being honest—with oneself as much as with others—is essential to progress. Experiments do not always come out as one expects, but the facts must stand and the expectations fall. The subject matter, not the scientist, knows best. The same practical consequences have created the scientific atmosphere in which statements are constantly submitted to check, where nothing is put above a precise description of the facts, and where facts are accepted no matter how distasteful their momentary consequences.

Scientists have also discovered the value of remaining without an answer until a satisfactory one can be found. This is a difficult lesson. It takes considerable training to avoid premature conclusions, to refrain from making statements on insufficient evidence, and to avoid explanations which are pure invention. Yet the history of science has demonstrated again and again the advantage of these practices.

Science is, of course, more than a set of attitudes. It is a search for order, for uniformities, for lawful relations among the events in nature. It begins, as we all begin, by observing single episodes, but it quickly passes on to the general rule, to scientific law. Something very much like the order expressed in a scientific law appears in our behavior at an early age. We learn the rough geometry of the space in which we move. We learn the "laws of motion" as we move about, or push and pull objects, or throw and catch them. If we could not find some uniformity in the world, our conduct would remain haphazard and ineffective. Science sharpens and supplements this experience by demonstrating more and more relations among events and by demonstrating them more and more precisely. As Ernst Mach showed in tracing the history of the science of mechanics, the earliest laws of science were probably the rules used by craftsmen and artisans in training apprentices. The rules saved time because the experienced craftsman could teach an apprentice a variety of details in a single formula. By learning a rule the apprentice could deal with particular cases as they arose.

In a later stage science advances from the collection of rules or laws to larger systematic arrangements. Not only does it make statements about the world, it makes statements about statements. It sets up a "model" of its subject matter, which helps to generate new rules very much as the rules themselves generate new practices in dealing with single cases. A science may not reach this stage for some time.

The scientific "system," like the law, is designed to enable us to handle a subject matter more efficiently. What we call the scientific conception of a thing is not passive knowledge. Science is not concerned with contemplation. When we have discovered the laws which govern a part of the world about us, and when we have organized these laws into a system, we are then ready to deal effectively with that part of the world. By predicting the occurrence of an event we are able to prepare for it. By arranging conditions in ways specified by the laws of a system, we not only predict, we control: we "cause" an event to occur or to assume certain characteristics.

BEHAVIOR AS A SCIENTIFIC SUBJECT MATTER

Behavior is not one of those subject matters which become accessible only with the invention of an instrument such as the telescope or microscope. We all know thousands of facts about behavior. Actually there is no subject matter with which we could be better acquainted, for we are always in the presence of at least one behaving organism. But this familiarity is something of a disadvantage, for it means that we have probably jumped to conclusions which will not be supported by the cautious methods of science. Even though we have observed behavior for many years, we are not necessarily able, without help, to express useful uniformities or lawful relations. We may show considerable skill in making plausible guesses about what our friends and acquaintances will do under various circumstances or what we ourselves will do. We may make plausible generalizations about the conduct of people in general. But very few of these will survive careful analysis. A great deal of unlearning generally takes place in our early contact with a science of behavior.

Behavior is a difficult subject matter, not because it is inaccessible, but because it is extremely complex. Since it is a process, rather than a thing, it cannot easily be held still for observation. It is changing, fluid, and evanescent, and for this reason it makes great technical demands upon the ingenuity and energy of the scientist. But there is nothing essentially insoluble about the problems which arise from this fact.

Several kinds of statements about behavior are commonly made. When we tell an anecdote or pass along a bit of gossip, we report a *single event*— what someone did upon such and such an occasion: "She slammed the door and walked off without a word." Our report is a small bit of history. History itself is often nothing more than similar reporting on a broad scale. The biographer often confines himself to a series of episodes in the life of his subject. The case history, which occupies an important place in several fields of psychology, is a kind of biography which is also concerned mainly with what a particular person did at particular times and places: "When she was eleven, Mary went to live with her maiden aunt in Winchester." Novels and short stories may be thought of as veiled biography or history, since the ingredients of even a highly fanciful work of fiction are somehow or other taken from life. The narrative reporting of the behavior of people at particular times and places is also part of the sciences of archeology, ethnology, sociology, and anthropology.

These accounts have their uses. They broaden the experience of those who have not had firsthand access to similar data. But they are only the beginnings of a science. No matter how accurate or quantitative it may be, the report of the single case is only a preliminary step. The next step is the discovery of some sort of uniformity. When we tell an anecdote to support an argument, or report a case history to exemplify a principle, we imply a general rule, no matter how vaguely it may be expressed. The historian is seldom content with mere narration. He reports his facts to support a theory—of cycles, trends, or patterns of history. In doing so he passes from the single instance to the rule. When a biographer traces the influence of an early event upon a man's later life, he transcends simple reporting and asserts, no matter how hesitantly, that one thing has caused another. Fable and allegory are more than storytelling if they imply some kind of uniformity in human behavior, as they generally do. Our preference for "consistency of character" and our rejection of implausible coincidences in literature show that we expect lawfulness. The "manners" and "customs" of the sociologist and anthropologist report the *general* behavior of groups of people.

A vague sense of order emerges from any sustained observation of human behavior. Any plausible guess about what a friend will do or say in a given circumstance is a prediction based upon some such uniformity. If a reasonable order was not discoverable, we could scarcely be effective in dealing with human affairs. The methods of science are designed to clarify these uniformities and make them explicit. The techniques of field study of the anthropologist and social psychologist, the procedures of the psychological clinic, and the controlled experimental methods of the laboratory are all directed toward this end, as are also the mathematical and logical tools of science.

Many people interested in human behavior do not feel the need for the standards of proof characteristic of an exact science; the uniformities in behavior are "obvious" without them. At the same time, they are reluctant to accept the conclusions toward which such proof inescapably points if they do not "sense" the uniformity themselves. But these idiosyncrasies are a costly luxury. We need not defend the methods of science in their application to behavior. The experimental and mathematical techniques used in discovering and expressing uniformities are the common property of science in general. Almost every discipline has contributed to this pool of resources, and all disciplines borrow from it. The advantages are well established.

SOME OBJECTIONS TO A SCIENCE
OF BEHAVIOR

The report of a single event raises no theoretical problems and comes into no conflict with philosophies of human behavior. The scientific laws or systems which express uniformities are likely to conflict with theory because they claim the same territory. When a science of behavior reaches the point of dealing with lawful relationships, it meets the resistance of those who give their allegiance to prescientific or extrascientific conceptions. The resistance does not always take the form of an overt rejection of science. It may be transmuted into claims of limitations, often expressed in highly scientific terms.

It has sometimes been pointed out, for example, that physical science has been unable to maintain its philosophy of determinism, particularly at the subatomic level. The Principle of Indeterminacy states that there are circumstances under which the physicist cannot put himself in possession of all relevant information: if he chooses to observe one event, he must relinquish the possibility of observing another. In our present state of knowledge, certain events therefore appear to be unpredictable. It does not follow that these events are free or capricious. Since human behavior is enormously complex and the human organism is of limited dimensions, many acts may involve processes to which the Principle of Indeterminacy applies. It does not follow that human behavior is free, but only that it may be beyond the range of a predictive or controlling science. Most students of behavior, however, would be willing to settle for the degree of prediction and control achieved by the physical sciences in spite of this limitation. A final answer to the problem of lawfulness is to be sought, not in the limits of any hypothetical mechanism within the organism, but in our ability to demonstrate lawfulness in the behavior of the organism as a whole.

A similar objection has a logical flavor. It is contended that reason cannot comprehend itself or—in somewhat more substantial terms—that the behavior required in understanding one's own behavior must be something beyond the behavior which is understood. It is true that knowledge is limited by the limitations of the knowing organism. The number of things in the world which might be known certainly exceeds the number of possible different states in all possible knowers. But the laws and systems of science are designed to make a knowledge of particular events unimportant. It is by no means necessary that one man should understand all the facts in a given field, but only that he should understand all the *kinds* of facts. We have no reason to suppose that the human intellect is incapable of formulating or comprehending the basic principles of human behavior—certainly not until we have a clearer notion of what those principles are.

The assumption that behavior is a lawful scientific datum sometimes meets with another objection. Science is concerned with the general, but the behavior of the individual is necessarily unique. The "case history" has a richness and flavor which are in decided contrast with general principles. It is easy to convince oneself that there are two distinct worlds and that one is beyond the reach of science. This distinction is not peculiar to the study of behavior. It can always be made in the early stages of any science, when it is not clear what we may deduce from a general principle with respect to a particular case. What the science of physics has to say about the world is dull and colorless to the beginning student when compared with his daily experience, but he later discovers that it is actually a more incisive account of even the single instance. When we wish to deal effectively with the single instance, we turn to science for help. The argument will lose cogency as a science of behavior progresses and as the implications of its general laws become clear. A comparable argument against the possibility of a science of medicine has already lost its significance. In *War and Peace,* Tolstoy wrote of the illness of a favorite character as follows:

> Doctors came to see Natasha, both separately and in consultation. They said a great deal in French, in German, and in Latin. They criticized one another, and prescribed the most diverse remedies for all the diseases they were familiar with. But it never occurred to one of them to make the simple reflection that they could not understand the disease from which Natasha was suffering, as no single disease can be fully understood in a living person; for every living person has his individual peculiarities and always has his own peculiar, new, complex complaints unknown to medicine—not a disease of the lungs, of the kidneys, of the skin, of the heart, and so on, as described in medical books, but a disease that consists of one out of the innumerable combinations of ailments of those organs.

Tolstoy was justified in calling every sickness a unique event. Every action of the individual is unique, as well as every event in physics and chemistry. But his objection to a science of medicine in terms of uniqueness was unwarranted. The argument was plausible enough at the time; no one could then contradict him by supplying the necessary general principles. But a great deal has happened in medical science since then, and today few people would care to argue that a disease cannot be described in general terms or that a single case cannot be discussed by referring to factors common to many cases. The intuitive wisdom of the old-style diagnostician has been largely replaced by the analytical procedures of the clinic, just as a scientific analysis of behavior will eventually replace the personal interpretation of unique instances.

A similar argument is leveled at the use of statistics in a science of behavior. A prediction of what the average individual will do is often of little or no value in dealing with a particular individual. The actuarial tables of life-insurance companies are of no value to a physician in predicting the death or survival of a particular patient. This issue is still alive in the physical sciences, where it is associated with the concepts of causality and probability. It is seldom that the science of physics deals with the behavior of individual molecules, atoms, or subatomic particles. When it is occasionally called upon to do so, all the problems of the particular event arise. In general a science is helpful in dealing with the individual only insofar as its laws refer to individuals. A science of behavior which concerns only the behavior of groups is not likely to be of help in our understanding of the particular case. But a science may also deal with the behavior of the individual, and its successes in doing so must be evaluated in terms of its achievements rather than any a priori contentions.

The extraordinary complexity of behavior is sometimes held to be an added source of difficulty. Even though behavior may be lawful, it may be too complex to be dealt with in terms of law. Sir Oliver Lodge once asserted that "though an astronomer can calculate the orbit of a planet or comet or even a meteor, although a physicist can deal with the structure of atoms and a chemist with their possible combinations, neither a biologist nor any scientific man can calculate the orbit of a common fly." This is a statement about the limitations of scientists or about their aspirations, not about the suitability of a subject matter. Even so, it is wrong. It may be said with some assurance that if no one has calculated the orbit of a fly, it is only because no one has been sufficiently interested in doing so. The tropistic movements of many insects are now fairly well understood, but the instrumentation needed to record the flight of a fly and to give an account of all the conditions affecting it would cost more than the importance of the subject justifies. There is, therefore, no reason to conclude, as the author does, that "an incalculable element of self-determination thus makes its appearance quite low down on the animal scale." Self-determination does not follow from complexity. Difficulty in calculating the orbit of the fly does not prove capriciousness, though it may make it impossible to prove anything else. The problems imposed by the complexity of a subject matter must be dealt with as they arise. Apparently hopeless cases often become manageable in time. It is only recently that any sort of lawful account of the weather has been possible. We often succeed in reducing complexity to a reasonable degree by simplifying conditions in the laboratory; but where this is impossible, a statistical analysis may be used to achieve an inferior, but in many ways acceptable, prediction. Certainly no one is prepared to say now what a science of behavior can or cannot accomplish eventually. Advance estimates of the limits of science have generally proved inaccurate. The issue is in the long run pragmatic: we cannot tell until we have tried.

Still another objection to the use of scientific method in the study of human behavior is that behavior is an anomalous subject matter because a prediction made about it may alter it. If we tell a friend that he is going to buy a particular kind of car, he may react to our prediction by buying a different kind. The same effect has been used to explain the failures of public opinion polls. In the presidential election of 1948 it was confidently predicted that a majority of the voters would vote for a candidate who, as it turned out, lost the election. It has been asserted that the electorate reacted to the prediction in a contrary way and that the published prediction therefore had an effect upon the predicted event. But it is by no means necessary that a prediction of behavior be permitted to affect the behaving individual. There may have been practical reasons why the results of the poll in question could not be withheld until after the election, but this would not be the case in a purely scientific endeavor.

There are other ways in which observer and observed interact. Study distorts the thing studied. But there is no special problem here peculiar to human behavior. It is now accepted as a general principle in scientific method that it is necessary to interfere in some degree with any phenomenon in the act of observing it. A scientist may have an effect upon behavior in the act of observing or analyzing it, and he must certainly take this effect into account. But behavior may also be observed with a minimum of interaction between subject and scientist, and this is the case with which one naturally tries to begin.

A final objection deals with the practical application of a scientific analysis. Even if we assume that behavior is lawful and that the methods of science will reveal the rules which govern it, we may be unable to make any technological use of these rules unless certain conditions can be brought under control. In the laboratory many conditions are simplified and irrelevant conditions often eliminated. But of what value are laboratory studies if we must predict and control behavior where a comparable simplification is impossible? It is true that we can gain control over behavior only insofar as we can control the factors responsible for it. What a scientific study does is to enable us to make optimal use of the control we possess. The laboratory simplification reveals the relevance of factors which we might otherwise overlook.

We cannot avoid the problems raised by a science of behavior by simply denying that the necessary conditions can be controlled. In actual fact there is a considerable degree of control over many relevant conditions. In penal institutions and military organizations the control is extensive. We control the environment of the human organism in the nursery and in institutions which care for those to whom the conditions of the nursery remain necessary in later life. Fairly extensive control of conditions relevant to human behavior is maintained in industry in the form of wages and conditions of work, in schools in the form of grades and conditions of work, in commerce by anyone in possession of goods or money, by governmental agencies through the police and military, in the psychological clinic through the consent of the controllee, and so on. A degree of effective control, not so easily identified, rests in the hands of entertainers, writers, advertisers, and propagandists. These controls, which are often all too evident in their practical application, are more than sufficient to permit us to extend the results of a laboratory science to the interpretation of human behavior in daily affairs—for either theoretical or practical purposes. Since a science of behavior will continue to increase the effective use of this control, it is now more important than ever to understand the processes involved and to prepare ourselves for the problems which will certainly arise.

TOWARD
QUALITY
EDUCATION

AUTHOR:

Arthur Bestor (*1908–*   )

WORK:

THE RESTORATION
OF LEARNING (1955)

. . . In a document that I presented to the American Historical Association
in December, 1952, I attempted to summarize the educational principles and
beliefs to which scholars and scientists subscribe. The eight points of this
statement may appropriately be reprinted here to constitute, as it were, a
prospectus of the present volume:

> 1. An indispensable function of education, at every level, is to pro-
> vide sound training in the fundamental ways of thinking represented
> by history, science, mathematics, literature, language, art, and the other
> disciplines evolved in the course of mankind's long quest for usable

From *The Restoration of Learning* by Arthur Bestor (New York: Alfred A. Knopf,
Inc., 1955), pp. 7–9, 23–25. Footnotes omitted. Copyright 1955 by Arthur Bestor.
Reprinted by permission.

knowledge, cultural understanding, and intellectual power. To advance moral conduct, responsible citizenship, and social adjustment is, of course, a vital function of education. But, like the other agencies which contribute to these ends, the school must work within the context provided by its own characteristic activity. In other words, the particular contribution which the school can make is determined by, and related to, the primary fact that it is an agency of intellectual training.

2. The ability to handle and apply complex ideas, to make use of a wide range of accurate knowledge, and to command the means of effective expression is valuable not only to the scholar or scientist, but equally to the citizen, the businessman, the skilled worker, the farmer, the housewife, and the parent. Their practical needs cannot be effectively served by vocational and utilitarian training unless such training includes a conscious intellectual component. Only if men are led to grasp the theory behind the practice can they achieve the superior efficiency in every activity of life which comes, as Horace Mann said, "where *mind* is a member of the partnership."

3. An educational philosophy is both anti-intellectual and anti-democratic if it asserts that sound training in the fundamental intellectual disciplines is appropriate only for the minority of students who are preparing for college and the professions, and if it proposes to deprive the rest of the children of our people of such training by substituting programs that minimize intellectual aims.

4. The content of the public-school curriculum is of such vital importance to the entire intellectual, scientific, and professional life of the nation that control of secondary-school educational policy ought not to be vested exclusively in a narrow group of secondary-school administrators and professional educators. Scholars, scientists, and other professional men must assume responsibility for advising the public clearly and continuously concerning the scientific and scholarly soundness of proposed changes in the curricula of the public schools. And universities and colleges must preserve and strengthen their entrance requirements in the basic fields of knowledge not merely to maintain their own standards but also to prevent, so far as possible, the deterioration of the secondary-school education which is provided for students not planning to enter college.

5. The great intellectual disciplines are not mere collections of facts and formulas, but ways of thinking with organized structures of their own. The learning of facts is not intellectual training, unless those facts are seen as the conclusions of systematic inquiry and as part of a larger structure of knowledge. Reorganizations of the curriculum are destructive if they cause the student to lose sight of the ordered relationships that exist, and of the methods of investigation that are employed, within each of the basic fields of knowledge. In particular, no genuine knowledge of history is imparted by an omnibus course that

uses isolated historical facts merely as illustrations, that presents no conception of historical development, or that treats history itself as irrelevant to an understanding of contemporary society.

6. "It being, of course, the first requisite of a teacher that he should himself know well that which he is to aid others in learning" (to quote the words spoken at the opening of one of the two original institutions for teacher training established in the United States), all programs for the training and certification of teachers must emphasize competence in the subject to be taught. Experienced teachers, in particular, ought not to be permited to achieve professional advancement by piling up additional credits in pedagogical courses when their greatest need is to acquire a more thorough and advanced knowledge of the disciplines they are responsible for teaching.

7. Freedom implies responsibility, and freedom of teaching implies a responsibility on the teacher's part of knowing the facts and of applying the critical methods of scholarship to the subjects that come up for discussion in the classroom. The freedom of all teachers is placed in jeopardy whenever teachers who are inadequately trained in subject matter undertake to handle controversial topics. Especially in history and the social studies, where practically all topics are controversial, freedom of teaching can be convincingly defended only if teachers are held to rigorous standards of competence in the disciplines involved.

8. To insist that instruction must meet the exacting standards of scholarship is not to infringe upon freedom of teaching. Such infringements occur when pressure groups—whether reactionary or radical—force the schools to conform to their preconceived ideas, to limit the curriculum, to censor textbooks, or to forbid the teaching of controversial subjects. Scientists and scholars must vigorously resist such efforts to impose upon the schools any narrow dogma in politics, economics, religion, or science, for learning itself is thereby threatened with destruction. They must also resist anti-intellectualism in the schools themselves, for if freedom of thinking and respect for intellectual effort are undermined there, it will be easy for demagogues to convince a larger public that intellectual effort is of little value in any case, and that freedom of thought is not worth preserving.

.   .   .

To anyone but an educationist the unchanging character of the criticism directed against the schools is proof that educational administrators have failed to put first things first. The persistent cry that schools should provide more adequate training in the basic skills of reading, writing, and arithmetic can be interpreted in no other way than as a mandate from the public to devote the full resources of the public schools to improved and intensified training in the fundamental intellectual disciplines, before venturing upon new experiments. Leading educationists arrogantly refuse to heed this mandate. They profess to be obeying the wishes of the public when they divert the schools from fundamental studies to "consumer education" and "life adjustment." They can make this assertion only by contemptuously ignoring the most clear-cut of all the expressions of public opinion in the matter—the unending complaints about inadequate teaching of basic intellectual skills. The fact of the matter is that there is no evidence of public pressure for "life-adjustment" education so long-continued, so universal, and so intense as the demand for better training in the "three R's."

Educational progress requires much more than money. The public schools of the United States are in need, above all, of adequate aims. In the sciences, in scholarship, in the learned professions, the men responsible for educational progress have been scholars and scientists in their own right. They have begun by accepting the traditional aims of their respective disciplines and professions, and they have defined their task as the carrying out of these recognized aims in a manner more effective than ever before. They have deliberately measured their achievement, not in terms of some slight improvement over the past, but in terms of the best that could possibly be done by any man, in any place, at any time. Until public-school educationists learn to think in the same way—until they acquire sufficient intellectual humility to accept the guidance of past experience and of the considered judgment of the modern learned world—no amount of financial support can possibly raise our schools above mediocrity. And mediocrity, given the possibilities that America offers to public education, is nothing else than downright failure.

Mediocrity is not an inescapable characteristic of democratic education. It is simply a characteristic of any educational system whose leaders have lost their faith and lowered their aims. Such a disastrous weakening of purpose has occurred, I believe, during the last two or three decades of American public education. In their policy-making role, the recently dominant group of professional educationists have adjusted downward the goals of the public schools, not out of necessity but because of a certain paralysis of will that results from confused thinking about the nature of education and of democracy. If we are to enter, as we should, upon the new qualitative phase of American educational development, we must seek guidance less narrow, less provincial, less backward-looking, and less timid than that which is furnished by the entrenched defenders of the educational *status quo*.

The founders of our Republic and of our school system betrayed no such uncertainty of purpose and no such confusion of values as we find in the educational world today. "If a nation expects to be ignorant and free," wrote Thomas Jefferson, ". . . it expects what never was and never will be." Jefferson intended his words to be taken literally. He knew, moreover, what he meant by "education." It is, first of all, the opposite of ignorance. Its positive meaning is indicated by the various synonyms that Jefferson employed in his letters. The kind of schooling that is vital to a democratic society is the kind that results in the "spread of information" and the "diffusion of knowledge"; the kind that regards "science . . . [as] more important in a republican than than in any other government"; the kind that recognizes that "the general mind must be strengthened by education"; the kind that aims to make the people "enlightened" and to "inform their discretion." These are the ends that the schools must serve if a free people are to remain free. These, be it noted, are intellectual ends. Genuine education, in short, is intellectual training.

The founders of our public-school system meant by "education" exactly what Jefferson meant by education and exactly what thoughtful men had always meant by it. They believed, quite simply, that ignorance is a handicap, and disciplined intelligence a source of power. A democracy, they argued, should make intellectual training available to every citizen, whether poor or rich. So great would be the benefit to the state from such a diffusion of knowledge and intelligence that it was legitimate to support the educational system by taxation, and even to use the coercive authority of law to compel every future citizen to secure an education by attending school for a substantial period of time.

A school that waters down its curriculum is not upholding but denying this time-honored ideal of democratic education, for it is in practice depriving our young men and women of that abundant educational opportunity which democracy promised. A school that furnishes only a narrow, vocational, workaday training to children of humble parentage is effectually denying the innate dignity of man—a doctrine which asserts that every individual, whatever his trade or his income, is entitled to share in the high, humane tradition of the liberal arts and sciences. A school that puts the trivia of "life-adjustment" education on a par with rigorous study of the fundamental intellectual disciplines is not vindicating democracy but is doing its best to demonstrate that the opponents of democracy were right when they predicted that a democratic society would be a society without standards or values.

A new era is about to commence in American education. If it is to be an era of light and not of darkness, we must reaffirm, for the benefit of our tired and faltering educational leaders, our continuing faith in intellectual values. The American people must go forward to prove, what they originally set out to prove, that democratic schools can be as sound and enlightened in their learning and as vigorous in their intellectual life as the schools of any society on earth.

EDUCATIONAL POWER STRUCTURE

AUTHOR:

David Riesman (1909–   )

WORK:

CONSTRAINT AND VARIETY IN AMERICAN EDUCATION
(1956)

. . . It is obvious that not all secondary school systems are alike: they differ as much among themselves as the colleges do. A few big-city and suburban public high schools (such as Boston Latin, Winnetka's New Trier, the Scarsdale schools, New York City's High School of Music and Art or Stuyvesant High, etc.) have quite as much of a tradition of intellectual distinction and even as devoted and protective alumni as all but a small handful of private schools—and offer a far better education than many col-

Reprinted from *Constraint and Variety in American Education* by David Riesman by permission of University of Nebraska Press. Copyright © 1956, 1958 by the University of Nebraska Press. Selection from 1965 edition, pp. 90–95, 100–101, 104–106.

leges do. Occasionally, as happened in Pasadena, such schools may lose a fight for freedom and experimentalism, but they recognize the fight as theirs.

In many ways the high schools are today in the position the colleges were a hundred years ago. In their need to monitor idly prankish youth, in their "collegiate" razzle-dazzle of sports and dating, in their fear of being called "godless," in their need (not financial but political) to accept whoever comes, in their unavoidable concern with morals, they recall many vignettes we have of nineteenth-century college life. Of course, the differences are great, too: the high schools today involve the whole community in a way that even the colleges with the most vociferous subway alumni neither did nor do; and one could argue that in some ways high school youth is presently more mature and more sober than college youth of the collegiate generations. Moreover, when we read W. Lloyd Warner's *Democracy in Jonesville* and August B. Hollingshead's description of the same Midwest small town in *Elmtown's Youth,* we are reminded of still another feature of the early American college, namely, its emphasis on parental social standing as the basis for seating and even for honors; for these books show the high school and its teachers to be almost completely dominated by the "better element," to the extent of influencing grades given and such honors as leading the band, according to the social-class position of the family. The same theme of class (and in the South, caste) domination of the schools appears in other books of the Warner group, such as Allison Davis and John Dollard's *Children of Bondage,* and in John Gillin's chapter on "The School in the Context of the Community" in *Education and Anthropology.*

Which Public Runs the Schools?

Other studies, however, have shown rapid democratizing tendencies to be at work in the control of the schools just as these tendencies have also, in hardly more than a generation, altered the high school from a college preparatory institution for one-fifth or so of the teen-agers (or an occasional terminal institution for the girls) to the taken-for-granted pattern for four-fifths or more. In a number of communities the school boards have become highly democratic in the sense of reflecting, with at least equal voice, the less educated and the less privileged strata. Thus, in one New England manufacturing city, the superintendency and the school board have become the symbols, even more than such an office as the mayoralty, of ethnic and class conflict, with the Irish and to a lesser degree the French Canadians getting their revenge on the Beacon Hill-type snobs of earlier generations. Since the lower-class parent has no interest in the schools, save as a political symbol, unless his own children are of school age, this means that the superintendent of schools must, if he lasts that long, educate a new group of constituents every few years—a totally different situation from that of the private school headmaster who has managed to cultivate a self-perpetuating body of trustees.

Likewise, an unpublished study done on the West Coast has shown how the school board in an expanding industrial town became the representative agency in the town, speaking not only for the newcomer industrialists but for the farmers and others of lesser education who didn't want to see any "new-fangled notions" in the schools, any more than they wanted to see the town's water monkeyed with by fluoridation—this last being, as I mentioned in my second lecture, as issue on which the more parochial have in some towns mobilized to defeat the more cosmopolitan and science-minded higher status groups.

The handful of studies we have (including the Lynds' close scrutiny of the control of the "Middletown" schools) do not allow us to triangulate the entire area or even readily to interpret the data we already have; thus, we know that Middletown and Elmtown are (or were) to some degree company towns and possibly not representative even of their regions. We do know that there are schools so located as to be able to profit from a balance of powers in the community—that is, to be powers themselves, able to give a cagey and purposeful superintendent quite a free hand within very broad limits—so long at least as no dramatic issue presents a group in the community with a chance to make trouble for him and capture votes and symbolic vindications for itself. Indeed, the teachers themselves, in alliance with school board members, have been known to drive a superintendent out, though on the whole they tend to stay out of fights at the hierarchy's peak and, like the conscientious civil servants they often are, to fall into line with any workable mandate from "downtown."

In rural areas, matters are again different. Warren Peterson found, in his study of women high school teachers in Kansas City, that many had entered the Kansas City system after sad experiences of rural and small-town politics, where a single shift in the school board might eliminate a school principal and virtually dispossess his teachers; in comparison, a metropolitan school system offered the security of tenure, often enforced by a union, as well as greater opportunity to specialize.

Altered Patterns of Pressure on the Teacher

The harassment of the public school teacher has been traditional in the smaller American communities, but this used to take the form (particularly if the teacher was a woman) of policing her private life, her smoking and gallivanting and church-going, without much direct interference in her conduct in the classroom. Today, especially in the larger places, the teacher is much freer to lead her own private life, but what we might term her academic freedom is under a great deal of pressure. Lack of concern over the teacher's private life reflects the general urbanization of America and the decline of puritanical vigilance over teachers, ministers, and other exemplars; meanwhile, however, concern over the teacher as a person has taken on a new aspect; the teacher is required today to be a "good guy," warm and friendly, not too eccentrically dedicated to interests in which the community cannot share. Moreover, the personality of the teacher has become more closely intertwined with the subjects taught: the high schools, which could remain fairly remote from immediate community preoccupations when attended only by a few, are now under a service-minded pressure to teach the social studies, and in many places they are also under pressure to teach a kind of syncretistic and neutral religion, as well as to teach tolerance, democracy and citizenship, and all other good things.

Teaching these topics, which contain more obvious dynamite than the limited traditional curriculum did, however, both draws on what is in the papers and risks getting into them. High school teachers can become labeled by their students as "controversial" as soon as any discussion in the social area gets at all heated or comes close to home. While a college student usually has to take the trouble to write home before he can get a parent steamed up about what a teacher has said in class, and in fact is quite likely to protect his teacher against his less enlightened parents, the secondary school student is still living at home with parents whose jealousy of the teacher is not mediated by distance either of space or of status. The high school teacher has in fact lost relative status in recent years as more and more parents themselves are high school graduates. And while the kindergarten teacher gains admiration because she can control several dozen preliterates whose mothers cannot always manage even one, the high school social studies teacher has a harder time being one-up on American-born parents who can claim to know as much as she about civics or UNESCO.

. . .

Fighting Fire with Water

The school's vulnerability is in part a matter of the rhetoric of community controversy. Suppose, as now often happens, a demand is made for religious instruction in the schools. The superintendent or school principal is against this: he thinks it can only be mushy, not truly religious—that, if anything, it will turn the kids against religion and against each other. To explain all this would take time and require some audience sophistication, while his critics will label him as "godless" if he resists. Or, to take another instance, there was a typical letter a short while ago (March 12, 1956, by Nancy McGannon) in the Chicago *Daily News* attacking the President of a division of the Illinois Education Association for resisting one of the Broyles Bills requiring all teachers to take a loyalty oath; the writer said she couldn't understand how academic freedom was abridged and ended by declaring: "I'm afraid there are a lot of parents and taxpayers who do not understand it." It is hard to imagine this "parent and taxpayer" writing a similar letter about her inability to grasp the import of one of the Hoover Commission reports or the Report of the President's Council of Economic Advisors, yet the "parents and taxpayers" do suppose that they can advise on matters having to do with education. When the President of the Illinois Education Association sought to answer her, the reply took nine paragraphs; it spelled out the ambiguity of requiring a special test oath of teachers, while at the same time it met the parent on the common ground of patriotism and anti-Communism. The very fact that the more complex positions take longer to state puts the teacher on the defensive to start with, for at best the teacher's position will be given equal chronological time and that will not suffice for clarification (unless she has the rare ingenuity for putting complex matters simply). The closer a word is to a blow, the greater its impact in the short run and the harm is done; in many controversies over the schools, there is no long run, little distance between the partisans, and few constitutional barriers to impetuosity.

THE COUNTERVAILING POWER OF THE SCHOOLS

And yet, despite all I have said, despite all the pressures and pieties to which the schools must be subservient, we know from a great accumulation of public opinion data that differences of education differentiate Americans more sharply than any other single factor. The college-educated person, whatever his religion, race, or region, tends to become internationalist and cosmopolitan in outlook, to be liberal on civil liberties issues, and in general to be tolerant. (If he terms himself conservative, it is rather because of his stand on economic and social welfare issues.) By contrast, the person who has gone only to grammar school is frequently xenophobic and suspicious—against giveaway programs and ties to foreign countries or to "foreigners" within this country. The high school and junior college graduates are between these extremes.

It is hard to separate out the effects of further schooling from the causes: we know from Kinsey's studies that the high school boy who will in all probability go to college already has different sexual patterns from the boy who will not. Income alone, apart from motivation, is not decisive, and it is clear that schooling attracts some and repels others at every point in the educational career. Certainly, one factor in the influence of high school and college is sheer size and movement; as the Junior Division *Bulletin* (of the University of Nebraska) states: college will bring "a mingling with young people from other communities and from foreign countries, whose backgrounds are different from yours and from whom you will learn just as they will learn from you" (p. 7, 1955–6). We know that this growth of mutual understanding by no means happens as a regular thing, but, coupled with whatever broadening influence the teachers have, it does make the feeling of the bigot that teachers and education in general must be watched, at least a comprehensible if not a forgivable one. We who are college teachers are all too aware how little impact we and our ideas ordinarily have on the young, but the polls show us that we are part of an apparatus in our society that sorts people out into very different styles of life and thought.

And even at the secondary school level, as I have already implied, the teachers are not quite so powerless in controlling the customers as might appear. Any subordinate finds ways, along with his fellows, to frustrate superior authority, just as an Uncle Tom Negro can annoy his betters by being tardy, "stupid," and careless. In the "Blackboard Jungle" type schools studied by Howard C. Becker, the "old pro" teachers showed the young ones how to beat a child's head against the wall so it wouldn't show, and how, in general, to turn dreadful conditions into an apathetic sinecure. Likewise, Warren Peterson's study of Kansas City high school teachers gives many hints as to how, like other working groups, they set standards of performance, on the one hand, to make difficulties for the uncommitted teacher who is insufficiently related to her colleagues (he studied only the women) and, on the other hand, to put brakes on a "rate-buster" who becomes too devoted to her subject-matter or otherwise sets too exalted standards. Such solidarity often testifies to the very vulnerability of the group of colleagues, and it may be especially strong when there is little support for the teacher against parental pressure—little support from the principal or superintendent or school board. Understandably, this solidarity is seldom used to protect freedom or excellence of teaching, but in good trade union fashion to minimize exploitation, though it will be a long time before teachers, perhaps the most harassed of the big white-collar cadres, get a forty-hour week with a lessening of extra-curricular obligations and all the fringe benefits of the nurse, stenographer, dental technician, and airline hostess.

Furthermore, public-school teachers have done better than professors in organizing into unions which overleap the local community—this is, as just implied, in part because they are not academic, not attached to specific disciplines. In the state education departments, teachers have powerful lobbies. And in the National Education Association and the nationally known teachers colleges, the embattled teachers have begun to find support when they get into a local jam. The PTA often serves teachers as a public relations device, just as the school superintendent does. Indeed, the superintendent (and his wife) must be ceaselessly conciliatory, while fearing, like our foreign service officials, that he can never be diplomatic enough. Such men, as I have seen them, sometimes forget what they themselves think or even who they are, lest they disturb some constituent, some paranoid parent, some self-styled "taxpayer."

THE ANTHROPOLOGICAL FRONTIER

AUTHOR:

Ashley Montagu (*1905–*   )

WORK:

EDUCATION AND HUMAN RELATIONS

(1958)

I believe that one of the most important developments in our time for the educator is the discovery of culture. I mean the culture that is the domain of the anthropologist—not the "culture" that so many people talk about and so few seem to possess. I believe that the kind of culture, that private civilization of the person which we sometimes call his personality, will be assisted to become a reality when educators have fully grasped the significance of the anthropological conception of culture. What, then, is the anthropological conception of culture?

To begin with a brief definition, the shortest and the best I know: Culture is the way of life of a people. It is a people's ideas, sentiments, religious and secular beliefs, its language, tools, pots and pans, its institutions. It is largely what makes a human being out of the organism perhaps too prematurely defined as *Homo sapiens*. Culture achieves this extraordinary feat owing to the fact that this creature called *Homo sapiens* is equipped, not so much with a unique capacity, as with a capacity which is developed to a uniquely high degree, namely, the capacity to use symbols. This highly developed capacity or potentiality for symbol usage is one of the species characters of man, but it is not this symbol-using capacity which makes him the kind of human being he is capable of becoming. The other distinctively human trait is man's plasticity, his educability, the fact that he is born pretty much free of that instinctive equipment which in lower animals so largely predetermines their responses to their environment. Man has to learn his responses—if he does not he fails to develop any which are recognizably human. The fact is that you have to be taught to be human. The potentialities for being human may be there, but, if they are not humanly stimulated, conditioned, and organized, they do not develop a human form. The stimulator, the conditioner, and the organizer of human potentialities is culture.

This represents one of the most important discoveries made by man *for* man in the entire history of man. Consider what it means. It means that men can make of man anything that, within the limits of what is human, they desire. It means that human beings are *not* predestined by their so-called biological heredity to be what they become, but that they largely become what their social heredity conditions them to become, socializes or culturizes them to become. It means that human nature is not what is biologically given, but it means rather the organization by a cultural process of what is biologically given to function in a particular series of social ways at an increasingly higher level of integration. Or put in plain English, human nature has to be acquired. Purely genetic potentialities will not of themselves produce human nature. This does not mean that the human organism is a *tabula rasa* in Locke's or any other sense, but it does mean that human nature is something that we, as human beings, can, at least, have the major part in making.

This fundamental statement presents to educators the challenge of the most newly discovered frontier of knowledge. If man is so malleable, so plastic, so educable an organism, then the challenge and the choice are squarely before the educators of the world: To stop instructing and to begin discovering and thinking about the kind of human nature it is best for human beings to have. For it should be clear to everyone that it is critically important that, because man is so impressionably plastic a creature, because he is so precariously dependent for his development as a human being upon others, we be quite sure we know what kind of a human being we want him to become. That is one thing, but it is not enough. We must be quite sure that we fully understand the means of helping him to become so. Those of you who have read George Orwell's important and terrifying novel *1984* will have obtained a good idea of the kind of automata it is possible, under certain forms of socialization processes, to make of human beings. Orwell gives a perfectly sound description of the manner in which human beings could be turned into automata. Because man is so educable, so plastic a creature, he is constantly in danger of being harmed, of harming himself, and of harming others. It is therefore vital for us to discover whether there are any universally applicable laws in the organism potentially human which may help us to understand how it should be educated in order to function at its optimum as an harmonic human being.

And this is where the second great advance upon a new frontier has been made. This may be termed the discovery of the directiveness of human development. This discovery is the joint contribution of anthropologists, biologists, psychoanalysts, psychiatrists, and psychologists. It is so recent a discovery that I am not sure it is known to more than a small proportion of the members of the professions I have just named, and it is probably known to still fewer persons outside these professions. So perhaps we had better speak of this discovery as one in process of being made.

This discovery is that the organism potentially human requires to be socialized (that is to say, humanized, turned upon the lathe of human experience into a human being) in a very special way. What is that way? It is the way of love. The organism requires, demands, and must receive love. If it does not receive love it becomes disequilibrated and disharmonic. Its socialization, its educative process must be a loving one; otherwise it learns with great difficulty.

What is love? And how has it come to be known that the organism potentially human must be loved if it is to develop harmoniously, creatively, and as itself a loving, co-operative human being? This is like asking what electricity is, but there is no one who can really define it to the satisfaction of a physicist. We know how to make electricity, or at least to induce it, but it still defies definition. The best that a physicist can do is to define it in terms of the operations he uses to induce it operationally. And perhaps we can best answer the question, What is love? by stating: What the organism operationally demands in order to fulfill itself and develop as a harmonic human being.

The organism is born with certain basic needs which must be satisfied if it is to survive. These needs are: oxygen, food and liquids, bowel and bladder elimination, activity, rest, sleep, avoidance of pain and danger. It has been discovered that these basic needs must be satisfied in a dependency relationship such that the organism becomes increasingly aware of the fact that it is receiving its satisfactions whenever it requires them in a supportive manner; that it is being satisfied by persons who want to satisfy it, and who are—to put it in the best way I know—all for it; that it is being satisfied by persons on whom it can rely in the increasing awareness that its expected satisfactions will be met and not thwarted, that is to say, not frustrated. This is what every baby, every child, every adolescent, and every adult wants, and this is love. The synonyms are security, support, co-operation, the confidence that other human beings will support one actively and interestedly, the confidence that no one will ever willingly commit the supreme of all treasons against one, that is, to let one down when most needed.

We have learned, chiefly from the work of the psychoanalysts, that it is the first six years that are critical here. The years during which the foundations of character and personality are being laid and solidified. This is the period during which the foundations are being laid for what may later develop as a harmonic personality or a neurotic. This is undoubtedly the most important period in the development of the human being as a person, the period during which he builds up his own ego, his own self, from the selves of others. As educators, therefore, this is the period to which, in the future, we must pay much more attention than we have in the past. And if we recognize the importance of this period for what it is, we shall see to it that the nursery school becomes part of the educational system of the land. It is during these first six years of life that the human being may be made or broken. We have learned this by following the socialization histories of many different persons and by correlating the details of their socialization with their traits of character and personality. Experimental studies, premeditated and unpremeditated, on lower animals and similar correlation studies on whole families, institution and noninstitution children, and on whole cultures have corroborated those findings.

But the years of later childhood and adolescence have an importance of their own, for much of the good and much of the damage that may have been done during the preceding developmental periods may be undone in the succeeding periods. The growing organism, at all times, desires co-operation, and it needs this co-operation no less during one developmental period than another. The educator's task, then, should be clear: He must be a co-operator, a lover, an inspirer of confidence, and a drawer-out of the best that is within those whom he educates; and he must educate for co-operation, for community. For we know that persons who are not so educated are malfunctional, sick, inefficient, unhappy, anxious, and dangerous.

Biologists, social biologists, ecologists have shown us that contrary to the muscular Darwinian viewpoint, the drives to co-operation, to sociability, to community are present in all forms of life and are much stronger than what are generally considered to be competitive drives. The tough Darwinian viewpoint with its emphasis on competition is badly out of focus and is replete with misinterpretations of the evidence. The aggressive, hostile kind of competition which is associated with the Darwinian viewpoint, we now have good reason to believe, is produced only under certain conditions, conditions that may be resumed under the one rubric: *frustration*. Hostility, in fact, is love frustrated. Those who are not frustrated are not hostile. To be not frustrated one must have one's needs satisfied, one must be loved. Frustrating physical conditions can make one quite as hostile as those produced by persons. This is what the muscular Darwinians, and some of their modern successors, never realized, and so competition between animals, and by extrapolation from them to men, was set down as an innate drive. The evidence today strongly indicates that this is not true, and that it is almost certainly not true for man.

Children are not born selfish little egotists whose drives are mainly aggressive and competitive, "original sinners," evil, destructive creatures, brats who have to be "disciplined" into human beings by being sedulously and efficiently frustrated for the good of their actual or metaphoric souls. Aggressors are made not born. On the other hand, the baby is born with drives which properly satisfied lead to co-operation. It is we, in our ignorance, who, failing to satisfy those needs, produce anxiety and hostility and then blame the child for being hostile! And so on at every stage of the process.

. . . The next great step which I forsee in the future of human education is the redefinition of its scope as the development of the organism potentially human in the science and art of being human, the remaking of our institutions of instruction in the three R's into institutes in human relations, in which the three R's are made part and parcel of the process of education in human relations, in humanity. For unless these "subjects" are humanized, of what further use can they be to mankind?

EDUCATION
FOR DEMOCRATIC
IDEALS

AUTHOR:

I. B. Berkson (*1891–*   )

WORK:

THE IDEAL
AND THE COMMUNITY (1958)

Experimentalism moved in the direction of an emphasis on the cultural; in his later writings Dewey referred to his view as "cultural naturalism." But it never crossed the bridge into the new territory. Its stress on naturalism with its Darwinian undertow represented in part an attack against supernaturalism with its connotation of an extramundane source of authority. It was this preoccupation with opposition to traditional religious conceptions and forms which diverted the experimentalist from a consistent following of the positive and social emphasis. The true antithesis to supernaturalism, it is suggested, is not naturalism but humanism. An unqualified cultural humanism is proposed as a substitute for the ambiguous cultural naturalism of the experimentalist.

Man is a creature of culture and not of nature. What man's original nature is can never be divined from a study of his biological constitution or from an inquiry into man's origin in the distant past of evolutionary development. Man's nature can be inferred only indirectly from a study of his achievements in civilized society. Man's unique character is revealed in two dimensions: through the institutions he has developed to fulfill his biological needs in distinctive human ways; and in his aspirations for beauty, for truth, and for goodness, as expressed in literature and science, in music and art, in philosophy and religion.

As a creature of culture, man is also a "historical animal." To achieve full stature as men, we need to identify ourselves with the career of man in time. It is necessary to add that history is not only a recollection of events that are past and gone, but also a recovery of the prophets' vision of man's future destiny. Besides cultural and historical, a third term, namely "communal," is needed to give full-bodied meaning to the concept of man as a social being. Men live in communities—not merely in societies. Community implies "belonging" as well as associating; it involves a sense of common destiny and imposes an obligation of loyalty. Community implies common material interests and at the same time a bond of common ideas and aspirations.

The pivotal communities in our society are the family, the church, and the nation. Each represents a compound of material interests and ideal concerns, each supplements and checks the other. The loyalties which each community inspires and demands may become narrow and fanatical negating the humane ethics which it is their intent to embody. But if the purpose of drawing out our common human nature is not to evaporate into an empty intellectual abstraction and if the initiation into the great society of mankind is to be more than a sentimental hope, the individual must become involved in a plurality of communal loyalties. It is through identification with the communities of family, church, and nation, not through transcending them, that one becomes part of the historical and international world order.

The self cannot develop morally or spiritually in separation from the responsibilities and opportunities of community life. Neither the concept of self-realization through interpersonal relations nor the idea of self-transcendence through the identification with cosmic forces provides a basis for educational development. Two roads are open to the growth and humanization of the self—one is through participation in the life of organized society, the other is through self-identification with the pattern of ideas correlated with the social organization. Both ways are indispensable. Through the struggle of the self to reconcile its several communal loyalties, and through the conflict between concern for the survival of the communities to which the individual belongs and commitment to their cultural, ethical and spiritual values, the individual achieves self-realization.

The self retains a consciousness of uniqueness never perhaps identifying itself completely with any single historical or social order. A residue of alienation may remain and the need of communion with the Source of Being may persist. The sense of unity with a transcendent reality may accompany our activities as with a sustaining obbligato. But when, in the endeavor to attain spiritual perfection, the self becomes separated from the community, it must in the end fall back into the pit of self-annihilation, as in the meditative ecstasy of the Nirvana of Buddhism, or, far worse, as in the despairing negations of contemporary existentialism.

EDUCATION AS ACCULTURATION AND IDEALIZATION

Education involves inducting the individual into the communities on which he depends for his material welfare, his cultural development, and his spiritual growth. The process of socialization includes two overlapping aspects which may be respectively designated "acculturation" and "idealization."

Acculturation signifies bringing up the individual to live on a satisfactory level of effectiveness and decency in the existing state of society. It includes the essentialist's purpose of the transmission of the social heritage, or looking at the matter from the point of view of the learner, as "the acquisition of the arts, the sciences, and the moral attitudes of civilization." It connotes the concept of adjustment to the existing society, to enable the individual "to get on in the world" and "to keep society as a going concern." It involves the study of literature and music, of the civic and religious institutions. No definition of the purpose of education is adequate which does not include these fundamentals as a prerequisite purpose.

In the conservative versions of the definition of acculturation, the purpose of the school is limited to the "reproduction of the social type." The second term "idealization" is introduced to emphasize that the school has the purpose also of "growth beyond the type." As Jacques Maritain says: "If an accepted culture is permeated with errors, cruelty or slavery, the task of education is not to perpetuate it but to strive to change it." To change society, means not only to correct errors—it implies reform in the light of the ideal implicit in its own cultural heritage. Idealization means transcending the conventional and the local. It requires seeing the present in its historical perspective; this means viewing it in relation not only to the past but also in relation to dynamic possibilities.

Both these conceptions, education as acculturation and education as idealization require relating education to a definite society and to a definite cultural pattern of values, not to society in general or to ideals in general. Only as we see the universal within the particular—the national ideal within the local, the international within the national, the enduring within the present, can we avoid meaningless generalities. Every definition of education—transmission of the social heritage, education as social adjustment, or as personal growth, moral development, intellectual discipline—remains formal and empty of content unless the definition is related to a definite society, marked by a definite political system and economic order.

THE AMERICAN NATION AND THE UNIVERSAL DEMOCRATIC IDEAL

Applying the foregoing assumptions to the problem of education in the United States means relating the philosophy and the content of school work to the national life. Only as we view the task of education in terms of the practical and cultural, the social and spiritual needs of children and youth as potential members of American society in its various institutional and communal manifestations, is it possible to formulate the aims, the content, and the methods of education with any degree of clarity or definiteness. Only as we do so can we nurture the necessary moral commitments as well as develop the relevant knowledge, inspire loyalties as well as enlarge the outlook.

To make the nation the core of consideration implies neither a narrow patriotism nor a policy of isolation. America represents for its citizens an inclusive community of economic, political, and cultural interests which transcend the limitations of region, race, and denomination. Through the American heritage of history and literature, we become linked with the course of European thought and Western civilization. Through America's involvement in international affairs we are made part of the emerging world order. It is a function of education to promote a concern for the national security and well-being and to nourish a respect for its institutions and traditions. At the same time, it is imperative to guard against abetting any inclination toward chauvinism or sanctioning blind worship of the past. Education has a positive task to develop an understanding of how deeply-rooted American spiritual values are in the history of Western civilization and how closely bound is our destiny with that of the rest of the world.

Education for American life entails the affirmation of democracy as the unifying and directing principle. Democracy, as a social philosophy, represents the contemporary embodiment of the Western ethical and political tradition. Its twofold theme of the unique value of each person and of the unity of the human race may be traced to Biblical origins. Its high appreciation of the scientific attitude of inquiry is the modern version of the Hellenic devotion to the pursuit of truth through reason. Its conception of law as based on universal principles amenable in application to the will of the people in public assembly is likewise an outgrowth of classical conceptions. The democratic constitution represents the accumulated political wisdom of the ages. It is founded on the principle of inalienable human rights and it provides for the application of these principles to changing conditions of life and thought. It places responsibility for decisions in the hands of the majority, protects the minority in its elementary rights and in its place in government, and gives a basis for support of family and church communities. American democracy recognizes the importance of education for the maintenance of the constitution of the state, but allows the school a measure of autonomy; it protects the right of parents to bring up their children in harmony with their spiritual beliefs.

To instill faith in these principles is a primary responsibility of the school. In no smaller degree, is it the school's duty to subject the existing achievement to critical analysis—to point out failures as well as successes and to lead to an understanding of the problems involved in a better embodiment of democratic principles.

As we view the course of development of the democratic idea since its formulation in the opening paragraphs of the Declaration of Independence and in the Constitution we may assert with confidence that progress has been made in the implementation of the humane conceptions of these historic documents. But as we face the new era with its demand for equality, freedom, and well-being for all peoples, the gap between promise and fulfilment looms large. The principles of equality have been flagrantly violated in racial relations; discrimination against religious minorities, though less virulent than against colored peoples, remains a characteristic feature of American life in many sections of the country. Whatever advances have been made, have been forced by the pressure of "politics" and the need of survival rather than by regard for the principle of "a general equality of condition" as basic for true democracy. The social scene is still marred by class inequality and by a compulsive drive for financial success as a prerequisite for social position. Our support of measures designed to strengthen international comity has been halting and vacillating, comporting ill with the role of democratic world leadership which the course of history has assigned to us. As a result of compromise, expediency, and indecision, the influence of the idea of democracy as a moral force in the world has seriously weakened.

It is imperative in this age to go beyond the liberalism of the nineteen twenties which in the words of James Harvey Robinson, one of its outstanding exponents, had "no reforms to recommend, except the liberation of intelligence." The following broad principles must be made directives:

1. Affirmation of the principles of the Constitution—subject to interpretation by the courts and to legislative enactments—as the framework of government.

2. Renewal of emphasis on the Bill of Rights, particularly on freedom

of political and economic discussion in the public forum and in the academic hall.

3. Commitment to the unqualified application of the principle of equality for all races and nations in law, politics, economics, education, and social relations, at home and abroad.

4. Promotion of a welfare economy through extension of social security, public housing, health services, and educational facilities, and redirection of the free-enterprise system under government leadership toward an ever more satisfactory realization of equality of opportunity and of condition.

5. Support of the United Nations and of the Universal Declaration of Human Rights and encouragement of all other regional and international agencies devoted to the advancement of a world economic order, the maintenance of international law, and the strengthening of collective security.

Taken together, these principles represent a pattern of values and imply a program of action. They are not, of course, to be inculcated as abstract doctrines or interpreted in utopian terms. What each principle means in application is to be determined empirically with full consideration of technical advice; the strategy of implementation must have a regard for national public opinion. The school cannot of itself build a new social order. But there are already forces in the community—trends of thought and political activities— working toward a more consistent embodiment of the democratic promise. Cooperating with the liberal movements in the community—cultivating competent knowledge related to democratic purposes, upholding the national welfare against partisan and regional interests, relating the national good to international perspective—the school can aid greatly in transforming the climate of opinion and advancing the realization of avowed ideals. If, on the other hand, it remains beating about the bush in evasive neutralism, it becomes a negative force compounding the confusion and the disillusionment of the age.

LOCAL CONTROL
OF EDUCATION

AUTHOR:

Myron Lieberman (*1919–*   )

WORK:

THE FUTURE
OF PUBLIC EDUCATION (1960)

One of the most important educational trends in the next few decades is likely to be the decline of local control of education. Such a development is long overdue. Local control of education has clearly outlived its usefulness on the American scene. Practically, it must give way to a system of educational controls in which local communities play ceremonial rather than policy-making roles. *Intellectually,* it is already a corpse. At least, I propose to treat it as such in this book. The proper way to treat a corpse is to conduct an autopsy upon it and then bury it promptly. Having done this, we can better understand the rationale for the school system which will emerge from the present chaos in education.

An autopsy of local control reveals several reasons for its demise. In the

Reprinted from *The Future of Public Education* by Myron Lieberman by permission of The University of Chicago Press. © 1960 by The University of Chicago. Published 1960.

first place, mobility and interdependence have completely undermined the notion that local communities ought to have a free hand in educating their children. Second, national survival now requires educational policies and programs which are not subject to local veto. Third, it is becoming increasingly clear that local control cannot in practice be reconciled with the ideals of a democratic society. Finally, local control is a major cause of the dull parochialism and attenuated totalitarianism that characterizes public education in operation.

Let us analyze these reasons briefly. In order to do so, consider carefully the following question: *Who* should decide whether the children in a given community should be required to learn to read and write?

Some persons would undoubtedly argue that parents should have the right to raise their children as illiterates if they wish to do so. Most people would probably feel that the public ought to have the right of final decision in this matter. Still, there are many publics: local, state, regional, national, international, and even publics which are not defined geographically. Which of these publics should be authorized to have the last word in the matter?

Until a short time ago, every state had a compulsory education law. These laws took the power to decide our hypothetical question out of the hands of parents and local communities. Recently, however, some states have passed standby legislation which would enable them to abolish compulsory education in order to avoid racial integration in their public schools. States cannot be prevented by the federal government from abolishing public education. There is no way that the federal government can force a state legislature or local community to appropriate money to operate public schools. But what about our basic question—should the decision as to whether children shall learn to read and write be properly regarded as one for local communities or even state governments to make?

The reasons why the power to make this decision was taken away from parents and later from local communities will help us to answer this question. One reason was based upon the concept of fair play for the individual child. There was growing acceptance of the belief that a child's chances in life should not depend upon whether his parents or his local community were willing and able to educate him.

Should a child's chances depend upon whether he lives in a state which is willing to educate him? Certainly not as long as we adhere to the concept of an open society, one in which the individual's chances are not determined by fortuitous factors. As far as the individual child is concerned, the extent to which his state government is willing to provide him with an education is as much a fortuitous matter as the socioeconomic status of his parents or the educational values of his local community.

Consider the problem from a social standpoint instead of an individual one. We are an extremely mobile people. Most of us eventually move away from the community in which we received our education. In the year ending April, 1958, 30,800,000 Americans changed their residence. Over 11,000,-000 moved from one county to another; about half this number moved to a different state. Thus, on the average, every American moves to a different state two times during his life. Under these circumstances, does it make sense to insist that the citizens of one state have no right to insist upon literacy for the children of other states? Today, we plead for federal aid to education in order to equalize opportunities between states. Tomorrow, we could hardly contend that the federal government must stand by idly while a state legislature compounded the inequity by depriving children of an education altogether.

As an abstract proposition, it has always been clear that it is undemocratic to permit educational opportunity to be determined by circumstances of race, geographical location, or economic status. It has also been clear that our national welfare was dependent upon the extent to which individual talents were able to flourish, regardless of their social, economic, racial, or geographical origins. Neither the ideal of equality of opportunity nor the fact of our interdependence is new. What is new is the urgency of these things. Proposals for federal aid to education in order to equalize educational opportunities between states have been ignored by Congress for generations. The same proposals, advanced as a counterpoise to Russian scientific progress, are now regarded as insufficient by panic-stricken congressmen who never supported them on equalitarian grounds.

. . .

The prevailing point of view is that anything but local control of education, with perhaps a few concessions made to control at the state level, would be a step toward totalitarianism. This view is profoundly mistaken. Our present system of local control is far more conducive to totalitarianism than a national system of schools would be. I know that this statement is not acceptable to the overwhelming majority of the American people, including the teachers, but I am willing to stand on it.

The assertion that our educational system tends toward totalitarianism seems absurd on its face. A totalitarian system is one which develops a massive uniformity of outlook. It is based upon a policy of intellectual protection for a point of view that cannot stand the test of free discussion. We have a multitude of schools of all denominations or no denomination at all. Among the teachers and students in our public schools, there are adherents to every major political, economic, and religious point of view. What could be further from totalitarianism than this?

In most states the purposes and the content of education are left to local school boards to determine. Undoubtedly, there are some constitutional limits to the purposes for which communities may operate public schools. However, these limits have never been spelled out, and there is great latitude in what a community might require of its schools. Since the purposes of education are set forth locally, the predominant groups in the community tend to establish purposes which accord with their particular religious, political, economic, or social points of view. As a practical matter, therefore, local control results in the same kind of intellectual protectionism that characterizes schools in totalitarian countries.

The basic problem is not that communities define the purpose of education to be the acceptance of the Protestant faith or unswerving devotion to the single tax or the inculcation of the tenets of the Democratic party. Some communities have not blinked at adopting purposes as sectarian as these, but this is not where the problem lies. Even where a community accepts the most liberal educational purposes for its public schools, its interpretation of what intermediate objectives and what educational programs fulfil these purposes may have the same stultifying effect as outright adherence to a sectarian purpose. Every pressure group is for the general welfare, but each has its own version of what measures do in fact promote the general welfare. Similarly, every pressure group is for a liberal or a democratic education, but has a special version of what intermediate objectives and what educational programs lead to this result.

What is crucial is that, at the local level, it is relatively easy for a preponderant group to enforce a policy of intellectual protectionism for its sacred cows. Thus the white majorities in Southern communities exclude instruction that is critical of racial segregation. Communities in which fundamentalist sects predominate exclude instruction [favorable to] evolution. Some communities have prohibited the study of the United Nations or of UNESCO. Ours is a heterogeneous country, but in most communities the predominant racial, religious, economic, or political groups are able to veto whatever in the school program displeases them.

Looking at our system as a whole and seeing the existence of public schools teaching diverse doctrines, one might infer that our schools are free. We do not readily recognize the totalitarianism implicit in our situation because not all schools protect the same dogmas. Nonetheless, a diversity of schools based upon intellectual protectionism for different dogmas does not constitute a "democratic school system." At least, it does not do so if "democratic" refers to the education actually provided in these schools instead of to the legal structure which encourages a variety of one-sided programs.

The diversity of our undemocratic schools is not the only factor which maintains the fiction that we have a democratic school system. No matter how successful a group may be in excluding certain facts and ideas from the public schools, television, radio, and other mass media are almost certain to expose students to these facts and ideas. The power structure of American society is such that no single group is able to enforce or to indoctrinate its dogmas on the population as a whole. People look at this situation and say "Our schools have kept us free." They should say "Our freedoms have survived our schools."

THE MYTHOLOGY OF LOCAL CONTROL

Many persons believe that public education was not made a federal responsibility in the Constitution because the founding fathers feared the potentialities for dictatorship in a federal school system. Actually, education was not included as a federal function in the Constitution because the idea of free public education had not even occurred to the founding fathers. At the time of the American Revolution, the concept of universal public education was receiving attention for the first time and then only from a few frontier thinkers. Our decentralized school system was not an inspired stroke of genius but a historical accident, resulting from the fact that the ideal of free public education for all became widely accepted only long after the American Revolution.

Our schools have never been an important foundation of our free society. Our freedom is partly due to a separation of powers which enables us to transact public business reasonably well while avoiding excessive subjection to government officials. Perhaps for this reason we tend to regard the diffusion of power over our schools as an essential element of our free society. But adherence to the general principle that we must avoid excessive concentration of power does not automatically justify every separation or diffusion of it. Everything depends upon the circumstances—what powers are involved, who is to wield them, and so on. It is preposterous to think that merely because their political genius was expressed through a constitution embodying a remarkably successful separation of powers, the founding fathers would align themselves today with the supporters of local control of education.

People are seldom aware of the non-public character of public education. They tend to regard it as a legal concept and to neglect it as an educational concept. However, the ideal of public education means more than having some governmental unit—local, state, or federal—provide the funds to operate schools. Public education has a referent in the quality of education as well as in its financial basis. The qualitative referent is an education in which the search for truth is carried on regardless of what empires topple, interests collapse, or heads roll. Without this, public education is a delusion, as dangerous as the notion that mere government ownership of the means of production will automatically result in their operation for the public welfare instead of for private interests. The socialization of a service at any level of government is no automatic guarantee that the service will be performed in the public interest. The "new class" should have ended all of our illusions on this score.

Public schools, then, are not necessarily infused with a public spirit. Likewise, the fact that a school is privately controlled does not mean that its program is necessarily sectarian in character. The program of some privately controlled institutions such as Harvard is more free of parochial limitations than the programs in most publicly controlled institutions. In short, we cannot assume anything about the educational program of a school merely from a knowledge of whether the school is publicly or privately controlled. Nor can we infer that the educational program of a school is undemocratic merely because the school is locally controlled or that it is democratic merely because the schools are part of a national system. The relationship between the legal status of a school and the quality of its educational program is never one of strict logical implication.

The system of legal controls under which schools operate is only one factor which serves to shape their educational programs. However, it is an extremely important factor. Because a national system of controls is more likely to broaden the purposes of education and to preserve the professional autonomy of teachers, it is much more likely to provide a truly liberal education than a multitude of totalitarian systems under local control. It is a striking fact that in England, which has a national system of education, the teachers are on record as being opposed to local control of education precisely because they fear that it would undermine their professional autonomy. Meanwhile, teachers in the United States, who lack any substantial measure of professional autonomy, continue to act as if local control must be maintained inviolate lest academic freedom (which they do not possess) be imperiled.

. . .

In general, the trend has been for local sources to provide a decreasing percentage of the total expenditures for public education. Expenditures by the state governments tend to constitute a much larger percentage of the total, while the percentage from federal sources has been increasing but at a much slower rate than that coming from the state governments. There are several reasons why this structure is not working and can never be made to work.

In the first place, some states have four to five times as much taxable wealth, on the average, as other states. The differences between school districts are even greater; some school districts have several hundred times as much taxable wealth as others. Ability to support education has also been studied in terms of what educators call "personal income payments per pupil enrolled," that is, the total income received by the residents of a state divided by the number of pupils enrolled in its public schools. In 1956–57, "personal income payments per pupil enrolled" amounted to $17,432 in Delaware and

$3,754 in Mississippi. Needless to say, there were even greater differences between the richest and the poorest school districts.

For many years, authorities on school finance have pointed out that the poorest states and school districts usually devote a higher proportion of their resources to education than do the wealthier ones. Theoretically, one might argue that this is not very significant because all states and school districts should be making a greater effort to support education. However, this argument overlooks many important considerations relating to our tax structure.

One such consideration is the competitive aspect of state and local taxation. In New York City, there is a concentration of high incomes unequaled anywhere in the country. Nearly 20 percent of all internal revenue is collected in New York State. Thus it would appear that New York City, which is permitted to levy an income tax but does not, and New York State, which does levy an income tax, could easily have the very best schools in the nation. The difficulty is, however, that many high-income persons and corporations would move if tax rates were raised substantially. This is why it is often fallacious to criticize states and communities for not raising taxes; if they did so, they would lose people and businesses to areas less concerned about education. The need for, and justice of, federal taxation for education would thus remain even if there were substantial equality in wealth and revenues among all states and school districts. The fact that a federal tax cannot be evaded at the expense of children in a particular school district is one of the most compelling reasons why we must move toward an educational system financed by the federal government.

Still another factor makes it very unlikely that an adequate educational system could be financed without massive federal support. School districts have been forced to raise most of their funds (54 percent in 1953–54) by means of the property tax. Unlike most other taxes, property taxes must usually be submitted to popular vote. As is usual in this type of situation, the people who are badly hurt by a substantial tax increase are more effective politically than the diffuse majority which benefits from the increase. The result is that an increasing number of bond issues for school funds are being defeated in communities sympathetic to public education. Here is some indication of the rising (and often justified) tide of resentment against such discriminatory taxation.

The need for federal support of public education, if not for a federal system, is also related to the way in which the federal government supports non-educational activities. In the new highway program, for example, the federal government will spend $9.00 for every dollar appropriated by the state governments. Obviously, this will result in a bigger share of the state dollar being spent on highways. And, in general, states are tending to appropriate funds for projects which will receive substantial support from the federal government. Thus the only way that education can compete for funds, even at the state level, is for the federal government to assume a much larger share of the educational budget.

. . .

It is difficult to predict the form which centralization will take. It is possible that centralization may take place while much of our present educational structure is formally left intact. To understand this, bear in mind that a national system of education is not necessarily the same thing as a federal system of education. A federal system would be one in which the schools were operated by the federal government. However, education might continue to be the legal responsibility of states and local communities, while it also became substantially similar over the country as a result of non-governmental pressures.

The point can be illustrated by the situation in medicine. Legally, medical education and licensure are controlled by the various state medical boards. In actuality, these state boards are so dominated by the American Medical Association that we have a national system of medical education. There are some variations from state to state, but nothing compared to the chaos in teacher education and licensure. There are other occupations wherein the legal control of professional training and entry is a state function but wherein the activities of national professional organizations and accrediting agencies have brought about a national system of professional training and licensure.

The same possibility exists for elementary and secondary education. That is, even though education at these levels may continue to be the legal responsibility of state and local governments, various organizations and social pressures may force the different states and communities to adopt the same basic educational program. Under these circumstances, it would make sense to speak of an educational system that was national but not federal.

It is unlikely that in the next few decades we shall have a federal school system covering the entire country. Such a development would occur only if the failures of states and communities to carry out their educational responsibilities were to be brought home dramatically to the American people by some such event as the abolition of public education in the South. I am convinced, however, that we are about to move rapidly toward a national system of education. What is certain is not the form but the fact that we shall have a much more centralized system of education in the future than we have had in the past. The idea that the present chaos in education is the price one has to pay for living in a democracy, or the even more nonsensical notion that the prevailing educational chaos is one of the foundations of democracy, will linger on but without any real force in our society.

AFTER JOHN DEWEY, WHAT?

AUTHOR:

Jerome S. Bruner (*1915–*   )

WORK:

ON KNOWING:
ESSAYS FOR
THE LEFT HAND (1962)

In 1897, at the age of thirty-eight, John Dewey published a stirring and prophetic work entitled *My Pedagogic Creed.* Much of his later writing on education is foreshadowed in this brief document. Five articles of faith are set forth. The first defines the educational process: "All education proceeds by the participation of the individual in the social consciousness of the race. This process begins unconsciously almost at birth, and is continually shaping the individual's powers, saturating his consciousness, forming his habits, training his ideas, and arousing his feelings and emotions."

The second article of faith embodies Dewey's concept of the school: "Education being a social process, the school is simply that form of com-

Reprinted by permission of the publishers from Jerome S. Bruner *On Knowing,* Cambridge, Mass.: Harvard University Press, Copyright, 1962, by the President and Fellows of Harvard College.

munity life in which all those agencies are concentrated that will be most effective in bringing the child to share in the inherited resources of the race, and to use his own powers for social ends. Education, therefore, is a process of living and not a preparation for future living." In the third thesis Dewey speaks to the subject matter of education: "The social life of the child is the basis of concentration or correlation in all his training or growth. The social life gives the unconscious unity and the background of all his efforts and all his attainments. . . . The true center . . . is not science, nor literature, nor history, nor geography, but the child's own social activities." A view of educational method gives form to Dewey's fourth article: "The law for presenting and treating material is the law implicit in the child's own nature." For Dewey, the law was that of action: "the active side precedes the passive in the development of the child-nature. I believe that consciousness is essentially motor or impulsive; that conscious states tend to project themselves in action." And, finally, Dewey's fifth thesis: "Education is the fundamental method of social progress and reform."

One reads the document today with mixed feelings. Its optimism is classically American in its rejection of the tragic view of life. It defines truth in the pragmatic spirit: truth is the fruit of inquiry into the consequences of action. It expresses a firm faith not only in the individual's capacity to grow but in society's capacity to shape man in its own best image. The final lines of the creed are these: "Every teacher should realize the dignity of his calling; that he is a social servant set apart for the maintenance of proper social order and the securing of the right social growth. In this way the teacher always is the prophet of the true God and the usherer in of the true kingdom of heaven."

Yet the very wholesomeness—the optimism, the pragmatism, the acceptance of man's harmonious continuity with society—leaves one uneasy. For in two thirds of a century between 1897 and today, there has been a profound change not only in our conception of nature but also of society and the world of social institutions. Perhaps more important, we have lived through a revolution in our understanding of the nature of man, his intelligence, his capabilities, his passions, and the forms of his growth.

Dewey's thinking reflected the changes, though he was limited by the premises of his philosophical position. But between Dewey's first premises and our day, there bristles a series of revolutionary doctrines and cataclysmic events that change the very character of the inquiry. Two world wars, the dark episode of Hitler and genocide, the Russian revolution, the relativistic revolution in physics and psychology, the Age of Energy with its new technology, the sardonic reign of skeptical philosophy—all of these have forced a reappraisal of the underlying terms by which we construct a philosophy of education.

Let us then re-examine the terms, guided by what we know today of the world and of human nature. There is matter here, however, that is liable to some misinterpretation and we do well to clear it up at the outset. One writes against the background of one's day. Dewey was writing with an eye to the sterility and rigidity of school instruction in the 1890s—particularly its failure to appreciate the nature of the child. His emphasis upon the importance of direct experience and social action was an implied critique of the empty formalism that did little to relate learning to the child's world of experience. Dewey did mighty service in inspiring a correction. But an excess of virtue is vice. We, in our day, are reconsidering education against the background of such an excess.

Then, too, misunderstanding often converted Dewey's ideas into the sentimental practices he so deplored: "Next to deadness and dullness, formalism and routine," he wrote in his creed, "our education is threatened by no greater evil than sentimentalism." The sentimental cult of "the class project," of "life adjustment" courses, the reluctance to expose the child to the startling sweep of man and nature for fear it might violate the comfortable domain of his direct experience, the cloying concept of "readiness"—these are conceptions about children, often with no experimental support, that are justified in the name of Dewey. His was a noble yet tender view in his time. But what of our times? In what form shall we speak our beliefs?

WHAT EDUCATION IS

Education seeks to develop the power and sensibility of mind. On the one hand, the educational process transmits to the individual some part of the accumulation of knowledge, style, and values that constitutes the culture of a people. In doing so, it shapes the impulses, the consciousness, and the way of life of the individual. But education must also seek to develop the processes of intelligence so that the individual is capable of going beyond the cultural ways of his social world, able to innovate in however modest a way so that he can create an interior culture of his own. For whatever the art, the science, the literature, the history, and the geography of a culture, each man must be his own artist, his own scientist, his own historian, his own navigator. No person is master of the whole culture; indeed, this is almost a defining characteristic of that form of social memory that we speak of as culture. Each man lives a fragment of it. To be whole, he must create his own version of the world, using that part of his cultural heritage he has made his own through education.

In our time, the requirements of technology constrain the freedom of the individual to create images of the world that are satisfying in the deepest sense. Our era has also witnessed the rise of ideologies that subordinate the individual to the defined aims of a society, a form of subordination that is without compassion for idiosyncracy and respects only the instrumental contribution of a man to the progress of the society. At the same time, and in spite of ideologies, man's understanding of himself and of his world—both the natural and social world—has deepened to a degree that warrants calling our age an intellectually golden one. The need is now to employ our deeper understanding not only for the enrichment of society but also for the enrichment of the individual.

It is true, as Dewey said, that all education proceeds by the participation of the individual in the social consciousness of the race, but it is a truth with a double edge. For all education, good and bad alike, is of this order. We know now to what degree this is so. To take but one example, the very language one speaks conditions the style and structure of thought and experience. Indeed, as we have seen, there is reason to believe that thought processes themselves are internalizations of social intercourse, an inner colloquy patterned by early external dialogues. It is this that makes education possible. But education, by giving shape and expression to our experience, can also be the principal instrument for setting limits on the enterprise of mind. The guarantee against limits is the sense of alternatives. Education must, then, be not only a process that transmits culture but also one that provides alternative views of the world and strengthens the will to explore them.

After a half century of startling progress in the psychological sciences, we know that mental health is only a minimum condition for the growth of mind. The tragedy of mental illness is that it so preoccupies the person with the need to fend off realities with which he cannot cope that it leaves him without either the nerve or the zest to learn. But mental health is only a state from which to start: the powers of mind grow with their exercise. Adjustment is too modest an ideal, if it is an ideal at all. Competence in the use of one's powers for the development of individually defined and socially relevant excellence is much more to the point. After a half century of Freud, we know that the freeing of instinct and inclination is not an end in itself but a way station along the road to competence. What is most prophetic for us about Freud in this second half of the century is not his battle against the fetters of rigid moralism, but his formula: "Where there was id, let there be ego."

Education must begin, as Dewey concluded his first article of belief, "with a psychological insight into the child's capacities, interests, habits," but a point of departure is not an itinerary. It is just as mistaken to sacrifice the adult to the child as to sacrifice the child to the adult. It is sentimentalism to assume that the teaching of life can be fitted always to the child's interests just as it is empty formalism to force the child to parrot the formulas of adult society. Interests can be created and stimulated. In this sphere it is not far from the truth to say that supply creates demand, that the provocation of what is available creates response. One seeks to equip the child with deeper, more gripping, and sublter ways of knowing the world and himself.

WHAT THE SCHOOL IS

The school is an entry into the life of the mind. It is, to be sure, life itself and not merely a preparation for living. But it is a special form of living, one carefully devised for making the most of those plastic years that characterize the development of *Homo sapiens* and distinguish our species from all others. School should provide more than a continuity with the broader community or with everyday experience. It is primarily the special community where one experiences discovery by the use of intelligence, where one leaps into new and unimagined realms of experience, experience that is discontinuous with what went before. A child recognizes this when he first understands what a poem is, or what beauty and simplicity inhere in the idea of the conservation theorems, or that measure is universally applicable. If there is one continuity to be singled out, it is the slow converting of the child's artistic sense of the omnipotence of thought into the realistic confidence in the use of thought that characterizes the effective man.

In insisting upon the continuity of the school with the community on the one side and the family on the other, John Dewey overlooked the special function of education as an opener of new perspectives. If the school were merely a transition zone from the intimacy of the family to the life of the community, it would be a way of life easily enough arranged. In the educational systems of primitive societies, there almost always comes a point, usually at puberty, where there is a sharp change in the life of the boy, marked by a *rite de passage* that establishes a boundary between childhood ways and the ways of the adolescent.

It would be romantic nonsense to pattern our practices upon those found in preliterate societies. I would only ask that we attend to one parallel: education must not confuse the child with the adult and must recognize that the transition to adulthood involves an introduction to new realms of experience, the discovery and exploration of new mysteries, the gaining of new powers.

In the *shtetl* of Eastern Europe, the traditional Jewish ghetto, the scholar was a particularly important figure—the *talmid khokhem*. In his mien, his mode of conversation so rich in allusion, his form of poise, the wise man was the image not of a competent but, rather, of a beautiful person. Traditional Chinese society also had its image of the beautiful person, one who blended knowledge and sentiment and action in a beautiful way of life. The ideal of the gentleman served much the same function in the Europe of the seventeenth and eighteenth centuries. It is perhaps in this spirit that Alfred North

Whitehead declared that education must involve an exposure to greatness if it is to leave its mark. For me the yeast of education is the idea of excellence, and that comprises as many forms as there are individuals to develop a personal image of excellence. The school must have as one of its principal functions the nurturing of images of excellence.

A detached conception of idealized excellence is not enough. A doctrine of excellence, to be effective, must be translatable into the individual lives of those who come in contact with it. What is compelling about the *talmid khokhem,* the Chinese scholar-administrator, and the eighteenth-century gentleman is that they embody ways of life to which any man can aspire in his own way and from which he can draw in his own style. I believe, then, that the school must also contain men and women who, in their own way, seek and embody excellence. This does not mean that we shall have to staff our schools with men and women of great genius but that the teacher must embody in his own approach to learning a pursuit of excellence. And, indeed, with the technical resources opened by television and its adjuncts, one can present the student and also his teacher with the working version of excellence in its highest sense. In the years ahead, we shall find that the great scholar, scientist, or artist can speak as easily and honestly to the beginner as to the graduate student.

THE SUBJECT MATTER OF EDUCATION

The issue of subject matter in education can be resolved only by reference to one's view of the nature of knowledge. Knowledge is a model we construct to give meaning and structure to regularities in experience. The organizing ideas of any body of knowledge are inventions for rendering experience economical and connected. We invent concepts such as force in physics, the bond in chemistry, motives in psychology, style in literature as means to the end of comprehension.

The history of culture is the history of the development of great organizing ideas, ideas that inevitably stem from deeper values and points of view about man and nature. The power of great organizing concepts is in large part that they permit us to understand and sometimes to predict or change the world in which we live. But their power lies also in the fact that ideas provide instruments for experience. Having grown up in a culture dominated by the ideas of Newton, and so with a conception of time flowing equably, we experience time moving inexorably and steadily, marked by a one-way arrow. Indeed, we know now, after a quarter of a century of research on perception, that experience is not to be had directly and neatly, but filtered through the programmed readiness of our senses. The program is constructed with our expectations and these are derived from our models or ideas about what exists and what follows what.

From this, two convictions follow. The first is that the structure of knowledge—its connectedness and the derivations that make one idea follow from another—is the proper emphasis in education. For it is structure, the great conceptual inventions that bring order to the congeries of disconnected observations, that gives meaning to what we may learn and makes possible the opening up of new realms of experience. The second conviction is that the unity of knowledge is to be found within knowledge itself, if the knowledge is worth mastering.

To attempt a justification of subject matter, as Dewey did, in terms of its relation to the child's social activities is to misunderstand what knowledge is and how it may be mastered. The significance of the concept of commutativity in mathematics does not derive from the social insight that two houses with fourteen people in each is not the same as fourteen houses with two people in each. Rather, it inheres in the power of the idea to create a way of thinking about number that is lithe and beautiful and immensely generative—an idea at least as powerful as, say, the future conditional tense in formal grammar. Without the idea of commutativity, algebra would be impossible. If set theory—now often the introductory section in newer curriculums in mathematics—had to be justified in terms of its relation to immediate experience and social life, it would not be worth teaching. Yet set theory lays a foundation for the understanding of order and number that could never be achieved with the social arithmetic of interest rates and bales of hay at so much per bale. Mathematics, like any other subject, must begin with experience, but progress toward abstraction and understanding requires precisely that there be a weaning away from the obviousness of superficial experience.

There is one consideration of cognitive economy, discussed in an earlier chapter, that is paramount. One cannot "cover" any subject in full, not even in a lifetime, if coverage means visiting all the facts and events and morsels. Subject matter presented so as to emphasize its structure will perforce be of that generative kind that permits reconstruction of the details or, at very least, prepares a place into which the details, when encountered, can be put.

What then of subject matter in the conventional sense? The answer to the question, "What shall be taught?" turns out to be the answer to the question, "What is nontrivial?" If one can first answer the question, "What is worth knowing about?" then it is not difficult to distinguish between the aspects of it that are worth teaching and learning and those that are not. Surely, knowledge of the natural world, knowledge of the human condition, knowledge of the nature and dynamics of society, knowledge of the past so that it may be used in experiencing the present and aspiring to the future—all of these, it would seem reasonable to suppose, are essential to an educated man. To these must be added another: knowledge of the products of our artistic heritage that mark the history of our aesthetic wonder and delight.

A problem immediately arises concerning the symbolism in terms of which knowledge is understood and talked about. There is language in its natural sense and language in its mathematical sense. I cannot imagine an educated man a century from now who will not be largely bilingual in this special sense—concise and adept in both a natural language and mathematics. For these two are the tools essential to the unlocking of new experience and the gaining of new powers. As such, they must have a central place in any curriculum.

Finally, it is as true today as it was when Dewey wrote that one cannot foresee the world in which the child we educate will live. Informed powers of mind and a sense of potency in action are the only instruments we can give the child that will be invariable across the transformations of time and circumstance. The succession of studies that we give the child in the ideal school need be fixed in only one way: whatever is introduced, let it be pursued continuously enough to give the student a sense of the power of mind that comes from a deepening of understanding. It is this, rather than any form of extensive coverage, that matters most.

THE NATURE OF METHOD

The process and the goal of education are one and the same thing. The goal of education is disciplined understanding; that is the process as well.

Let us recognize that the opposite of understanding is not ignorance or simply "not knowing." To understand something is, first, to give up some other way of conceiving of it. Confusion all too often lies between one way of conceiving and another, better way. It is one of our biological inheritances that confusion produces emergency anxiety, and with anxiety there come the defensive measures—flight, fright, or freezing—that are antithetical to the free and zestful use of mind. The binding fact of mental life in child and adult alike is that there is a limited capacity for processing information—our span, as it is called, can comprise six or seven unrelated items simultaneously. Go beyond that and there is overload, confusion, forgetting. As George Miller has put it, the principle of economy is to fill our seven mental-input slots with gold rather than dross. The degree to which material to be learned is put into structures by the learner will determine whether he is working with gold or dross.

For this reason, as well as for reasons already stated, it is essential that, before being exposed to a wide range of material on a topic, the child first have a general idea of how and where things fit. It is often the case that the development of the general idea comes from a first round of experience with concrete embodiments of ideas that are close to a child's life. The cycle of learning begins, then, with particulars and immediately moves toward abstraction. It comes to a temporary goal when the abstraction can then be used in grasping new particulars in the deeper way that abstraction permits.

Insofar as possible, a method of instruction should have the objective of leading the child to discover for himself. Telling children and then testing them on what they have been told inevitably has the effect of producing bench-bound learners whose motivation for learning is likely to be extrinsic to the task—pleasing the teacher, getting into college, artificially maintaining self-esteem. The virtues of encouraging discovery are of two kinds. In the first place, the child will make what he learns his own, will fit his discovery into the interior world of culture that he creates for himself. Equally important, discovery and the sense of confidence it provides is the proper reward for learning. It is a reward that, moreover, strengthens the very process that is at the heart of education—disciplined inquiry.

The child must be encouraged to get the full benefit from what he learns. This is not to say that he should be required to put it to immediate use in his daily life, though so much the better if he has the happy opportunity to do so. Rather, it is a way of honoring the connectedness of knowledge. Two facts and a relation joining them is and should be an invitation to generalize, to extrapolate, to make a tentative intuitive leap, even to build a tentative theory. The leap from mere learning to using what one has learned in thinking is an essential step in the use of the mind. Indeed, plausible guessing, the use of the heuristic hunch, the best employment of necessarily insufficient evidence—these are activities in which the child needs practice and guidance. They are among the great antidotes to passivity.

Most important of all, the educational process must be free of intellectual dishonesty and those forms of cheating that explain without providing understanding. I have expressed the conviction elsewhere that any subject can be taught to anybody at any age in some form that is honest. It is not honest to present a fifth-grade social-studies class with an image of town government as if it were a den of cub scouts presided over by a parent figure interpreting the charter—even if the image set forth does happen to mesh with the child's immediate social experience. A lie is still a lie—even if it sounds like familiar truth. Nor is it honest to present a sixth-grade science class with a garbled but concrete picture of the atom that is, in its way, as sweeteningly false as the suburban image of town government given them the year before. A dishonest image can only discourage the self-generating intellectual inquiry out of which real understanding grows.

THE SCHOOL AND SOCIAL PROGRESS

I believe that education is the fundamental method of social change. Revolutions themselves are no better and are often less good than the ideas they embody and the means invented for their application. Change is swifter in our times than ever before in human history and news of it is almost instantaneous. If we are to be serious in the belief that school must be life itself and not merely preparation for life, then school must reflect the changes through which we are living.

The first implication of this belief is that means must be found to feed back into our schools the ever deepening insights that are developed on the frontiers of knowledge. This is an obvious point in science and mathematics, and continuing efforts are now being instituted to assure that new, more powerful, and often simpler ways of understanding find their way back into the classrooms of our primary and secondary schools. But it is equally important to have this constant refreshment from fields other than the sciences—where the frontiers of knowledge are not always the universities and research laboratories but political and social life, the arts, literary endeavor, and the rapidly changing business and industrial community. Everywhere there is change, and with change we are learning.

I see the need for a new type of institution, a new conception in curriculum. What we have not had and what we are beginning to recognize as needed is something that is perhaps best called an "institute for curriculum studies"—not one of them, but many. Let it be the place where scholars, scientists, men of affairs, and artists come together with talented teachers continually to revise and refresh our curriculums. It is an activity that transcends the limits of any of our particular university faculties—be they faculties of education, arts and science, medicine, or engineering. We have been negligent in coming to a sense of the quickening change of life in our time and its implications for the educational process. We have not shared with our teachers the benefits of new discovery, new insight, new artistic triumph. Not only have we operated with the notion of the self-contained classroom but also with the idea of the self-contained school—and even the self-contained educational system.

The Nobel poet or the ambassador to the United Nations, the brilliant cellist or the perceptive playwright, the historian making use of the past or the sociologist seeking a pattern in the present—these men, like the student, are seeking understanding and mastery over new problems. They represent excellence at the frontiers of endeavor. If a sense of progress and change toward greater excellence is to illuminate our schools, there must be a constant return of their wisdom and effort to enliven and inform teacher and student alike. There is no difference in kind between the man at the frontier and the young student at his own frontier, each attempting to understand. Let the educational process be life itself as fully as we can make it.

NATIONAL STANDARDS FOR EDUCATION

AUTHOR:

H. G. Rickover (1900–   )

WORK:

AMERICAN EDUCATION— A NATIONAL FAILURE (1963)

At the end of the Hearings before the House Appropriations Committee, Mr. Cannon asked me: "By way of summary, Admiral Rickover, may I ask, do you feel that while some communities have taken steps to raise scholastic levels, the rate of progress is too slow? What practical means do you think Congress could take to speed up school reform?

"We in the committee are aware that as Aristotle said, 'Nobody could doubt that the chief concern of the lawgiver must be the education of the young.' What specific action do you suggest that this committee or the Congress can take to aid in correcting the deficiencies which you see in our educational system?"

I answered him as follows: "Mr. Chairman, I know from the many times I have appeared before this and other committees of Congress how deeply concerned Members of Congress are about the education of our children. Over the years, in the many private discussions I have been privileged to have with individual members, I have also felt their concern. I feel that no real and timely improvement will be made unless *you* take the lead and show the way. You are the highest and most representative organ in the United States for getting things done and you have the power of the purse to make your deliberations effective. Congress has rightly been called the 'potent and omnipresent teacher.'

"All great philosophers have understood that the education of youth is the primary function of society—the means by which humanity's inheritance is transmitted from one generation to another. When one reflects on the matter he must see that each one of us is heir to all of the ideas and accomplishments of every human being who has ever lived. This is why education is so important, why it is our responsibility as human beings to assure that our own heirs receive their full human inheritance.

"Further, as Plato said, 'most issues exercising the lawgiver can be settled only by reference to the basic problem of the citizen's education.'

"If we adult Americans are not intelligent enough to figure out a way to improve American education, we cannot hope that our children will be intelligent enough to keep our Nation strong and prosperous and capable of living up to its task of leading the free world.

"I do not wish to deprecate the importance of high moral standards, of good character, of kindliness, of humaneness, of ability to get along well with fellow citizens—there are innumerable virtues I should like to see inculcated in American youth. But the one thing which I believe will be of the greatest importance for the future of our Nation and of the free world, the one *indispensable* thing, is to bring all our children to markedly higher intellectual levels. Most of the problems they will have to cope with as individuals and as citizens of this great democracy will involve use of their minds. Whitehead wrote half a century ago that 'in the modern complex social organism, the adventure of life cannot be disjoined from intellectual adventure.'

"To pull their weight as democratic citizens with rights, but also with civic responsibilities, our young people must be brought intellectually to a point where they can understand complex national issues, evaluate the various positions taken on these issues by individuals and organizations, and judge whether their positions are based on sincere conviction or on naked self-interest; they must learn the difficult art of collectively choosing the best course of action that is feasible and do this for many diverse national issues. In all this the mind is the most important factor.

"In fact, civilization has reached the point where the frontier now lies in the mind itself. Americans must conquer knowledge as formerly they conquered the wilderness. Bacon's saying, 'the mind is the man,' is now literally true for each man and for all of mankind. Our future depends squarely on how well we succeed in developing the minds of our young men and women. We must not, we cannot permit anything to stand in the way.

"I think we must be realistic and face the fact that most people do not like very much to work with their minds; this is something we must try to teach children at school; we must get them into the habit of using their minds whenever a problem requires application of reason and logic. It is this very practical necessity that makes me insist on the importance of establishing national scholastic standards, for academic excellence does not just happen. It must be actively promoted and nothing will do this better than setting children standards and rewarding them—with class promotion, good marks, diplomas, et cetera—if they work hard and thus succeed in meeting the standards.

"You know the Greeks in classical times were convinced they were superior to every other nation. Herodotus is said to have been the first Greek who had the temerity to suggest they might learn something from another people. He wrote his history from that point of view. I imagine this made him a 'controversial person.' I do feel that there are things we can learn from English education. I would include the following:

"1. Elimination of 'ability to pay' from public education; retention of 'ability to learn'; separate secondary schools.

"2. Highly qualified teachers to whom much freedom is given in their work and whose influence on all aspects of education is great, notably in setting scholastic standards through national examinations. Total absence of nonteaching school principals and administrators.

"3. The use of Government grants as a means of raising national standards in education, by making acceptance of standards and of inspection to check on standards a condition for awarding grants.

"4. National examinations leading to national diplomas, designed to permit great variety in selection of test subjects, yet clear-cut indication on the diploma of the type of examination taken and passed. Cooperation of all interested parties in setting up the examinations and great care in evaluating them.

"These are the principal features of English education by means of which they maintain high standards while permitting decentralized management of public education. I take it these are also our own objectives. One or more of the above measures may prove acceptable to us; this is why I list them here."

I then went on to suggest that Congress set up a National Standards Committee, a small Committee composed of men of national stature and eminence—trustworthy, intelligent, scholarly, and devoted to the ideal of an American education second to none. The Committee would have two tasks:

The first would be purely informational; it would act as an educational watchtower announcing danger when it saw it approaching. The members would keep under continuous scrutiny and periodically report on the state of American education. Does it meet the needs of our times? Is it competitive with education in countries at similar levels of culture and technology with whom we compete economically, politically, or militarily? How do American children compare in academic knowledge with children in Europe or Russia, say at age 12, or 16, or 18—of course, taking into consideration different ability levels?

The Committee's second task would be to formulate a national scholastic standard on the basis of its findings, a standard which would make us internationally competitive and would also respond to our specific domestic needs. The Committee would do this by means of examinations set at different ability levels. No one would have to take them, but those who passed would receive national accreditation. The Committee would in no way interfere with established institutions now granting diplomas or degrees. It would simply set up a higher standard, offer it to anyone who wished to meet it, and certify those who had successfully done so.

Neither the Committee's informational nor its standard-setting function would represent a radical departure from established practice. Many Federal agencies collect and distribute information. We need a disinterested agency to tell us the unvarnished truth about the true state of American education. The Committee would help prevent complacency and illusions of superiority, thus saving us from the kind of painful shocks that were administered by Sputnik and other evidences of Russian scientific proficiency in the past few years. There is precedent, too, for the Committee's setting of permissive national standards. We have something very like it in the 1961 amendment to the 1956 Water Pollution Act.

This amendment authorizes the Federal Government—*if so requested by a State*—to research and develop new methods of pollution control and to award grants-in-aid to localities and states wishing to use these federally established methods. In principle, you have here a national standard very much like the scholastic standard of the proposed Committee, in that it is not *imposed* but merely *offered as a service* on a take-it-or-leave-it basis.

Water pollution and mediocre education have this in common: they are problems that cannot be solved by local and State authorities *alone* but require some assistance from the Federal Government. Population growth threatens us with a severe water shortage unless we devise better means to preserve the quality of our water resources, so that they may be used over and over again. Pollution abatement has therefore become a national problem and we accept a new kind of Federal aid. I believe improvement of the quality of American education is at least as pressing as the need for an assured supply of clean water. "Education," says the Ford Foundation report for 1959, "is now the indispensable medium for survival and progress." Education is so basic to the quality of our national life that by steering it in the right direction we can change America's future; we can make it secure. To steer it right, I believe we need a new kind of Federal aid—the kind of aid that the proposed National Standards Committee would offer.

A NATIONWIDE EDUCATIONAL POLICY

AUTHOR:

James Bryant Conant (*1893–*   )

WORK:

SHAPING EDUCATIONAL POLICY (1964)

It is my thesis that such a jumble of influential private and public bodies does not correspond to the needs of the nation in the 1960s. Some degree of order needs to be brought out of this chaos, primarily for the benefit of the oncoming generations, but also, to achieve a more effective use of public and private moneys.

At the high school level and below, policy should not be determined solely by either "public school people" or state officials, but wise decisions cannot be made if either is excluded. At the level beyond the high school, plans cannot be made by the state alone, nor by private institutions alone, nor by Washington alone. But no nationwide policy can be successfully formu-

From *Shaping Educational Policy* by James Bryant Conant (New York: McGraw-Hill Publishing Company, 1964), pp. 109–114, 123–124, 128–130. Footnotes omitted. Copyright 1964 by James Bryant Conant. Reprinted by permission.

lated if any one of the three is excluded. A single state, as the California action shows, can develop a master plan for higher education; any single state can, as New York has shown, keep its schools well up-to-date with the educational revolution. Congress can help meet the problems presented by the revolution by grants for specific purposes and a handsome assist to institutions of higher education. But all this does not add up to a nationwide educational policy, let alone a national educational policy which would be the equivalent of the national policy in Great Britain or France.

The fact is, of course, that without a drastic Constitutional amendment nobody is in a position to establish an educational policy in the United States. It is my contention that some form of cooperative exploration of educational problems between the states and the Federal government is imperative. We cannot have a national educational policy, but we might be able to evolve a *nationwide policy*. The concluding pages of this chapter give my suggestions as to how this might be accomplished without an amendment to the Constitution of the United States. Before presenting my radical proposal, however, I must devote some pages to an analysis of the present situation.

Let me start with an examination of the powers of the Federal government to establish a national educational policy through the formation of a commission or committee appointed by the Congress or the President. Until one examines the Constitutional and political realities, such proposals seem quite persuasive. And it is true, of course, that for more than 100 years Congress, by its granting of land or its appropriation of money for the individual states, has enormously influenced the development of our educational system. But Congrees has not the power, without an amendment to the Federal Constitution, to determine a total national educational policy. Why not? Because in government, as in business, authority to establish a policy requires full power (1) to establish a structure and to alter it as conditions change; (2) to appoint personnel; (3) to issue directions to the personnel; (4) to provide for the financing of the entire operation. It is the essence of our system of government, with its checks and balances and division of powers, that neither a single state nor the Federal government has the power to establish, maintain, and operate a system of education in the way a free nation without a federalized structure can establish educational policy.

The educational powers of each of the single states in practice is far greater than that of the Federal government. There are, however, three limitations on these powers. The first derives from the Federal Constitution as interpreted by the Supreme Court; the second is the power of Congress to pass laws affecting individuals as citizens of the United States, as for example the power to draft men into military service; the third is the practical limitations of a state's ability to raise money. There are a number of recent examples of Supreme Court decisions that limit the power of a state to determine its educational policy. These decisions, which have attracted widespread interest, involve the Court's interpretation of the First and Fourteenth Amendments of the Federal Constitution. The questions they raise concern state and local provisons as to the use of school time for ceremonies or instruction considered to be religious. It is interesting to note that no one now argues that a state would be free to establish a state-supported system of schools which were frankly connected with a religious denomination. Yet before the Fourteenth Amendment was passed after the Civil War, such a possibility existed, since the First Amendment originally was only a limitation on the power of the Federal government.

The decisions of the Supreme Court on racial segregation in the schools are clearly a limitation on a state's power to establish and maintain completely separate Negro schools, colleges, and universities. One of the earliest decisions in which the Court reversed a state educational policy held that the Fourteenth Amendment guaranteed to a parent a right to send his children to a private school of his own choice, notwithstanding any state law. The attempt of a state legislature (Oregon) to outlaw private schools was thus thwarted. The same issue had arisen in a less dramatic form in Nebraska, where the state legislature had by law regulated the teaching of foreign languages. The Court held that the legislature could not prevent a private school from offering instruction in German, since to do so would be to deprive a parent of a right to have his child so instructed. The power of the state to regulate the curriculum of the public schools was not contested.

The impact of Federal legislation for purposes of defense on schools and colleges was clearly evident during the two World Wars. The drafting of young men into the armed services does, in a sense, place a restriction on the power of the state to plan the education of its young people. To a certain extent the same may be said of Federal laws affecting the employment of youth in industries engaged in interstate commerce.

The greatest limitation on the ability of the state to provide for education of its youth at public expense comes from the limitations on the ability of the state to raise funds. (One need not dwell on the restraints imposed by the Federal Constitution, such as the prohibition of post-facto laws and the requiring of due process; these stand as a guard against arbitrary confiscation of personal property.) The practical limitations of the Federal income tax is most often in the minds of educators when they discuss the impact of the Federal power on state power. A generation ago conservative school people, deeply committed to the principle of local control of the public schools, openly deplored the amendment which authorized the Federal income tax. This amendment, it was said, would destroy the basic structure of our public schools.

There can be no doubt that the Federal taxing power, broadened by the

Sixteenth Amendment, does mean that a state is not as independent a sovereign power as it once was insofar as supporting state activities is concerned. Not only does the Federal government absorb a large portion of the income available for taxation, but the methods by which some of this money is sent back to the states affects indirectly the way the state spends what money it collects. I refer to such measures as the Federal road-building program. The basis for this program is such that state funds are drawn into this type of expenditure because Federal money comes to the state only if the state itself provides money for the same purpose. The advocates of general Federal aid for public education have made much of the implication of such arrangements, and this argument has never been adequately answered by the opponents of Federal aid.

In writing of the limitations of the power of a state to establish an educational policy, I have made no reference to the state constitutional limitations on the power of the state legislature and the organs of government created by the legislature, such as the local school boards. In theory, the people of a state can change their constitution; therefore, in contrasting state with Federal power, it is unnecessary to consider the state constitution. This is fortunate as I doubt if the provisions of any two of the fifty state constitutions are alike, even on such basic matters as schools and colleges.

Because of the Federal Constitution and certain rights of the Federal government connected with defense and interstate commerce, it is evident that a state is not completely free to provide and regulate education. On the other hand, let it be noted that the Federal government is powerless to interfere with many aspects of state-supported schools, colleges, and universities. It has been pointed out more than once that a state need not provide any public instruction at all. Some states have no compulsory attendance laws. Therefore one might say that it is a happy accident that in all states, at present, there are free public schools and at least one state university and several state colleges. It is further a happy accident that in all but a few states children must attend school (public or private) from approximately six years of age until at least sixteen (in some states until eighteen).

· · ·

To be quite specific, let me be bold and make a suggestion for a possible way by which the road to the development of a nationwide educational policy might be opened up. *Let the fifty states, or at least fifteen to twenty of the more populous states, enter into a compact for the creation of an "Interstate Commission for Planning a Nationwide Educational Policy."* The compact would have to be drawn up by the states and approved by Congress. The document would provide for the membership of the commission and provide the guidelines for its operation. Each state would be represented, though a group of less populous states might decide to be represented by one person. Each state would be ready to listen to any conclusions of the commission but, of course, would not be bound to follow its recommendations.

Since such an interstate commission would be concerned with the drawing up of plans, *not* with administration, I see no constitutional or legal reason against a state legislature authorizing one or more persons to participate in it. Nor do I see any obstacles to a legislature expressing its willingness to examine any reports coming from such a group. The matter of finances might raise issues. It might be difficult to get any considerable number of state legislatures to appropriate the money; but I hope not, for if it were proposed that the Congress of the United States do so, certainly the cry of states' rights might be raised. Yet I would hope the commission would invite the chief United States school officer, the Commissioner of Education, as well as other Federal officials to attend each conference.

. . .

. . . Therefore I suggest that Congress appoint first a National Advisory Committee to explore the workings of the present interstate compacts and to list the problems to be met. I am frank to say that I believe the report of such a preliminary survey would lead to the formation of the type of commission I have recommended based on an interstate compact.

I must admit that the record of national committees on education, however authorized and however appointed, is not such as to lead one to be optimistic about the results to be accomplished by still another committee. Yet the creation of a national commission which would be an interstate educational planning commission whose existence was the result of a compact between the states would be something quite new. It differs from schemes for appointing a Presidential or Congressional advisory commission in several respects. In the first place, because the commission would be an interstate commission, the reports of the working parties would be automatically concerned with state-by-state variations and would recognize the realities of the conditions in each state. In the second place, the recommendations would be directed to the state legislatures or state boards of education and would be considered by the state authorities because each state had been involved in the creation of the undertaking. In the third place, the magnitude and detailed nature of the financial demands required would be spelled out in such a way that Congress (through its own committees) and the Office of Education (through its own staff) could explore the significance of each item in terms of the function of the Federal governmental agencies.

Each working party would have to start with certain premises agreed upon by the commission. Within the framework thus established, the working party would be required first to make an exhaustive factual study of the structure state by state, second to come up with specific recommendations to the state authorities (the chief state school officer, the state school board, or the legislature). There might well be dissenting opinions on many points. The right to public dissent would be inherent in accepting an appointment on the working party. The more controversial the area, the more necessary would be such a provision.

Admittedly, in setting up any working party, the most difficult task for the interstate commission would be an agreement on what I have called the framework. And to let a working party loose in any controversial area without some guidelines would be to insure catastrophic failure at the onset. Certain premises could be agreed on without much difficulty. These would constitute part of the framework for all of the working parties. In my opinion, these premises might be formulated somewhat as follows:

1. It is assumed that our present form of government should be perpetuated; to that end all future citizens of the nation should receive an education that will prepare them to function as responsible members of a free society, as intelligent voters and, if appointed or elected to public office, as honest reliable servants of the nation, state or locality.

2. It is assumed that each state is committed to the proposition of providing free schooling to all the children in the state through twelve grades. (Though the Federal government has no power to proclaim the doctrine of free schools, practically the action of all the states during the last 100 years enables the interstate commission to declare that providing free public schooling is a nationwide policy of the United States.)

3. It is assumed that in every state the parents have a right to send their children to private schools, colleges, and universities instead of to the publicly supported institutions. This assumption follows from the interpretation of the Federal Constitution by the Supreme Court on more than one occasion.

4. It is assumed that each state *desires* to have all normal children in the state attend school at least five hours a day, 150 days a year, at least until they reach the age of 18, but that the states differ and will continue to differ in regard to the laws requiring school attendance and the way special provisions are provided for physically and mentally handicapped children.

5. It is assumed that each state accepts the responsibility of providing for the education of at least some of its youth beyond high school; the organization and financing of such education, however, differs and will continue to differ state by state; in each state opportunities for education beyond high school now includes at least one university chartered by the state and largely supported by public funds; the continuation of such universities as centers of research, advanced study, and above all, fearless free inquiry is essential to the welfare of the state and the nation.

6. It is assumed that the education provided in high school and beyond

by public institutions is designed to develop the potentialities of all the youth to fit them for employment in a highly industrialized society.

7. The financing of education, including research and scholarly work in the universities, is a concern of private universities, the states, and the Federal government.

The declaration of some such set of premises by an interstate commission would be the first step in shaping a nationwide educational policy. If each state legislature would pass a resolution accepting such a declaration, we should for the first time as a nation be officially committed to certain basic principles of educational policy. We now assume these principles to be valid, but in fact they have never been promulgated by representative assemblies and could not be promulgated by the Congress.

THE
CONTEMPORARY
PERIOD
(20th Century)

SIGNIFICANT
ACTIONS

THE OREGON CASE
DECISION

Pierce (Governor of Oregon) et. al. *v. Society of Sisters* (1925) (*also Pierce* et al. *v. Hill Military Academy*)

Mr. Justice McReynolds delivered the opinion of a unanimous Court.

. . . The challenged Act, effective September 1, 1926, requires every parent, guardian or other person having control or charge or custody of a child between eight and sixteen years to send him to "a public school for the period of time a public school shall be held during the current year" in the district where the child resides; and failure so to do is declared a misdemeanor. . . . The manifest purpose is to compel general attendance at public schools by normal children, between eight and sixteen, who have not completed the eighth grade. And without doubt enforcement of the statute would seriously impair, perhaps destroy, the profitable features of appellees' business and greatly diminish the value of their property.

. . .

No question is raised concerning the power of the State reasonably to regulate all schools, to inspect, supervise and examine them, their teachers and pupils; to require that all children of proper age attend some school, that

---

268 U.S. 510.

teachers shall be of good moral character and patriotic disposition, that certain studies plainly essential to good citizenship must be taught, and that nothing be taught which is manifestly inimical to the public welfare.

The inevitable practical result of enforcing the Act under consideration would be destruction of appellees' primary schools, and perhaps all other private primary schools for normal children within the State of Oregon. These parties are engaged in a kind of undertaking not inherently harmful, but long regarded as useful and meritorious. Certainly there is nothing in the present records to indicate that they have failed to discharge their obligations to patrons, students or the State. And there are no peculiar circumstances or present emergencies which demand extraordinary measures relative to primary education.

. . . We think it entirely plain that the Act . . . unreasonably interferes with the liberty of parents and guardians to direct the upbringing and education of children under their control. As often heretofore pointed out, rights guaranteed by the Constitution may not be abridged by legislation which has no reasonable relation to some purpose within the competency of the State. The fundamental theory of liberty upon which all governments in this Union repose excludes any general power of the State to standardize its children by forcing them to accept instruction from public teachers only. The child is not the mere creature of the State; those who nurture him and direct his destiny have the right, coupled with the high duty, to recognize and prepare him for additional obligations.

. . .

The suits were not premature. The injury to appellees was present and very real, not a mere possibility in the remote future. If no relief had been possible prior to the effective date of the Act, the injury would have become irreparable. Prevention of impending injury by unlawful action is a well recognized function of courts of equity.

Affirmed.

PUBLIC SCHOOL BOOKS
FOR PRIVATE SCHOOL
STUDENTS

Cochran et al. *v. Louisiana State Board of
Education* (1930)

Mr. Chief Justice Hughes delivered the opinion of a unanimous Court.

The appellants, as citizens and taxpayers of the State of Louisiana, brought this suit to restrain the State Board of Education and other state officials from expending any part of the severance tax fund in purchasing school books and in supplying them free of cost to the school children of the State, under Acts No. 100 and No. 143 of 1928, upon the ground that the legislation violated specified provisions of the constitution of the State, and also section 4 of Article IV and the Fourteenth Amendment of the Federal Constitution. The Supreme Court of the State affirmed the judgment of the trial court, which refused to issue an injunction.

. . .

Act No. 100 of 1928 provided that the severance tax fund of the State, after allowing funds and appropriations as required by the state constitution, should be devoted, "first, to supplying school books to the school children of the State." The Board of Education was directed to provide "school books for school children free of cost to such children." Act No. 143 of 1928 made appropriations in accordance with the above provisions.

The Supreme Court of the State, . . . held that these acts were not repugnant to either the state or the Federal Constitution.

. . .

The contention of the appellant under the Fourteenth Amendment is that taxation for the purchase of schools books constituted a taking of private property for a private purpose. . . . The purpose is said to be to aid private, religious, sectarian and other schools not embraced in the public educational system of the State by furnishing textbooks free to the children attending such private schools. The operation and effect of the legislation in question were described by the Supreme Court of the State as follows:

> One may scan the acts in vain to ascertain where any money is appropriated for the purchase of school books for the use of any church, private, sectarian or even public school. The appropriations were made for the specific purpose of purchasing school books for the use of the school children of the state, free of cost to them. It was for their benefit and the resulting benefit to the state that the appropriations were made. True, these children attend some school, public or private, the latter, sectarian or nonsectarian, and that the books are to be furnished them for their use, free of cost, whichever they attend. The schools, however, are not the beneficiaries of these appropriations. They obtain nothing from them, nor are they relieved of a single obligation because of them. The school children and the state alone are the beneficiaries. It is also true that the sectarian schools, which some of the children attend, instruct their pupils in religion, and books are used for that purpose, but one may search diligently the acts, though without result, in an effort to find anything to the effect that it is the purpose of the state to furnish religious books for the use of such children. . . .

Viewing the statute as having the effect thus attributed to it, we cannot doubt that the taxing power of the state is exerted for a public purpose. The legislation does not segregate private schools, or their pupils, as its beneficiaries or attempt to interfere with any matters of exclusively private concern. Its interest is education, broadly; its method, comprehensive. Individual interests are aided only as the common interest is safeguarded.

Judgment affirmed.

THE BUS
TRANSPORTATION CASE

*Everson v. Board of Education of Ewing
Township, N.J.* (1947)

Mr. Justice Black delivered the [5–4] opinion of the Court.

A New Jersey statute authorizes its local school districts to make rules and contracts for the transportation of children to and from schools. The appellee, a township board of education, acting pursuant to this statute, authorized reimbursement to parents of money expended by them for the bus transportation of their children on regular buses operated by the public transportation system. Part of this money was for the payment of transportation of some children in the community to Catholic parochial schools. These church schools give their students, in addition to secular education, regular religious instruction conforming to the religious tenets and modes of worship of the Catholic Faith. The superintendent of these schools is a Catholic priest.

The appellant, in his capacity as a district taxpayer, filed suit in a state court challenging the right of the Board to reimburse parents of parochial school students. He contended that the statute and the resolution passed pursuant to it violated both the State and the Federal Constitutions. That court held that the legislature was without power to authorize such payment under the state constitution. . . . The New Jersey Court of Errors and Appeals

---

330 U.S. 1.

reversed, holding that neither the statute nor the resolution passed pursuant to it was in conflict with the State constitution or the provisions of the Federal Constitution in issue.

. . .

The only contention here is that the state statute and the resolution, insofar as they authorized reimbursement to parents of children attending parochial schools, violate the Federal Constitution in these two respects, which to some extent overlap. *First.* They authorize the State to take by taxation the private property of some and bestow it upon others, to be used for their own private purposes. This, it is alleged, violates the due process clause of the Fourteenth Amendment. *Second.* The statute and the resolution forced inhabitants to pay taxes to help support and maintain schools which are dedicated to, and which regularly teach, the Catholic Faith. This is alleged to be a use of state power to support church schools contrary to the prohibition of the First Amendment which the Fourteenth Amendment made applicable to the states.

. . . But, the New Jersey legislature has decided that a public purpose will be served by using tax-raised funds to pay the bus fares of all school children, including those who attend parochial schools. The New Jersey Court of Errors and Appeals has reached the same conclusion. The fact that a state law, passed to satisfy a public need, coincides with the personal desires of the individuals most directly affected is certainly an inadequate reason for us to say that a legislature has erroneously appraised the public need.

. . .

It is much too late to argue that legislation intended to facilitate the opportunity of children to get a secular education serves no public purpose. . . . The same thing is no less true of legislation to reimburse needy parents, or all parents, for the payment of the fares of their children so that they can ride in public buses to and from schools rather than run the risk of traffic and other hazards incident to walking or "hitchhiking." . . .

Insofar as the second phase of the due process argument may differ from the first, it is by suggesting that taxation for transportation of children to church schools constitutes support of a religion by the State. But if the law is invalid for this reason, it is because it violates the First Amendment's prohibition against the establishment of religion by law. This is the exact question raised by appellant's second contention, to consideration of which we now turn.

. . . The New Jersey statute is challenged as a "law respecting an establishment of religion." The First Amendment, as made applicable to the states by the Fourteenth, . . . commands that a state "shall make no law respecting an establishment of religion, or prohibiting the free exercise thereof." . . . Whether this New Jersey law is one respecting an "establishment of religion" requires an understanding of the meaning of that language, particularly with respect to the imposition of taxes. Once again, therefore, it is not inappropriate briefly to review the background and environment of the period in which that constitutional language was fashioned and adopted.

. . .

The "establishment of religion" clause of the First Amendment means at least this: Neither a state nor the Federal Government can set up a church. Neither can pass laws which aid one religion, aid all religions, or prefer one religion over another. Neither can force nor influence a person to go to or to remain away from church against his will or force him to profess a belief or disbelief in any religion. No person can be punished for entertaining or professing religious beliefs or disbeliefs, for church attendance or non-attendance. No tax in any amount, large or small, can be levied to support any religious activities or institutions, whatever they may be called, or whatever form they may adopt to teach or practice religion. Neither a state nor the Federal Government can, openly or secretly, participate in the affairs of any religious organizations or groups and *vice versa*. In the words of Jefferson, the clause against establishment of religion by law was intended to erect "a wall of separation between church and State."

. . .

We must consider the New Jersey statute in accordance with the foregoing limitations imposed by the First Amendment. But we must not strike that state statute down if it is within the State's constitutional power even though it approaches the verge of that power. . . . New Jersey cannot consistently with the "establishment of religion" clause of the First Amendment contribute tax-raised funds to the support of an institution which teaches the tenets and faith of any church. On the other hand, other language of the amendment commands that New Jersey cannot hamper its citizens in the free exercise of their own religion. Consequently, it cannot exclude individual Catholics, Lutherans, Mohammedans, Baptists, Jews, Methodists, Non-believers, Presbyterians, or the members of any other faith, *because of their faith, or lack of it,* from receiving the benefits of public welfare legislation. While we do not mean to intimate that a state could not provide transportation only to children attending public schools, we must be careful, in protecting the citizens of New Jersey against state-established churches, to be sure that we do not inadvertently prohibit New Jersey from extending its general state law benefits to all its citizens without regard to their religious belief.

Measured by these standards, we cannot say that the First Amendment prohibits New Jersey from spending tax-raised funds to pay the bus fares of parochial school pupils as a part of a general program under which it pays the fares of pupils attending public and other schools. . . . [The First] Amendment requires the state to be a neutral in its relations with groups of religious believers and non-believers; it does not require the state to be their adversary. State power is no more to be used so as to handicap religions than it is to favor them.

This Court has said that parents may, in the discharge of their duty under state compulsory education laws, send their children to a religious rather than a public school if the school meets the secular educational requirements which the state has power to impose. See *Pierce v. Society of Sisters.* . . . It appears that these parochial schools meet New Jersey's requirements. The State contributes no money to the schools. It does not support them. Its legislation, as applied, does no more than provide a general program to help parents get their children, regardless of their religion, safely and expeditiously to and from accredited schools.

The First Amendment has erected a wall between church and state. That wall must be kept high and impregnable. We could not approve the slightest breach. New Jersey has not breached it here.

Affirmed.

Mr. Justice Jackson, dissenting.

I find myself, contrary to first impressions, unable to join in this decision. I have a sympathy, though it is not ideological, with Catholic citizens who are compelled by law to pay taxes for public schools, and also feel constrained by conscience and discipline to support other schools for their own children. Such relief to them as this case involves is not in itself a serious burden to taxpayers and I had assumed it to be as little serious in principle. Study of this case convinces me otherwise. The Court's opinion marshals every argument in favor of state aid and puts the case in its most favorable light, but much of its reasoning confirms my conclusions that these are no good grounds upon which to support the present legislation. In fact, the undertones of the opinion, advocating complete and uncompromising separation of Church and State, seem utterly discordant with its conclusion yielding support to their commingling in educational matters. The case which irresistibly comes to mind as the most fitting precedent is that of Julia who, according to Byron's reports, "whispering 'I will ne'er consent,'—consented."

The Township of Ewing is not furnishing transportation to the children in any form; it is not operating school buses itself or contracting for their operation; and it is not performing any public service of any kind with this taxpayer's money. All school children are left to ride as ordinary paying passengers on the regular buses operated by the public transportation system. What the Township does, and what the taxpayer complains of, is at stated intervals to reimburse parents for fares paid, provided the children attend either public schools or Catholic Church schools. This expenditure of tax funds has no possible effect on the child's safety or expedition in transit. As passengers on the public buses they travel as fast and no faster, and are as safe and no safer, since their parents are reimbursed as before.

.   .   .

The New Jersey Act in question makes the character of the school, not the needs of the children, determine the eligibility of parents to reimbursement. The Act permits payment for transportation to parochial schools or public schools but prohibits it to private schools operated in whole or in part for profit. . . .

.   .   .

I should be surprised if any Catholic would deny that the parochial school is a vital, if not the most vital, part of the Roman Catholic Church. If put to the choice, that venerable institution, I should expect, would forego its whole service for mature persons before it would give up education of the young, and it would be a wise choice. Its growth and cohesion, discipline and loyalty, spring from its schools. Catholic education is the rock on which the whole structure rests, and to render tax aid to its Church school is indistinguishable to me from rendering the same aid to the Church itself.

.   .   .

It seems to me that the basic fallacy in the Court's reasoning, which accounts for its failure to apply the principles it avows, is in ignoring the essentially religious test by which beneficiaries of this expenditure are selected. A policeman protects a Catholic, of course—but not because he is a Catholic; it is because he is a man and a member of our society. The fireman protects the Church school—but not because it is a Church school; it is because it is property, part of the assets of our society. Neither the fireman nor the policeman has to ask before he renders aid "Is this man or building identified with the Catholic Church?" But before these school authorities draw a check to reimburse for a student's fare they must ask just that question, and if the school is a Catholic one they may render aid because it is such, while if it is of any other faith or is run for profit, the help must be withheld. . . .

.   .   .

. . . Religious teaching cannot be a private affair when the state seeks to impose regulations which infringe on it indirectly, and a public affair when it comes to taxing citizens of one faith to aid another, or those of no faith to aid all. If these principles seem harsh in prohibiting aid to Catholic education, it must not be forgotten that it is the same Constitution that alone assures Catholics the right to maintain these schools at all when predominant local sentiment would forbit them. *Pierce v. Society of Sisters.* . . . Nor should I think that those who have done so well without this aid would want to see this separation between Church and State broken down. If the state may aid these religious schools, it may therefore regulate them. Many groups have sought aid from tax funds only to find that it carried political controls with it.

Mr. Justice Frankfurter joins in this opinion.

RELIGIOUS INSTRUCTION
IN PUBLIC SCHOOLS

People of State of Illinois ex rel. *McCollum v.*
Board of Education of School District No. 71,
Champaign County, Illinois et al. (1948)

Mr. Justice Black delivered the [8–1] opinion of the Court.

This case relates to the power of a state to utilize its tax-supported public school system in aid of religious instruction insofar as that power may be restricted by the First and Fourteenth Amendments to the Federal Constitution.

The appellant, Vashti McCollum, began this action for mandamus against the Champaign Board of Education in the Circuit Court of Champaign County, Illinois. Her asserted interest was that of a resident and taxpayer of Champaign and of a parent whose child was then enrolled in the Champaign public schools. Illinois has a compulsory education law which, with exceptions, requires parents to send their children, aged seven to sixteen, to its tax-supported public schools where the children are to remain in attendance during the hours when the schools are regularly in session. Parents who violate this law commit a misdemeanor punishable by fine unless the children attend private or parochial schools which meet educational standards fixed by the State. District boards of education are given general supervisory

---

333 U.S. 203.

powers over the use of the public school buildings within the school districts. . . .

Appellant's petition for mandamus alleged that religious teachers, employed by private religious groups, were permitted to come weekly into the school buildings during the regular hours set apart for secular teaching, and then and there for a period of thirty minutes substitute their religious teaching for the secular education provided under the compulsory education law. The petitioner charged that this joint public-school religious-group program violated the First and Fourteenth Amendments to the United States Constitution. . . .

Although there are disputes between the parties as to various inferences that may or may not properly be drawn from the evidence concerning the religious program, the following facts are shown by the record without dispute. In 1940 interested members of the Jewish, Roman Catholic, and a few of the Protestant faiths formed a voluntary association called the Champaign Council on Religious Education. They obtained permission from the Board of Education to offer classes in religious instruction to public school pupils in grades four to nine inclusive. Classes were made up of pupils whose parents signed printed cards requesting that their children be permitted to attend; they were held weekly, thirty minutes for the lower grades, forty-five minutes for the higher. The council employed the religious teachers at no expense to the school authorities, but the instructors were subject to the approval and supervision of the superintendent of schools. The classes were taught in three separate religious groups by Protestant teachers, Catholic priests, and a Jewish rabbi, although for the past several years there have apparently been no classes instructed in the Jewish religion. Classes were conducted in the regular classrooms of the school building. Students who did not choose to take the religious instruction were not released from public school duties; they were required to leave their classrooms and go to some other place in the school building for pursuit of their secular studies. On the other hand, students who were released from secular study for the religious instructions were required to be present at the religious classes. Reports of their presence or absence were to be made to their secular teachers.

The foregoing facts, without reference to others that appear in the record, show the use of tax-supported property for religious instruction and the close cooperation between the school authorities and the religious council in promoting religious education. The operation of the State's compulsory education system thus assists and is integrated with the program of religious instruction carried on by separate religious sects. Pupils compelled by law to go to school for secular education are released in part from their legal duty upon the condition that they attend the religious classes. This is beyond all question a utilization of the tax-established and tax-supported public school system to aid religious groups to spread their faith. And it falls squarely under the ban of the First Amendment (made applicable to the States by the Fourteenth) as we interpreted it in *Everson v. Board of Education.* . . .

. . .

To hold that a state cannot consistently with the First and Fourteenth Amendments utilize its public school system to aid any or all religious faiths or sects in the dissemination of their doctrines and ideals does not, as counsel urge, manifest a governmental hostility to religion or religious teachings. A manifestation of such hostility would be at war with our national tradition as embodied in the First Amendment's guaranty of the free exercise of religion. For the First Amendment rests upon the premise that both religion and government can best work to achieve their lofty aims if each is left free from the other within its respective sphere. Or, as we said in the *Everson* case, the First Amendment has erected a wall between Church and State which must be kept high and impregnable.

Here not only are the State's tax-supported public school buildings used for the dissemination of religious doctrines. The State also affords sectarian groups an invaluable aid in that it helps to provide pupils for their religious classes through use of the State's compulsory public school machinery. This is not separation of Church and State.

The cause is reversed and remanded to the State Supreme Court for proceedings not inconsistent with this opinion.

Reversed and remanded.

Mr. Justice Frankfurter *et al.,* concurring.

We dissented in *Everson v. Board of Education.* . . . because in our view the Constitutional principle requiring separation of Church and State compelled invalidation of the ordinance sustained by the majority. Illinois has here authorized the commingling of sectarian with secular instruction in the public schools. The Constitution of the United States forbids this.

This case, in the light of the *Everson* decision, demonstrates anew that the mere formulation of a relevant Constitutional principle is the beginning of the solution of a problem, not its answer. This is so because the meaning of a spacious conception like that of the separation of Church from State is unfolded as appeal is made to the principle from case to case. We are all agreed that the First and the Fourteenth Amendments have a secular reach far more penetrating in the conduct of Government than merely to forbid an "established church." But agreement, in the abstract, that the First Amendment was designed to erect a "wall of separation between Church and State," does not preclude a clash of views as to what the wall separates. . . .

Of course, "released time" as a generalized conception, undefined by differentiating particularities, is not an issue for Constitutional adjudication. Local programs differ from each other in many and crucial respects. Some "released time" classes are under separate denominational auspices, others are conducted jointly by several denominations, often embracing all the religious affiliations of a community. Some classes in religion teach a limited sectarianism; others emphasize democracy, unity and spiritual values not anchored in a particular creed. Insofar as these are manifestations merely of the free exercise of religion, they are quite outside the scope of judicial concern, except insofar as the Court may be called upon to protect the right of religious freedom. It is only when challenge is made to the share that the public schools have in the execution of a particular "released time" program that close judicial scrutiny is demanded of the exact relation between the religious instruction and the public educational system in the specific situation before the Court.

. . .

. . . The Champaign arrangement thus presents powerful elements of inherent pressure by the school system in the interest of religious sects. The fact that this power has not been used to discriminate is beside the point. Separation is a requirement to abstain from fusing functions of Government and of religious sects, not merely to treat them all equally. That a child is offered an alternative may reduce the constraint; it does not eliminate the operation of influence by the school in matters sacred to conscience and outside the school's domain. The law of imitation operates, and non-conformity is not an outstanding characteristic of children. The result is an obvious pressure upon children to attend. Again, while the Champaign school population represents only a fraction of the more than two hundred and fifty sects of the nation, not even all the practicing sects in Champaign are willing or able to provide religious instruction. The children belonging to these non-participating sects will thus have inculcated in them a feeling of separatism when the school should be the training ground for habits of community, or they will have religious instruction in a faith which is not that of their parents. As a result, the public school system of Champaign actively furthers inculcation in the religious tenets of some faiths, and in the process sharpens the consciousness of religious differences at least among some of the children committed to its care. . . .

Mention should not be omitted that the integration of religious instruction within the school system as practiced in Champaign is supported by arguments drawn from educational theories as diverse as those derived from Catholic conceptions and from the writings of John Dewey. Movements like "released time" are seldom single in origin or aim. Nor can the intrusion of religious instruction into the public school system of Champaign be minimized by saying that it absorbs less than an hour a week; in fact, that affords evidence of a design constitutionally objectionable. If it were merely a question of enabling a child to obtain religious instruction with a receptive mind the thirty or forty-five minutes could readily be found on Saturday or Sunday. If that were all, Champaign might have drawn upon the French system, known in its American manifestation as "dismissed time," whereby one school day is shortened to allow all children to go where they please, leaving those who so desire to go to a religious school. The momentum of the whole school atmosphere and school planning is presumably put behind religious instruction, as given in Champaign, precisely in order to secure for the religious instruction such momentum and planning. To speak of "released time" as being only half or three quarters of an hour is to draw a thread from a fabric.

. . . We do not now attempt to weigh in the Constitutional scale every separate detail or various combination of factors which may establish a valid "released time" program. We find that the basic Constitutional principle of absolute Separation was violated when the State of Illinois, speaking through its Supreme Court, sustained the school authorities of Champaign in sponsoring and effectively furthering religious beliefs by its educational arrangement.

Separation means separation, not something else. . . .

Mr. Justice Jackson, concurring.

I join the opinion of Mr. Justice Frankfurter, and concur in the result reached by the Court, but with these reservations: I think it is doubtful whether the facts of this case establish jurisdiction in this Court, but in any event that we should place some bounds on the demands for interference with local schools that we are empowered or willing to entertain. I make these reservations a matter of record in view of the number of litigations likely to be started as a result of this decision.

A Federal Court may interfere with local school authorities only when they invade either a personal liberty or a property right protected by the Federal Constitution. Ordinarily this will come about in either of two ways:

First. When a person is required to submit to some religious rite or instruction or is deprived or threatened with deprivation of his freedom for resisting such unconstitutional requirement. . . . But here, complainant's son may join religious classes if he chooses and if his parents so request, or he may stay out of them. The complaint is that when others join and he does not, it sets him apart as a dissenter, which is humiliating. Even admitting this to be true, it may be doubted whether the Constitution which, of course, protects the right to dissent, can be construed also to protect one from the embarrassment that always attends nonconformity, whether in religion, politics, behavior or dress. Since no legal compulsion is applied to complainant's son himself and no penalty is imposed or threatened from which we may relieve him, we can hardly base jurisdiction on this ground.

Second. Where a complainant is deprived of property by being taxed for unconstitutional purposes, such as directly or indirectly to support a religious establishment. We can protect a taxpayer against such a levy. This was the *Everson* case . . . as I saw it then and see it now. . . .

In this case, however, any cost of this plan to the taxpayers is incalculable and negligible. It can be argued, perhaps, that religious classes add some wear and tear on public buildings and that they should be charged with some expense for heat and light, even though the sessions devoted to religious instruction do not add to the length of the school day. But the cost is neither substantial nor measurable, and no one seriously can say that the complainant's tax bill has been proved to be increased because of this plan. I think it is doubtful whether the taxpayer in this case has shown any substantial property injury.

. . .

While we may and should end such formal and explicit instruction as the Champaign plan and can at all times prohibit teaching of creed and catechism and ceremonial and can forbid forthright proselyting in the schools, I think it remains to be demonstrated whether it is possible, even if desirable, to comply with such demands as plaintiff's completely to isolate and cast out of secular education all that some people may reasonably regard as religious instruction. Perhaps subjects such as mathematics, physics or chemistry are, or can be, completely secularized. But it would not seem practical to teach either practice or appreciation of the arts if we are to forbid exposure of youth to any religious influences. . . . The fact is that, for good or for ill, nearly everything in our culture worth transmitting, everything which gives meaning to life, is saturated with religious influences, derived from paganism, Judaism, Christianity—both Catholic and Protestant—and other faiths accepted by a large part of the world's peoples. One can hardly respect a system of education that would leave the student wholly ignorant of the currents of religious thought that move the world society for a part in which he is being prepared.

But how one can teach, with satisfaction or even with justice to all faiths, such subjects as the story of the Reformation, the Inquisition, or even the New England effort to found "a Church without a Bishop and a State without a King," is more than I know. . . .

. . . We must leave some flexibility to meet local conditions, some chance to progress by trial and error. While I agree that the religious classes involved here go beyond permissible limits, I also think the complaint demands more than plaintiff is entitled to have granted. So far as I can see this Court does not tell the State court where it may stop, nor does it set up any standards by which the State court may determine that question for itself.

The task of separating the secular from the religious in education is one of magnitude, intricacy and delicacy. To lay down a sweeping constitutional doctrine as demanded by complainant and apparently approved by the Court, applicable alike to all school boards of the nation, "to immediately adopt and enforce rules and regulations prohibiting all instruction in and teaching of religious education in all public schools," is to decree a uniform, rigid and, if we are consistent, an unchanging standard for countless school boards representing and serving highly localized groups which not only differ from each other but which themselves from time to time change attitudes. It seems to me that to do so is to allow zeal for our own ideas of what is good in public instruction to induce us to accept the role of a super board of education for every school district in the nation.

It is idle to pretend that this task is one for which we can find in the Constitution one word to help us as judges decide where the secular ends and the sectarian begins in education. Nor can we find guidance in any other legal source. It is a matter on which we can find no law but our own prepossessions. If with no surer legal guidance we are to take up and decide every variation of this controversy, raised by persons not subject to penalty or tax but who are dissatisfied with the way schools are dealing with the problem, we are likely to have much business of the sort. And, more importantly, we are likely to make the legal "wall of separation between church and state" as winding as the famous serpentine wall designed by Mr. Jefferson for the University he founded.

Mr. Justice Reed, dissenting.

. . . . I find it difficult to extract from the opinions any conclusion as to what it is in the Champaign plan that is unconstitutional. Is it the use of school buildings for religious instruction; the release of pupils by the schools for religious instruction during school hours; the so-called assistance by teachers in handing out the request cards to pupils, in keeping lists of them for release and records of their attendance; or the action of the principals in arranging an opportunity for the classes and the appearance of the Council's instructors? None of the reversing opinions say whether the purpose of the Champaign plan for religious instruction during school hours is unconstitutional or whether it is some ingredient used in or omitted from the formula that makes the plan unconstitutional.

. . .

With the general statements in the opinions concerning the constitutional requirement that the nation and the states, by virtue of the First and Fourteenth Amendments, may "make no law respecting an establishment of religion," I am in agreement. But, in the light of the meaning given to those words by precedents, customs, and practices . . . I cannot agree with the Court's conclusion that when pupils compelled by law to go to school for secular education are released from school so as to attend the religious classes, churches are unconstitutionally aided. Whatever may be the wisdom of the arrangement as to the use of the school buildings made with The Champaign Council of Religious Education, it is clear to me that past practice shows such cooperation between the schools and a non-ecclesiastical body is not forbidden by the First Amendment. . . . This Court cannot be too cautious in upsetting practices embedded in our society by many years of experience. A state is entitled to have great leeway in its legislation when dealing with the important social problems of its population. A definite violation of legislative limits must be established. The Constitution should not be stretched to forbid national customs in the way courts act to reach arrangements to avoid federal taxation. Devotion to the great principle of religious liberty should not lead us into a rigid interpretation of the constitutional guarantee that conflicts with accepted habits of our people. This is an instance where, for me, the history of past practices is determinative of the meaning of a constitutional clause not a decorous introduction to the study of its text. The judgment should be affirmed.

THE "RELEASED TIME" DECISION

Zorach et al. *v. Clauson* et al. (1952)

Mr. Justice Douglas delivered the [6–3] opinion of the Court.

New York City has a program which permits its public schools to release students during the school day so that they may leave the school buildings and school grounds and go to religious centers for religious instruction or devotional exercises. A student is released on written request of his parents. Those not released stay in the classrooms. The churches make weekly reports to the schools, sending a list of children who have been released from public school but who have not reported for religious instruction.

This "released time" program involves neither religious instruction in public school classrooms nor the expenditure of public funds. All costs, including the application blanks, are paid by the religious organizations. The case is therefore unlike *McCollum v. Board of Education* . . . which involved a "released time" program from Illinois. In that case the classrooms were turned over to religious instructors. We accordingly held that the program violated the First Amendment which (by reason of the Fourteenth Amendment) prohibits the states from establishing religion or prohibiting its free exercise.

Appellants, who are taxpayers and residents of New York City and

343 U.S. 306.

whose children attend its public schools, challenge the present law, contending it is in essence not different from the one involved in the *McCollum* case. Their argument, stated elaborately in various ways, reduces itself to this: the weight and influence of the school is put behind a program for religious instruction; public school teachers police it, keeping tab on students who are released; the classroom activities come to a halt while the students who are released for religious instruction are on leave; the school is a crutch on which the churches are leaning for support in their religious training; without the cooperation of the schools this "released time" program, like the one in the *McCollum* case, would be futile and ineffective. The New York Court of Appeals sustained the law against this claim of unconstitutionality. . . .

. . .

It takes obtuse reasoning to inject any issue of the "free exercise" of religion into the present case. No one is forced to go to the religious classroom and no religious exercise or instruction is brought to the classrooms of the public schools. A student need not take religious instruction. He is left to his own desires as to the manner or time of his religious devotions, if any.

There is a suggestion that the system involves the use of coercion to get public school students into religious classrooms. There is no evidence in the record before us that supports that conclusion. The present record indeed tells us that the school authorities are neutral in this regard and do no more than release students whose parents so request. If in fact coercion were used, if it were established that any one or more teachers were using their office to persuade or force students to take the religious instruction, a wholly different case would be presented. Hence we put aside that claim of coercion both as respects the "free exercise" of religion and "an establishment of religion" within the meaning of the First Amendment.

. . . The First Amendment within the scope of its coverage permits no exception; the prohibition is absolute. The First Amendment, however, does not say that in every and all aspects there shall be a separation of Church and State. Rather, it studiously defines the manner, the specific ways, in which there shall be no concert or union or dependency one on the other. That is the common sense of the matter. Otherwise the state and religion would be aliens to each other—hostile, suspicious, and even unfriendly. Churches could not be required to pay even property taxes. Municipalities would not be permitted to render police or fire protection to religious groups. Policemen who helped parishioners into their places of worship would violate the Constitution. Prayers in our legislative halls; the appeals to the Almighty in the messages of the Chief Executive; the proclamations making Thanksgiving Day a holiday; "so help me God" in our courtroom oaths—these and all other references to the Almighty that run through our laws, our public rituals, our ceremonies would be flouting the First Amendment. A fastidious atheist or agnostic could even object to the supplication with which the Court opens each session: "God save the United States and this Honorable Court."

We would have to press the concept of separation of Church and State to these extremes to condemn the present law on constitutional grounds. . . .

. . . When the state encourages religious instruction or cooperates with religious authorities by adjusting the schedule of public events to sectarian needs, it follows the best of our traditions. For it then respects the religious nature of our people and accommodates the public service to their spiritual needs. To hold that it may not would be to find in the Constitution a requirement that the government show a callous indifference to religious groups. That would be preferring those who believe in no religion over those who do believe. Government may not finance religious groups nor undertake religious instruction nor blend secular and sectarian education nor use secular institutions to force one or some religion on any person. But we find no constitutional requirement which makes it necessary for government to be hostile to religion and to throw its weight against efforts to widen the effective scope of religious influence. The government must be neutral when it comes to competition between sects. It may not thrust any sect on any person. It may not make a religious observance compulsory. It may not coerce anyone to attend church, to observe a religious holiday, or to take religious instruction. But it can close its doors or suspend its operations as to those who want to repair to their religious sanctuary for worship or instruction. No more than that is undertaken here.

This program may be unwise and improvident from an educational or a community viewpoint. . . . Our individual preferences, however, are not the constitutional standard. The constitutional standard is the separation of Church and State. . . .

Affirmed.

Mr. Justice Black, dissenting.

I see no significant difference between the invalid Illinois system and that of New York here sustained. Except for the use of the school buildings in Illinois, there is no difference between the systems which I consider even worthy of mention. In the New York program, as in that of Illinois, the school authorities release some of the children on the condition that they attend the religious classes, get reports on whether they attend, and hold the other children in the school building until the religious hour is over. As we attempted to make categorically clear, the *McCollum* decision would have been the same if the religious classes had not been held in the school buildings.

. . .

I am aware that our *McCollum* decision on separation of Church and State has been subjected to a most searching examination throughout the country. Probably few opinions from this Court in recent years have attracted more attention or stirred wider debate. Our insistence on "a wall between Church and State which must be kept high and impregnable" has seemed to some a correct exposition of the philosophy and a true interpretation of the language of the First Amendment to which we should strictly adhere. With equal conviction and sincerity, others have thought the *McCollum* decision fundamentally wrong and have pledged continuous warfare against it. The opinions in the court below and the briefs here reflect these diverse viewpoints. . . .

Here the sole question is whether New York can use its compulsory education laws to help religious sects get attendants presumably too unenthusiastic to go unless moved to do so by the pressure of this state machinery. That this is the plan, purpose, design and consequence of the New York program cannot be denied. The state thus makes religious sects beneficiaries of its power to compel children to attend secular schools. Any use of such coercive power by the state to help or hinder some religious sects or to prefer all religious sects over non-believers or vice versa is just what I think the First Amendment forbids. . . .

. . .

State help to religion injects political and party prejudices into a holy field. It too often substitutes force for prayer, hate for love, and persecution for persuasion. Government should not be allowed, under cover of the soft euphemism of "cooperation," to steal into the sacred area of religious choice.

Mr. Justice Frankfurter, dissenting.

Of course, a State may provide that the classes in its schools shall be dismissed, for any reason, or no reason, on fixed days, or for special occasions. The essence of this case is that the school system did not "close its doors" and did not "suspend its operations." There is all the difference in the world between letting the children out of school and letting some of them out of school into religious classes. If every one is free to make what use he will of time wholly unconnected from schooling required by law—those who wish sectarian instruction devoting it to that purpose, those who have ethical instruction at home, to that, those who study music, to that—then of course there is no conflict with the Fourteenth Amendment.

The pith of the case is that formalized religious instruction is substituted for other school activity which those who do not participate in the released-time program are compelled to attend. The school system is very much in operation during this kind of released time. If its doors are closed, they are closed upon those students who do not attend the religious instruction, in order to keep them within the school. That is the very thing which raises the constitutional issue. It is not met by disregarding it. . . .

Mr. Justice Jackson, dissenting.

This released time program is founded upon a use of the State's power of coercion, which, for me, determines its unconstitutionality. . . .

If public education were taking so much of the pupils' time as to injure the public or the students' welfare by encroaching upon their religious opportunity, simply shortening everyone's school day would facilitate voluntary and optional attendance at Church classes. But that suggestion is rejected upon the ground that if they are made free many students will not go to the Church. Hence, they must be deprived of freedom for this period, with Church attendance put to them as one of the two permissible ways of using it.

The greater effectiveness of this system over voluntary attendance after school hours is due to the truant officer who, if the youngster fails to go to the Church school, dogs him back to the public schoolroom. Here schooling is more or less suspended during the "released time" so that nonreligious attendants will not forge ahead of the churchgoing absentees. But it serves as a temporary jail for a pupil who will not go to Church. It takes more subtlety of mind than I possess to deny that this is governmental constraint in support of religion. It is as unconstitutional, in my view, when exerted by indirection as when exercised forthrightly.

As one whose children, as a matter of free choice, have been sent to privately supported Church schools, I may challenge the Court's suggestion that opposition to this plan can only be antireligious, atheistic, or agnostic. My evangelistic brethren confuse an objection to compulsion with an objection to religion. It is possible to hold a faith with enough confidence to believe that what should be rendered to God does not need to be decided and collected by Caesar.

The day that this country ceases to be free for irreligion it will cease to be free for religion—except for the sect that can win political power. The same epithetical jurisprudence used by the Court today to beat down those who oppose pressuring children into some religion can devise as good epithets tomorrow against those who object to pressuring them into a favored religion. And, after all, if we concede to the State power and wisdom to single out "duly constituted religious" bodies as exclusive alternatives for compulsory secular instruction, it would be logical to also uphold the power and wisdom to choose the true faith among those "duly constituted." We start down a rough road when we begin to mix compulsory public education with compulsory godliness. . . .

The wall which the Court was professing to erect between Church and State has become even more warped and twisted than I expected. Today's judgment will be more interesting to students of psychology and of the judicial process than to students of constitutional law.

THE DESEGREGATION
DECISION

Brown v. Board of Education of Topeka (1954)
(also *Briggs v. Elliott, Davis v. County School
Board of Prince Edward County, Va.,* and
Gebhart v. Benton)

Mr. Chief Justice Warren delivered the opinion of a unanimous Court.

These cases come to us from the States of Kansas, South Carolina, Virginia, and Delaware. They are premised on different facts and different local conditions, but a common legal question justifies their consideration together in this consolidated opinion.

In each of the cases, minors of the Negro race, through their legal representatives, seek the aid of the courts in obtaining admission to the public schools of their community on a nonsegregated basis. In each instance, they have been denied admission to schools attended by white children under laws requiring or permitting segregation according to race. This segregation was alleged to deprive the plaintiffs of the equal protection of the laws under the Fourteenth Amendment. In each of the cases other than the Delaware case, a three-judge federal district court denied relief to the plaintiffs on the so-called "separate but equal" doctrine announced by this Court in *Plessy v. Ferguson,* 163 U.S. 537. Under that doctrine, equality of treatment is accorded when the

347 U.S. 483.

447

races are provided substantially equal facilities, even though these facilities be separate. In the Delaware case, the Supreme Court of Delaware adhered to that doctrine, but ordered that the plaintiffs be admitted to the white schools because of their superiority to the Negro schools.

The plaintiffs contend that segregated public schools are not "equal" and cannot be made "equal," and that hence they are deprived of the equal protection of the laws. Because of the obvious importance of the question presented, the Court took jurisdiction. Argument was heard in the 1952 Term, and reargument was heard this Term on certain questions propounded by the Court.

Reargument was largely devoted to the circumstances surrounding the adoption of the Fourteenth Amendment in 1868. It covered exhaustively consideration of the Amendment in Congress, ratification by the states, then existing practices in racial segregation, and the views of proponents and opponents of the Amendment. This discussion and our own investigation convince us that, although these sources cast some light, it is not enough to resolve the problem with which we are faced. At best, they are inconclusive. The most avid proponents of the post-War Amendments undoubtedly intended them to remove all legal distinctions among "all persons born or naturalized in the United States." Their opponents, just as certainly, were antagonistic to both the letter and the spirit of the Amendments and wished them to have the most limited effect. What others in Congress and the state legislatures had in mind cannot be determined with any degree of certainty.

. . .

In the first cases in this Court construing the Fourteenth Amendment, decided shortly after its adoption, the Court interpreted it as proscribing all state-imposed discriminations against the Negro race. The doctrine of "separate but equal" did not make its appearance in this Court until 1896 in the case of *Plessy v. Ferguson,* supra, involving not education but transportation. American courts have since labored with the doctrine for over half a century. In this Court, there have been six cases involving the "separate but equal" doctrine in the field of public education. . . .

. . . Here, unlike *Sweatt v. Painter,* there are findings below that the Negro and white schools involved have been equalized, or are being equalized, with respect to buildings, curricula, qualifications and salaries of teachers, and other "tangible" factors. Our decision, therefore, cannot turn on merely a comparison of these tangible factors in the Negro and white schools involved in each of these cases. We must look instead to the effect of segregation itself on public education.

. . . We must consider public education in the light of its full development and its present place in American life throughout the Nation. Only in this way can it be determined if segregation in public schools deprives these plaintiffs of the equal protection of the laws.

Today, education is perhaps the most important function of state and local governments. . . . In these days, it is doubtful that any child may reasonably be expected to succeed in life if he is denied the opportunity of an education. Such an opportunity, where the state has undertaken to provide it, is a right which must be made available to all on equal terms.

We come then to the question presented: Does segregation of children in public schools solely on the basis of race, even though the physical facilities and other "tangible" factors may be equal, deprive the children of the minority group of equal educational opportunities? We believe that it does.

In *Sweatt v. Painter,* . . . in finding that a segregated law school for Negroes could not provide them equal educational opportunities, this Court relied in large part on "those qualities which are incapable of objective measurement but which make for greatness in a law school." In *McLaurin v. Oklahoma State Regents,* . . . the Court, in requiring that a Negro admitted to a white graduate school be treated like all other students, again resorted to intangible considerations: ". . . his ability to study, to engage in discussions and exchange views with other students, and, in general, to learn his profession." Such considerations apply with added force to children in grade and high schools. To separate them from others of similar age and qualifications solely because of their race generates a feeling of inferiority as to their status in the community that may affect their hearts and minds in a way unlikely ever to be undone. The effect of this separation on their educational opportunities was well stated by a finding in the Kansas case by a court which nevertheless felt compelled to rule against the Negro plaintiffs:

> Segregation of white and colored children in public schools has a detrimental effect upon the colored children. The impact is greater when it has the sanction of the law; for the policy of separating the races is usually interpreted as denoting the inferiority of the Negro group. A sense of inferiority affects the motivation of a child to learn. Segregation with the sanction of law, therefore, has a tendency to retard the educational and mental development of Negro children and to deprive them of some of the benefits they would receive in a racially integrated school system.

Whatever may have been the extent of psychological knowledge at the time of *Plessy v. Ferguson,* this finding is amply supported by modern authority. Any language in *Plessy v. Ferguson* contrary to this finding is rejected.

We conclude that in the field of public education the doctrine of "separate but equal" has no place. Separate educational facilities are inherently unequal. Therefore, we hold that the plaintiffs and others similarly situated for whom the actions have been brought are, by reason of the segregation complained of, deprived of the equal protection of the laws guaranteed by the Fourteenth Amendment. This disposition makes unnecessary any discussion whether such segregation also violates the Due Process Clause of the Fourteenth Amendment.

OFFICIAL PRAYERS
IN PUBLIC SCHOOLS

Engel et al. *v. Vitale* et al. (1962)

Mr. Justice Black delivered the [6–1] opinion of the Court.

The respondent Board of Education of Union Free School District No. 9, New Hyde Park, New York, acting in its official capacity under state law, directed the School District's principal to cause the following prayer to be said aloud by each class in the presence of a teacher at the beginning of each school day:

"Almighty God, we acknowledge our dependence upon Thee, and we beg Thy blessings upon us, our parents, our teachers and our Country."

This daily procedure was adopted on the recommendation of the State Board of Regents, a governmental agency created by the State Constitution to which the New York Legislature has granted broad supervisory, executive, and legislative powers over the State's public school system. These state officials composed the prayer which they recommended and published as a part of their "Statement on Moral and Spiritual Training in the Schools," saying: "We believe that this Statement will be subscribed to by all men and women of good will, and we call upon all of them to aid in giving life to our program."

Shortly after practice of reciting the Regents' prayer was adopted by

370 U.S. 421.

the School District, the parents of ten pupils brought this action in a New York State Court insisting that use of this official prayer in the public schools was contrary to the beliefs, religions, or religious practices of both themselves and their children. . . . The New York Court of Appeals, over the dissents of Judges Dye and Fuld, sustained an order of the lower state courts which had upheld the power of New York to use the Regents' prayer as a part of the daily procedures of its public schools so long as the schools did not compel any pupil to join in the prayer over his or his parents' objection. We granted certiorari to review this important decision involving rights protected by the First and Fourteenth Amendments.

We think that by using its public school system to encourage recitation of the Regents' prayer, the State of New York has adopted a practice wholly inconsistent with the Establishment Clause. There can, of course, be no doubt that New York's program of daily classroom invocation of God's blessings as prescribed in the Regents' prayer is a religious activity. It is a solemn avowal of divine faith and supplication for the blessings of the Almighty. . . .

The petitioners contend among other things that the state laws requiring or permitting use of the Regents' prayer must be struck down as a violation of the Establishment Clause because that prayer was composed by governmental officials as a part of a governmental program to further religious beliefs. For this reason, petitioners argue, the State's use of the Regents' prayer in its public school system breaches the constitutional wall of separation between Church and State. We agree with that contention since we think that the constitutional prohibition against laws respecting an establishment of religion must at least mean that in this country it is no part of the business of government to compose official prayers for any group of the American people to recite as a part of a religious program carried on by the government.

It is a matter of history that this very practice of establishing governmentally composed prayers for religious services was one of the reasons which caused many of our early colonists to leave England and seek religious freedom in America. . . .

. . .

By the time of the adoption of the Constitution, our history shows that there was a widespread awareness among many Americans of the dangers of a union of Church and State. . . . The First Amendment was added to the Constitution to stand as a guarantee that neither the power nor the prestige of the Federal Government would be used to control, support or influence the kinds of prayer the American people can say—that the people's religions must not be subjected to the pressures of government for change each time a new political administration is elected to office. Under that Amendment's prohibition against governmental establishment of religion, as reinforced by the provisions of the Fourteenth Amendment, government in this country, be it state or federal, is without power to prescribe by law any particular form of prayer which is to be used as an official prayer in carrying on any program of governmentally sponsored religious activity.

There can be no doubt that New York's state prayer program officially establishes the religious beliefs embodied in the Regents' prayer. The respondents' argument to the contrary, which is largely based upon the contention that the Regents' prayer is "non-denominational" and the fact that the program, as modified and approved by state courts, does not require all pupils to recite the prayer but permits those who wish to do so to remain silent or be excused from the room, ignores the essential nature of the program's constitutional defects. Neither the fact that the prayer may be denominationally neutral nor the fact that its observance on the part of the students is voluntary can serve to free it from the limitations of the Establishment Clause, as it might from the Free Exercise Clause, of the First Amendment, both of which are operative against the States by virtue of the Fourteenth Amendment. Although these two clauses may in certain instances overlap, they forbid two quite different kinds of governmental encroachment upon religious freedom. The Establishment Clause, unlike the Free Exercise Clause, does not depend upon any showing of direct governmental compulsion and is violated by the enactment of laws which establish an official religion whether those laws operate directly to coerce nonobserving individuals or not. This is not to say, of course, that laws officially prescribing a particular form of religious worship do not involve coercion of such individuals. When the power, prestige and financial support of government is placed behind a particular religious belief, the indirect coercive pressure upon religious minorities to conform to the prevailing officially approved religion is plain. . . . The New York laws officially prescribing the Regents' prayer are inconsistent both with the purposes of the Establishment Clause and with the Establishment Clause itself.

. . . It is neither sacrilegious nor antireligious to say that each separate government in this country should stay out of the business of writing or sanctioning official prayers and leave that purely religious function to the people themselves and to those the people choose to look to for religious guidance.

. . . To those who may subscribe to the view that because the Regents' prayer is so brief and general there can be no danger to religious freedom in its governmental establishment, however, it may be appropriate to say in the words of James Madison, the author of the First Amendment:

"[It] is proper to take alarm at the first experiment on our liberties. . . . Who does not see that the same authority which can establish Christianity, in exclusion of all other Religions, may establish with the same ease any particular sect of Christians, in exclusion of all other Sects? That the same authority which can force a citizen to contribute three pence only of his property for the support of any one establishment, may force him to conform to any other establishment in all cases whatsoever?"

The judgment of the Court of Appeals of New York is reversed and the cause remanded for further proceedings not inconsistent with this opinion.

Reversed and remanded.

Mr. Justice Frankfurter took no part in the decision of this case.

Mr. Justice White took no part in the consideration or decision of this case.

Mr. Justice Stewart, dissenting.

With all respect, I think the Court has misapplied a great constitutional principle. I cannot see how an "official religion" is established by letting those who want to say a prayer say it. On the contrary, I think that to deny the wish of these school children to join in reciting this prayer is to deny them the opportunity of sharing in the spiritual heritage of our Nation.

The Court's historical review of the quarrels over the Book of Common Prayer in England throws no light for me on the issue before us in this case. England had then and has now an established church. Equally unenlightening, I think, is the history of the early establishment and later rejection of an official church in our own States. For we deal here not with the establishment of a state church, which would, of course, be constitutionally impermissible, but with whether school children who want to begin their day by joining in prayer must be prohibited from doing so. Moreover, I think that the Court's task, in this as in all areas of constitutional adjudication, is not responsibly aided by the uncritical invocation of metaphors like the "wall of separation," a phrase nowhere to be found in the Constitution. What is relevant to the issue here is not the history of an established church in sixteenth century England or in eighteenth century America, but the history of the religious traditions of our people, reflected in countless practices of the institutions and officials of our government.

· · ·

I do not believe that this Court, or the Congress, or the President has by the actions and practices I have mentioned established an "official religion" in violation of the Constitution. And I do not believe the State of New York has done so in this case. What each has done has been to recognize and to follow the deeply entrenched and highly cherished spiritual traditions of our Nation —traditions which come down to us from those who almost two hundred years ago avowed their "firm reliance on the Protection of Divine Providence" when they proclaimed the freedom and independence of this brave new world.

I dissent.

RELIGIOUS CEREMONIES
IN PUBLIC SCHOOLS

School District of Abington Township, Pa. et al.
v. Schempp et al. and *Murray* et al. *v. Curlett*
*(President, Baltimore City Board of School
Commissioners)* (1963)

Mr. Justice Clark delivered the [8–1] opinion of the Court.

Once again we are called upon to consider the scope of the provision of the First Amendment to the United States Constitution which declares that "Congress shall make no law respecting an establishment of religion, or prohibiting the free exercise thereof. . . ." These companion cases present the issues in the context of state action requiring that schools begin each day with readings from the Bible. While raising the basic questions under slightly different factual situations, the cases permit of joint treatment. In light of the history of the First Amendment and of our cases interpreting and applying its requirements, we hold that the practices at issue and the laws requiring them are unconstitutional under the Establishment Clause, as applied to the States through the Fourteenth Amendment.

The Facts in Each Case: No. 142. The Commonwealth of Pennsylvania by law . . . requires that "At least ten verses from the Holy Bible shall be read, without comment, at the opening of each public school on each school

---
374 U.S. 203.

day. Any child shall be excused from such Bible reading, or attending such Bible reading, upon the written request of his parent or guardian." The Schempp family, husband and wife and two of their three children, brought suit to enjoin enforcement of the statute, contending that their rights under the Fourteenth Amendment to the Constitution of the United States are, have been, and will continue to be violated unless this statute be declared unconstitutional as violative of these provisions of the First Amendment. . . . A three-judge statutory District Court for the Eastern District of Pennsylvania held that the statute is violative of the Establishment Clause of the First Amendment as applied to the States by the Due Process Clause of the Fourteenth Amendment and directed that appropriate injunctive relief issue. . . .

. . .

No. 119. In 1905 the Board of School Commissioners of Baltimore City adopted a rule . . . [which] provided for the holding of opening exercises in the schools of the city, consisting primarily of the "reading, without comment, of a chapter in the Holy Bible and/or the use of the Lord's Prayer." The petitioners, Mrs. Madalyn Murray and her son, William J. Murray III, are both professed atheists. Following unsuccessful attempts to have the respondent school board rescind the rule, this suit was filed for mandamus to compel its rescission and cancellation. It was alleged that William was a student in a public school of the city and Mrs. Murray, his mother, was a taxpayer therein; that it was the practice under the rule to have a reading on each school morning from the King James version of the Bible; that at petitioner's insistence the rule was amended to permit children to be excused from the exercise on request of the parent and that William had been excused pursuant thereto; that nevertheless the rule as amended was in violation of the petitioner's rights "to freedom of religion under the First and Fourteenth Amendments" and in violation of "the principle of separation between church and state, contained therein. . . ."

The respondents demurred and the trial court, recognizing that the demurred admitted all facts well pleaded, sustained it without leave to amend. The Maryland Court of Appeals affirmed, the majority of four justices holding the exercise not in violation of the First and Fourteenth Amendments, with three justices dissenting. . . .

. . .

The wholesome "neutrality" of which this Court's cases speak thus stems from a recognition of the teachings of history that powerful sects or groups might bring about a fusion of governmental and religious functions or a concert or dependency of one upon the other to the end that official support of the State or Federal Government would be placed behind the tenets of one or of all orthodoxies. This the Establishment Clause prohibits. And a further reason for neutrality is found in the Free Exercise Clause, which recognizes the value of religious training, teaching and observance and, more particularly, the right of every person to freely choose his own course with reference thereto, free from any compulsion from the state. This the Free Exercise Clause guarantees. Thus, as we have seen, the two clauses may overlap. As we have indicated, the Establishment Clause has been directly considered by this Court eight times in the past score of years and, with only one Justice dissenting on the point, it has consistently held that the clause withdrew all legislative power respecting religious belief or the expression thereof. The test may be stated as follows: what are the purpose and the primary effect of the enactment? If either is the advancement or inhibition of religion then the enactment exceeds the scope of legislative power as circumscribed by the Constitution. That is to say that to withstand the strictures of the Establishment Clause there must be a secular legislative purpose and a primary effect that neither advances nor inhibits religion. . . . The Free Exercise Clause, likewise considered many times here, withdraws from legislative power, state and federal, the exertion of any restraint on the free exercise of religion. Its purpose is to secure religious liberty in the individual by prohibiting any invasions thereof by civil authority. Hence it is necessary in a free exercise case for one to show the coercive effect of the enactment as it operates against him in the practice of his religion. The distinction between the two clauses is apparent—a violation of the Free Exercise Clause is predicted on coercion while the Establishment Clause violation need not be so attended.

Applying the Establishment Clause principles to the cases at bar we find that the States are requiring the selection and reading at the opening of the school day of verses from the Holy Bible and the recitation of the Lord's Prayer by the students in unison. These exercises are prescribed as part of the curricular activities of students who are required by law to attend school. They are held in the school buildings under the supervision and with the participation of teachers employed in those schools. None of these factors, other than compulsory school attendance, was present in the program upheld in *Zorach v. Clauson*. The trial court in No. 142 has found that such an opening exercise is a religious ceremony and was intended by the State to be so. We agree with the trial court's finding as to the religious character of the exercises. Given that finding, the exercises and the law requiring them are in violation of the Establishment Clause.

There is no such specific finding as to the religious character of the exercises in No. 119, and the State contends (as does the State in No. 142) that the program is an effort to extend its benefits to all public school children without regard to their religious belief. Included within its secular purposes, it says, are the promotion of moral values, the contradiction to the materialistic trends of our times, the perpetuation of our institutions and the teaching of literature. The case came up on demurrer, of course, to a petition which alleged that the uniform practice under the rule had been to read from the King James version of the Bible and that the exercise was sectarian. The short answer, therefore, is that the religious character of the exercise was admitted by the State. But even if its purpose is not strictly religious, it is sought to be accomplished through readings, without comment, from the Bible. Surely the place of the Bible as an instrument of religion cannot be gainsaid, and the State's recognition of the pervading religious character of the ceremony is evident from the rule's specific permission of the alternative use of the Catholic Douay version as well as the recent amendment permitting non-attendance at the exercises. None of these factors is consistent with the contention that the Bible is here used either as an instrument for nonreligious moral inspiration or as a reference for the teaching of secular subjects.

The conclusion follows that in both cases the laws require religious exercises and such exercises are being conducted in direct violation of the rights of the appellees and petitioners. Nor are these required exercises mitigated by the fact that students may absent themselves upon parental request, for that fact furnishes no defense to a claim of unconstitutionality under the Establishment Clause. . . . Further, it is no defense to urge that the religious practices here may be relatively minor encroachments on the First Amendment. The breach of neutrality that is today a trickling stream may all too soon become a raging torrent and, in the words of Madison, "it is proper to take alarm at the first experiment on our liberties." . . .

It is insisted that unless these religious exercises are permitted a "religion of secularism" is established in the schools. We agree of course that the State may not establish a "religion of secularism" in the sense of affirmatively opposing or showing hostility to religion, thus "preferring those who believe in no religion over those who do believe." . . . We do not agree, however, that this decision in any sense has that effect. In addition, it might well be said that one's education is not complete without a study of comparative religion or the history of religion and its relationship to the advancement of civilization. It certainly may be said that the Bible is worthy of study for its literary and historic qualities. Nothing we have said here indicates that such study of the Bible or of religion, when presented objectively as part of a secular program of education, may not be effected consistently with the First Amendment. But the exercises here do not fall into those categories. . . .

·   ·   ·

The place of religion in our society is an exalted one, achieved through a long tradition of reliance on the home, the church and the inviolable citadel of the individual heart and mind. We have come to recognize through bitter experience that it is not within the power of government to invade that citadel, whether its purpose or effect be to aid or oppose, to advance or retard. In the relationship between man and religion, the State is firmly committed to a position of neutrality. Though the application of that rule requires interpretation of a delicate sort, the rule itself is clearly and concisely stated in the words of the First Amendment. Applying that rule to the facts of these cases, we affirm the judgment in No. 142. In No. 119, the judgment is reversed and the cause remanded to the Maryland Court of Appeals for further proceedings consistent with this opinion.

CARDINAL PRINCIPLES
OF SECONDARY EDUCATION

Report of the Commission on the Reorganization
of Secondary Education (1918)

I. THE NEED FOR REORGANIZATION

Secondary education should be determined by the needs of the society to be
served, the character of the individuals to be educated, and the knowledge of
educational theory and practice available. These factors are by no means static.
Society is always in process of development; the character of the secondary-
school population undergoes modification; and the sciences on which educational theory and practice depend constantly furnish new information. Secondary education, however, like any other established agency of society, is
conservative and tends to resist modification. Failure to make adjustments
when the need arises leads to the necessity for extensive reorganization at
irregular intervals. The evidence is strong that such a comprehensive reorganization of secondary education is imperative at the present time.

· · ·

From *Cardinal Principles of Secondary Education,* A Report of the Commission on
the Reorganization of Secondary Education, Appointed by the National Education
Association, Bureau of Education Bulletin No. 35 (Washington, D.C.: U.S. Government Printing Office, 1918).

II. THE GOAL OF EDUCATION IN A DEMOCRACY

Education in the United States should be guided by a clear conception of the meaning of democracy. It is the ideal of democracy that the individual and society may find fulfillment each in the other. Democracy sanctions neither the exploitation of the individual by society, nor the disregard of the interests of society by the individual. More explicitly—

The purpose of democracy is so to organize society that each member may develop his personality primarily through activities designed for the well-being of his fellow members and of society as a whole.

This ideal demands that human activities be placed upon a high level of efficiency; that to this efficiency be added an appreciation of the significance of these activities and loyalty to the best ideals involved; and that the individual choose that vocation and those forms of social service in which his personality may develop and become most effective. For the achievement of these ends democracy must place chief reliance upon education.

Consequently, education in a democracy, both within and without the school, should develop in each individual the knowledge, interests, ideals, habits, and powers whereby he will find his place and use that place to shape both himself and society toward ever nobler ends.

III. THE MAIN OBJECTIVES OF EDUCATION

In order to determine the main objectives that should guide education in a democracy it is necessary to analyze the activities of the individual. Normally he is a member of a family, of a vocational group, and of various civic groups, and by virtue of these relationships he is called upon to engage in activities that enrich the family life, to render important vocational services to his fellows, and to promote the common welfare. It follows, therefore, that worthy home-membership, vocation, and citizenship, demand attention as three of the leading objectives.

Aside from the immediate discharge of these specific duties, every individual should have a margin of time for the cultivation of personal and social interests. This leisure, if worthily used, will recreate his powers and enlarge and enrich life, thereby making him better able to meet his responsibilities. The unworthy use of leisure impairs health, disrupts home life, lessens vocational efficiency, and destroys civic-mindedness. The tendency in industrial life, aided by legislation, is to decrease the working hours of large groups of people. While shortened hours tend to lessen the harmful reactions that arise from prolonged strain, they increase, if possible, the importance of preparation for leisure. In view of these considerations, education for the worthy use of leisure is of increasing importance as an objective.

To discharge the duties of life and to benefit from leisure, one must have good health. The health of the individual is essential also to the vitality of the race and to the defense of the Nation. Health education is, therefore, fundamental.

There are various processes, such as reading, writing, arithmetical computations, and oral and written expression, that are needed as tools in the affairs of life. Consequently, command of these fundamental processes, while not an end in itself, is nevertheless an indispensable objective.

And, finally, the realization of the objectives already named is dependent upon ethical character, that is, upon conduct founded upon right principles, clearly perceived and loyally adhered to. Good citizenship, vocational excellence, and the worthy use of leisure go hand in hand with ethical character; they are at once the fruits of sterling character and the channels through which such character is developed and made manifest. On the one hand, character is meaningless apart from the will to discharge the duties of life, and, on the other hand, there is no guarantee that these duties will be rightly discharged unless principles are substituted for impulses, however well-intentioned such impulses may be. Consequently ethical character is at once involved in all the other objectives and at the same time requires specific consideration in any program of national education.

This commission, therefore, regards the following as the main objectives of education: 1. Health. 2. Command of fundamental processes. 3. Worthy home-membership. 4. Vocation. 5. Citizenship. 6. Worthy use of leisure. 7. Ethical character.

. . .

XVIII. SECONDARY EDUCATION ESSENTIAL FOR ALL YOUTH

To the extent to which the objectives outlined herein are adopted as the controlling aims of education, to that extent will it be recognized that an extended education for every boy and girl is essential to the welfare, and even to the existence, of democratic society. The significance of these objectives is becoming more and more apparent under modern conditions in our democracy. These conditions grow out of increased knowledge of science with its rapidly extending applications to all the affairs of life, keener competition with its attendant dangers, closer contacts of peoples of varied racial and religious types, and greater assertiveness of all men and women in the control of their own destinies. These and many other tendencies increase the significance of health, worthy home-membership, vocation, citizenship, the worthy use of leisure, and ethical character.

Each of these objectives requires for its realization not only the training and habit formation that the child may secure, but also the intelligence and efficiency that can not be developed before adolescence. In fact, their realization calls for the full period allotted to both the junior and senior high schools.

Consequently, this commission holds that education should be so reorganized that every normal boy and girl will be encouraged to remain in school to the age of 18, on full time if possible, otherwise on part time.

GENERAL EDUCATION
IN A FREE SOCIETY

The Harvard Committee Report of 1945

LETTER OF TRANSMITTAL
President James Bryant Conant
Harvard University

Sir:

In the spring of 1943 you appointed a University Committee on the Objectives of a General Education in a Free Society, with members drawn from the faculties of Arts and Sciences and of Education. Your instructions to the committee were as expansive as its name was long. We were urged to consider the problem of general education in both the school and the college. We were cautioned that the general education of the great majority of each generation in the high schools was vastly more important than that of the comparatively small minority who attend our four-year colleges. You advised us that the educational process falls short of its ideal unless it includes at each stage of maturity some continuing contact with liberal and humane studies. The goals of these studies, you said, had been the topic of prolonged discussion; so much so that the peculiar character of the problem was in danger of being missed. "There is nothing new," you asserted, "in such educational goals; what is new in this century in the United States is their application to a system of universal education."

In short, we were directed not so much to make recommendations for general education in Harvard College as to venture into the vast field of American educational experience in quest of a concept of general education that would have validity for the free society which we cherish. . . .

Finally, we should like to remind you of the words you used to the Board of Overseers in your *Annual Report* of January 11, 1943, in describing your purpose in appointing the committee. You then wrote: "The primary concern of American education today is not the development of the appreciation of the 'good life' on young gentlemen born to the purple. It is the infusion of the liberal and humane tradition into our entire educational system. Our purpose is to cultivate in the largest possible number of our future citizens an appreciation of both the responsibilities and the benefits which come to them because they are Americans and are free."

You will find this theme dominant in the report now submitted to you. Such a concept of general education is the imperative need of the American educational system. It alone can give cohesion to our efforts and guide the contribution of our youth to the nation's future.

Respectfully submitted, . . .

. . .

BASIC PLAN FOR THE SCHOOLS

It therefore remains only to draw the scheme of general education that follows from these premises. At the center of it, at school and again at college, would be the three inevitable areas of man's life and knowledge which were sketched in the previous chapter and will be discussed in detail in the next: the physical world, man's corporate life, his inner visions and standards. That these should be taken up at school and again at college seems to us to follow both from their importance and from the quick growth of students in these years. But if so, the duty will rest on colleges to find ways of treating these great themes which will build on rather than duplicate what the schools have done. Exactly that, in effect, was argued in the previous chapter when it was said that, if these three areas differ not only in subject matter but in the values to which they look and in the methods which they follow, then mere encyclopedism is not enough, and the only adequate treatment of them will be one which concerns itself with values and methods quite as much as with facts. In other words, college courses on these subjects must be partly philosophic if they are to deal not only with information but with kinds of truth (e.g. the values and norms of literature as contrasted to the demonstrable truth of science). The same holds of course to some extent for schools, and no teacher can shake the responsibility of making very clear what is involved in judgment and value on the one hand, and in fact and measurement on the other. But schools have, after all, a huge task of plain exposition to perform if students are to have in their hands the main tools and elements of knowledge, and, instead of repeating this work, colleges should move on to new relationships and new stages of understanding.

In school, in our opinion, general education in these three areas should form a continuing core for all, taking up at least half a student's time. That does not mean that all should have exactly the same courses. In the present high school there is a great difference between general mathematics and algebra, between English as studied by commercial students and English in a college-preparatory course, and what has been said of the range of ability among students justifies the distinction. But just here applies what was also said about the crucial need for new and authentic treatments of these great subjects, not simply waterings-down of harder courses, for the less able. Here, to repeat, is the basic question facing our school system, and on its success in answering this question the wider success of general education, as a bond between all future citizens and all sharers of the common culture, will largely depend. It can be objected that an education which is not shared by all exactly in the same way is not a truly common education. This objection has some force, since sharing of experience is certainly, within limits, an ideal of all education, notably in a democracy. Yet, if thoroughly carried out, this ideal would be disastrous. It would mean that in general education, and only in general education, would the quick and the slow be thrown helter-skelter together, the ones held back, the others forced beyond their speed, and neither satisfied. The ideal of commonness must therefore show itself chiefly in a common requirement rather than in a common way of carrying it out. There must be courses of different difficulty and different method in each of the three spheres of general education, and the criterion for membership in these should be neither a student's intentions in life nor his background nor the kind of diploma for which he is aiming, but simply whether or not a given course is the best for him—which is to say, a criterion of ability. Extracurricular activities and the general atmosphere of the school, both important for general education, are perhaps the only truly identical experiences, but even these will be stronger when they rest on common aims of study.

.   .   .

We come at last to the heart of the subject, the curriculum. It has been a long road, though, even as it is, we have pushed like hardened tourists through much that mutely asked for delay, and we have left out much. When every question is inexhaustible, it is hard to keep a sense of proportion. But whether too long or too short, these preliminary chapters have served, or were meant to serve, a strictly necessary purpose. It is fruitless to think about any such practical step as a curriculum without having in mind specifications or points of reference, in this case the ends toward which the curriculum should look and the students for whom it is intended. It is these two points of reference that we have tried to establish so far. The first is a view of society as depending on both heritage and change. The second is a view of students as both united and divided: united, as heirs of a common past and agents in a joint future; divided, as varying in gifts, interests, and hopes. From these premises comes the idea of education as, for all and at all stages beyond the earliest, both general and special. These two sides of education should be thought of as connected, the special forever flowing out of the general and forever returning to and enriching it. Certainly their separation maims and impoverishes each, since higher and more universal relationships are empty except as they bear on particulars, and particulars in turn run to chaos and conflict unless they find place in a larger whole.

. . .

It is obvious that our account of education in its bearing on the entire human being presupposes a general theory of human nature and of human values. It is equally obvious that in the nature of the case such a theory had to be assumed rather than explicitly formulated in this report. A contrast with current tendencies may help clarify our views. In a natural reaction against the inherited type of formal and bookish learning, educational practice has tended to swing to the opposite extreme and to replace the traditional courses of the curriculum with highly specific and practical courses. The danger here is that training is being substituted for education. More recently a reaction to the reaction has appeared, which would place great books in a central, even monopolistic, position and which tends to identify education exclusively with cultivating the ability to think. We have stated that education looks to the whole man and not to his reason alone; yet we have maintained that the whole man is integrated only in so far as his life is presided over by his reason. While we thus regard the cultivation of the mind as the chief function of the school, we view reason as a means to the mastery of life; and we define wisdom as the art of living.

We have stressed the importance of the trait of relevance; and we have urged that, while in school, the pupil should be helped to see beyond conceptual frameworks and make concrete applications. Yet since the school by its nature cannot reproduce the complexity of actual life, a merely functional approach to teaching is inadequate also.

An extreme and one-sided view easily calls attention to itself and gains fervent adherents; but a balanced view is apt to be less immediately striking. Reasonableness does not lead to exciting conclusions because it aims to do justice to the whole truth in all its shadings. By the same token, reasonableness may legitimately hope to attain at least to part of the truth.

NATIONAL SCIENCE
FOUNDATION ACT OF 1950

(Public Law 81–507)

AN ACT

To promote the progress of science; to advance the national health, prosperity, and welfare; to secure the national defense; and for other purposes.

   Be it enacted by the Senate and House of Representatives of the United States of America in Congress assembled, That this Act may be cited as the "National Science Foundation Act of 1950."

ESTABLISHMENT OF NATIONAL SCIENCE FOUNDATION

SEC. 2.   There is hereby established in the executive branch of the Government an independent agency to be known as the National Science Foundation (hereinafter referred to as the "Foundation"). The Foundation shall consist of a National Science Board (hereinafter referred to as the "Board") and a Director.

64 Stat. 149

FUNCTIONS OF THE FOUNDATION

SEC. 3.   (a) The Foundation is authorized and directed—

(1) to develop and encourage the pursuit of a national policy for the promotion of basic research and education in the sciences;

(2) to initiate and support basic scientific research and programs to strengthen scientific research potential in the mathematical, physical, medical, biological, engineering, and other sciences, by making contracts or other arrangements (including grants, loans, and other forms of assistance) to support such scientific activities and to appraise the impact of research upon industrial development and upon the general welfare;

(3) at the request of the Secretary of Defense, to initiate and support specific scientific research activities in connection with matters relating to the national defense by making contracts or other arrangements (including grants, loans, and other forms of assistance) for the conduct of such scientific research;

(4) to award, as provided in section 10, scholarships and graduate fellowships in the mathematical, physical, medical, biological, engineering, and other sciences;

(5) to foster the interchange of scientific information among scientists in the United States and foreign countries;

(6) to evaluate scientific research programs undertaken by agencies of the Federal Government, and to correlate the Foundation's scientific research programs with those undertaken by individuals and by public and private research groups;

(7) to establish such special commissions as the Board may from time to time deem necessary for the purposes of this Act;

(8) to maintain a register of scientific and technical personnel and in other ways provide a central clearing house for information covering all scientific and technical personnel in the United States, including its Territories and possessions;

(9) to initiate and support a program of study, research, and evaluation in the field of weather modification, giving particular attention to areas that have experienced floods, drought, hail, lightning, fog, tornadoes, hurricanes, or other weather phenomena, and to report annually to the President and the Congress thereon.

(b) In exercising the authority and discharging the functions referred to in subsection (a) of this section, it shall be one of the objectives of the Foundation to strengthen basic research and education in the sciences, including independent research by individuals, throughout the United States, including its Territories and possessions, and to avoid undue concentration of such research and education.

. . .

SCHOLARSHIPS AND GRADUATE FELLOWSHIPS

SEC. 10.   The Foundation is authorized to award, within the limits of funds made available specifically for such purpose pursuant to section 17, scholarships and graduate fellowships for scientific study or scientific work in the mathematical, physical, medical, biological, engineering, and other sciences at appropriate nonprofit American or nonprofit foreign institutions selected by the recepient of such aid, for stated periods of time. Persons shall be selected for such scholarships and fellowships from among citizens or nationals of the United States, and such selections shall be made solely on the basis of ability; but in any case in which two or more applicants for scholarships or fellowships, as the case may be, are deemed by the Foundation to be possessed of substantially equal ability, and there are not sufficient scholarships or fellowships, as the case may be, available to grant one to each of such applicants, the available scholarship or scholarships or fellowship or fellowships shall be awarded to the applicants in such manner as will tend to result in a wide distribution of scholarships and fellowships among the States, Territories, possessions, and the District of Columbia. Nothing contained in this Act shall prohibit the Foundation from refusing or revoking a scholarship or fellowship award, in whole or in part, in the case of any applicant or recipient, if the Board is of the opinion that such award is not in the best interests of the United States.

NATIONAL DEFENSE EDUCATION ACT OF 1958

(Public Law 85–864)

AN ACT

To strengthen the national defense and to encourage and assist in the expansion and improvement of educational programs to meet critical national needs; and for other purposes.

Be it enacted by the Senate and House of Representatives of the United States of America in Congress assembled, That this Act, divided into titles and sections according to the following tables of contents, may be cited as the "National Defense Education Act of 1958."

---

72 Stat. 1580

472

Title VII—Research and Experimentation in More Effective Utilization
of Television, Radio, Motion Pictures, and Related Media
for Educational Purposes
Title VIII—Area Vocational Education Programs
Title IX—Science Information Service
Title X—Miscellaneous Provisions
Title XI—Institutes

TITLE I—GENERAL PROVISIONS

Findings and Declaration of Policy

SEC. 101.   The Congress hereby finds and declares that the security of the
Nation requires the fullest development of the mental resources and technical
skills of its young men and women. The present emergency demands that
additional and more adequate educational opportunities be made available.
The defense of this Nation depends upon the mastery of modern techniques
developed from complex scientific principles. It depends as well upon the
discovery and development of new principles, new techniques, and new
knowledge.

We must increase our efforts to identify and educate more of the talent
of our Nation. This requires programs that will give assurance that no student
of ability will be denied an opportunity for higher education because of
financial need; will correct as rapidly as possible the existing imbalances in
our educational programs which have led to an insufficient proportion of our
population educated in science, mathematics, and modern languages and
trained in technology.

The Congress reaffirms the principle and declares that the States and
local communities have and must retain control over and primary responsibility for public education. The national interest requires, however, that the
Federal Government give assistance to education for programs which are
important to our defense.

To meet the present educational emergency requires additional effort at
all levels of government. It is therefore the purpose of this Act to provide
substantial assistance in various forms to individuals, and to States and their
subdivisions, in order to insure trained manpower of sufficient quality and
quantity to meet the national defense needs of the United States.

FEDERAL CONTROL OF EDUCATION PROHIBITED

SEC. 102.   Nothing contained in this Act shall be construed to authorize any
department, agency, officer, or employee of the United States to exercise any
direction, supervision, or control over the curriculum, program of instruction,
administration, or personnel of any educational institution or school system.

ECONOMIC OPPORTUNITY ACT OF 1964

(Public Law 88–452)

AN ACT

To mobilize the human and financial resources of the Nation to combat poverty in the United States.

Be it enacted by the Senate and House of Representatives of the United States of America in Congress assembled, That this Act may be cited as the "Economic Opportunity Act of 1964."

. . .

TITLE I—YOUTH PROGRAMS

Part A—Job Corps

SEC. 101.   The purpose of this part is to prepare for the responsibilities of citizenship and to increase the employability of young men and young women aged sixteen through twenty-one by providing them in rural and urban residential centers with education, vocational training, useful work experience, including work directed toward the conservation of natural resources, and other appropriate activities.

---

78 Stat. 508

. . .

STATE-OPERATED YOUTH CAMPS

SEC. 108 The Director is authorized to enter into agreements with States to assist in the operation or administration of State-operated programs which carry out the purpose of this part. The Director may, pursuant to such regulations as he may adopt, pay part or all of the operative or administrative costs of such programs.

. . .

Part B—Work-Training Programs

STATEMENT OF PURPOSE

SEC. 111. The purpose of this part is to provide useful work experience opportunities for unemployed young men and young women, through participation in State and community work-training programs, so that their employability may be increased or their education resumed or continued and so that public agencies and private nonprofit organizations (other than political parties) will be enabled to carry out programs which will permit or contribute to an undertaking or service in the public interest that would not otherwise be provided, or will contribute to the conservation and development of natural resources and recreational areas.

DEVELOPMENT OF PROGRAMS

SEC. 112. In order to carry out the purposes of this part, the Director shall assist and cooperate with State and local agencies and private nonprofit organizations (other than political parties) in developing programs for the employment of young people in State and community activities hereinafter authorized, which, whenever appropriate, shall be coordinated with programs of training and education provided by local public educational agencies.

. . .

Part C—Work-Study Programs

STATEMENT OF PURPOSE

SEC. 121. The purpose of this part is to stimulate and promote the part-time employment of students in institutions of higher education who are from low-income families and are in need of the earnings from such employment to pursue courses of study at such institutions.

. . .

GRANTS FOR WORK-STUDY PROGRAMS

SEC. 123.   The Director is authorized to enter into agreements with institutions of higher education . . . under which the Director will make grants to such institutions to assist in the operaton of work-study programs as hereinafter provided.

CONDITIONS OF AGREEMENTS

SEC. 124.   An agreement entered into pursuant to section 123 shall—
(a) provide for the operation by the institution of a program for the part-time employment of its students in work—
　(1) for the institution itself, or
　(2) for a public or private nonprofit organization when the position is obtained through an arrangement between the institution and such an organization and—
　　(A) the work is related to the student's educational objective, or
　　(B) such work (i) will be in the public interest and is work which would not otherwise be provided, (ii) will not result in the displacement of employed workers or impair existing contracts for services, and (iii) will be governed by such conditions of employment as will be appropriate and reasonable in light of such factors as the type of work performed, geographical region, and proficiency of the employee:
　　Provided, however, That no such work shall involve the construction, operation, or maintenance of so much of any facility used or to be used for sectarian instruction or as a place for religious worship. . . .

TITLE II—URBAN AND RURAL COMMUNITY ACTION PROGRAMS

Part A—General Community Action Programs

STATEMENT OF PURPOSE

SEC. 201.   The purpose of this part is to provide stimulation and incentive for urban and rural communities to mobilize their resources to combat poverty through community action programs.

. . .

RESEARCH, TRAINING, AND DEMONSTRATIONS

SEC. 207.   The Director is authorized to conduct, or to make grants to or enter into contracts with institutions of higher education or other appropriate public agencies or private organizations for the conduct of research, training and demonstrations pertaining to the purposes of this part. Expenditures under this section in any fiscal year shall not exceed 15 per centum of the sums appropriated or allocated for such year to carry out the purposes of this part.

.   .   .

Part B—Adult Basic Education Programs

DECLARATION OF PURPOSE

SEC. 212.   It is the purpose of this part to initiate programs of instruction for individuals who have attained age eighteen and whose inability to read and write the English language constitutes a substantial impairment of their ability to get or retain employment commensurate with their real ability, so as to help eliminate such inability and raise the level of education of such individuals with a view to making them less likely to become dependent on others, improving their ability to benefit from occupational training and otherwise increasing their opportunities for more productive and profitable employment, and making them better able to meet their adult responsibilities.

GRANTS TO STATES

SEC. 213.   (a) From the sums appropriated to carry out this title, the Director shall make grants to States which have State plans approved by him under this section.

RECOMMENDATIONS
OF PRESIDENT
LYNDON JOHNSON

Education Program Message—January 12, 1965
Excerpts

In 1787, the Continental Congress declared in the Northwest Ordinance: "Schools and the means of education shall forever be encouraged."

America is strong and prosperous and free because for 178 years we have honored that commitment.

In the United States today—

One-quarter of all Americans are in the Nation's classrooms.

High school attendance has grown eighteenfold since the turn of the century—six times as fast as the population.

College enrollment has advanced eightyfold. Americans today support a fourth of the world's institutions of higher learning and a third of its professors and college students.

In the life of the individual, education is always an unfinished task.

And in the life of this Nation, the advancement of education is a continuing challenge.

There is a darker side to education in America:

One student out of every three now in the fifth grade will drop out before finishing high school—if the present rate continues.

Almost a million young people will continue to quit school each year—if our schools fail to stimulate their desire to learn.

Message to Congress, January 12, 1965, reprinted from the *Congressional Record*.

Over 100,000 of our brightest high school graduates each year will not go to college—and many others will leave college—if the opportunity for higher education is not expanded.

The cost of this neglect runs high—both for the youth and the Nation. . . .

I propose that the 89th Congress join me in extending the commitment still further. I propose that we declare a national goal of

FULL EDUCATIONAL OPPORTUNITY

Every child must be encouraged to get as much education as he has the ability to take.

We want this not only for his sake—but for the Nation's sake.

Nothing matters more to the future of our country: not our military preparedness, for armed might is worthless if we lack the brainpower to build a world of peace; not our productive economy, for we cannot sustain growth without trained manpower; not our democratic system of government, for freedom is fragile if citizens are ignorant.

We must demand that our schools increase not only the quantity but the quality of America's education. For we recognize that nuclear age problems cannot be solved with horse-and-buggy learning. The three R's of our school system must be supported by the three T's—teachers who are superior, techniques of instruction that are modern, and thinking about education which places it first in all our plans and hopes.

Specifically, four major tasks confront us—

to bring better education to millions of disadvantaged youth who need it most;

to put the best educational equipment and ideas and innovations within reach of all students;

to advance the technology of teaching and the training of teachers; and

to provide incentives for those who wish to learn at every stage along the road to learning. . . .

In all that we do, we mean to strengthen our State and community education systems. Federal assistance does not mean Federal control—as past programs have proven. The late Senator Robert Taft declared:

"Education is primarily a State function—but in the field of education, as in the fields of health, relief, and medical care, the Federal Government has a secondary obligation to see that there is a basic floor under those essential services for all adults and children in the United States."

In this spirit, I urge that we now push ahead with the No. 1 business of the American people—the education of our youth in preschools, elementary and secondary schools, and in the colleges and universities.

ELEMENTARY AND SECONDARY EDUCATION ACT OF 1965

(Public Law 89-10)

AN ACT

To strengthen and improve educational quality and educational opportunities in the Nation's elementary and secondary schools.

Be it enacted by the Senate and House of Representatives of the United States of America in Congress assembled, That this Act may be cited as the "Elementary and Secondary Education Act of 1965."

TITLE I—FINANCIAL ASSISTANCE TO LOCAL EDUCATIONAL AGENCIES FOR THE EDUCATION OF CHILDREN OF LOW-INCOME FAMILIES AND EXTENSION OF PUBLIC LAW 874, EIGHTY-FIRST CONGRESS

Declaration of Policy.

SEC. 201.   In recognition of the special educational needs of children of low-income families and the impact that concentrations of low-income families

79 Stat. 27

have on the ability of local educational agencies to support adequate educational programs, the Congress hereby declares it to be the policy of the United States to provide financial assistance (as set forth in this title) to local educational agencies serving areas with concentrations of children from low-income families to expand and improve their educational programs by various means (including preschool programs) which contribute particularly to meeting the special educational needs of educationally deprived children.

. . .

National Advisory Council

SEC. 212. (a) The President shall, within ninety days after the enactment of this title, appoint a National Advisory Council on the Education of Disadvantaged Children for the purpose of reviewing the administration and operation of this title, including its effectiveness in improving the educational attainment of educationally deprived children, and making recommendations for the improvement of this title and its administration and operation. These recommendations shall take into consideration experience gained under this and other Federal educational programs for disadvantaged children and, to the extent appropriate, experience gained under other public and private educational programs for disadvantaged children.

. . .

TITLE II—SCHOOL LIBRARY RESOURCES, TEXTBOOKS, AND OTHER INSTRUCTIONAL MATERIALS

Appropriations Authorized

SEC. 201. (a) The Commissioner shall carry out during the fiscal year ending June 30, 1966, and each of the four succeeding fiscal years, a program for making grants for the acquisition of school library resources, textbooks, and other printed and published instructional materials for the use of children and teachers in public and private elementary and secondary schools.

(b) For the purpose of making grants under this title, there is hereby authorized to be appropriated the sum of $100,000,000 for the fiscal year ending June 30, 1966; but for the fiscal year ending June 30, 1967, and the three succeeding fiscal years, only such sums may be appropriated as the Congress may hereafter authorize by law.

. . .

State Plans

SEC. 203.   (a) Any State which desires to receive grants under this title shall submit to the Commissioner a State plan. . . .

TITLE III—SUPPLEMENTARY EDUCATIONAL CENTERS AND SERVICES

Appropriations Authorized

SEC. 301.   (a) The Commissioner shall carry out during the fiscal year ending June 30, 1966, and each of the four succeeding fiscal years, a program for making grants for supplementary educational centers and services, to stimulate and assist in the provision of vitally needed educational services not available in sufficient quantity or quality, and to stimulate and assist in the development and establishment of exemplary elementary and secondary school educational programs to serve as models for regular school programs. (b) For the purpose of making grants under this title, there is hereby authorized to be appropriated the sum of $100,000,000, for the fiscal year ending June 30, 1966, . . .

Advisory Committee

SEC. 306.   (a) The Commissioner shall establish in the Office of Education an Advisory Committee on Supplementary Education Centers and Services, consisting of the Commissioner, who shall be Chairman, and eight members appointed, without regard to the civil service laws, by the Commissioner with the approval of the Secretary.

. . .

TITLE IV—EDUCATIONAL RESEARCH AND TRAINING

SEC. 401.   . . . The Act of July 26, 1954 (20 U.S.C. 332), entitled "An Act to authorize cooperative research in education," . . . is amended. . . . SEC. 2.   (a) (1) The Commissioner of Education . . . is authorized to make grants to universities and colleges and other public or private agencies, institutions, and organizations and to individuals, for research, surveys, and demonstrations in the field of education . . . and for the dissemination of information derived from educational research (including but not limited to information concerning promising educational practices. . . .)

(2) No grant shall be made or contract or jointly financed cooperative arrangement entered into under this subsection until the Commissioner has obtained the advice and recommendations of a panel of specialists who are not employees of the Federal Government and who are competent to evaluate the proposals. . . .

TITLE V—GRANTS TO STRENGTHEN STATE DEPARTMENTS OF EDUCATION

Appropriations Authorized

SEC. 501.   (a) The Commissioner shall carry out during the fiscal year ending June 30, 1966, and each of the four succeeding fiscal years, a program for making grants to stimulate and assist States in strengthening the leadership resources of their State educational agencies, and to assist those agencies in the establishment and improvement of programs to identify and meet the educational needs of States.

(b) For the purpose of making grants under this title, there is hereby authorized to be appropriated the sum of $25,000,000 for the fiscal year ending June 30, 1966, . . .

. . .

Limitation on Payments Under This Act

SEC. 605.   Nothing contained in this Act shall be construed to authorize the making of any payment under this Act, or under any Act amended by this Act, for religious worship or instruction.

NATIONAL ARTS AND HUMANITIES FOUNDATION ACT OF 1965

(Public Law 89–209)

AN ACT

To provide for the establishment of the National Foundation on the Arts and the Humanities to promote progress and scholarship in the humanities and the arts in the United States, and for other purposes.

Be it enacted by the Senate and House of Representatives of the United States of America in Congress assembled, That this Act may be cited as the "National Foundation on the Arts and the Humanities Act of 1965."

DECLARATION OF PURPOSE

SEC. 2. The Congress hereby finds and declares—

(1) that the encouragement and support of national progress and scholarship in the humanities and the arts, while primarily a matter for private and local initiative, is also an appropriate matter of concern to the Federal Government;

(2) that a high civilization must not limit its efforts to science and tech-

79 Stat. 845

nology alone but must give full value and support to the other great branches of man's scholarly and cultural activity;

(3) that democracy demands wisdom and vision in its citizens and that it must therefore foster and support a form of education designed to make men masters of their technology and not its unthinking servant;

(4) that it is necessary and appropriate for the Federal Government to complement, assist, and add to programs for the advancement of the humanities and the arts by local, State, regional, and private agencies and their organizations;

(5) that the practice of art and the study of the humanities requires constant dedication and devotion and that, while no government can call a great artist or scholar into existence, it is necessary and appropriate for the Federal Government to help create and sustain not only a climate encouraging freedom of thought, imagination, and inquiry but also the material conditions facilitating the release of this creative talent;

(6) that the world leadership which has come to the United States cannot rest solely upon superior power, wealth, and technology, but must be solidly founded upon worldwide respect and admiration for the Nation's high qualities as a leader in the realm of ideas and of the spirit; and

(7) that, in order to implement these findings, it is desirable to establish a National Foundation on the Arts and the Humanities and to strengthen the responsibilities of the Office of Education with respect to education in the arts and the humanities.

.   .   .

SEC. 4.   (a) There is established a National Foundation on the Arts and the Humanities (hereinafter referred to as the "Foundation"), which shall be composed of a National Endowment for the Arts, a National Endowment for the Humanities, and a Federal Council on the Arts and the Humanities (hereinafter established).

.   .   .

SEC. 5.   (a) There is established within the Foundation a National Endowment for the Arts.

(b) The Endowment shall be headed by a Chairman, to be known as the Chairman of the National Endowment for the Arts.

(c) The Chairman, with the advice of the Federal Council on the Arts and the Humanities and the National Council on the Arts, is authorized to establish and carry out a program of grants-in-aid to groups or, in appropriate cases, to individuals engaged in or concerned with the arts, for the purpose of enabling them to provide or support in the United States—

(1) productions which have substantial artistic and cultural significance,

giving emphasis to American creativity and the maintenance and encouragement of professional excellence;

(2) productions, meeting professional standards or standards of authen-
ticity, irrespective of origin which are of significant merit and which, without
such assistance, would otherwise be unavailable to our citizens in many areas
of the country;

(3) projects that will encourage and assist artists and enable them to
achieve standards of professional excellence;

(4) workshops that will encourage and develop the appreciation and
enjoyment of the arts by our citizens;

(5) other relevant projects, including surveys, research, and planning in
the arts.

. . .

SEC. 7. (a) There is established within the Foundation a National Endowment for the Humanities.

(b) (1) The Endowment shall be headed by a chairman. . . .

(c) The Chairman, with the advice of the Federal Council on the Arts and the
Humanities and the National Council on the Humanities (hereinafter established), is authorized to—

(1) develop and encourage the pursuit of a national policy for the promotion of progress and scholarship in the humanities;

(2) initiate and support research and programs to strengthen the research
potential of the United States in the humanities by making arrangements
(including grants, loans, and other forms of assistance) with individuals or
groups to support such activities;

(3) award fellowships and grants to institutions or individuals for training
and workshops in the humanities. Fellowships awarded to individuals under
this authority may be for the purpose of study or research at appropriate
nonprofit institutions selected by the recipient of such aid, for stated periods
of time;

(4) foster the interchange of information in the humanities;

(5) foster, through grants or other arrangements with groups, public
understanding and appreciation of the humanities; and

(6) support the publication of scholarly works in the humanities. . . .

. . .

SEC. 11. (a) For the purpose of carrying out sections 5 (c) and 7 (c) and
the functions transferred by section 6 (a) of this Act, there is authorized to be
appropriated for the fiscal year ending June 30, 1966, and each of the two
succeeding fiscal years the sum of $10,000,000; but for the fiscal year ending
June 30, 1969, and each subsequent fiscal year, only such sums may be
appropriated as the Congress may hereafter authorize by law. . . .

HIGHER EDUCATION ACT OF 1965

(Public Law 89–329)

AN ACT

To strengthen the educational resources of our colleges and universities and to provide financial assistance for students in postsecondary and higher education.

Be it enacted by the Senate and House of Representatives of the United States of America in Congress assembled, That this Act may be cited as the "Higher Education Act of 1965."

TITLE I—COMMUNITY SERVICE AND CONTINUING EDUCATION PROGRAMS

Appropriations Authorized

SEC. 101.   For the purpose of assisting the people of the United States in the solution of community problems such as housing, poverty, government, recreation, employment, youth opportunities, transportation, health, and land use by enabling the Commissioner to make grants under this title to strengthen community service programs of colleges and universities, there are

79 Stat. 1219

authorized to be appropriated $25,000,000 for the fiscal year ending June 30, 1966, and $50,000,000 for the fiscal year ending June 30, 1967, and for the succeeding fiscal year. For the fiscal year ending June 30, 1969, and the succeeding fiscal year, there may be appropriated, to enable the Commissioner to make such grants, only such sums as the Congress may hereafter authorize by law.

. . .

TITLE II—COLLEGE LIBRARY ASSISTANCE AND LIBRARY TRAINING AND RESEARCH

Part A—College Library Resources

APPROPRIATIONS AUTHORIZED

SEC. 201.   There are authorized to be appropriated $50,000,000 for the fiscal year ending June 30, 1966, and for each of the two succeeding fiscal years, to enable the Commissioner to make grants under this part to institutions of higher education to assist and encourage such institutions in the acquisition for library purposes of books, periodicals, documents, magnetic tapes, phonograph records, audiovisual materials, and other related library materials (including necessary binding). . . .

TITLE III—STRENGTHENING DEVELOPING INSTITUTIONS

Statement of Purpose and Appropriations Authorized

SEC. 301.   (a) The purpose of this title is to assist in raising the academic quality of colleges which have the desire and potential to make a substantial contribution to the higher education resources of our Nation but which for financial and other reasons are struggling for survival and are isolated from the main currents of academic life, and to do so by enabling the Commissioner to establish a national teaching fellow program and to encourage and assist in the establishment of cooperative arrangements under which these colleges may draw on the talent and experience of our finest colleges and universities, and on the educational resources of business and industry, in their effort to improve their academic quality.

(b) (1) There is authorized to be appropriated the sum of $55,000,000 for the fiscal year ending June 30, 1966, to carry out the provisions of this title. . . .

TITLE IV—STUDENT ASSISTANCE

Part A—Educational Opportunity Grants

STATEMENT OF PURPOSE AND APPROPRIATIONS AUTHORIZED

SEC. 401.   (a) It is the purpose of this part to provide, through institutions of higher education, educational opportunity grants to assist in making available the benefits of higher education to qualified high school graduates of exceptional financial need, who for lack of financial means of their own or of their families would be unable to obtain such benefits without such aid.

(b) There are hereby authorized to be appropriated $70,000,000 for the fiscal year ending June 30, 1966, and for each of the two succeeding fiscal years, to enable the Commissioner to make payments to institutions of higher education that have agreements with him entered into under section 407, for use by such institutions for payments to undergraduate students for the initial academic year of educational opportunity grants awarded to them under this part. . . .

TITLE V—TEACHER PROGRAMS

Part A—General Provisions

ADVISORY COUNCIL ON QUALITY TEACHER PREPARATION

SEC. 501.   (a) The Commissioner shall establish in the Office of Education an Advisory Council on Quality Teacher Preparation for the purpose of reviewing the administration and operation of the programs carried out under this title and of all other Federal programs for complementary purposes. This review shall pay particular attention to the effectiveness of these programs in attracting, preparing, and retaining highly qualified elementary and secondary school teachers, and it shall include recommendations for the improvement of these programs. The Council shall consist of the Commissioner, who shall be Chairman, and twelve members appointed for staggered terms and without regard to the civil service laws, by the Commissioner with the approval of the Secretary. Such twelve members shall include persons knowledgeable with respect to teacher preparation and the needs of urban and rural schools, and representatives of the general public. . . .

TITLE VI—FINANCIAL ASSISTANCE FOR THE IMPROVEMENT OF UNDERGRADUATE INSTRUCTION

Part A—Equipment

STATEMENT OF PURPOSE AND AUTHORIZATION OF APPROPRIATIONS

SEC. 601.   (a) The purpose of this part is to improve the quality of classroom instruction in selected subject areas in institutions of higher education. (b) There are hereby authorized to be appropriated $35,000,000 for the fiscal year ending June 30, 1966, $50,000,000 for the fiscal year ending June 30, 1967, and $60,000,000 for the fiscal year ending June 30, 1968, to enable the Commissioner to make grants to institutions of higher education pursuant to this part for the acquisition of equipment and for minor remodeling described in section 603 (2) (A). . . .

STATE COMMISSIONS AND PLANS

SEC. 603.   Any State desiring to participate in the program under this part shall designate for that purpose an existing State agency which is broadly representative of the public and of institutions of higher education in the State, or, if no such State agency exists, shall establish such a State agency, and submit to the Commissioner through the agency so designated or established (hereafter in this part referred to as the "State commission"), a State plan for such participation. The Commissioner shall approve any such plan which—

   (1) provides that it shall be administered by the State commission;
   (2) sets forth, consistently with basic criteria prescribed by regulation pursuant to section 604, objective standards and methods (A) for determining the relative priorities of eligible projects for the acquisition of laboratory and other special equipment (other than supplies consumed in use), including audiovisual materials and equipment for classrooms or audiovisual centers, and printed and published materials (other than textbooks) for classrooms or libraries, suitable for use in providing education in science, mathematics, foreign languages, history, geography, government, English, other humanities, the arts, or education at the undergraduate level in institutions of higher education, and minor remodeling of classroom or other space used for such materials or equipment. . . .

JUDICIAL STANDARDS AND STUDENT DISCIPLINE

General Order on Judicial Standards of
Procedure and Substance in Review of Student
Discipline in Tax Supported Institutions of
Higher Education (1968)

DEFINITIONS

"Education" as used herein means tax supported formal higher education unless the context indicates another meaning.

"Institution" and "educational institution" as used herein mean a tax supported school, college, university, or multiversity.

"Mission" as used herein means a goal, purpose, task, or objective.

INTRODUCTION

The number of actions for review of student disciplinary action has been increasing in this and other courts. . . .

These cases reflect rapid development and much controversy concerning appropriate procedural and substantive standards of judicial review in such cases. Because of the importance in this district of clearly enunciated reliable standards, this Court scheduled hearings . . . for the purpose of hearing

U.S. District Court for the Western District of Missouri, 1968. Footnotes abridged.

arguments and suggestions . . . on the standards which would be applied regardless of the judge to whom the cases are assigned by lot. This was done for the purpose of uniformity of decision in this district.

The following memorandum represents a statement of judicial standards of procedure and substance applicable, in the absence of exceptional circumstances, to actions concerning discipline of students in tax supported educational institutions of higher learning.

RELATIONS OF COURTS AND EDUCATION

Achieving the ideal of justice is the highest goal of humanity. Justice is not the concern solely of the courts. Education is equally concerned with the achievement of ideal justice. The administration of justice by the courts in the United States represents the people's best efforts to achieve the ideal of justice in the field of civil and criminal law. It is generally accepted that the courts are necessary to this administration of justice and for the protection of individual liberties. Nevertheless, the contributions of the modern courts in achieving the ideals of justice are primarily the products of higher education. The modern courts are, and will continue to be, greatly indebted to higher education for their personnel, their innovations, their processes, their political support, and their future in the political and social order. Higher education is the primary source of study and support of improvement in the courts. For this reason, among others, the courts should exercise caution when importuned to intervene in the important processes and functions of education. A court should never intervene in the processes of education without understanding the nature of education.

Before undertaking to intervene in the educational processes, and to impose judicial restraints and mandates on the educational community, the courts should acquire a general knowledge of the lawful missions and the continually changing processes, functions, and problems of education. Judicial action without such knowledge would endanger the public interest and be likely to lead to gross injustice.

Education is the living and growing source of our progressive civilization, of our open repository of increasing knowledge, culture and our salutary democratic traditions. As such, education deserves the highest respect and the fullest protection of the courts in the performance of its lawful missions.

There have been, and no doubt in the future there will be, instances of erroneous and unwise misuse of power by those invested with powers of management and teaching in the academic community, as in the case of all human fallible institutions. When such misuse of power is threatened or occurs, our political and social order has made available a wide variety of lawful, non-violent, political, economic, and social means to prevent or end the misuse of power. These same lawful, non-violent, political, economic, and social means are available to correct an unwise, but lawful choice of educational policy or action by those charged with the powers of management and teaching in the academic community. Only where the erroneous and unwise actions in the field of education deprive students of federally protected rights or privileges does a federal court have power to intervene in the educational process.[1]

LAWFUL MISSIONS OF TAX SUPPORTED HIGHER EDUCATION

The lawful missions of tax supported public education in the United States are constantly growing and changing. For the purposes of this analysis, it is sufficient to note some of the widely recognized traditional missions of tax supported higher education in this country. Included in these lawful missions of education, the following are summarized:

(1) To maintain, support, critically examine, and to improve the existing social and political system;

(2) To train students and faculty for leadership and superior service in public service, science, agriculture, commerce and industry;

(3) To develop students to well rounded maturity, physically, socially, emotionally, spiritually, intellectually and vocationally;

(4) To develop, refine and teach ethical and cultural values;

(5) To provide fullest possible realization of democracy in every phase of living;

(6) To teach principles of patriotism, civil obligation and respect for the law;

(7) To teach the practice of excellence in thought, behavior and performance;

(8) To develop, cultivate, and stimulate the use of imagination;

(9) To stimulate reasoning and critical faculties of students and to encourage their use in improvement of the existing political and social order;

(10) To develop and teach methods of change and improvement in the existing political and social order;

(11) To provide by study and research for increase of knowledge;

(12) To provide by study and research for development and improvement of technology, production and distribution for increased national production of goods and services desirable for national civilian consumption, for export, for exploration, and for national military purposes;

---

[1] These principles are not applicable where influences outside the educational community seek to impose unlawful and irrelevant conditions on the educational institution. . . .

(13) To teach methods of experiment in meeting the problems of a changing environment;

(14) To promote directly and explicity international understanding and cooperation;

(15) To provide the knowledge, personnel, and policy for planning and managing the destiny of our society with a maximum of individual freedom; and

(16) To transfer the wealth of knowledge and tradition from one generation to another.

The tax supported educational institution is an agency of the national and state governments. Its missions include, by teaching, research and action, assisting in the declared purposes of government in this nation, namely:

To form a more perfect union,

To establish justice,

To insure domestic tranquility,

To provide for the common defense,

To promote the general welfare, and

To secure the blessing of liberty to ourselves and to posterity.

The nihilist and the anarchist, determined to destroy the existing political and social order, who directs his primary attack on the educational institutions, understands fully the mission of education in the United States.

Federal law recognizes the powers of the tax supported institutions to accomplish these missions and has frequently furnished economic assistance for these purposes.

The genius of American education employing the manifold ideas and works of the great Jefferson,[2] Mann, Dewey and many others living, has made the United States the most powerful nation in history. In so doing, it

---

[2] Thomas Jefferson, the earliest and greatest advocate of tax supported higher education and the unequalled defender of personal liberty, reported in his correspondence on an early instance of a student riot at his creation, the University of Virginia, in these words: . . .

From letter of October 13, 1825, to Joseph Coolidge, Jr.:

"The news of our neighborhood can hardly be interesting to you, except what may relate to our University. And it happens that a serious incident has just taken place there, which I will state to you the rather, as of the thousand versions which will be given not one will be true. My position enables me to say what is so, but with the most absolute concealment from whence it comes; regard to my own peace requiring that,—except with friends whom I can trust and wish to gratify with the truth.

"The University had gone on with a degree of order and harmony which had strengthened the hope that much of self government might be trusted to the discretion of the students of the age of 16 and upwards, until the 1st instant. In the night of that day a party of fourteen students, animated first with wine, masked themselves so as not to be known, and turned out on the lawn of the University, with no intention, it is believed, but of childish noise and uproar. Two professors hearing it went out to see

has in a relatively few years expanded the area of knowledge at a revolutionary rate.

With education the primary force, the means to provide the necessities of life and many luxuries to all our national population, and to many other

---

what was the matter. They were received with insult, and even brick-bats were thrown at them. Each of them seized an offender, demanded their names (for they could not distinguish them under their disguise), but were refused, abused, and the culprits calling on their companions for a rescue, got loose, and withdrew to their chambers. The Faculty of Professors met the next day, called the whole before them, and in address, rather harsh, required them to denounce the offenders. They refused, answered the address in writing and in the rudest terms, and charged the Professors themselves with false statements. Fifty others, who were in their rooms, no ways implicated in the riot and knowing nothing about it, immediately signed the answer, making common cause with the rioters, and declaring their belief of their assertions in opposition to those of the Professors. The next day chanced to be that of the meeting of the Visitors; the Faculty sent a deputation to them, informing them of what had taken place. The Visitors called the whole body of students before them, exhorted them to make known the persons masked, the innocent to aid the cause of order by bearing witnesses to the truth, and the guilty to relieve their innocent brethren from censures which they were conscious that themselves alone deserved. On this the fourteen maskers stepped forward and avowed themselves the persons guilty of whatever had passed, but denying that any trespass had been committed. They were desired to appear before the Faculty, which they did. On the evidence resulting from this enquiry, three, the most culpable, were expelled; one of them, moreover, presented by the grand jury for civil punishment (for it happened that the district court was then about to meet). The eleven other maskers were sentenced to suspensions or reprimands, and the fifty who had so gratuitously obtruded their names into the offensive paper retracted them, and so the matter ended.

"The circumstances of this transaction enabled the Visitors to add much to the strictness of their system as yet new. The students have returned into perfect order under a salutary conviction they had not before felt that the laws will in future be rigorously enforced, and the institution is strengthened by the firmness manifested by its authorities on the occasion. It cannot, however, be expected that all breaches of order can be made to cease at once, but from the vigilance of the Faculty and energy of the civil power their restraint may very soon become satisfactory. It is not perceived that this riot has been more serious than has been experienced by other seminaries; but, whether more or less so, the exact truth should be told, and the institution be known to the public as neither better nor worse than it really is."

From letter of November 14, 1825, to Ellen W. Coolidge:

"My Dear Ellen,—In my letter of October 13 to Mr. Coolidge, I gave an account of the riot we had at the University and of its termination. You will both, of course, be under anxiety till you know how it has gone off. With the best effects in the world, having let it be understood from the beginning that we wished to trust very much to the discretion of the students themselves for their own government. With about four-fifths of them this did well, but there were about fifteen or twenty bad subjects who were disposed to try whether our indulgence was without limit. Hence the licentious transaction of which I gave an account to Mr. Coolidge; but when the whole mass saw the serious way in which that experiment was met, the peoples, has been created. This great progress has been accomplished by the provision to the educational community of general support, accompanied by diminishing interference in educational processes by political agencies outside the academic community.

If it is true, as it well may be, that man is in a race between education and catastrophe, it is imperative that educational institutions not be limited in the performance of their lawful missions by unwarranted judicial inter-ference.

OBLIGATIONS OF A STUDENT

Attendance at a tax supported educational institution of higher learning is not compulsory. The federal constitution protects the equality of opportunity of all qualified persons to attend. Whether this protected opportunity be called a qualified "right" or "privilege" is unimportant. It is optional and voluntary.

The voluntary attendance of a student in such institutions is a voluntary entrance into the academic community. By such voluntary entrance, the student voluntarily assumes obligations of performance and behavior reason-ably imposed by the institution of choice relevant to its lawful missions, processes, and functions. These obligations are generally much higher than those imposed on all citizens by the civil and criminal law. So long as there is no invidious discrimination, no deprival of due process, no abridgement of a right protected in the circumstances, and no capricious, clearly unreasonable or unlawful action employed, the institution may discipline students to secure compliance with these higher obligations as a teaching method or to sever the student from the academic community.

Faculty of Professors assembled, the Board of Visitors coming forward in support of that authority, a grand jury taking up the subject, four of the most guilty ex-pelled, the rest reprimanded, severer laws enacted and a rigorous execution of them declared in future,—it gave them a shock and struck a terror, the most severe as it was less expected. It determined the well-disposed among them to frown upon every-thing of the kind hereafter, and the ill-disposed returned to order from fear, if not from better motives. A perfect subordination has succeeded, entire respect towards the professors, and industry, order, and quiet the most exemplary, has prevailed ever since. Every one is sensible of the strength which the institution has derived from what appeared at first to threaten its foundation. We have no further fear of anything of the kind from the present set, but as at the next term their numbers will be more than doubled by the accession of an additional band, as unbroken as these were, we mean to be prepared, and to ask of the legislature a power to call in the civil authority in the first instant of disorder, and to quell it on the spot by imprison-ment and the same legal coercions provided against disorder generally committed by other citizens from whom, at their age, they have no right to distinction."

All the foregoing quotations are found in *The Writings of Thomas Jefferson,* Library Edition, The Thomas Jefferson Memorial Association, Washington, D.C., 1904, Volume 18, pp. 341–348.

No student may, without liability to lawful discipline, intentionally act to impair or prevent the accomplishment of any lawful mission, process, or function of an educational institution.

THE NATURE OF STUDENT DISCIPLINE COMPARED TO CRIMINAL LAW

The discipline of students in the educational community is, in all but the case of irrevocable explusion, a part of the teaching process. In the case of irrevocable explusion for misconduct, the process is not punitive or deterrent in the criminal law sense, but the process is rather the determination that the student is unqualified to continue as a member of the educational community. Even then, the disciplinary process is not equivalent to the criminal law of federal and state criminal law. For, while the expelled student may suffer damaging effects, sometimes irreparable, to his educational, social and economic future, he or she may not be imprisoned, fined, disenfranchised, or subjected to probationary supervision. The attempted analogy of student discipline to criminal proceedings against adults and juveniles is not sound.

In the lesser disciplinary procedures, including but not limited to guidance counseling, reprimand, suspension of social or academic privileges, probation, restriction to campus and dismissal with leave to apply for readmission, the lawful aim of discipline may be teaching in performance of a lawful mission of the institution. The nature and procedures of the disciplinary process in such cases should not be required to conform to federal processes of criminal law, which are far from perfect, and designed for circumstances and ends unrelated to the academic community. By judicial mandate to impose upon the academic community in student discipline the intricate, time consuming, sophisticated procedures, rules and safeguards of criminal law would frustrate the teaching process and render the institutional control impotent.

A federal court should not intervene to reverse or enjoin disciplinary actions relevant to a lawful mission of an educational institution unless there appears one of the following:

(1) a deprival of due process, that is, fundamental concepts of fair play;

(2) invidious discrimination, for example, on account of race or religion;

(3) denial of federal rights, constitutional or statutory, protected in the academic community; or

(4) clearly unreasonable, arbitrary or capricious action.

. . .

PROVISIONAL SUBSTANTIVE STANDARDS
IN STUDENT DISCIPLINE CASES
UNDER SECTION 1983, TITLE 42

1. Equal opportunity for admission and attendance by qualified persons at tax supported state educational institutions of higher learning is protected by the equal privileges and immunities, equal protection of laws, and due process clauses of the Fourteenth Amendment to the United States Constitution. It is unimportant whether this protected opportunity is defined as a right or a privilege. The protection of the opportunity is the important thing.

2. In an action under Section 1983 issues to be determined will be limited to determination whether, under color of any statute, ordinance, regulation, custom or usage of a state ("state action"), a student has been deprived of any rights, privileges, or immunities secured by the Constitution and laws of the United States.

3. State constitutional, statutory, and institutional delegation and distribution of disciplinary powers are not ordinarily matters of federal concern. Any such contentions based solely on claims of unlawful distribution and violation of state law in the exercise of state disciplinary power should be submitted to the state courts. Such contentions do not ordinarily involve a substantial federal question of which the district court has jurisdiction under Section 1983. This rule does not apply, however, to actions based on diversity jurisdiction under Sections 1331, 1332 or 2201, Title 28, U.S.C.

4. Disciplinary action by any institution, institutional agency, or officer will ordinarily be deemed under color of a statute, ordinance, regulation, custom or usage of a state ("state action") within the meaning of Section 1983, Title 42, U.S.C.

5. In the field of discipline, scholastic and behavioral, an institution may establish any standards reasonably relevant to the lawful missions, processes, and functions of the institution. It is not a lawful mission, process, or function of an institution to prohibit the exercise of a right guaranteed by the Constitution or a law of the United States to a member of the academic community under the circumstances. Therefore, such prohibitions are not reasonably relevant to any lawful mission, process or function of an institution.

6. Standards so established may apply to student behavior on and off the campus when relevant to any lawful mission, process, or function of the institution. By such standards of student conduct the institution may prohibit any action or omission which impairs, interferes with, or obstructs the missions, processes and functions of the institution.

Standards so established may require scholastic attainments higher than the average of the population and may require superior ethical and moral behavior. In establishing standards of behavior, the institution is not limited to the standards or the forms of criminal laws.

7. An institution may establish appropriate standards of conduct (scholastic and behavioral) in any form and manner reasonably calculated to give adequate notice of the scholastic attainments and behavior expected of the student.

The notice of the scholastic and behavioral standards to the students may be written or oral, or partly written and partly oral, but preferably written. The standards may be positive or negative in form.

Different standards, scholastic and behavioral, may be established for different divisions, schools, colleges, and classes of an institution if the differences are reasonably relevant to the missions, processes, and functions of the particular divisions, schools, colleges, and classes concerned.

8. When a challenged standard of student conduct limits or forbids the exercise of a right guaranteed by the Constitution or a law of the United States to persons generally, the institution must demonstrate that the standard is recognized as relevant to a lawful mission of the institution, and is recognized as reasonable by some reputable authority or school of thought in the field of higher education. This may be determined by expert opinion or by judicial notice in proper circumstances. It is not necessary that all authorities and schools of thought agree that the standard is reasonable.

9. Outstanding educational authorities in the field of higher education believe, on the basis of experience, that detailed codes of prohibited student conduct are provocative and should not be employed in higher education.

For this reason, general affirmative statements of what is expected of a student may in some areas be preferable in higher education. Such affirmative standards may be employed, and discipline of students based thereon.

10. The legal doctrine that a prohibitory statute is void if it is overly broad or unconstitutionally broad does not, in the absence of exceptional circumstances, apply to standards of student conduct. The validity of the form of standards of student conduct, relevant to the lawful missions of higher education, ordinarily should be determined by recognized educational standards.

11. In severe cases of student discipline for alleged misconduct, such as final expulsion, indefinite or long-term suspension, dismissal with deferred leave to reapply, the institution is obligated to give to the student minimal procedural requirements of due process of law. The requirements of due process do not demand an inflexible procedure for all such cases. "But 'due process' unlike some legal rules, is not a technical conception with a fixed content unrelated to time, place and circumstances." Three minimal requirements apply in cases of severe discipline, growing out of fundamental

conceptions of fairness implicit in procedural due process. First, the student should be given adequate notice in writing of the specific ground or grounds and the nature of the evidence on which the disciplinary proceedings are based. Second, the student should be given an opportunity for a hearing in which the disciplinary authority provides a fair opportunity for hearing of the student's position, explanations and evidence. The third requirement is that no disciplinary action be taken on grounds which are not supported by any substantial evidence. Within limits of due process, institutions must be free to devise various types of disciplinary procedures relevant to their lawful missions, consistent with their varying processes and functions, and not an unreasonable strain on their resources and personnel.

There is no general requirement that procedural due process in student disciplinary cases provide for legal representation, a public hearing, confrontation and cross-examination of witnesses, warnings about privileges, self-incrimination, application of principles of former or double jeopardy, compulsory production of witnesses, or any of the remaining features of federal criminal jurisprudence. Rare and exceptional circumstances, however, may require provision of one or more of these features in a particular case to guarantee the fundamental concepts of fair play.

It is encouraging to note the current unusual efforts of the institutions and the interested organizations which are devising and recommending procedures and policies in student discipline which are based on standards, in many features, far higher than the requirements of due process.

Joint Statement on Rights and Freedoms of Students, 54 A.A.U.P. Bulletin No. 2, Summer 1968, 258, a report of a joint committee of representatives of the U.S. National Students Association, Association of American Colleges, American Association of University Professors, National Association of Student Personnel Administrators, National Association of Womens Deans and Counselors, American Association of Higher Education, Jesuit Education Association, American College Personnel Association, Executive Committee, College and University Department, National Catholic Education Association, Commission on Student Personnel, American Association of Junior Colleges; University of Missouri, *Provisional Rules of Procedure In Student Disciplinary Matters.*

Many of these recommendations and procedures represent wise matters of policy and procedure far above the minimum requirements of federal law, calculated to ensure the confidence of all concerned with student discipline.

The excellent briefs and arguments, including those of *amici curiae,* have been of great assistance in the preparation of this memorandum.

CONCLUSION

In two centuries, America has achieved—through great effort and struggle —one major educational advance after another: free public schooling; the land-grant colleges; the extension of the universities into the nation's farms and homes: the unique venture that has placed a high school education within the reach of every young person.

. . .

The Congress has approved more than 40 laws to support education from the pre-school project to the postgraduate laboratory;

The federal government has raised its investment in education to nearly $12-billion annually, ...

Yet for all of our progress, we still face enormous problems in education: stubborn, lingering, unyielding problems.

The phrase "equal educational opportunity," to the poor family in Appalachia and to the Negro family in the city, is a promise—not a reality.

Our schools are turning out too many young men and women whose years in the classroom have not equipped them for useful work.

Growing enrollments and rising expenses are straining the resources of our colleges—and the strain is being felt by families across America.

Each of these problems will be difficult to solve. Their solution may take years—and almost certainly will bring new problems. But the challenge of our generation is to lead the way.

And in leading the way, we must carefully set our priorities. . . .

President Johnson's 1968
Education Message to Congress

Progress, yes! In America there are more students attending school and at more levels than ever before. More support than ever is being given education. More than ever before, scholars, civic leaders, and ordinary citizens are concerned with the many aspects of education. Paralleling private and state concern with education, the federal government in less than a decade has undertaken such wide-ranging programs of educational support as:

new programs for nursery school through graduate school
classroom, library and special facilities construction

programs like Head Start, the Teacher Corps, and Upward Bound that
   attempt to attack directly the consequences of poverty and underprivilege
student loans, fellowships for prospective teachers, educational opportunity
   grants, medical and counseling assistance to students
financial assistance for schools and colleges to obtain special equipment for a
   variety of instructional and remedial programs
increased funding of vocational education
increased assistance to international education programs and exchanges
educational research support and a network of regional educational laboratories and services to assist local school districts
financial assistance to both science and the humanities

In short, a significant increase to public and private education by the government has been undertaken to supplement private and local resources, with
built-in legal guarantees of equality of opportunity and assistance.

Yet there also seem to be more problems and issues than ever before.
The whole matter of appropriate education, for the disadvantaged as well as
for all students, is unresolved. The Negro, the Indian, the Spanish-American,
the poor of all races, creeds and ethnic backgrounds demand better answers
and solutions than we have been able or willing to provide. So acute is the
issue that racial separatism is often proposed, both socially and educationally,
by various groups. This would be a bitter and ironic consequence of the efforts
that are being made, even though the attempts are as yet inadequate. And the
riots, the college protests and demands for greater voice in institutional
government, the disagreements and difficulties over financing education, the
promises of educational advance through technological means that raise the
fear of dehumanization of learning—these and a host of key educational and
social concerns now face a society that over time has turned to education as its
best prospect for creating equality and advancement among its people.

Basic educational issues have long cultural roots; thus while many issues
and problems appear in new guises, often they remain at core quite constant,
particularly in their philosophical and moral dimensions. It has been demonstrated in the preceding sections that there is a long history to such issues as:
what is a suitable education? what educational goals are social and which are
essentially academic? what is there about the nature of man and of knowledge
that must be taken into account by the educator and in what measure? how can
education be assured to minority groups or underprivileged groups, and what
measures must be taken to effect such a guarantee? We continue to raise
questions about education, more penetrating and more precise questions
perhaps, but answers are slow to come and when provided they are even
slower of acceptance. For education is more than what occurs in schools; it is
also a shaping of social attitudes and expectations.

One does not start *de novo* in attempting to resolve educational problems and issues. The documents in this anthology show the evolution of issues and offer a variety of suggestions and positions. They provide no totally acceptable and unchanging blueprint, for society and its educational demands constantly are changing. But these contents have been influential in shaping both the current issues and practices of American education, and they provide a proper starting point for examining our present educational system, its accomplishments and its dilemmas.

CUMULATIVE
INDEX OF
BASIC ISSUES

RELATION OF EDUCATION AND SOCIETY

A SELECTED BIBLIOGRAPHY OF MODERN WORKS

BASIS FOR LEARNING AND CURRICULUM

NATURE OF REALITY, KNOWLEDGE, AND MAN

Dewey, John, *Art as Experience,* New York: Minton, Balch, 1934; Putnam Capricorn, 1959.

Dewey, John, *Human Nature and Conduct,* New York: Modern Library, 1930, 1950, 1957.

Dewey, John, *The Quest for Certainty,* New York: Minton, Balch, 1929; Putnam Capricorn, 1960.

Dewey, John, *Democracy and Education,* New York: Macmillan, 1916.

Horne, Herman H., *Idealism in Education,* New York: Macmillan, 1910.

Kelley, Earl, *Education for What Is Real,* New York: Harper & Row, 1947.

Kilpatrick, William H., *Philosophy of Education,* New York: Macmillan, 1951.

Kneller, George F., *Existentialism and Education,* New York: Philosophical Library, 1958.

Maritain, Jacques, *The Education of Man,* Garden City, N.Y.: Doubleday, 1962.

Morris, Van Cleve, *Existentialism in Education,* New York: Harper & Row, 1966.

Price, Kingsley, *Education and Philosophical Thought,* 2nd ed., Boston: Allyn and Bacon, 1967.

Rusk, Robert R., *Doctrines of the Great Educators,* revised and enlarged 3rd ed., Melbourne: Macmillan, New York: St. Martin's Press, 1965.

Scheffler, Israel, *Conditions of Knowledge,* Chicago: Scott, Foresman, 1965.

PURPOSES OF EDUCATION

Brameld, Theodore, *Education for the Emerging Age,* New York: Harper & Row, 1961.

Childs, John L., *Education and Morals,* New York: Appleton-Century-Crofts, 1950.

Counts, George S., *Education and American Civilization,* New York: Bureau of Publications, Teachers College, 1952.

Frank, Lawrence K., *The School as Agent for Cultural Renewal,* Cambridge, Mass.: Harvard University Press, 1959.

Gardner, John W., *Self-Renewal,* New York: Harper & Row, 1964.

Hook, Sidney, *Education for Modern Man: A New Perspective,* New York: Knopf, 1963.

Hutchins, Robert M., *Education for Freedom,* Baton Rouge: Louisiana State University Press, 1943.

Kimball, Solon T. and McClellan, James E., Jr., *Education and the New America,* New York: Random House, 1962.

Lerner, Max, *Education and a Radical Humanism,* Columbus: Ohio State University Press, 1962.

Maritain, Jacques, *Education at the Crossroads,* New Haven: Yale University Press, 1943.

Mead, Margaret, *The School in American Culture,* Cambridge, Mass.: Harvard University Press, 1951.

Russell, Bertrand, *Education and the Good Life,* London: Boni and Live-right, 1926.

Thelen, Herbert, *Education and the Human Quest,* New York: Harper & Row, 1960.

SELECTION OF SUBJECT MATTER AND METHODOLOGY

Bruner, Jerome, *The Process of Education,* Cambridge, Mass.: Harvard University Press, 1960.

Bruner, Jerome, *Toward a Theory of Instruction,* Cambridge, Mass.: Belknap Press of Harvard University, 1966.

Cantor, Nathaniel, *The Teaching-Learning Process,* New York: Holt, Rinehart & Winston, 1953.

DeHaan, Robert F. and Havighurst, Robert J., *Educating Gifted Children,* revised and enlarged ed., Chicago: University of Chicago Press, 1961.

Dewey, John, *The Child and the Curriculum,* Chicago: University of Chicago Press, 1902, 1956.

Freud, Anna, *Introduction to Psychoanalysis for Teachers,* London: Allen and Unwin, 1931.

Freud, Sigmund, *New Introductory Lectures on Psycho-analysis,* New York: Norton, 1933.

Getzels, Jacob W. and Jackson, Philip W., *Creativity and Intelligence,* New York: Wiley, 1962.

Green, Edward J., *The Learning Process and Programmed Instruction,* New York: Holt, Rinehart & Winston, 1962.

Lee, J. Murray and Lee, Dorris May, *The Child and His Curriculum,* New York: Appleton-Century-Crofts, 1950.

Rugg, Harold O. and Schumaker, Ann, *The Child-Centered School,* Yonkers-on-Hudson, N.Y., and Chicago, Illinois: World, 1928.

Stratemeyer, Florence B., *et al., Developing a Curriculum for Modern Living,* New York: Bureau of Publications, Teachers College, 1947.

RELATION OF EDUCATION AND SOCIETY

GOVERNMENT AND EDUCATION

American Academy of Arts and Sciences, *Students and Politics (Daedalus,* v. 97, #1), 1968.

Bailey, Stephen K., *Schoolmen and Politics,* New York: Syracuse University Press, 1962.

Barzun, Jacques, *Teacher in America,* Boston: Little, Brown, 1945. Garden City: N.Y., Doubleday, 1954.

Benson, C. S., *The Economics of Public Education,* Boston: Houghton Mifflin, 1961.

Burke, Arvid J., *Financing Public Schools in the U.S.,* New York: Harper & Row, 1951.

Cahill, Robert S. and Hencley, Stephen P. (eds.), *The Politics of Education in the Local Community,* Danville, Ill.: Interstate Printers and Publishers, 1964.

Carter, Richard F., *Voters and Their Schools,* Stanford, Calif.: Stanford University, Institute for Communication Research, 1960.

Clark, Burton, *Educating the Expert Society,* San Francisco: Chandler, 1962.

Conant, James Bryant, *The Child, the Parent, and the State,* Cambridge, Mass.: Harvard University Press, 1959.

Fiske, Majorie, *Book Selection and Censorship,* Berkeley: University of California Press, 1959.

Gross, Neal, *Who Runs Our Schools?* New York: Wiley, 1958.

Hofstadter, Richard, *Academic Freedom in the Age of the Colleges,* New York: Columbia University Press, 1955, 1961.

Hollingshead, A. B., *Elmtown's Youth,* New York: Wiley, 1949.

Jones, Howard Mumford (ed.), *Primer of Intellectual Freedom,* Cambridge: Harvard University Press, 1949.

Kimbrough, Ralph, *Political Power and Educational Decision Making,* New York: Rand McNally, 1964.

Lieberman, Myron, *Education as a Profession,* Englewood Cliffs, N.J.: Prentice-Hall, 1956.

MacIver, Robert M., *Academic Freedom in Our Time,* New York: Columbia University Press, 1955.

Martin, Roscoe C., *Government and the Suburban School,* Syracuse, N.Y.: Syracuse University Press, 1962.

Reutter, E. Edmund, Jr., *Schools and the Law,* New York: Oceana Publications, 1962.

Stiles, Lindley (ed.), *The Teacher's Role in American Society,* New York: Harper & Row, 1957.

Vidich, Arthur J. and Bensman, Joseph, *Small Town in Mass Society,* Princeton: Princeton University Press, 1958. Garden City, N.Y.: Anchor, 1960.

PRINCIPLE OF CHURCH-STATE SEPARATION

The American Association of School Administrators, *Religion in the Public Schools,* Washington: American Association of School Administrators, 1964.

Barker, Sir Ernest, *Church, State, and Education,* Ann Arbor: University of Michigan Press, 1957.

Blanshard, Paul, *Religion and the Schools,* Boston: Beacon Press, 1963.

Boles, Donald E., *The Bible, Religion and the Public Schools,* 2nd ed., Ames: Iowa State University Press, 1963.

Butts, R. Freeman, *The American Tradition in Religion and Education,* Boston: Beacon Press, 1950.

Dierenfeld, R. B., *Religion in American Public Schools,* Washington: Public Affairs Press, 1962.

Drinan, Robert F., *Religion, the Courts, and Public Policy,* New York: McGraw-Hill, 1963.

Duker, Sam, *The Public Schools and Religion,* New York: Harper & Row, 1966.

Educational Policies Commission, *Moral and Spiritual Values in the Public Schools,* Washington: National Education Association, 1951.

Frommer, Arthur B., *The Bible and the Public Schools,* New York: The Frommer Publishing Corp., 1963.

The Fund for the Republic, *Religion and the Schools,* New York: The Fund for the Republic, 1959.

Herberg, Will, *Protestant, Catholic, Jew,* Garden City, New York: Doubleday, 1955.

Johnson, F. E. (ed.), *American Education and Religion,* New York: Harper & Row, 1952.

Kauper, Paul G., *Religion and the Constitution,* Baton Rouge: Louisiana State University Press, 1964.

LaNoue, George R., *Public Funds for Parochial Schools?* New York: National Council of Churches, 1963.

Lenski, Gerhard, *The Religious Factor,* Garden City, N.Y.: Doubleday, 1961.

McCluskey, Neil G., *The Catholic Viewpoint on Education,* Garden City, N.Y.: Hanover House, 1959.

Oaks, D. H. (ed.), *The Wall Between Church and State,* Chicago: University of Chicago Press, 1963.

Pfeffer, Leo, *Church, State and Freedom,* Boston: Beacon Press, 1953.

Phenix, Philip H., *Religious Concerns in Contemporary Education,* New York: Bureau of Publications, Teachers College, Columbia University, 1959.

Powell, Theodore, *The School Bus Law,* Middletown, Conn.: Wesleyan University Press, 1960.

Spurlock, Clark, *Education and the Supreme Court,* Urbana: University of Illinois Press, 1955.

Stokes, Anson P., *Church and State in the United States, Vol. II,* New York: Harper & Row, 1950.

Thayer, V. T., *Religion in Public Education,* New York: Viking, Inc., 1947.

Van Dusen, Henry P., *God in Education,* New York: Scribner's, 1951.

PRINCIPLE OF EQUAL OPPORTUNITY

Ashmore, Harry S., *The Negro and the Schools,* 2nd ed., Chapel Hill: University of North Carolina Press, 1954.

Baldwin, James, *Nobody Knows My Name,* New York: Dial Press, 1961.

Blaustein, Albert P. and Ferguson, Clarence C., *Desegregation and the Law,* New Brunswick, New Jersey: Rutgers University Press, 1957; New York: Vintage Books, 1962.

Conant, James Bryant, *Slums and Suburbs,* New York: McGraw-Hill, 1959.

Davis, Allison, *Social Class Influences Upon Learning,* Cambridge, Mass.: Harvard University Press, 1948.

DuBois, W. E. B., *The Souls of Black Folk,* Chicago: A. C. McClurg and Co., 1903, 1929, 1931.

Edwards, Newton, *The Courts and the Public Schools,* Chicago: University of Chicago Press, 1955.

Ellison, Ralph, *Invisible Man,* New York: McGraw-Hill, 1959.

Harrington, Michael, *The Other America,* New York: Macmillan, 1963.

Kahn, Thomas, *The Economics of Equality,* New York: League for Industrial Democracy, 1964.

King, Martin Luther, Jr., *Why We Can't Wait,* New York: Harper & Row, 1964.

Lomax, Louis E., *The Negro Revolt,* New York: Harper & Row, 1962.

Muse, Benjamin, *Ten Years of Prelude: The Story of Integration Since the Supreme Court's 1954 Decision,* New York: Viking, 1964.

Myrdal, Gunnar, et al., *An American Dilemma,* New York: Harper & Row, 1944.

Passow, Harry A., *Education in Depressed Areas,* New York: Bureau of Publications, Teachers College, 1963.

Redding, Saunders, *On Being Negro in America,* Indianapolis: Bobbs-Merrill, 1951.

Riessman, Frank, *The Culturally Deprived Child,* New York: Harper & Row, 1963.

Silberman, Charles E., *Crisis in Black and White,* New York: Random House, 1964.

Warner, William Lloyd, Havighurst, Robert J., and Loeb, Martin B., *Who Shall Be Educated?* New York: Harper & Row, 1944.

Washington, Booker T., *Up From Slavery,* New York: A. L. Burt Co., 1901; New York: Doubleday, 1901, 1909, 1915; Garden City, N.Y.: The Sun Dial Press, 1937.

FEDERAL INVOLVEMENT IN EDUCATION

Allen, Hollis P., *The Federal Government and Education,* New York: McGraw-Hill, 1950.

Campbell, Ronald F. and Bunnell, Robert A., *Nationalizing Influences on Secondary Education,* Chicago: Midwest Administration Center, University of Chicago, 1963.

Lee, Gordon C., *The Struggle for Federal Aid,* New York: Bureau of Publications, Teachers College, Columbia University, 1949.

Munger, Frank J. and Fenno, Richard F., *National Politics and Federal Aid to Education,* Syracuse, N.Y.: Syracuse University Press, 1962.

Rockefeller Brothers Fund, *The Pursuit of Excellence,* Garden City, N.Y.: Doubleday, 1958.

Sufrin, Sidney C., *Issues in Federal Aid to Education,* Syracuse, N.Y.: Syracuse University Press, 1962.

HISTORY OF AMERICAN EDUCATION

Bailyn, Bernard, *Education in the Forming of American Society,* Chapel Hill: University of North Carolina Press, 1960; New York: Vintage Books, 1960.

Butts, R. Freeman and Cremin, Lawrence A., *A History of Education in American Culture,* New York: Holt, Rinehart & Winston, 1953, 1961.

Cremin, Lawrence A., *The Transformation of the School,* New York: Knopf, 1961, 1962.

Cremin, Lawrence A., *The American Common School, An Historic Conception,* New York: Bureau of Publications, Teachers College, Columbia University, 1951.

Cubberley, Elwood P., *Public Education in the United States,* Boston, New York: Houghton Mifflin, 1919, 1934.

Curti, Merle, *The Social Ideas of American Educators,* Paterson, N.J.: Pageant Books, 1959.

Good, H. G., *A History of American Education,* New York: Macmillan, 1956, 1962.

Greene, Maxine, *The Public School and the Private Vision,* New York: Random House, 1965.

Meyer, Adolph, *An Educational History of the American People,* New York: McGraw-Hill, 1957.

Morison, Samuel Eliot, *The Intellectual Life of Colonial New England,* 2nd ed., New York: New York University Press, 1956.

Nye, Russel Blaine, *The Cultural Life of the New Nation,* New York: Harper & Row, 1960.

Thayer, Vivian T. and Levit, Martin, *The Role of the School in American Society,* 2nd ed., New York: Dodd, Mead, 1966.

Welter, Rush, *Popular Education and Democratic Thought in America,* New York: Columbia University Press, 1962.

Wiggin, Gladys, *Education and Nationalism,* New York: McGraw-Hill, 1962.

RELATED RECOMMENDED BOOKS

Callahan, Raymond E., *An Introduction to Education in American Society,* New York: Knopf, 1956, 1960.

Gross, Richard E. (ed.), *Heritage of American Education,* Boston: Allyn and Bacon, 1962.

Gruber, Frederick C., *Anthropology and Education,* Philadelphia: University of Pennsylvania Press, 1961.

Havighurst, Robert J. and Neugarten, Bernice L., *Society and Education,* 3rd ed., Boston: Allyn and Bacon, 1967.

King, Edmund J., *Other Schools and Ours,* Revised edition. New York: Holt, Rinehart & Winston, 1963.

King, Edmund J., *World Perspective in Education,* Indianapolis: Bobbs-Merrill, 1962.

Mallinson, Vernan, *An Introduction to the Study of Comparative Education,* Melbourne: Heinemann, 1957; 2nd ed., London: Heinemann, 1960.

Marrou, H. I., *A History of Education in Antiquity,* translated by George Lamb. New York: Sheed and Ward, 1956.

Myers, Edward D. and Toynbee, Arnold J., *Education in the Perspective of History,* New York: Harper & Row, 1960.

National Society for the Study of Education, *Social Forces Influencing American Education, Sixtieth Yearbook, Part II,* Chicago: University of Chicago Press, 1961.

Ulich, Robert, *The Education of Nations: A Comparison in Historical Perspective,* Cambridge, Mass.: Harvard University Press, 1961.

RECOMMENDED BOOKS OF GENERAL INTEREST

Allen, George N., *Undercover Teacher,* Garden City, N.Y.: Doubleday, 1960.

Allport, Gordon, *Becoming,* New Haven: Yale University Press, 1955.

Ashton-Warner, Sylvia, *Teacher,* New York: Simon & Schuster, 1963.

Ashton-Warner, Sylvia, *Spinster,* New York: Simon & Schuster, 1958, 1959.

Belth, Marc, *Education as a Discipline,* Boston: Allyn and Bacon, 1965.

Callahan, Raymond E., *Education and the Cult of Efficiency,* Chicago: University of Chicago Press, 1962.

Coleman, James S., *The Adolescent Society,* New York: Free Press of Glencoe, 1961.

Denney, Reuel, *The Astonished Muse,* Chicago: University of Chicago Press, 1957.

Fromm, Erich, *Man for Himself,* New York: Holt, Rinehart & Winston, 1947.

Goodman, Paul, *Growing Up Absurd,* New York: Random House, 1960.

Goodman, Paul, *Compulsory Mis-Education,* New York: Horizon Press, Inc., 1964.

Henry, Jules, *Culture Against Man,* New York: Random House, 1963.

Hofstadter, Richard, *Anti-Intellectualism in American Life,* New York: Knopf, 1963.

Koerner, James, *The Case for Basic Education,* Boston: Little, Brown, 1959.

Maslow, Abraham, *Toward a Psychology of Being,* Princeton, N.J.: Van Nostrand, 1962.

May, Rollo, *Man's Search for Himself,* New York: Holt, Rinehart & Winston, 1953.

Mayer, Martin, *The Schools,* New York: Harper & Row, 1961.

Phenix, Philip, *Realms of Meaning,* New York: McGraw-Hill, 1964.

Rafferty, Max, *Suffer, Little Children,* New York: Devin-Adair, 1962.

Rafferty, Max, *What They Are Doing to Your Children,* The New American Library of World Literature, 1964.

Scheffler, Israel, *The Language of Education,* Springfield, Ill.: Charles C Thomas, 1960.

Skinner, B. F., *Walden Two,* New York: Macmillan, 1948.

Smith, B. Othanel and Ennis, Robert H., *Language and Concepts in Education,* Chicago: Rand McNally, 1961.

Spindler, George, *Education and Culture,* New York: Holt, Rinehart & Winston, 1963.

Waller, Willard, *The Sociology of Teaching,* New York: Wiley, Inc., 1932.

Whyte, William, *The Organization Man,* New York: Simon & Schuster, 1953.

Woodring, Paul, *A Fourth of a Nation,* New York: McGraw-Hill, 1957.

Veblen, Thorstein, *The Higher Learning in America,* New York: Sagamore Press, 1957.